Alan

Thanks and best wishes

Clive

GOLDEN YEARS

Front cover photograph: *Kelly Holmes celebrates winning the 800m, the first of her two gold medals in Athens in 2004. Courtesy of Press Association.*

Back cover photograph: *James Cracknell looks on as Matthew Pinsent embraces Steve Redgrave after the coxless four's victory in Sydney in 2000. Courtesy of Press Association.*

BRITAIN'S SUMMER
OLYMPIC CHAMPIONS
1948-2008

GOLDEN YEARS

CLIVE ELLIS

First published in the United Kingdom in 2012 by
Greenwich Publishing,
2 Arlington Place, London SE10 8NR

British Library Cataloguing in Publication Data. A Catalogue
record for this book is available from the British Library.

ISBN 978-0-9564081-1-2

All inside photographs are Press Association
unless otherwise stated

Cover design, typesetting and origination by Graham Hales
(www.grahamhales.co.uk)

Printed and bound in Great Britain by
Jellyfish Print Solutions, Swanmore, Hampshire.

CONTENTS

ACKNOWLEDGEMENTS

The author is immensely grateful to the following gold medallists (listed alphabetically) for sharing their memories so generously: David Bond, Bob Braithwaite, Ann Brightwell (née Packer), Lynn Davies, Sarah Dempsey (née Ayton), Gillian Donaldson (née Sheen), Richard Faulds, Jim Fox, Sally Gunnell, David Hemery, Jane Holderness-Roddam (née Bullen), Ben Hunt-Davis, Richard Leman, Anita Lonsbrough, Mary Low (née Gordon-Watson), Mike McIntyre, Dick McTaggart, Ken Matthews, Richard Meade, Adrian Parker, Bridget Parker, Rodney Pattisson, Mary Peters, Mary Reese (formerly Rand), Shirley Robertson, Judy Roe (née Grinham), Jonny Searle, Bryn Vaile, Allan Wells.

Husbands, widows, sons, daughters, relations, team-mates and friends also helped immeasurably to put flesh on the bones of the gold medal winning performances. These are again listed alphabetically: Dorothy Bond, Kathleen Braithwaite, Robbie Brightwell, Peter Burnell, Sarah Cooper, John Disley, Rosemary Ellmore, Alan French, Janet Hesketh, Mick Hill, Sarah Hobbs, Hugh Laurie, Jacqueline Page, Sara Ridao, Bobby Stewart, Maggie Thompson, Rob White, James Wilson, Peter Wilson.

Thanks are also due to the following: Shirley Berry, John Bryant, Simon Clegg, Chris Dodd, Celia Edgington, Graham Hales, Colin Kennedy, Bob Lonkhurst, Alan Smith, Laura Wagg, Miriam Walton.

INTRODUCTION

"To put it bluntly and briefly, we just don't take our sports seriously enough. Americans have swept the Olympic board because running, jumping and discus throwing have become as important in their school and university curriculum as modern languages. Two hours a day is the minimum trackmen – they don't bother so much about their women – spend with their coaches, many of whom earn almost £2,000 a year. I can see a lot of people giving a casual shoulder shrug and saying, 'So what?' It matters a lot. It is a humiliating business sitting through an Olympiad and listening to the medley of foreign anthems. These games have a great prestige value, and we could get much nearer the front if we discarded our casual outlook."

Sunday Graphic, Aug 8 1948

BRITAIN'S gold cupboard was embarrassingly bare when the *Sunday Graphic* delivered its verdict midway through the London Olympics in 1948. Although four rowers and two sailors restored a little national pride in the second week of the Games, the criticism was no less apposite, and an updated version of the argument was being aired 48 years later in the wake of a feeble showing in Atlanta.

Nothing much changed in between – Olympic gold medals were won by Britain in spite of rather than because of the system. Their most successful post-war Games prior to Sydney were also in Australia, but there was no reason to draw longer-term encouragement from the random successes of two boxers, a steeplechaser, swimmer and fencer in Melbourne. The three-day event team had won in Stockholm earlier in the year.

If anything, the six gold medals from 1956 were an unhelpful diversion from the general malaise. British athletics, in particular, was heading towards civil war (and the foundation of the International Athletes' Club in 1958). On one side were the increasingly disillusioned athletes; on the other were the 'Blazerati', personified by Harold Abrahams, himself a gold medallist at the 1924 Olympics, and Jack Crump, secretary of the British Amateur Athletic Board and team manager in Melbourne. Both were able to peddle the party line, largely unchallenged, as athletics correspondents – Crump wrote for *The Daily Telegraph*. On the flight out to Melbourne he insisted that the male and female athletes were segregated; only university graduates were allowed to join him in the first class lounge.

The steeplechaser, John Disley, co-founder of the London Marathon with Chris Brasher in 1981, wrote in the book, *The Road to Rome*, published just before the 1960 Games: "It was not as if 1956 was a particularly black year, it was just that at Melbourne we had time to organise our bickerings. With only one table-tennis table and three dart boards for four thousand competitors, we needed some occupation!

"We had time to find out that we did not enjoy the privileges taken for granted by other national teams. We could see that where other teams had half-a-dozen coaches to cast a critical eye over training workouts, the British had only one [Geoff Dyson], supplemented by the willing but uninformed assistant team manager. Moreover we were not receiving the unofficial daily cash allowance received by many other teams. After agitation we were given limited free postal facilities."

There was no gold medal blueprint for British sportsmen to follow and – long after more pragmatic countries had chosen to bend the rules – a stringent insistence on whiter-than-white amateurism persisted. The Americans had the collegiate system, the Eastern Bloc countries showered their athletes with state support; we relied on talent, ingenuity and enormous sacrifice. Gillian Sheen, who in 1956 became Britain's lone fencing gold medallist, says: "In my day you damn well paid for everything."

David Hemery heralded an era in which British Olympians began to tap into, rather than just envy, the American experience; David Wilkie and Duncan Goodhew followed suit in the 1970s. Others, like Steve Ovett and Daley Thompson, chose to stay at home. Hemery was also one of the first British gold medallists to be plunged into the post-Olympic "goldfish bowl of three or four interviews, dinners,

HOW DID WE DO

LEADING NATION

	G	S	B	Position			G	S	B
1948	3	14	6	12th		US	38	27	19
1952	1	2	8	18th		US	40	19	17
1956	6	7	11	8th		USSR	37	29	32
1960	2	6	12	12th		USSR	43	29	31
1964	4	12	2	10th		US	36	26	28
1968	5	5	3	10th		US	45	28	34
1972	4	5	9	12th		USSR	50	27	22
1976	3	5	5	13th		USSR	49	41	35
1980	5	7	9	9th		USSR	80	69	46
1984	5	10	22	11th		US	83	61	30
1988	5	10	9	12th		USSR	55	31	46
1992	5	3	12	13th		USSR	45	38	28
1996	1	8	6	36th		US	44	32	25
2000	11	10	7	10th		US	37	24	33
2004	9	9	12	10th		US	36	39	27
2008	19	13	15	4th		China	51	21	28

luncheons, receptions, openings a day, all for nothing because it was an amateur era".

There was no handbook explaining how to deal with the attention. Sally Gunnell, a winner in 1992, learned the hard way "that a lot of people do not have your best interests at heart. They offer you things – right, left and centre. You wonder why they are doing it. Why would someone want to give me a car?" Bradley Wiggins went on a "nine-month bender" after winning three medals in Athens; fellow cyclist Chris Hoy reckoned, in the wake of his triple triumph in Beijing, that over a 12-week period he did not sleep in the same bed for successive nights.

The era of the professional Olympian has brought a uniformity of opportunity – at the expense of the romantic plot. The gold medallists whose stories are recounted in the first part of this book – although comparatively few in number – were ordinary people who achieved the extraordinary; they were war heroes, war babies and the children of rationing. They came back to their civic receptions, token appearance on *Desert Island Discs,* and modelling session for Madame Tussauds, then rejoined the real world as lawyers, teachers, civil servants, doctors, nurses, dentists and vets. Ann Packer was only 22 when she retired after winning the 800m at the Tokyo Games in 1964.

In some cases, they bore witness to the Olympics' loss of innocence: in 1960 swimmer Anita Lonsbrough won her gold medal 24 hours after the Danish cyclist, Knud Enemark Jensen, had collapsed and died during the cycling road race. The initial verdict was that he had suffered sunstroke, but the autopsy showed traces of amphetamine. Sailors Rodney Pattisson and Chris Davies received their gold medals on the same day, in August 1972, that terrorists killed nine Israeli athletes at the Munich Games. Four years later, Britain's modern pentathlon team were the main witnesses for the prosecution when Boris Onischenko was found to have rigged his fencing weapon. In 1988, attention was diverted from Mike McIntyre and Bryn Vaile's Star class victory by the news that Canadian sprinter Ben Johnson had tested positive for anabolic steroids.

Only in the last 30 years have Britain's Olympic champions learned – via the ubiquitous agent – how to put a value on their success. They book in for their *Hello!* subsidised weddings, negotiate their contracts with Lucozade and Horlicks and reinvent themselves as ambassadors, spokesmen and motivational speakers. Only since the infusion of Lottery funding have they found themselves competing on a largely level playing field. There are still excuses for failure, but the financial get-out clause has largely vanished. The rewards, for the new breed of serial champions in particular, can be enormous.

Down-to-early humility is an endangered species. Step forward Pete Reed, a member of the winning coxless four in Beijing. A few months later he was asked what the gold medal had meant in practical terms. "I got a free TV from Panasonic [given to all of Britain's gold medallists in 2008] and a set of golf clubs from TaylorMade – that's about it," he said. "But there are people out there right now who are desperately worried about their jobs. What's the worst that could happen to me: that I'll have to stop shopping at Waitrose and downsize to Aldi or the Co-Op?"

1948

Aug 9: Coxless pairs, Ran Laurie, Jack Wilson

A PHOTOGRAPH sits on actor Hugh Laurie's desk, showing his father, Ran, and rowing partner, Jack Wilson, at the medal ceremony after their victory in the Olympic coxless pairs at Henley in 1948. Laurie sketches the scene: "Jack is loose-limbed and grooving and looks like he should be mixing a martini. My father is very rigid, standing to attention."

Laurie jnr was unaware that his father had ever held an oar until he saw him in action on a family holiday. "I was 10, perhaps younger," he recalls, "setting out on a Scottish trout loch with my parents, two rods and a picnic. My father took the oars as we pushed away from the jetty and, like every boy anticipating familial embarrassment, I nervously whispered to my mother: 'Does dad know how to row?' The two of them smiled at each other and my mother simply said, 'Yes'. That's all. No further word on the subject for several years. When finally they came clean and confessed, I asked if I could see the medal. My dad told me to go and look in his sock drawer. Sure enough there it was. I think the enveloping sock may have been Leander pink but I can't swear to it."

The story of Laurie and Wilson may lack the class tension and antipathy of *Bert and Dickie*, the BBC film based on the odd-couple pairing of Bert Bushnell and Richard Burnell in the double sculls in 1948, but it is every bit as compelling in its way: an old-fashioned yarn of chums on a rattling adventure. In the scene-setting chapter they are separated by an ocean. William George Ranald Mundell Laurie was born in Grantchester, on the outskirts of Cambridge; John Hyrne Tucker Wilson, eight months older, spent the first nine years of his life in the United States, where his English father worked as a cotton exporter. In the mid-Twenties the family uprooted from Galveston, Texas and returned to England.

They were both public school educated, Laurie at Monkton Combe, in Somerset, and Wilson at Shrewsbury. Although Wilson had already been singled out as an oarsman/sculler of rare talent, his scheduled arrival to read engineering at Pembroke College, Cambridge, in the autumn of 1932, was delayed by a badly poisoned leg which also prevented him from rowing in the 1933 Boat Race. Six months later Laurie began a natural sciences degree at Selwyn College. He and Wilson gelled on and off the water, helping Cambridge to win for the 11th, 12th and 13th successive times, an unparalleled streak in the long history of the race.

They both committed to the Sudan Political Service, the old boys' network which imposed Britain's imperial interests until the country's independence in 1956. Wilson took up his job just before the 1936 Olympics, Laurie stayed long enough to be able to stroke the British eight to fourth place in Berlin (he insisted that with Wilson on board they could have won the gold medal).

In his unpublished memoirs, Laurie recalled that as his crew were preparing to launch their boat for the final the National Anthem played in recognition of Jack Beresford and Dick Southwood's victory in the double sculls. "There was a large German next to me who didn't take his hat off," wrote Laurie, "and I snatched his hat and threw it away into the crowds as far as I could, and we then lifted the boat and launched it and I heard no more of it."

Wilson and Laurie's work as assistant district commissioners involved what Laurie's daughter, Janet Hesketh, describes as "an amazing amount of responsibility for young men who had just left university". New recruits to the service had to prove they were conversant with the Sudanese penal code and fluent in written and spoken Arabic before qualifying for their first pay rise (Wilson received a £60 bonus for mastering Dinka and Nuer). They arbitrated in disputes over grazing rights and land ownership and, on a more sensitive level, meted out justice after tribal fights. Wilson wrote: "We used to say if after a heated boundary dispute both sides were equally unhappy the judgment was about right." He even had to show surgical expertise on one occasion, using a darning needle and giraffe hair plucked from a servant's bracelet to stitch up a barge captain's scrotum which had been cut open by a cow's horn.

Witch doctors were all-powerful and dangerous, as Wilson discovered to his cost when he almost lost his life in a bizarre incident (described in greater detail below) in 1942. A message was sent to Laurie, who feared the worst when he arrived at the hospital after an arduous journey to find his friend's bed unoccupied. He was relieved – and amazed – to be told that Wilson was outside playing tennis.

Wilson was thwarted in his ambition to join the RAF during the war, but he came uncomfortably close to the action when the convoy in which he and his new wife, Anne, were travelling on their return for leave in Britain, was attacked by U-boats. Laurie also got a taste of conflict as a political officer for the Occupied Enemy Territory Administration, who oversaw the collaboration between British forces and Abyssinian partisans to end the Italian occupation of Ethiopia in 1941. In a letter to Laurie a colleague wrote: "I am sorry your account-ant is worried by the loneliness of the wilderness, snakes, lions etc."

Although their jobs kept them largely apart during their time in Sudan, their lives followed similar paths. Wilson married in 1943, Laurie the following year. Anne Wilson was also, according to the couple's son, James, responsible for teaching the waltz to the reticent Laurie after he met his wife-to-be, Pat. Both women adapted stoically to what Janet Hesketh calls "a pretty extreme posting". She adds: "My mother claimed she was the only white woman within 300 miles."

Rowing was largely off the agenda for Laurie and Wilson, though they discussed the possibility of teaming up for the 1940 Olympics, which were switched from Tokyo to Helsinki when Japan invaded China in 1937. The vague ambition assumed sharper focus when they

Ran Laurie and Jack Wilson (first and second left) in training before the 1936 Boat Race PRIVATE COLLECTION

returned to Britain on leave in 1938 and, despite minimal training, won the prestigious Silver Goblets at Henley. Laurie recorded that they were loaned a boat by a Leander member who "behaved very kindly to us when I steered it into a post and completely ruined it". The Second World War appeared to have scuppered the pair's Olympic plans: first the Helsinki Games were cancelled then the proposed 1944 Olympics in London suffered a similar fate.

An exchange of letters (the only form of correspondence available to Laurie and Wilson in the Sudan) persuaded them to have what Laurie described as "a last fling" in 1948 – despite the fact that they would both be 33 by the time of the Games and had not set foot in a boat for 10 years. Laurie's secondary incentive for gaining selection was that it would enable him to be in England for the birth of his second child. He and Wilson began basic training at the start of the year; Laurie would run in front of his car while on trek and became used to concerned old men on donkeys stopping to offer him a ride.

They returned to Britain in May, three months before the Olympics but, as in 1938, the early signs were not encouraging. Laurie recalled: "Once again our preparations included rowing at Marlow Regatta and, once again, we were disastrously beaten – by some Australians – and we were in pretty low spirits. When reviewing the situation the next day Mac McCulloch [the pair's coach] advanced the extraordinary idea that we should change places, that is to say that I should row at bow and Jack should row at stroke, and this we did with astonishing results." They earned their Olympic place by winning the Silver Goblets again.

Richard Burnell, whose own selection remained in doubt, wrote in the *Times*: "Perhaps the most welcome nomination to the rowing world generally is that of W.G.R.M Laurie and J.H.T. Wilson for the coxwainless pairs. Their victories in the '30s have become rowing legend, but it did look at one time as though they had left too long a gap in their racing careers. It is too early to say what opposition they will face next month, but it is certain that they will not easily break their winning tradition at this stage of their rowing careers."

They were dubbed the 'Desert Rats', the nickname given to the 7th Armoured Division for their heroism in the North African Campaign during the Second World War. Laurie felt anything but heroic the night before their first race. He was up repeatedly with an upset stomach and almost passed out as he and Wilson held off the challenge of a skilful Italian pair, who protested in vain that the Britons had changed station.

Laurie wrote: "I can just remember, in the last 100 yards, throwing the rudder against Jack and just hoping that he would get home, which we did by half a length."

Laurie and Wilson won their semi-final comfortably two days later, but Laurie had more than rowing on his mind on Aug 7 – it was also the day on which his wife was due to give birth to their second child. Although Janet obligingly delayed her entrance until the 14th, five days after the final, Pat Laurie relied on Raymond Glendenning's radio commentary to follow her husband's fortunes from the family home in Cambridge.

On the eve of the final Wilson went to get his hair cut in Henley. The barber, oblivious to the identity of his customer, said, 'I'm looking forward to the finals tomorrow, I'm backing Laurie and Wilson.' After Wilson had owned up, the hairdresser said, 'Right, if you win, you can have free hair cuts for the rest of your life.'

Wilson made sure that he kept his part of the bargain; his wife nervously knitted a Union flag as she waited for the off. The *Times* reported: "It was a wonderful race, with the veterans being led all the way by the Swiss up to the 1,150 metres mark when, rowing in masterly style, Wilson spurted. It was perfectly timed and Great Britain went ahead." Laurie described it as "straightforward" and their best ever performance, while Roland Allen, writing in the *Daily Graphic*, noted that Laurie and Wilson "sat bowed in their shell just

Ran Laurie and Jack Wilson (nearest the camera) on their way to victory in the coxless pairs at Henley

past the winning post, hardly aware of the loud cheering. They could hardly raise their arms to acknowledge the congratulations of the losing pairs. They remained motionless for a long minute, then paddled slowly down to the winners' platform to receive their medals. We heard our National Anthem and it sounded good. The sun came through, for the first time during the regatta, as they passed the post." The only jarring note for Hylton Cleaver, who covered the race for the *Evening Standard*, was that the anthem was played on a *gramophone* (his italics). The band, an integral part of festival week, had been sacrificed when the booms were dismantled to allow crews to row three rather than two abreast.

The day of the final finished on a comically anti-climactic note. After the end-of-regatta meal laid on by the Mayor of Henley, Laurie, who in deference to his heavily pregnant wife had traded in his motorbike and sidecar for a Standard 12 saloon, picked up his mother from friends nearby. "Unfortunately, at Luton, on the way back to Cambridge," he recalled, "the lights gave out at about two o'clock in the morning, and I didn't know what to do. I saw a policeman and he said, 'Come with me', and he was on a motorbike and we followed him to the main police station. There they received us very kindly and provided each of us with a cell to sleep in, and called us at dawn with cups of hot tea and set us on our way."

A few days after Janet's birth, Laurie went back to the Sudan. He had put an intended medical career on hold when he moved to Africa and he returned to England in 1950 so that he could retrain as a doctor. He worked as a general practitioner in Oxford for more than 30 years and lent his rowing experience to the Henley Regatta as an unfailingly polite steward and umpire.

Laurie betrayed an almost deferential admiration for Wilson in a letter he wrote to Cleaver in the mid-Fifties: "It was my privilege to be his second fiddle," he said. "He was a genius and had no twin." He also highlighted Wilson's "supreme and unique quality", explaining: "He was not only the greatest mover of a boat I have ever seen, but he was, above all, the Gay Amateur. He rowed so hard because he loved it. Rowing was such fun to him and that made it fun for anyone who rowed with him."

Wilson stayed on for another four years, leaving shortly before the Sudan gained independence; his final posting was as deputy governor of Wau, a multi-ethnic southern Sudanese city/province in which 25 different languages were spoken. "When we left the Sudan in

'INCIDENT IN WESTERN NUER DISTRICT, SEPTEMBER 1942'

JACK WILSON was checking grain in an Arab merchants' compound when, without warning, a woman picked up a spear lying nearby and thrust it into his back. Believing only that someone had bumped into him, Wilson turned to say, 'Be careful.' A porter caught the spear as she lunged again. The woman was knocked to the ground and Wilson's cook's boy had to be dissuaded from decapitating her with an axe.

The medical dresser who regularly accompanied Wilson on trek lifted his shirt, saw a large hole spouting blood and declared, 'Well, you won't be any use any more', before going off to seek vengeance against a subversive witch doctor believed to have inspired the attack. The dresser and Wilson's interpreter killed both the witch doctor's brother and an innocent visitor to the village (conspicuous because he was wearing clothes) before their ammunition ran out. Wilson's house boy, meanwhile, used the merchant's turban to bind the wound and he was carried six miles on a string bed to less hostile territory before nightfall.

Under questioning from local chiefs, Wilson's attacker explained that the witch doctor, fearful that he would lose his magic powers if he was forced to leave home ground, issued a curse on everyone he held responsible, including Wilson and the woman's husband, a sub-chief. He also withdrew his beneficial influence on the couple's 10-year-old son, whom he had previously 'cured' of fits. A few days later the boy had a convulsion and dropped dead at his mother's feet. She believed that if she killed the district commissioner the British authorities would exact summary punishment on the witch doctor and his tribe.

Wilson was carried for a further two days on the angarib (string bed) before reaching the river at Lake No. Finally, he was picked up by a medical steamer which had responded to an SOS message relayed to the nearest telephone, two days' walk away. He was given antibiotics which saved his life and taken on to the hospital in Malakal before being transferred to Khartoum. He discovered that the spear had passed right through his liver and penetrated far enough to raise the skin on his stomach. His attacker was sentenced to 12 years' imprisonment for attempted homicide. In his detailed account of what he referred to as, 'Incident in Western Nuer District, Upper Nile Province, Sudan, September 1942', Wilson wrote:

> I used to see her and pass the time of day when I went into Malakal to replenish my food stores; after all she had no personal animosity against me; I was merely a tool in her plan for revenge. When my wife arrived at the end of 1943 she could not understand how I could talk to a woman who had tried to kill me.

Ran Laurie looks on as Jack Wilson receives his gold medal
GETTY IMAGES

September 1954," he wrote, "I had to decide how to allot my assets. I decided to give my house to the head Arab boy and keep my wife." He worked for Stewarts and Lloyds, the steel manufacturing company based in Corby, Northamptonshire, but took early retirement when it was absorbed into British Steel. "He hated being in a business that wasn't being run for profit," says his son, James. "He spent a lot of his time dealing with unions, so he retired when he was 55 and moved down to Devon, where he had an enormously fulfilling life. He was able to do all the things he hadn't had time for previously."

Although their gold medal winning boat was discovered some years later at King's School Ely, north of Cambridge, and is on permanent display in the River and Rowing Museum in Henley, neither Wilson nor the equally modest Laurie was interested in dwelling on past achievements. Wilson's nephew, Peter, remembers that his uncle was "happier to show his scars than his medals". Laurie was godfather to James Wilson, who was a contemporary of Hugh Laurie at Eton in the Seventies and remained a friend. Laurie admits that his own rowing ambitions – he competed in the World Junior Championships and rowed (on the losing side) in the 1980 Boat Race after following his father to Selwyn College – were fuelled by his father's achievements. "Every boy seeks to please their father, don't they?" he says. "Unless they have a reason to rebel and antagonise and my father was much too kind to deserve that."

Six years after his father's death in 1998 (Wilson had died 18 months earlier), Laurie appeared for the first time on screen as the misanthropic physician Gregory House. What would his father's verdict have been? "I hope he would have enjoyed it," says Laurie. "He was certainly a very logical man, and I think he would have approved of the show's rationality. He might have tutted at House's incivility, but that's partly the point. He certainly had none of House's cynicism."

Laurie doubts that he would volunteer for the role of his father if the film *Jack and Ran* were ever made. "I suspect that an actor portraying his own father might be a pretty short route to the psychiatrist's coach. It feels strange enough pretending to be a doctor when he was the real thing."

Aug 9: Double sculls, Bert Bushnell, Richard Burnell

THERE was nothing particularly controversial about journalist Richard Burnell's reflections on the Henley Regatta, but his *Times* article on July 5 1948 proved to be a cleverly coded exercise in self-advancement. It also helped to set in train the series of events which ended with Burnell winning an Olympic gold medal five weeks later.

He wrote, in the no-nonsense way which was typical of sports reporting at the time: "M.T. Wood, the Australian policeman, won the Diamond Sculls in most convincing fashion. He beat Bushnell, of Maidenhead, easily in 8min 24sec. The only time we have seen Wood extended was in his race with Rowe, of Leander. Then we saw what a grand sculler the Australian is, and also what magnificent material we have in Rowe."

Burnell's fellow old Etonian may have been high on potential but he was low on experience. He made no secret of the fact that he had only taken up sculling "for fun" after being left out of Oxford's Boat Race crew in 1947. When the selection committee opted for Rowe, Bushnell could have been forgiven for thinking that the old boys' network was conspiring against him. At this stage there was no certainty that either he or Burnell would figure; Burnell had failed to impress at Henley with his latest double sculls partner and turned to Bushnell in a desperate attempt to put together a competitive combination. They had just two weeks to prepare for the selection trials.

By background, education and stature, they were incompatible. Burnell was the second generation of a formidable rowing dynasty; both his father, Charles, and father-in-law to be, Stanley Garton, had rowed in the British eights who won Olympic gold medals before the First World War. He was automatically welcomed into the exclusive Leander club. Membership was denied to Bushnell, a product of Henley Grammar School. There was, however, a sporting alchemy which smoothed over the bumps in the relationship. Writer William Ivory was so struck by the contrasts, and feel-good finale, that he conceived *Bert and Dickie*, a BBC film which was due to air for the first time just before the 2012 Games. Bushnell, keen to establish a semblance of equality in their relationship, plumped for 'Dickie' rather than the more deferential Richard. Burnell's children believe that everyone else called him Richard or Dick.

Burnell, four years older than his new partner, was 21 when he won a lone Oxford Blue just before war broke out in 1939. He served as a captain with the Rifle Brigade and Northumberland Fusiliers and, in the absence of a top-class coach, decided after leaving the Army in 1946 that he would concentrate on the double sculls. He became the *Times*'s rowing correspondent in the same year and also worked for the British Council, who deeply resented the time he took off during the Olympics.

Bushnell was a child of the Thames. A reluctant schoolboy – his daughter, Jacqueline Page, is convinced that he was an undiagnosed dyslexic – he expressed himself more articulately through sport. In normal circumstances he would have joined the family boat-making business, but in order to guarantee that his amateur status was not compromised he was apprenticed during the war to the Southampton-based firm Thornycroft, testing engines for torpedo boats.

He was presented to President Juan Peron and his wife Eva, while training and competing in Argentina in 1947 – it was also here that he discovered the benefits of a daily massage. There was even better anecdotal material in his meeting with Grace Kelly, the would-be actress who later found worldwide fame when she married Prince Rainier of Monaco. In 1947 she was the arrestingly beautiful 17-year-old who cheered on her elder brother, Jack, at the Henley Regatta. Bushnell claimed that he was the charmer who beat off the opposition to win a date with Grace. He also felt an affinity with her brother, who won the Diamond Sculls in 1947. Kelly's father, Jack snr, was an outstanding sculler between the wars and won gold medals at successive Olympics, but he was not allowed to compete in the

Diamond Sculls because he had served an apprenticeship as a bricklayer. From such humble beginnings he built a multi-million dollar business in Philadelphia. Jack jnr was back at Henley the following year, helping to supplement Bushnell's rations allowance in the build-up to the Olympics.

Despite their differences, Bushnell fulfilled most of the criteria which Burnell outlined in a book four years later: "If I was to double up for sculls it would have to be with someone younger than myself, someone who might benefit from my strength and experience, and in return contribute youthful exuberance and zest. The problem which ultimately presented itself was how to find two people who could scull fairly well together, who lived within reach of the same bit of river, who could get off work at the same time, and finally who could bear the sight of each other's faces for 10 months."

Six weeks, the actual length of their sculling partnership, was the limit of their forbearance. Bushnell recalled, in a 2004 interview: "We were complete opposites. After about our third or fourth outing we had had three or four arguments. I told Dickie I was going to re-rig the boat, and he ordered me not to touch it. I just waited until he walked off and re-rigged it anyway, because I was three stone lighter than the previous fellow who had sculled with him. I was proved right about that and he was proved right about the extra mileage he insisted on doing in training." Given that Burnell could have chosen the Theory of Rigging as his *Mastermind* special subject, Bushnell was risking all.

He was quoted in one interview as saying: "There was class tension there and it came from me being bloody awkward." His daughter, though, is adamant that if he caricatured himself as the uppity shop steward to Burnell's haughty managing director he was just pandering to the audience. "My father clearly did not like Richard Burnell, but the tension was based on education, nothing more. He was very resentful that he was being made to do double sculls rather than single sculls and he projected some of that resentment on to Burnell. It could have been anybody; it could have been another working-class lad. He thought he was being robbed of his individual glory." She also complained that an *Independent* obituary in 2010 painted her father as "a whingeing oick".

They were easy enough to tell apart – Burnell was 6ft 4in and 14½st, Bushnell seven inches shorter and four stone lighter – but the physical differences were emphasised by Bushnell's glasses and white sculling cap. Somehow it worked, Burnell observing: "Our respective weak points seemed to cancel themselves out, and our strong points were complementary. Bushnell was inclined to over-reach. I was on the short side in my forward swing and the result was we reached naturally to about the same place. Our sculling was soon the most enjoyable I had ever experienced."

After winning the trials they were coached by Jack Beresford, the closest thing to a Steve Redgrave equivalent between the wars. He had won his third and final gold medal, also in the double sculls, at the Berlin Games, and though he had no great reputation as a coach he had some prescient observations to make after the 1948 Olympics: "In America professional coaches operate on results, and hold their job only if they succeed. Oarsmen over there are under coaches who study everything, diet, exercise and rowing. Here, discipline is voluntary and guidance, other than for rowing, almost negligible. Until we realise that the detailed study of every aspect of sport is essential we shall not be successful."

The *Times* was not alone in devoting minimal space to the 1948 Olympics and Burnell did nothing to put flesh on the factual bones when he wrote in the BOA's official report: "Bushnell and myself, of Great Britain, won safely." The special correspondent who stood in for Burnell reported the British pair's day-to-day progress like this:

Aug 5

Burnell and Bushnell, of Great Britain, disappointed in their row with France and Italy. They were beaten by France and will have to row much better to-day. [The writer was obviously oblivious to Burnell's cunning plan: lose deliberately to the French, build rhythm in the repechage and avoid the dangerous Danes until the final].

Aug 6

Burnell and Bushnell, sculling excellently, won the doubles and became the sixth British crew in seven events to pass into the semi-finals.

Aug 7

Burnell and Bushnell, improving with every race and rowing well within themselves, beat the United States and the famous Belgians in the double sculls.

Aug 9

R.D. Burnell and B.H.T. Bushnell gave Great Britain her second victory of the regatta in the double sculls. Cracking off the mark at 43 against 38 by Uruguay and 40 by Denmark they took the lead at once, being one length ahead at the 250 metres mark. Burnell then settled down to 32 and rowing with immense power and length won convincingly, with Denmark second, two lengths in front of Uruguay.

Burnell and Bushnell were handed a bottle of champagne by a Leander club member as they left the course. The crowds were big, the aftermath decidedly low-key – until, that was, a celebration dinner for all the rowers, in a tent beside the Thames, descended into anarchy. Bushnell's version of events was: "It was bloody awful food and after a while the Americans started throwing the bread rolls around, saying they weren't fit to eat. So we all started pelting each other with the food. In the end somebody shoved a custard tart down some bloke's neck and he turned round and sloshed him, so I left before it got any nastier, and it did."

Ran Laurie, fresh from his victory in the coxless pairs with Jack Wilson, called it "good-natured chaos". His abiding memory was of an official calling out, 'Attention messieurs!' in an effort to silence the multi-national diners for a planned speech. Although the rowers struggled to communicate with each other in a dozen or more different languages, they were all familiar with the default French used to start a race, "Attention! Êtes-vous prêts. Partez.' Each time the official said, 'Attention', they responded *en masse*, 'Êtes-vous prêts…' and there were no speeches.

Burnell's son, Peter, says the British pair's paths may have crossed at various Henley Regattas but, in essence, they reverted to being very different individuals on their very distinct journeys through life. "They certainly didn't have 25-year reunions or anything like that," he confirms. Despite the richest of rowing genes, Peter's achievements on the water were restricted to an Oxford Blue in 1962, though he, too, came reasonably close to Olympic action. "I was the spare man when the Oxford crew represented GB in Rome in 1960. The other spare man and I had to stay in training at Henley and then the crew got knocked out in the first round in Rome so it wasn't the greatest Olympic experience."

Richard Burnell was still rowing competitively in the early Fifties and he remained an integral part of the Henley and Boat Race scene for the rest of his life (he died in 1995). He was a mushroom farmer for a time, but writing dominated his working life. He was attached to the *Times* and *Sunday Times* until 1990 and his books on sculling were

Richard Burnell and (right) Bert Bushnell stand to attention as the National Anthem is played

regularly reprinted. He pointed out, rather wistfully, that they were made necessary by the lamentable lack of coaching expertise available to British scullers.

The deal when Bert Bushnell got married a month after the 1948 Olympics, or so his wife Margaret claimed, was that he would give up sculling. The gold medal was not the painkiller it might have been; he clung to the conviction that he should have been competing in the single sculls instead. Nevertheless, he threw himself whole-heartedly into business, sporting and domestic challenges.

He set up a highly successful company which hired out river cruisers (the innovative use of pump-out toilets earned him the nickname Recirc Bert). He became an obsessive golfer, ballroom dancer, gardener and cook. After selling the business he settled in the Algarve, only to have his gold medal stolen. Lateral thinking helped to reclaim the prize. "I went down to the local boozer and told everybody my medal had been stolen by people who didn't realise it was only lead sprayed with gold. Nobody in the bar said a word, but two days later the medal came back in the post." When he returned to Britain, he donated the medal to the River and Rowing Museum in Henley.

Aug 12: Swallow class sailing, Stewart Morris, David Bond

DAVID BOND was the forgotten man in 1948, when his role as Stewart Morris's crew in the Swallow class winning boat was largely overlooked. Bond's indignant Aunt Tulla tried to drum up a little belated publicity by alerting the *Bournemouth Echo* to her nephew's achievement and a rookie reporter was despatched to interview him at the British Overseas Airways Corporation offices in Poole. "She didn't really know what to ask," he remembers, "and all they used was a few lines saying how excited I was."

He had only kept his job on the understanding that the eight weeks he took off to prepare for and compete in the Games classed as unpaid leave. When he returned to work, his boss said sarcastically, 'I suppose you won the bloody thing, did you?' Bond responded, 'Yes, we did actually.' The sceptic was only convinced when Bond produced his medal as irrefutable evidence. He was bypassed again early in 2010 when obituaries for sculler Bert Bushnell hailed him as the last survivor from Britain's 1948 gold medallists. This time the 87-year-old Bond responded with a gentle, chiding letter which featured in the *Guardian*'s Corrections and Clarifications.

Finally, last summer, as news organisations became aware of this unique winning link with the last London Olympics, the requests for full-scale interviews honed in on the Cornish seaside village of Feock where he has lived for almost 60 years. In the few days prior to our conversation, exactly a year before the start of the 2012 Games, he had "spent all day posing with a picture frame in my hand" to help the Royal Mail promote their Olympic stamp issue, and received a letter asking him to carry the Olympic torch. 'Wheelchairs will be acceptable,' the invitation added, but Bond was unimpressed. "I don't think I want to be chased all over the country in a wheelchair," he said.

His hearing is poor, but his recollection of people and events either side of the Second World War is impressively lucid for someone due to celebrate his 90th birthday in March 2012. He was an impressionable 12-year-old schoolboy when Morris, already acknowledged as a small-boat maestro on the Norfolk Broads, came out west to compete. Morris had played a big part in popularising dinghies at Cambridge University in the late Twenties and Bond's father, Cyril, was credited with introducing dinghy racing to Cornwall; they were sailing soulmates and David Bond is not embarrassed to refer to Morris as a "boyhood hero". In 1932, when still only 23, Morris had pulled off the first of an unparalleled 12 victories in the prestigious Prince of Wales Cup, for International 14 dinghies. He was reserve in the centreboard dinghy class in 1936, when Britain's representative at the Berlin Olympics was Peter Scott, later to find greater fame as a conservationist.

After the war, designer Uffa Fox helped Morris to bring his undergraduate concept of an inexpensive dinghy class to fruition. The first four off the production line, which cost £65, were named Fe, Fi,

Fo and Fum. The Firefly was also adopted as the singlehanded class for the 1948 Olympics, allowing the legendary Danish skipper, Paul Elvstrom, to win the first of his four successive gold medals. Neither the Firefly nor the Swallow, a 26ft keelboat, was retained on the Olympic roster after the London Games.

David Bond lost both his parents to cancer in the early part of the war, when he helped to develop aircraft and gliders for the Airborne Forces Experimental Establishment. Morris rose to the rank of Commander in the Fleet Air Arm and in 1944 he was appointed OBE for his role in developing a successful air defence system for the carrier HMS Formidable; the system was subsequently adopted as a standard for all British aircraft carriers.

Bond recalls: "I ran into Stewart Morris again after the war when I was in Bournemouth and my brother came back from Ceylon. He bought himself an International 14 and I started crewing for him when I joined Itchenor Sailing Club." He confesses that until the winter of 1947 he was completely unaware that the Olympic Games were around the corner.

His path to selection presented itself in odd circumstances. "Stewart had a long-term crewman, Martin Beale, who'd been with me at Harrow, oddly enough. Out of the blue, he announced that he wanted to qualify with Stewart but he also fancied going for the singlehanded and seeing which one he liked best. Stewart was a bit narked by this and more or less told Martin, 'Pack it up, mate'.

"I'd told Stewart before that I'd rather like to have a go at this Olympic thing. I was going to have a try-out with another chap at Cowes, but then Stewart rang me in the office to say that Martin had let him down and did I want to have a bash at it." Bond rates the qualification process, and in particular the final trials, as harder than the Olympic Games themselves. One of their rivals in the trials was 66-year-old Tom Thornycroft, both the designer of the Swallow and a man who would have provided a unique competitive link between the London Games of 1908 and 1948. He had won both motor boat racing classes in 1908, though in each case the only other competitor failed to finish.

'I'd told Stewart before that I'd rather like to have a go at this Olympic thing'

Torquay, the venue for the Olympic sailing, was gripped by a strange mixture of excitement and bewilderment. The local paper, the *Herald Express*, described it as the town's "biggest event of the century" – and

David Bond and (right) Stewart Morris come ashore after winning the fourth race in the Olympic regatta

that was just the arrival of the Olympic flame. Holidaymakers, on the other hand, struggled to find an explanation for the multi-national invasion.

The British pair put in six weeks of hard training; on a mundane level Bond remembers hanging Swift's spinnakers from the top landing of their hotel down to the bottom level so that they could dry overnight. They quickly established themselves as the most consistent combination in the fleet, taking the overall lead after winning the second of seven races and finishing almost nine minutes clear in the fourth race.

All was going according to plan until the penultimate day, when Morris was disqualified for touching a mark. There were, according to Bond, "too many bits of rope to pull. Stewart actually let go of the main sheet, which was a bit silly, but he was already holding a couple of the spinnaker sheets. Anyway, the main sheet flew out from the end of the boom and just touched the tip of the flag which was actually lying in the water. The Canadian who was behind us protested so we were out of that race. There was a discard system but we weren't really in a position to take advantage of it."

It all made for an uncomfortably tense final day, especially as their closest rivals, Portugal, dominated the race. "I'd worked out the previous evening that we had to finish fourth and we had a hell of a job to do that," says Bond. "Everybody had told us to take it easy early on and we finished up virtually last at the start. We moved up to fifth and we were very lucky then. We picked up a little puff of wind going across the bottom leg and the boat started to plane and we just passed the Brazilian. We then covered him all the way up to the finish."

Another half hour passed while the jury considered a desperate protest from the Italian skipper, Dario Salata, who claimed the British pair had failed to re-cross the line after a recall. "I'm sure it was a bit of bad feeling," says Bond, "because Stewart didn't like him at all. He called him a little s***."

Morris confided afterwards: "I wish your father was here to see this." There may have been the odd trembling lip of emotion then, but the Charterhouse boy, Morris, and Old Harrovian, Bond, were dignified and composed for the medal ceremony. Bond recalls: "Just before *God Save the King*, Stewart said, 'Ready. Off caps…now!' I suppose we were awful prigs, but that's the way it was."

They never sailed again together. Bond was soon married with twin daughters and carried on working as a flight observer for BOAC and De Havillands before returning to Cornwall in 1954; he set up a "not very successful" market gardening company, built his first Shearwater catamaran in 1957 and continued competing with his wife, Elizabeth, until 1971. Morris, who managed the family hop-growing business, won the Prince of Wales Cup for the final time in 1965 and was as influential a helmsman off the water as he had been on it. He succeeded the Duke of Edinburgh as president of the Royal Yachting Association in 1980, at a time when they had just decided to boycott the Moscow Games, and also oversaw the RYA's adoption of windsurfing as it was welcomed into the Olympic fold.

1952

Aug 3: Team show-jumping, Harry Llewellyn, Duggie Stewart, Wilf White

WHEN asked to nominate his greatest achievement, Harry Llewellyn replied, 'Sleep'. This was no cure for a lifetime's insomnia; it was just an hour's relaxation which separated an Olympics of near misses and might-have-beens from a triumphant finale. The Helsinki Games were declared closed eight minutes after the show-jumping team claimed Britain's solitary gold medal.

Llewellyn had taken his cue from Foxhunter, the horse-superstar with which his name will be for ever linked. "I knew that Foxhunter would be having his midday nap – sighing peacefully as he did so," he wrote. "I lay on my bed, staring desperately at the white wall of my room and repeating over and over again, 'I must go to sleep, I must go to sleep.' And eventually I slept."

The irony was that Foxhunter himself had torn up the original script with a ragged morning round. He was like some equine hustler, feigning incompetence then raising his game when the stakes were at their highest. He earned even greater adulation for his brinkmanship, leaving an embarrassed Llewellyn to remind journalists that he did have team-mates, Wilf White and Duggie Stewart.

The chorus of general criticism was stifled but far from silenced. J.L Manning wrote in the *Daily Graphic*: "Britain has done badly largely by conforming to the rigid amateur laws which are unobserved or unwanted by other countries because they prevent an all-out effort." The odd near miss – Sheila Lerwill was, according to *The Daily Telegraph*, a "stocking's thickness" away from winning the high jump – could not obscure the malaise. Geoff Dyson, the chief coach for Britain's track and field team, said in a television interview: "If you people at home want Olympic gold medals you will have to give us the track facilities to train for them. Ours are the world's worst."

There was an object lesson in the British show-jumping team's meticulous preparations for the Helsinki Games: it was very much a pan-British affair. Llewellyn was Welsh, White was English, Stewart was Scottish, and the team manager, Mike Ansell, Irish-born. They all had engaging stories to tell.

Llewellyn's father, who was created a baronet in 1922, had company interests which impacted on half the coal produced in south Wales. He was impatient (a character trait passed on to his son) and a compulsive gambler (a weakness from which his son was spared). Harry Llewellyn was educated at Oundle and Cambridge, where his contemporaries included the future spies, Guy Burgess, Donald Maclean and Kim Philby. He became an expert on the classification of coal and had the unusual distinction of advising Winston Churchill, a family friend, on the best stoker to put in his swimming pool at Chartwell.

Llewellyn was introduced to horses at an early age and began riding an Irish-bred horse, Ego, over fences in 1933. When the chance came to ride Ego at the 1936 Grand National he dieted down from 14st to 10st 3lb; his breakfasts consisted of two eggs in a glass of vinegar. Ego was 100-1 in the ante-post betting and started the Aintree race at 50-1. He finished a remarkable second behind Reynoldstown and narrowly failed to claim third place the following year. Ego was also one of the favourites for the race in 1938 but dropped dead after finishing a warm-up race at Gatwick.

Harry Llewellyn's professional life followed a similar path to his father's, but the coal industry took a back seat when war broke out. Llewellyn joined the Warwickshire Yeomanry then became a senior liaison officer with the Eighth Army. This brought him into regular contact with General Montgomery and he also enjoyed a memorable encounter with the American, General Patton, in Sicily.

He recalled: "After waiting an hour I found out where his tent was and walked straight up to it and announced, 'Major Llewellyn, Liaison Officer, sent by General Montgomery.' Without any formality, a soft voice said, 'Come inside,' where I found Patton stripped to the waist. He said, 'Excuse me Major, but it's kinda hot.'

"I then outlined my business, and he learned that I had been in a horsed cavalry regiment. As a horse-lover himself he was motivated to ask if I knew the Llewellyn who rode Ego to second in the National in

1936 which he had seen. When I told him I was the same person, he forgot all about the war and we had a gossip about Americans and steeplechasing."

Llewellyn married just before the end of the war, during which Duggie Stewart, the son of a Brigadier General, excelled as a lead-from-the-front swashbuckler of a soldier. Between 1943 and 1945, largely spent fighting the Germans on various fronts with the Royal Scots Greys, he also managed to get married and produce two children, born only 11 months apart.

Stewart's wartime exploits – he was twice awarded the Military Cross and also received a Distinguished Service Order – were the stuff of legend. The Greys were forced to trade in their horses in 1941 and soon afterwards Stewart was drawn into a cat-and-mouse duel with a German tank at Nofilia. They found themselves on either side of a steep ridge, able to see only each other's heads and wireless aerials. With stalemate looming, Stewart waved in greeting to his adversary and saluted him. The German did likewise and they were able to reverse slowly out of each other's sights.

During the assault landings at Salerno, Stewart's craft was hit and sunk a few yards from the beach. Although badly burned to the face and hands he swam ashore, mounted another tank and reassumed control. He was only 31 when he commanded the regiment in the last six months of the war. As peace returned the Greys collected horses, many in a sad state of neglect, and set up a regimental riding school at Wismar. One of the equine refugees, whose name, Bones, fairly described the state he was in when rescued, would become a regular partner in competitions for Stewart.

His son, Bobby, remembers his parents as "two peas in a pod", adding: "My mother was as mad as a hatter: she raced, she hunted, she shot. It was to the detriment of my sister and me because that was how she died. She had a nasty fall from a horse and when she came round her doctor told her that she'd messed up her insides and shouldn't try to have any more children." Ignoring the advice, she became pregnant and gave herself even less chance of surviving by continuing to follow her husband from competition to competition. Gillian Stewart died in childbirth in 1950; the child, Rory, survived but, by the saddest of coincidences, became a cot death victim 10 days later. Duggie Stewart, showing extraordinary resilience, remarried in 1952 and the Olympics in Helsinki doubled as a honeymoon for him and his second wife, Phoebe.

Britain's winning show-jumping team on the medal podium in Helsinki

Wilf White neither fought nor bore children between 1939 and 1945, but his family had been dealt a cruel hand by the '14-'18 war. Two of White's three brothers were killed; the other was left crippled. There was an essential modesty about White, applicable as much to his upbringing as his demeanour. In a sport dominated by the haves he was very much a have-not, born (in 1904) and brought up on a council smallholding near Nantwich, Cheshire.

He had barely ridden before, at the age of 17, he was given a job by a local farmer which involved taking horses to and from shows. In time, he was given the chance to compete on them. His wife-to-be (White called her Jim because he did not like her real name, Dorothy) decided that she was in love when she saw him lying unconscious after a fall at Olympia.

The organisational genius behind the win in Helsinki was Mike Ansell, whose own riding career had been cut short after he was caught in a volley of friendly fire while taking shelter in a barn in northern France in 1940. Ansell was blinded and spent three years in a prisoner of war camp before being repatriated. Rather than dwelling on his misfortune, he dreamed up a master plan for the promotion of equestrian sport in Britain after the war. Ansell knew that competition success would accelerate the process – the victory in 1952 was the perfect catalyst – and gave equal thought to how teams could best prepare for major championships. He was show director for the International Horse of the Year Show for more than 25 years and archive footage from the Fifties shows him feeling his way across a miniature lay-out for the course as though it were a giant form of braille.

Llewellyn's post-war life was rich with memorable landmarks. He bought Gobion Manor, near Abergavenny, at the end of 1945. His wife Teeny, herself a capable and courageous rider, gave birth to Dai in 1946 and Roddy just over a year later. Both would outstrip their father in the celebrity stakes – Roddy's affair with Princess Margaret made him a household name in the Seventies – though neither came close to matching his achievements. The year 1947 was also a pivotal one for Harry Llewellyn's riding career; he was keen to compete inter-nationally but lacked a horse of sufficient quality, so he scoured the records of every registered horse at the British Show Jumping Association's London headquarters. He arrived at a short list of two, one of which was Foxhunter and, after taking advice from various expert quarters, paid what was then a formidable amount, £1,500, to buy him from a farmer in Thrussington, Leicestershire.

"I felt instantly that there was a feeling of friendship between us," Llewellyn said. "I noted that when I went up to him he examined me carefully; possibly he was just looking for sugar, but he had those charming, kind eyes which were always a feature of the horse. He was, quite obviously, a gentle, affectionate animal and I felt a little flattered by the interest he showed in me." The same placidity endeared Foxhunter to horse-lovers young and old. Even when rationing was still in full swing schoolgirls would send him sugar lumps by the lorry load. The 'distinguishing mark' entry on his passport would have read: 'Split ear' – the result of an accident when he was a yearling.

Llewellyn discovered that Foxhunter had been called Eelskin by his first owner; Nizefela was plain Bill when Wilf White paid just over £100 for him in 1946. Both horses were bay geldings, both around 16 hands, but Nizefela was a completely different temperamental beast. Early in their relationship, he almost broke White's leg when he kicked him. On the one occasion that another rider teamed up with Nizefela in competition, when White was injured, the horse refused then ran out of the arena. The rider was Harry Llewellyn.

Nizefela's calling card, a flamboyant touch completely at odds with his owner, was an instinctive kick-back as he cleared a jump. White was at a loss to explain the flourish, but wrote: "All I can say is that the horse is no clown, and is not trying to be funny. Does he know people are laughing at him? I think not. But he knows when he has made a mistake at a jump, and when he has jumped a clear round. All manner of explanations of that kick-back have been put forward, but the point is he never does it if he's in trouble."

Foxhunter, though still relatively inexperienced, helped Llewellyn and Britain to a team bronze at the 1948 Olympics. Llewellyn regarded it as a notable achievement, saying it "put British show jumping firmly on the Olympic map at a time when many people said that this should be a test of only human beings' prowess without involving other mammals to do the main work". A more cynical observation was that only three teams had finished. Duggie Stewart was picked for the three-day event team, only for his horse, Dark Seal, to go lame during the cross-country phase.

In 1949, the Horse of the Year Show was launched at Harringay Arena in east London; it was a television-friendly showcase and British successes at home and abroad fed a feverish enthusiasm for the sport; Princesses Elizabeth and Margaret were regularly attendees. Behind the scenes, 'Colonel Mike' Ansell was already preparing for the Helsinki Olympics.

Stewart forged a successful partnership with Kilgeddin, another of Llewellyn's horses, but broke three ribs in a competition which preceded the Nations Cup in Geneva in 1949. In his absence, Llewellyn rode both Foxhunter and Kilgeddin to a remarkable victory. "Today you have struck a blow for Great Britain," Ansell told him. "With those words ringing in my ears," Llewellyn remembered, "I went to my [hotel] room to be telephoned by Duggie Stewart, who said, 'You know, I'm absolutely furious because I really felt that I was fit enough' – he could hardly speak, incidentally – 'but, on the other hand, many, many congratulations.' " Kilgeddin, a potential partner for Stewart in Helsinki, had to be destroyed after breaking a femur in 1951.

Both Llewellyn and White were part of the British team who competed in the United States and Canada the previous year, a journey which involved 10-day boat crossings in both directions (White reckoned that Nizefela had been upright for 15 days solid when they

Harry Llewellyn and Foxhunter atone for their morning mistakes by going clear in Helsinki PRIVATE COLLECTION

finally returned to Cheshire). The horse's idiosyncratic style won him a new legion of fans and a clutch of victories.

The countdown to Helsinki effectively began in December 1951 when, according to White, "it was laid down that to ensure all the selected horses being in good condition, an allowance would be made for feeding and extra corn coupons were allowed." A series of training camps was arranged and reserve horses lined up. "I doubt if any team left any country so perfectly tuned up as the British in 1952," White said. "The horses in particular were the admiration of all countries." The team also had a formidable combination in reserve, Peter Robeson and Craven A.

Riders, wives and horses were all on the Skyways York which set out from Blackbushe Airport, in Surrey, on July 30, four days before the competition in Helsinki. Soon after take-off they were reminded that no amount of planning can control the forces of nature as a violent electrical storm began to buffet the plane. Also on board was Charlie Moffat, who had groomed for Stewart after joining the Greys in 1945. According to Moffat, a panicky Foxhunter demolished his box, prompting the pilot to order that he should be put out of his misery. Moffat responded: "Well you may as well shoot us all then, as living won't be an option if we arrive without Foxhunter."

The story, though too good to overlook, is not fully corroborated. Llewellyn insisted in his memoirs that the flight was smooth and incident-free. White confirmed the storm, but suggested that the prime casualty was human: farrier Bob Armstrong was badly traumatised by the experience. Foxhunter seemed none the worse for his ordeal, though he took an instant dislike to Finnish oats and hay; Llewellyn had to sneak back on to the plane to gather up a reserve supply of Spillers nuts.

The Prix des Nations occupied the same ground on which javelins had been thrown and on which a Hungarian all-stars team orchestrated by Ferenc Puskas had won the football final the previous day; the obstacles were installed overnight. There was a muted, muggy atmosphere – the stadium was less than half full – when the competition got under way at eight o'clock in the morning. Stewart and Aherlow were first out for the British team, incurring 12 faults on the tricky course, but White and Nizefela managed to get round with just a clipped gate counting against them. A regulation performance from Foxhunter was all that stood between Britain and a half-way lead, but he lacked his customary alertness.

Lainson Wood wrote in *The Daily Telegraph*: "Had Foxhunter been in anything remotely like his real form we should have had a formidable lead already, but he made a complete mess of it, and, apart from nearly unseating his well-loved master, forfeited 16.75 points for errors he has never made since becoming a star and will probably never make again." Britain were sixth in the team standings, a minor medal probably the limit of their ambitions. Teeny Llewellyn almost threw away her lucky horseshoe in disgust.

By the time the afternoon round began 70,000 spectators packed the stadium; Prince Philip and the Duke of Kent watched from the VIPs' section. The portents were good when Stewart conjured a brilliant round from Aherlow, whose fitness had been in doubt, marred only by a slight mistake in the middle of the treble. White, described by Ansell as his "full back" because of Nizefela's reliability in a crisis, believed his individual prospects were better than those of the team. He lost an iron when Nizefela jumped the penultimate fence, but negotiated the last obstacle safely. "I really thought we had brought it off," he recalled, "and then I heard the announcement over the loudspeaker: 'Four faults'."

Organisers had been ridiculed for employing soldiers, many of whom had never even seen an equestrian competition, as judges. In this case one said that Nizefela had put a hind foot in the water; the other maintained that he had simply touched the splash on the other side of the white tape which distinguished between four faults and safety. White found plenty of support, including from rival teams, and the British management went as far as raising the £10 deposit for a formal protest before backing down. Nizefela, built for accuracy rather than speed, finished last of the five horses, all with eight faults, who jumped off against the clock.

White reflected a few years later: "As far as I have ever been able to find out, this appeal never got to the arbitrators perhaps because Prince Philip was there, and it was felt that as we had won the team event anyhow, it would be more in keeping with British dignity to accept the verdict as it stood, or perhaps it was just turned down." In the absence of a tell-tale indentation or television evidence – the organising committee had been unable to sell the rights – Llewellyn took the view that it would have been a difficult verdict to overturn. He still felt enormous sympathy for his team-mate. "I think to this day," he wrote in 1977, "that Wilf White is the unluckiest man I have ever known not to have won an individual gold medal."

The inquest was still in full flow when Llewellyn and Foxhunter, reinvigorated by their lunchtime nap, came into the ring knowing that a clear round would secure the team gold medal ahead of Chile. They rose to the challenge magnificently; it was as if the morning debacle had been a figment of everyone's imagination. Cynical, battle-hardened journalists stood to sing the National Anthem with lumps in their throats before raising Foxhunter on to an even more exalted plane in their reports.

Llewellyn struggled to explain what had occurred: "Why Foxhunter was so bad this morning and so good this afternoon is a mystery," he said. "Not that I wasn't responsible for the morning run: the rider is always responsible. You might say the combination just didn't click. He seemed to know it was up to him when he came out for the second time – he was right on his toes. I swear he knew what was at stake."

White was left with a feeling of intense frustration. "For me the story is rather a sad one," he wrote, "because Nizefela on that day had his greatest opportunity and took it, yet was not awarded the prize. Nobody wants to win by a fluke, but to lose by one is tough." He and Stewart were also made to feel like extras in the Foxhunter blockbuster. White's typically understated verdict in his memoirs was: "I doubt whether these Games were reported in the press at home as realistically as they might have been. The British are faithful to their favourites. When we got back we found that Foxhunter was a front-page hero and had all the headlines to himself as the horse, the only horse, who had brought back Britain's only gold medal. The reporters had apparently not grasped that our three horses brought back a gold medal each, and that of the three Foxhunter's points were the worst.

'Nobody wants to win by a fluke but to lose by one is tough'

"Nobody was more anxious to make this clear than Harry Llewellyn, but it seemed that to do so would spoil a really good story and so it went on record that Foxhunter had won the medal, and even the BBC put it that way."

White's wife, fearful that her reticent husband might take flight if he knew that a civic reception had been arranged to coincide with their return to Nantwich, kept it under wraps until they were half a mile from the centre of the town. A crowd of 2,000 turned out and even Nizefela submitted without complaint to the pats and hugs. White succeeded Llewellyn as captain of the British team and made a second Olympic appearance on Nizefela at Stockholm in 1956, winning a bronze medal in the team competition and finishing fourth in the individual standings. He was made an OBE for his services to the sport in 1958. White later trained National Hunt horses and was still driving a wagon and caravan when he was 70; he competed at Olympia at the same age. He died in the Isle of Man in 1995.

One of Stewart's last initiatives as the Royal Scots Greys' commanding officer was to take groups of soldiers to Belsen – "not only for firing on the ranges," according to one of them, the future Labour MP, Tam Dalyell, "but to be taught the lurid facts of the concentration camp".

Stewart left the Greys in 1952 to go into farming, but never lost his sense of adventure. He got a private pilot's licence and had an extraordinary experience in 1963. His obituary in the *Times* – he died in 1991 – recorded: "Over the Home Counties one Saturday, on his way to visit his Lloyds underwriter, he circled round an isolated farmhouse, trying to place it on his map and find his bearings. By chance the Great Train Robbers were hiding in the farmhouse and, thinking themselves to be discovered and to be observed, panicked and fled after dark. In their hasty retreat they left behind much that was later to be used in evidence at their trial. Meanwhile, Stewart landed in the adjoining field, was picked up by his host in a large black car, returned three hours later after his meeting and took off again, blissfully unaware of the commotion."

Llewellyn was still doing his best to share the credit – "we went as a team, we won as team," he insisted – when the gold medallists returned to England the day after their triumph. Still the questioning focused obsessively on Foxhunter. How much is he worth, Col Llewellyn? "Please don't ask me that?" he said. "You might as well ask, what would you sell your wife for?"

Harry Llewellyn, Wilf White and (right) Duggie Stewart arrive back at Blackbushe Airport after their victory in Helsinki

Lucky horseshoes, or not, 1954 was a bad year for the Llewellyn family. Whereas Harry had avoided serious injury on horseback – he did have teeth knocked out on seven separate occasions – his wife was thoroughly accident-prone. Her misadventures in the saddle were matched behind the wheel and she all but died when her Land Rover collided with a lorry. In the same year Llewellyn retired Foxhunter from competitive show-jumping, though he had another two seasons' hunting in him. In 1955 Llewellyn acquired Aherlow and began competing on her.

He weaned himself off the routine of a 'good-night' pat for Foxhunter, reasoning in his memoirs: "I realised after he had retired from jumping and he was getting on in years that I ought to break myself of this habit because I knew I would miss him dreadfully when he died." Llewellyn had acquired a habit of answering journalists' questions through Foxhunter, as though the horse lacked only the power of speech. Judging by the response to an article in the *Daily Express*, claiming that Foxhunter was clever enough to sign his own autograph, the public were in on the artifice. Thousands of letters descended on the Llewellyn home before the Express took to sending out signed 'hoofprints'.

Foxhunter died at the age of 19, on Nov 28 1959; Llewellyn held his head as he expired. His skeleton was preserved and donated to the Royal Veterinary College, his hide placed in a steel casket with Llewellyn's book, *Foxhunter in Pictures*, and buried on the top of Blorenge mountain, overlooking the family homes, Gobion and Llanvair Grange. Llewellyn explained the joint burial thus: "In the Royal Veterinary College his skeleton will be a constant reminder of a great horse, whilst the burial on Blorenge mountain will remind many people that he was partly trained in this beautiful country of Wales."

The king of horses was also remembered through a class in his name at the Horse of Year Show and the Foxhunter Inn, close to his burial site and accompanying plaque. His owner retained his close ties with the equestrian world and was chef d'équipe for the British show-jumping team at the Mexico Olympics in 1968. He also helped to found Television Wales and West and became chairman of the Sports Council for Wales in 1971. He was knighted for his services to Wales in 1977 and, the following year, succeeded to the baronetcy after the death of his elder brother, Rhys. He himself died in 1999.

1956

June 14: Team three-day event, Bertie Hill, Laurence Rook, Frank Weldon

FEW, if any of the Olympic gold medals won by Britain during the Queen's reign, will have given her greater pleasure than the three-day event team's victory in Stockholm in 1956. As the part owner of Bertie Hill's horse, Countryman III, she even had a stake in the success. Diplomatic strings had been pulled to ensure that the Queen could fulfil her official duties on a state visit of Sweden before going on to watch the British team with all the nervous excitement of a proud parent.

It had been confirmed in August 1953 that Melbourne would be unable to stage the equestrian events because of a rigorously enforced six-month quarantine period. Harry Llewellyn, almost as well known in Australia as he was in Britain, lamented: "It is a great blow. If horsemen all over the world have no gold medal to aim at for eight years we may as well take up ping-pong. I feel very strongly about this – and so does Foxhunter." The opinion of Britain's best-loved horse was ignored, but at least the riders could put their table tennis bats down when, in May of the following year, Stockholm was chosen as a replacement venue.

The British team, battle-hardened by victories in the 1953, 1954 and 1955 European Championships, were strongly fancied to do well. Battle-hardened would also serve as an adjective to describe two of the three-man team. Laurence Rook, only 18 at the outbreak of war, won a Military Cross in 1944 while serving with the Royal Horse Guards. Frank Weldon's war is best summed up by this extract from his obituary in the *Times*: "Commissioned into the Royal Artillery, he won the Military Cross in 1940 during the retreat to St Valery. He was captured shortly afterwards, however, and spent the next five years in German prison camps, from which he escaped three times. He never got outside Germany, however, and was finally thrown into Colditz. There he was once more involved in attempted breakouts and was later awarded his military MBE for returning to help a fellow escapee trapped in a tunnel."

The junior member of the team was 29-year-old Hill, whose precocious skills as a horseman made him a very mobile member of the Home Guard on night patrols of Exmoor. He was a successful point-to-point rider immediately after the war and intensive schooling in dressage allowed him to join Rook in Britain's three-day event team at the 1952 Olympics.

A bronze medal, or better, was on the cards in Helsinki until an astonishingly quick cross-country ride by Rook on Starlight XV ended in an incident comparable to Devon Loch's stumble on the run-in at the Grand National in 1956; Starlight tripped over a hidden rut on the approach to the last fence. Wilf White, who three days later helped to give Britain their only gold medal of the Games, remembered: "Rook was tossed out of the saddle and so badly concussed that he didn't know where he was. Two Finnish soldiers had caught his horse, and Harry Llewellyn and Duggie Stewart hoisted him back into the saddle,

Britain's winning three-day event team in Stockholm, (from left to right) Laurence Rook, Bertie Hill and Frank Weldon

more dead than alive. Then someone gave Starlight a whack and the horse took the last jump with the reins loose, and Rook sitting in the saddle like a dummy."

It was confirmed afterwards that Rook had been unconscious for 30 seconds and, in his delirious state, had gone the wrong side of flags on the approach to the finish. Disqualification, while heartless, was largely irrelevant because Rook would have been in no fit state to take part in the show-jumping phase. The experience, though nothing more than gross misfortune, convinced Weldon that caution would be the watchword for the British trio on the cross-country section in Stockholm.

Although Rook was competing on a horse, Wild Venture, drafted in at the eleventh hour, his dressage test was impressive. On the following day Hill and Weldon gave Britain a lead which they would never sacrifice. *The Daily Telegraph* suggested that Countryman "may have been marked a little generously" and Weldon's Kilbarry a trifle harshly. It may have had something to do with the Queen's presence – Hill's start was even delayed so that she could watch.

Although Weldon appears to have been the victim of the judges' balancing act in Stockholm, he, too, knew what it was like to have friends in high places. He was having no success in convincing his commander that he should be allowed to miss a brigade exercise, until, that was, the brigadier received a letter backing up his request. "He is riding our horse at Badminton that day," it read. The letter was personally signed by the Queen Mother.

Hill's daughter, Sarah Hobbs, who is married to National Hunt trainer Philip Hobbs, tells the story of how Countryman was bought...and sold: "My father had gone down to Cornwall to buy another horse. The old boy who was showing him around had a broken leg. Dad said, 'I don't particularly like this horse you're showing me but I do like the head of that one beside him.' The chap said, 'That's the bugger who broke my leg. I can't get a saddle on him. You can have him for £90. Good riddance to him.'"

Countryman was broken in after being forced to jump onto the bank from a deep river. Under Hill's skilled tutelage he became such a capable eventer that he won the individual bronze medal when the European Championships were held at Windsor in 1955. It was there that the Queen took a shine to him and asked if he might be for sale. Hill, a natural wheeler-dealer, was offering no royal concessions and quoted a price of £1,000. The Queen is reported to have said, 'I can't afford that on my own, I'll get my mother to have a share.' The Duke of Beaufort also joined the syndicate. Hill's mighty profit went towards the purchase of a farm at Great Rapscott.

Countryman's new part owner again had her binoculars keenly trained as she and Princess Margaret willingly muddied shoes and stockings on a two-hour trudge around the sticky cross-country course in Stockholm. They were heard to shout out, 'Well done, Bertie' in unison and the Queen offered a delighted 'hooray' as Countryman cleared an obstacle in style. Mercifully, the royal party missed a heart-stopping moment for the British team, when Countryman slipped on his approach to the wide 'trakener' fence and became spreadeagled over the bar. Hill used exactly the same extrication method he had employed a few weeks earlier to rescue a similarly stricken bullock on his farm. The *Telegraph* reported: "Eventually he slipped back and was pulled out on the take-off side and at the second attempt cleared the jump with ease."

Hill admitted afterwards: "I was afraid he would not go on. I know I shouldn't have continued if I had been the horse. He slid back into a deep water-filled ditch and was almost submerged. I got him out and we scrambled back up the slope. I thought he would refuse to jump the fence – and that would have put the team out. Only a horse of great courage would have tackled it again, but that's Countryman. But for that unlucky slip and the three minutes it cost us it would have been the perfect round."

The *Times* correspondent struck an unctuous note in acknowledging the royal role in the campaign, writing: "The Queen was on the course to see her Countryman go round, and her gracious action in allowing our team to train and stable at Windsor has had the greatest influence on the progress and morale of our team. To see the British nations so well up in the hunt must have given satisfaction to her whose knowledge exceeds all but a few experts, and whose enthusiasm is an inspiration to us all."

According to the *Telegraph*, Rook went "unusually slowly" on Wild Venture and Kilbarry made an out-of-character error. The paper's correspondent wrote: "The chance of an individual gold was lost when Kilbarry unaccountably refused at the most innocuous fence 20, a simple post and rails on a road. I believe that this must be the first time Kilbarry had refused at a fence for at least two years."

If Britain had their problems, their rivals had far more. An 134-point advantage over Germany going into the final day was equivalent to 13 fences down. Rook and Hill hit one fence apiece and Weldon had two down as he failed narrowly to claim the individual silver medal.

Equestrians have been particularly dutiful in recycling their experiences for the benefit of the next generation of Olympians, and all three of the 1956 gold medallists did their bit. Frank Weldon was director of the Badminton Horse Trials and a forthright correspondent for *The Sunday Telegraph*. Rook, who made the familiar transition from soldiering to farming in the Fifties, was a technical delegate at the Olympics in 1964, 1968 and 1972. He was also chairman of Britain's horse trials committee from 1973 to 1980.

Wild Venture had someone new in the saddle at the Rome Olympics: Bertie Hill. The British team almost won the bronze medal, but should have done better; the meticulous planning so evident in 1956 was missing. The experience was a salutary one for Hill, who set up the Rapscott School of Equitation after retiring from international competition. Princess Anne and husband-to-be Mark Phillips were both inspired by his can-do brand of tuition but the Princess, according to Sarah Hobbs, was less impressed by Mary Hill's cooking and would often volunteer to stand in. In 1967 Bertie Hill was appointed official trainer to Britain's eventing team, sharing fully in the victory in Mexico the following year.

Nov 29: 3,000m steeplechase, Chris Brasher

HARRY CARPENTER, a man not given to empty hyperbole, described it in the *Daily Mail* as "the rottenest raw deal ever known in the Olympics". He was referring to Chris Brasher's groundless disqualification after winning the 3,000m steeplechase. Three hours passed before Brasher was reinstated; the medal ceremony had to be delayed until the following day.

He thought he had run the perfect race, working his way through the field before capitalising on a moment's hesitation from the world record holder, Sandor Rozsnyoi, to hit the front on the final bend. As he maintained his lead on the straight, Brasher screamed to himself, 'You've done it! You've done it! You've done it!' After finishing in an Olympic record time of 8min 41.2sec, he described himself as being "in a trance of happiness". Then came the jolting, unreal moment as the 1-2-3 was announced; his name was missing. Only when he went over to the jury table and spoke to the Marquess of Exeter, himself a gold medallist at the 1928 Olympics, did Brasher discover what had happened: a judge claimed that Brasher had impeded the Norwegian, Ernst Larsen, at the fourth hurdle from home. Michael Melford wrote in *The Daily Telegraph*: "One felt the same awful pang of disbelief as when Devon Loch slipped up at Aintree last spring."

Precedent was firmly against Brasher: the only previous example of a track disqualification being rescinded was when the American 4 x 100m relay team were reinstated in 1948, and that on the strength of filmed evidence. Brasher's case rested on the integrity of his rivals. Larsen insisted that he had not been impeded; Hans Laufer, the German who had been upgraded to third place, said he would throw the medal back if it was presented to him. Rozsynoi, who stood to inherit the gold medal, was interested only in knowing what had happened to his wife and family in the wake of the Hungarian uprising. "How can I run with that on my mind?" he said.

Forty years later Brasher reflected: "Had they been drug-testing athletes at Melbourne back in 1956, goodness knows what they would have made of me. No nandrolone, no EPO. Just an off-the-scale measure of Chardonnay and, since it is fashionable to refer to illicit substances by acronyms, G&T. Indeed, I may have the unique distinction of being the only athlete to have stood on the Olympic rostrum absolutely sloshed.

"The night I won I had quite a celebration with Chris Chataway and, at about 3am, a few journalists came to my room in the village, which was quite possible then because the whole place was open to everybody. They brought some wine and we sat up drinking. We met up again at lunchtime and all 12 or 13 journalists and friends brought a round of gin and tonics, so by the time of the medal ceremony in the afternoon I was well away. I was given my medal by a little Frenchman, and I was worried at the time that I was going to totter over and fall on top of him."

Brasher offered little evidence in his formative years that he was bound for greatness – in the sporting arena anyway. He was born in British Guiana, where his father helped to establish the state's post and telegraph service, and educated at Rugby School and Cambridge. While he was at St John's College, Brasher met John Disley, a fellow athlete and conspirator in many of Brasher's later business ventures. Disley recalls: "We met at a climbing hut in North Wales in 1949. He was president of the Cambridge University Climbing Club at the time. He brought a group of students with him and I remember hearing this raucous voice, telling some poor young student how to make porridge.

Chris Brasher clears the water jump on his way to victory in the 3,000m steeplechase

I was asleep in my bunk and it was only later when I recognised Chris had no more idea about making porridge than anyone else. What he was trying to do was to establish himself as the leader."

If talent had been the sole determinant, Brasher's claim to fame as an athlete would have rested on his selfless pacemaker's role in the first sub-four-minute mile in 1954; Chataway took up the running on the third lap, allowing Roger Bannister to surge through in the final straight. "He wasn't a good enough miler," says Disley, "so I suggested that he tried the steeplechase. Geoff Dyson, my coach, taught him how to take hurdles." Disley finished third in the steeplechase at the 1952 Games; Brasher was a distant 11th.

He knew that 1956 – he was 28 at the time – represented his last realistic opportunity to win an Olympic medal. "Fourteen months before Melbourne I decided I would become more serious," he wrote. "I took a less demanding job at Mobil, where I was a management trainee, gave up smoking, split with my girlfriend of the time and stopped mountaineering, which was my favourite hobby." Showing forensic attention to detail, he persuaded a scientist friend to produce titanium running spikes which were an ounce lighter than conventional spikes and used the lightest kangaroo leather available. Brasher was also able to draw on the innovative coaching methods of the Austrian-born Franz Stampfl. Disley insists that Stampfl has been given too much credit. "Most of us who were involved with coaching regarded Franz Stampfl as a hanger-on. He was a javelin thrower who knew nothing about running really."

Disley, who was suffering from the after-effects of viral pneumonia in Melbourne, played a crucial, remarkably charitable role in Brasher's selection for Melbourne. He explains:

> Chris was regarded as the third option for the Games. In fact he wasn't picked until the last race of the summer. We worked out on paper how much a lap would cost you to put toward your airfare – what he had to do to get on that plane. I just coached him all the way round, chopping off a bit when he was off the pace. We got back on schedule and by the last hurdle he was back with me. I beat him by a couple of seconds but he got the qualification time. If I hadn't done that he wouldn't have been in Melbourne. Lots of people said, why did you do it? It's not the kind of thing you do normally: to help a competitor to get into the team. Eric Shirley [Britain's other representative in Melbourne] always regrets not running in that race because he then probably would have stopped Brasher getting in.

It surprised no one who knew Brasher that he continued to excel, innovate and challenge the status quo for the rest of his life. He was described in a *Times* obituary in 2003 as bringing "a potent combination of idealism and cussedness to almost everything he did". As each Olympic Games passed, the idealist in Brasher saw something else to depress and disappoint him. The line was finally crossed in a welter of American excess at Atlanta in 1996. "I believe hugely in

Olympism," he said, "but my love affair with the Games themselves has finally hit the divorce courts. All the magic has dissolved."

Brasher was often a maverick voice of reason during his 35 years of writing for the *Observer's* sports section. "He was abrasive and very few of his colleagues liked him," says Disley. "They complained that he stole their stories, wasn't really a journalist and had used his gold medal to get where he did on the *Observer*." Disley, already a devotee of orienteering, was the catalyst for Brasher's highly influential article in 1957, in praise of the then uniquely Nordic sport. Two years later Brasher married Shirley Bloomer, the British tennis player who had won the French Open in 1957; she did not share her husband's love of the great outdoors.

He worked as a reporter on BBC Television's *Tonight* programme in the Sixties and stamped his mark even more indelibly in the Seventies and Eighties, first founding Chris Brasher's Sporting Emporium, which was soon rebranded as Sweatshop. He also designed the hybrid Brasher Boot, but his ultimate sporting legacy is the London Marathon, which he founded in 1981 after witnessing the mass participation appeal of the New York race. Brasher and John Disley, his fellow steeplechaser turned business partner, won £1.1 million in damages from Channel 4 and the *New Statesman* after being accused of using the London Marathon to feather their own nests. Brasher, who was made a CBE in 1996, discovered a new passion in the last chapter of his life: as a racehorse owner. By the mid-Nineties, he had eight horses in training.

Nov 30: Individual foil fencing, Gillian Sheen

GILLIAN SHEEN accepts that she would preach a more abstinent message if her book *Instructions to Young Fencers* were reprinted today. In 1958 her recipe for success sounded enticingly liberal. "Before going to the Olympic Games at Melbourne in 1956," she confided, "I used to fortify myself after a hard evening's training with a steak, watercress, and a glass of Burgundy." She also cringes at her observation that "the odd cigarette never hurt a fit person" before admitting, with a chuckle, that her gold medal sits in the lid of a cigarette box in her lakeside home in up-state New York.

Sheen was 14 when she took up fencing at a private school in Kent, North Foreland Lodge. Her first instructor was ex Foreign Legion. "We all thought he was a complete dragon, but he got results," she says. "Two of our three fencers at the 1952 Olympics were from the school." Sheen was immediately drawn to a sport which demanded both brawn and brain – she described it as "duelling without the need to have a doctor in attendance" – but Helsinki was not a high point in her budding career. "I hardly wanted to fight. It was terrible," she says. "I came back to London thinking I'd never make any progress."

Eventually she regained her appetite for a sport in transition. "They had only just brought in the electric foil which made a big difference. It certainly cleaned up the judging, which was definitely a plus. At the same time you had this heavy bit on the end of the tip of the foil which made it heavier and more cumbersome. The emphasis had been on fine finger work. It gradually became more athletic and these days there's much more footwork and much less handwork."

Sheen already had a clutch of university and national titles under her belt, but she only became convinced that she could compete effectively on the international stage when, a few months before the Melbourne Games, she beat all the top Soviet fencers in a team competition in London.

British journalists who barely knew their sabre from their épée, let alone the distinction between a *remise* and a *redoublement*, had to feign authority when Sheen converted that promise into the foil gold medal at St Kilda Town Hall. One report claimed that the same wrist action she employed as a dentist helped to strengthen her hold on the foil. Inevitable comparisons were made with Chris Brasher's steeplechase victory the previous day, the *Times* reporting: "If Brasher's win was unexpected, Miss Sheen's was a bombshell." By extraordinary coincidence, the two were born on the same day, Aug 21 1928.

Sheen had set her sights on a place in the final pool of eight fencers, but although she travelled out early to acclimatise she soon found that her preparations were hampered. "It was the usual thing with the British team," she remembers. "It was decided to send the fewest people possible out to Australia because it was so expensive, so we didn't have a trainer with us. We were having to train on our own, but then the Hungarian coach agreed to give us lessons. I felt a bit guilty when I beat their world champion, Lidia Domolki, in a barrage."

The victory over Domolki enabled Sheen to reach the final pool; her only defeat on the opening day of the competition had come against Olga Orban-Szabo. The outcome was the same when they met in the

***Gillian Sheen with (right) Melbourne team-mate Mary Glen-Haig,
who went on to become the first female member of the
International Olympic Committee***

final pool, but the Romanian also lost a bout, setting up a barrage
between her and Sheen to decide who would win the gold medal. "I
think the Romanians were pretty jubilant, thinking it would be a piece
of cake," she reflects. "I beat her 4-2 and I'd never been happier in my
life."

Her understated reaction at the time was: "I guess mother and
father will be pleased." The *Daily Mail* reported: "Laughing and crying
alternatively, Gillian said: 'It's all such a shock. I just can't think
properly. It's like a beautiful dream. I hope I don't wake up and find it's
untrue.' " Britain's team captain, Charles de Beaumont, a highly
influential figure in the sport, called it "the greatest thing that has ever

happened to British fencing". Sheen's coach/mentor, Leon Bertrand, a classicist who was fond of quoting great Italian instructors, glowed: "Her footwork is akin to ballet…and her finger work!"

Sheen recalls the aftermath to her victory: "All the British team came rushing up to hug me and I eventually went back to the village. When I went into the dining room for supper the whole of the British section got up and applauded. Then, if you won a medal, you got a cake presented to you. I remember we went out on the town and we eventually found this nightclub; the doorman wanted to say they were full up. Of course I'd got my gold medal with me – it was in a plastic box at that point – so we shone that around and immediately we were admitted. The celebrations went on practically all night."

Sheen had taken her accountant father's advice by quitting her job in a West End dental practice and as the other gold medallists went home she travelled round New Zealand before returning to England, and her flat overlooking Lord's cricket ground, by boat. "It was a wonderful trip, but when I got back it was February and horribly cold. I was met by the Mayor of Marylebone, who gave me a brooch with the Marylebone seal on it."

She has no doubt that her victory was beneficial for fencing in Britain and did her best to fuel the surge in popularity. "We gave demonstrations all over the place; we called it a fencing circus. I was in two minds about going to Rome: once you've won the ultimate prize you don't have that same incentive again. Perhaps I should have retired, but I didn't want to. I wanted to keep going and promote the sport." Her title defence ended when she was knocked out in the quarter-final pool.

Sheen had spent most of 1958 in the United States, working in a dental dispensary. She also met her husband-to-be, fellow dentist Robert Donaldson. "I wanted him to come to England, but I couldn't persuade him." The couple married in 1963 and settled in the US soon after. Even after almost 50 years on the other side of the pond, Sheen retains her well-heeled English accent and self-deprecating sense of humour. A little bit of England still resides in Albany, NY.

Dec 1: Flyweight boxing, Terry Spinks

TERRY SPINKS was the ridiculously young-looking boxer – he was 18 but could have passed for 12 – who shot to fame by winning the flyweight title at the 1956 Olympics. The high-tempo lifestyle which followed guaranteed that he would never fulfil his potential in the professional ranks and by the age of 24, when he should have been in his prime, he was already an ex-boxer.

His every decision seemed to have a ruinous side-effect: he was the boxer who always struggled to make the weight…and bought a sweet shop. He was the gambler who became a bookmaker at the height of the great freeze in 1963. He was debt-ridden and desperate when a Sunday newspaper offered him £1,500 for a four-part confessional. Already on the Inland Revenue's hit list, he now presented them with chapter-and-verse evidence of untaxed income and drink-fuelled excess.

At the bankruptcy hearing which sealed his fate, Spinks was floored by a simple line of inquiry from J.L. Williams, the Official Receiver: "I have read that by the time you were 19 or 20 you had drunk so much Scotch whisky that you spoke Cockney with a Scots accent. Did you say that?"

"No," insisted Spinks, ignoring the fact that the exact words had appeared under his name in the serialisation a few weeks earlier.

He was the binge drinker who bought a pub…and then another, before his licence was finally revoked in 1991. His mother died in the same year; he was hopelessly drunk at her funeral and by now the excuses for hitting the bottle were forming a disorderly queue. Spinks's second wife, Barbara, left him, taking with her their seven-year-old daughter, Claire.

The story would have ended, with grim certainty, soon afterwards but for the benign intervention of Spinks's cousin, Rosemary Ellmore. Although they had been regular playmates during school holidays, she had seen him only a handful of times in the previous 20 years, the last being when she witnessed Spinks's demeanour at his mother's funeral; she put it down to the grief of the moment.

After he was barred from the pub trade Spinks lived with his father. They were devoted to each other, but neither was suited to orderly domesticity. Terry continued to drink heavily and his proud father continued to insist that he was fighting fit. Tich himself was ageing and losing his sight. Ellmore arranged to have a drink with father and son in 1993 but had not prepared herself for the shocks which greeted her when she went to pick up her cousin.

"Terry could hardly walk," she remembers. "He was seven stone and his belt was pulled in. I'll never forget going into his bedroom: there were clothes and photographs strewn all over the place. It was absolutely heartbreaking. I went off on holiday the following week and the day I came back my mum called to say that Terry had been rushed into hospital after collapsing. They only gave him until the weekend."

He was incapable of washing or dressing himself and was hallucinating badly. Scans confirmed the diagnosis which could have been made years earlier: he was suffering from irreversible brain damage. The neurologist who briefed Rosemary Ellmore likened his liver and brain to a ripe pear and a bruised, soft pear (the typical legacy of years in the ring). The alcoholic onslaught spared Spinks's liver and attacked his brain instead.

When his condition stabilised he was admitted to a clinic which specialised in brain-damaged patients, though there was precious little stimulation for Spinks. He was more at ease in the family environment but needed round-the-clock supervision. Finally, when his father died in 1999, he moved in permanently with Rosemary Ellmore and her husband, also called Terry, in Chadwell Heath. Spinks had to undergo a series of operations after fluid on the brain was diagnosed six years ago, forcing Ellmore to admit: "He's really been through it."

The award of an MBE in 2002 was a much-needed tonic; Ellmore recalls how the campaign for belated recognition was launched: "Terry had stopped drinking, of course, but when he was in the clinic I used to take him out sometimes to a little country pub. It was owned by a friend of Terry's who asked me one day why he'd never got the MBE. I mentioned it to Reg Gutteridge and that started it all off, though it took us eight years to get there. We'd always said if Terry got the award we'd have the biggest party ever. There were 1,100 people in York Hall and Terry raised £6,200 and he gave every penny of it to charity." She remembers the trip to Buckingham Palace, which coincided with her birthday, as "a lovely, lovely day".

The remarkable turn-out at York Hall simply underlined that Spinks, for all his self-destructive frailties, was still a superstar in his manor: the East End of London. The brain was no longer able to articulate the wealth of memories, good and bad, but at heart he remained the same lovable lad who was once, in Ellmore's words, "as high profile as David Beckham is today".

Gambling was in the blood – Tich Spinks was a street bookmaker – and the eight-year-old Terry could be found running a book with sweets as stakes. His early ambition was to become a jockey; he was taken on as a stable lad at Newmarket in 1953, but weight problems, also the bane of his boxing career, soon blocked off that career path. He

Terry Spinks on the offensive during his flyweight final against Romania's Mircea Dobrescu

was working as a bin man in the London docks when he won the ABA flyweight title at the first attempt in 1956. He was not originally selected for the Olympic Games team, but journalist Gutteridge (later to become an ITV commentator) led a successful campaign for his inclusion.

It soon became clear that Spinks was not just there to make up the numbers. He was impressive in the ring and quotable out of it; the *Daily Mail* dubbed him the "Kid Philosopher". He found his opponents' names more difficult to master than his opponents. "Blimey," he said. "I can't pronounce any of them but they can all be walloped."

Suddenly, he was in the semi-finals. Harry Carpenter, then working for the *Mail*, wrote: "Visions of gold medals appeared suddenly last night when Cockney fly-weight Terry Spinks, wearing lucky No. 7 on his white vest, unexpectedly beat tough Russian Vladimir Stolnikov. In Moscow this year it had been the other way round and, without exaggeration, Spinks has had Stolnikov so much on his mind that, the night before his quarter-final, he had a nightmare. 'I woke up on the floor,' said Spinks, 'with my room-mate, Tommy Nicholls, standing over me counting me out. When I realised it wasn't Stolnikov I couldn't get back to sleep for laughing.' "

Showing great speed and remarkable ring craft for such a young boxer, he outpointed Frenchman René Libeer in his semi-final, but needed to skip for half an hour in 100 degree temperatures to make the weight for the final. Neil Allen's lyrical account of the fight for the *Times* is worth reproducing here:

> The first bell and there was the cherubic-looking Spinks dancing out to jab away at the swarthy Romanian [Mircea] Dobrescu, who is built like a boiler. As with the other two Romanian finalists Dobrescu never stopped moving in, throwing hooks and flailing away at close quarters like a buzz-saw, but Spinks rapped out his left hand and moved away swiftly on lightning feet. In the second round Dobrescu began to drop his damaging left hooks over Spinks's left shoulder and the British boxer had to whip away in retreat, stemming the onslaught with an occasional left hand. Finally, Spinks took refuge in clinches until the bell, and we could breathe again.
>
> The last round brought one long roar from the crowd as Spinks, ivory-white but still moving as elusively as a moth under the harsh ring lights, side-stepped the bobbing, weaving attack of Dobrescu. The crucial moment came when Spinks was really hurt for the first time by a right which stretched him limp across the ropes. Dobrescu moved in but the referee stopped the contest to warn Spinks for slapping, and the momentary respite was all the British boy needed. Soon he was back in his rhythm with his jabs and even some daring combinations to head and body which made Dobrescu shake his shaggy head.

Gutteridge made light of the fact that he had lost a leg during the war to dance on his desk at the *Evening News* offices in London, though he would later admit to Rosemary Ellmore that the gold medal was both the best and worst thing which happened to Spinks. His parents' Canning Town home became the hub of a party which still seemed to be going when their son arrived home 10 days later. London Zoo announced that they were going to name a baby giraffe after him.

Spinks did not enjoy the ceaseless attention which came with A-list celebrity, but he found the trappings of stardom seductive. "Terry was a real playboy," says Ellmore. "He was a good-looking boy, he wore sharp suits and he mixed with royalty and film stars." She also admits that it was an unsustainable lifestyle. "He'd come out of the clubs and pubs and go in the gym to take off the weight he'd just put on."

The same lack of self-discipline – "if I hadn't been a boxer I think I'd have looked like a barrel," he admitted – made it inevitable that his professional career would be short and unfulfilled. He won his first 11 pro fights, condensed into an eight-month period in 1957. He first won the British featherweight title, in September 1960, then lost it to future world champion Howard Winstone in a brutal encounter seven months later. He married shortly afterwards, but he was never temperamentally suited to a sedate family life. There were brief signs that he might forge a secondary career in boxing as a trainer – he coached the South Korean team for the 1972 Olympics in Munich – but it was just another what-might-have-been.

Rosemary Ellmore's selfless dedication has seen Terry Spinks into his seventies, an achievement for any boxer let alone one capable of such self-neglect. She has never looked for a pat on the back; she simply wishes that so-called friends, many of whom benefited from Spinks's generosity, had stepped in when he was drinking himself into oblivion. Spinks can no longer articulate his own story, but Ellmore is more qualified to speak on his behalf than anyone. "Terry is a genuinely nice man; he'd give everything away. He'd be the first to tell you, 'If I die tomorrow I've had a wonderful life.' "

Dec 1: Lightweight boxing, Dick McTaggart

THE archive footage of Dick McTaggart's lightweight final at the Melbourne Games shows a man in control. Uniquely, for a British boxer, he was to compete in two more Olympic Games before retiring in 1965 – still an amateur and still convinced that there was an unacceptable price to pay for chasing the pot of gold.

McTaggart's chaotic but largely contented upbringing in Dundee, as the third youngest of 18 children, could have made him easy prey for the promoters. He can't quite remember the brother-sister ratio – there were infant casualties – but reckons there were more girls than boys. When asked about his father's job, he quips, "To make love to his wife."

Five of his brothers shared his passion for boxing; at one point, extraordinarily, the McTaggarts held the Army, Navy and RAF titles. Dick, who spent five years as a cook at RAF Halton in Buckinghamshire, recalls that he was beaten by one of his brothers in regional championships...though he was only 17 at the time. Defeats were rare in any company: he lost only 24 of his 634 bouts. The 5ft 9in McTaggart confesses that he struggled throughout his career to make the 60kg limit for lightweights. By the time he made his final Olympic appearance in Tokyo he had moved up to light welterweight.

He was only 21 when he was picked for the Melbourne Games and could have been forgiven for treating it as a trans-global adventure. Not a bit of it. "You hear all this stuff about, it's not the winning, it's the taking part. I'm not going all that way just to take part. I wanted to win a medal of some sort. I've never been one to boast, but I boxed exceptionally well throughout; it was just one of those occasions when you feel right in yourself. After the semi-final I said, 'I'm going to win this.' " One of his brothers, Thomas, had jumped ship from the

Terry Spinks and (right) Dick McTaggart arrive home with the Val Barker Trophy awarded to McTaggart as the most stylish boxer at the Melbourne Games

merchant navy to watch him fight; the rest of the family tuned in to Raymond Glendenning's radio commentary on the final.

McTaggart had already seen off one tough opponent in the Soviet, Anatoly Lagetko, Another stood between him and the gold medal. The *Daily Mail* wrote of the "scrub-topped" Scot's adversary: "What a tartar he has to deal with in that battling bricklayer from Berlin, Homicide Harry Kurschat, who builds houses by day and knocks over opponents by night." As Neil Allen's report for the *Times* made plain, the Scot was the tactical master:

> McTaggart surprised everyone by the way in which he sailed into Kurschat, his right hook stunning the German again and again in the first round and sending him down twice. The second was mere repetition, with the immensely game Kurschat taking steady punishment, and it was only in the last minute of the third, when McTaggart invariably blows up, that the scales went the other way. Then Kurschat, at last giving instead of taking, hurled himself after McTaggart, who looked as weak as a landed fish. McTaggart huddled behind protective gloves and lasted out. It was a splendid performance and quite unlooked for by many who had seen McTaggart during the domestic season.

A huge bonus for McTaggart came with confirmation that he had won the prestigious Val Barker Trophy, awarded to the top stylist across all the weight categories. "It was fantastic to receive that," he says, "not just for me but for the whole team." Harry Carpenter, writing in the *Daily Mail*, went further: "I think the boxing boys are more proud of the Val Barker Trophy than they are of their five medals. When last, if ever, did a southpaw counter-puncher like McTaggart win their flinty hearts?"

On the long trip back, Britain's Olympians were transferred on to a large Japanese aircraft at Istanbul. McTaggart's fellow gold medallist, Terry Spinks, who has been a close friend ever since, discovered a bar in the upper section of the plane, shouting down to McTaggart: "Hey, Jock. Come quick. There's a bar up here...and it's free." McTaggart was so well oiled by the time they got back to London that he almost left behind the trophy.

"The celebrations seemed to go on for about a year after that," he says. In particular, he remembers being overwhelmed by the reception when he got back to Dundee. "It was like I was going to be crowned king. I came off the train and was carried shoulder-high to an open-topped bus and paraded through the streets." There were decisions to be made about his future, but he responds to the inevitable question – Why did you remain amateur? – with a few rhetorical questions of his own. He had a hereditary defect in his left eye, suggesting that a pro licence might not, anyway, have been granted, but insists that he was never remotely interested in joining the paid ranks.

"Do you want the truth? Do you ever see any punch-drunk managers? Do you ever see any punch-drunk promoters? No. But you see a lot of punch-drunk boxers, don't you? I wanted to keep my health, but I also realised that if I was going to be a good pro I'd have to sacrifice an awful lot. I used to smoke and drink." Nor did the sums ever add up for McTaggart. "I didn't fancy fighting and getting my 25 per cent of the purse, the promoters getting their 25 per cent. Then your trainer would want his share as well. Anyway, I didn't fancy fighting for money. I enjoyed it as a sport."

The bank balance has never been too healthy and after McTaggart left the RAF and married in 1958, he and his first wife, June, moved briefly to her home town, Bristol. "He had plenty of promises," she claimed at the time, "but the only jobs he has been able to get in Dundee have been as an assistant warehouseman and a builders' labourer at wages on which we could not bring up a family decently." The relationship did not last and McTaggart was soon back in Scotland. He and his second wife, Doreen, have been together since 1963.

A stint in pest control gave Carpenter, in his guise as BBC commentator, the excuse to dub McTaggart the 'Glasgow rat-catcher'.

> **'I wasn't a rat-catcher. I was a rodent exterminator. I didn't do it for long either'**

"I wasn't a rat-catcher," he says in mock protest, "I was a rodent exterminator for Glasgow Corporation. I didn't do it for long, either, but Harry was still calling me that a year after I'd left the job." McTaggart's boxing career almost came to an abrupt halt in 1962 when he injured his left hand unloading beer barrels.

He thought another gold medal was in his grasp in Rome, but had to settle for bronze after being beaten by the Pole, Kazimierz Pazdzior, who went on to win the competition. Another Pole en route to gold, Jerzy Kulej, blocked McTaggart's progress in 1964. The Ghanaian, Clement Quartey, was so shocked to win a points decision against McTaggart in the light-welterweight final at the Commonwealth

Games in 1962 that he fainted. McTaggart shook his head in disbelief and said afterwards: "I thought I had it won easily. No wonder he fainted."

McTaggart's career finished on a high in 1965, when he won a record-equalling fifth ABA title. The man he beat, Larry O'Connell, went on to become one of the best-known referees. Appropriately, Carpenter, who once described McTaggart as the finest amateur boxer he had seen, was describing the fight for the BBC. McTaggart retired from the ring soon afterwards, but he remained fully involved in boxing; he went to the Los Angeles Olympics as a coach and received the unusual accolade of a half-hour documentary on Soviet television in 1988 when he visited St Petersburg with a Scottish team. Unaware that the programme was being aired, he woke just in time for the closing credits. A sports centre was named after him and two years ago he received an honorary degree from Dundee's Abertay University.

McTaggart, who now lives in Troon, on the Ayrshire coast, believes that amateur boxing can re-establish itself in Britain, but says it more in hope than confidence. "These days they offer you quarter of a million to stay amateur," he says wistfully.

Dec 5: 100m backstroke, Judy Grinham

JUDY GRINHAM quit school to become a full-time swimmer in March 1956. Her single-minded approach might have been applauded elsewhere, but in Britain it simply provoked complaints that she had turned her back on education – in her case a sixth-form secretarial course – and embraced the sinister Soviet ethos.

Even the freedom came with strings attached. She still had to "battle through screaming, splashing masses of youngsters" wherever she trained. She wrote in her autobiography: "We tried to get special facilities from the various baths I visited, but it was hopeless. One pool finally offered me a roped-off lane, but it proved almost useless. Most of the other swimmers in the pool either wanted to swim in it with me or hang on to the corks, hindering me."

Twice in 1956 she went down with conjunctivitis, the legacy of the chemicals poured by the gallon into public baths. She was a naturally fretful 17-year-old and admitted that as the Melbourne Games drew closer she became "touchy and hysterical". Ten days before she flew out to Australia she was persuaded to visit a psychiatrist, who calmed her fears and prescribed tranquillisers. Only after the Games did she wonder whether the pills might have given her anything more than psychological assistance.

The curious prospect facing Grinham, as she made the multi-legged flight to the other side of the world, was that the greatest threat would come from a swimmer who lived and trained only a few miles away. Grinham was from Neasden, Margaret Edwards from neighbouring Heston. They were born only 23 days apart in 1939 and were united in their desire to be the best after competing against each other for the first time in 1952.

There was no personal animosity between them, but they were soon caught up in a hurtful and daft propaganda campaign. Grinham admitted: "It gave a sharp edge to a rivalry which was already keen enough in the water. The most serious aspect of it was that this over-enthusiasm on the part of the rival camp-followers opened a gulf between Margaret and me, which although never apparent to out-siders, nevertheless persisted and, unhappily, never really healed." Old tensions have been forgotten when the two have met in recent years.

Grinham always insisted that her parents rose above the squabbling and viewed their daughter's success with healthy detachment. "They never complained when I lost, they were no more than naturally proud when I won – and, wisely, they left my coaches alone." Grinham had been only six months old when her father, Norman, went away to war; he did not return home – bar a couple of weeks' leave after the evacuation of Dunkirk in 1944 – until she was six and a half. Grinham recalls:

> My family, during the time he was away at war, was my mother and grandmother, and this strange man who came into my life was an interloper. Dad told me that I was horrible to him. I can't believe that I was so mean and am appalled but, apparently, this was a common problem for soldiers coming back from the war. He had the foresight to find something to use as a bridge to a relationship with this child that he did not know. He found that I loved swimming and was at my side through all the ups and downs of my swimming career.

British officials showed at best insensitivity by asking Grinham and Edwards to be room-mates during their month-long stay in Melbourne's Olympic village. There were no tantrums but, in the absence of her trusted coach, Reg Laxton, Grinham was soon at odds with team manager Alf Price, resenting his accusations that she wasn't training hard enough.

The 100m backstroke had become marginally less competitive following the withdrawal of Holland, in protest at the Soviet Union's ruthless response to the Hungarian uprising, but Grinham was concerned only with securing a place in the final when the heats got under way. She promptly posted an Olympic record time of 1min

Judy Grinham, still Britain's youngest individual gold medallist at the Olympic Games

13.1sec, only for Edwards to go a tenth of a second faster in her heat and confirm her as the favourite for the gold medal.

Grinham welcomed the distraction of the freestyle relay heats the following day, but as she was driven to the Olympic Park for the final she was the same hyperactive bundle of nerves she had been before the heats. Price said later: "She sang at the top of her voice in the car all the way to the pool. She went through her whole repertoire from *Rule Britannia* to *Maybe It's Because I'm a Londoner*. She didn't fool me. I guessed she was putting on an act."

No sooner had Grinham dived into the pool than she felt her slip move under her costume. "I giggled," she recalled, "probably relieving some of my tension, and I was still giggling when the gun cracked." She started poorly and was still outside the medal positions at the turn, but halfway down the second length she drew level with the leaders. "I went beyond the pain barrier then, almost into a different world. I found inspiration and even increased my speed over the last few yards before flinging myself at the wall in a last desperate lunge." She fractionally beat the American, Carin Cone, to the touch, clocking a long-course world record time of 1min 12.9sec; Edwards was third. The *Times* reported: "Miss Grinham was accorded an ovation of a kind that has hitherto been reserved for the Australians."

She was Britain's first Olympic champion in the pool since Lucy Morton, whom she had met three years earlier, in 1924. At 17 years 277 days she remains the youngest British gold medallist in an individual event at the Games. Grinham's instinctive response, when offered a chair at the press conference afterwards, was more widely quoted than her considered reflections on the race. "I can't sit down, my bottom's wet," she insisted. Asked about her future plans in the pool, she said she would abandon the backstroke and concentrate on the freestyle in 1957.

Harry Carpenter wrote in the *Daily Mail*: "Judy Grinham, Britain's first gold-medal swimmer for 32 years, flies home next week to get herself measured for a wedding dress. But it doesn't mean marriage for this 17-year-old London lass. Let Judy explain: 'Before I came away a friend of my mother's said she would make me a wedding dress if I did well in the Olympics. So now I have my wedding gown – but no one to marry.' "

Her homecoming was marked by a street party in Neasden reminiscent of VE Day; she and Edwards were all smiles at a civic reception in their honour. Grinham turned down the chance to earn

£350 a week for a six-month contract as part of a touring 'aqua show'. Despite the difficulty of re-motivating herself, she still felt she had unfinished business in the pool. She became the first woman to duck under a minute for the 100 yards freestyle, though it could not count for record purposes as it was a relay anchor leg. Grinham then won the 110 yards backstroke title at the 1958 Commonwealth Games, helped England to a world record in the medley relay and completed a then unique triple of individual titles by winning the European crown in Budapest.

A newspaper publicity stunt, widely interpreted as Grinham's attempt to break into films, brought her a small part in the instantly forgettable *Operation Bullshine* and much speculation that her amateur status was under threat. The mumbling became irrelevant when she announced on the BBC's *Sportsview* programme that she had retired from swimming.

On March 5 1959, her 20th birthday, Grinham joined the *Daily Express* as a trainee journalist, quickly feeling the predictably protective backlash from seasoned reporters. She looks back on her two years with the paper as more "life experience" than enjoyable, but she did have the pleasure of covering Anita Lonsbrough's victory in Rome in 1960. "It was very hard to keep an objective reporter's view when I wanted to dance up and down in the press box," she recalls

Grinham married a fellow sports journalist, Pat Rowley, in 1960, and went on to work for the charity Barnardo's for 15 years. After she and Rowley divorced, Grinham married Michael Roe, moving to Cornwall in the mid-Nineties. Years of lobbying by her daughter, Alison Heeks, finally paid off when Grinham was awarded an MBE in 2006, the 50th anniversary of her victory in Melbourne. She settled in Hertfordshire when Michael Roe died in 2010.

1960

Aug 27: 200m breaststroke, Anita Lonsbrough

WINNING an Olympic gold medal was far from Anita Lonsbrough's thoughts the previous winter. She was too busy fighting off gastroenteritis, gastric flu and finally an attack of shingles which left her so weak that she could barely walk when she came out of hospital. "To be honest with you, only six months ago I would not have given tuppence for her chances," admitted Lonsbrough's mother, Maud, after seeing her daughter lift the 200m breaststroke title in Rome. "She had one illness after another. Then she damaged her shoulder, and I was all for telling her that her health was more important than swimming."

Lonsbrough, though, came from determined Yorkshire stock. Her mother was a capable cyclist and swimmer who competed in the long-distance race on the River Ouse; her father was a sergeant major in the Coldstream Guards and it was during the nine months when he was based at Mhow, in Central India, that six-year-old Anita had her first swimming lessons at the barracks pool. There was no preferential treatment at her local baths in Huddersfield – even when she was in full training for the Olympics. In the morning she would have to wait for the boilerman to open up, and then had to clear away the cockroaches; she swam again during her lunch break from her job with Huddersfield council and, pool availability permitting, returned in the evening for a third session.

She was calmness personified in the build-up to the evening final on Aug 27. In the previous day's heats 19-year-old Lonsbrough had recorded the second quickest time, beaten only by Wiltrud Urselmann, the West German who had taken Lonsbrough's world record two months earlier. "I never really thought of winning," she recalls, "but then I never really thought of losing either. I knew exactly what I'd got

Anita Lonsbrough arrives back in Britain after winning the 200m breaststroke in Rome

to do and it was just a question then of whether Wiltrud could do something different and beat me."

Lonsbrough's support, in the capacity crowd of 20,000 at the outdoor pool, consisted of her mother, Aunt Nora, cousin Joyce and a small party of fans from York. Her father, Sidney, convinced that he always put his daughter off when he watched her race, stayed at home. Urselmann was urged on by an estimated 2,000 Germans. In the descriptive shorthand of the *Daily Herald*'s Sam Leitch, she was the "blonde and beautiful grocery girl"; Lonsbrough was "broadshouldered"; Ada den Haan, the Dutch swimmer also expected to challenge for a medal, was the "slim perfectionist".

Leitch wrote that Lonsbrough "slept for four hours in the sweaty Italian night, breakfasted on steak and chips, grapes and orange juice, then waited for mum." Lonsbrough insists, less romantically, that she commandeered the room of a yet-to-arrive athlete and managed 12 hours' untroubled sleep. In the afternoon she painted her nails and by the time the swimmers marched out for the evening final the fierce heat had abated.

The tactics were already clear in her mind. "I knew if I tried to go out with Urselmann I would probably blow up because she was a better sprinter than I was. I planned to go out at a pace which was within my capacity and then catch her on the third length and pass her on the last length. It worked, up to a point. For the first time in our rivalry she came back at me on the last length." The chants of 'Bravo Wiltrud' died away as the German was hauled in, though Lonsbrough admitted afterwards that she had felt "a bit of a chump" rising out of the water with 20 metres to go to check where the fast-finishing Den Haan was. She still managed to clock a world record time of 2min 49.5sec, becoming the first female breaststroker to go under 2min 50sec.

Leitch, the Scot whose face and girth were to become familiar to BBC football-watchers, admitted: "Never in my sports globe-trotting have I felt so moved as I did when Anita, with a bold Yorkshire stride, walked the length of the luxury pool to take her gold medal." Lonsbrough remembers being caught up in the madness of the moment: "You get carried along, because suddenly your life's not your own anymore. It's go there, come here. After the medal ceremony I was whisked along to the BBC studios and had to sit there for quite a while in a wet bathing suit while the programme started. The next day I was amazed by the number of telegrams I received from people I didn't know. It was rather nice."

Mother and daughter were reunited to give the press their morning-after versions of events:

Maud: Do you know, if I saw our Anita win that race once I saw it a thousand times last night. Every time I tried to get to sleep I would see her just winning, and every time I had that same fear I had when she was trailing behind in the first two lengths. Then I would wake up and find I was either cheering or crying.

Anita: It's all right mum telling the tale now and looking all calm and cool, but you should have seen us when we met after the race. Cry? You could have filled a swimming pool with it before we dried up!

The one journalist who could claim genuine empathy was Judy Grinham, the 100m backstroke champion in Melbourne who was working as a fledgling reporter for the *Daily Express*. She had an unusual insight for her readers: "Anita did admit she had one moment of terror before she stood on her block for the start. Not because of her rivals, or because of the tremendous effort before her. She was scared that she might swallow a fly that was frantically swimming round and round in the water right below her. It was this silly diversion from the great trial ahead that must have helped Anita to relax from the pre-race tension."

The promised civic reception in Huddersfield was delayed until Maud Lonsbrough returned from Italy. Anita arrived back limping (courtesy of a painful insect bite on her ankle) and clutching a Koala bear which had been given to her by the Australian team. She joined her cricket-loving father at the Scarborough Festival. "When I went in one day people recognised me and they started to applaud just as Freddie Trueman [the famous fast bowler] was going out. He thought the applause was for him."

The mayor of Huddersfield, Norman Day, had despatched an immediate congratulatory telegram after the final, but instead of Huddersfield council gaining some reflected glory – Lonsbrough was employed in the motor car taxation office – they found themselves in the Fleet Street firing line. It was discovered that Lonsbrough had lost £12 13s 6d in wages after asking for her weekly hours to be cut from 38 to 31 three months before the Games. She *was* granted leave on full pay for the period immediately before and during the Olympics. A secondary charge of petty provincialism centred on the "tuppence halfpenny" reception laid on by the council. Mayor Day confessed gloomily: "I sometimes think that I never want to read a paper again."

A second function drew a crowd of 1,200 to the town hall. Anita Lonsbrough, addressing the throng from the balcony, confessed that she was more nervous than she had been before the final in Rome. The mayor read out a poem of dedication:

> Put out the flags and bunting,
> And let the bells be pealed;
> In honour of a grand young lass,
> Who hails from Huddersfield
> Anita Lonsbrough swam for us,
> And we were with her too;
> All through that long last toiling length,
> And now our thanks are due

Normality was soon restored, though a dynamic new life opened up for Lonsbrough when *The Sunday Telegraph* was launched in 1961 and she was asked to become the paper's first swimming correspondent. Although she made it clear that she wanted to carry on competing the offer was obligingly put on hold until she was ready.

In 1962 she completed the clean sweep of major titles by adding the European Championship to the Olympic and Commonwealth crowns; she also became the first female winner of the BBC Sports Personality of the Year award. Lonsbrough's chances of glory in the 400m medley at the 1964 Olympics in Tokyo vanished when she swallowed water in the final. The Games were, however, memorable for other reasons. On the flight out she met her husband-to-be, cyclist Hugh Porter, whose strong medal hopes in the 4,000m pursuit were dashed by a bout of bronchitis.

Lonsbrough also became the first woman to carry the British flag at the opening ceremony, greeting the invitation with almost regal solemnity. "This is a great victory for the women of Britain who sometimes feel they must always be a step behind the men folk," she said. On a less earnest note, she recalls: "I think they were concerned whether I'd have the strength to carry the flag. The other worry was that the flag might knock my hat off, so I was allowed to parade without a hat."

On Jan 1 1965, two months after the end of the Tokyo Games, she joined *The Sunday Telegraph* and soon became a radio regular as well, the summariser charged with lowering the temperature after Peter Jones's passionate race commentaries. Lonsbrough's 44-year stint with *Telegraph* newspapers – she began writing for the daily paper as well in the late Eighties – ended without ceremony or sentiment in 2009, just long enough for her to witness (with more than a tear) Rebecca Adlington's two gold medals in Beijing; she calls her "a lovely girl".

"It would have been nice to have covered a home Olympics," she says, "but it was not to be, so I will watch my first Olympics on television instead."

Sept 7: 50km walk, Don Thompson

EVEN in the masochists' playground of long-distance race walking, Don Thompson was a phenomenon. When the 5ft 5in Londoner won the Milan 100km race in 1955 he was dubbed 'il topolino' - a word which for Italians in the mid-Fifties represented not only Mickey

Mouse but also Fiat's mini-engined car. Five years later the 27-year-old insurance clerk was embraced like a native when he conquered the intense heat of Rome to win Britain's second gold medal of the Games.

The distance this time was 50km, roughly five miles further than a marathon but a stroll round the block compared to the ordeal which he let himself in for on his final international outing in 1991: the Bazancourt 200km (125 miles) in northern France. When the 24-hour time limit passed Thompson had managed only 188km…but he was 58 at the time.

In the words of team-mate Ken Matthews, a gold medallist over 20km in Tokyo, Thompson was "like a mechanical toy. You'd wind him up and he'd go all day." The batteries occasionally ran out, most famously when he dropped out of the Olympic final in Melbourne, so delirious and disorientated that he walked into the back of a car. He vowed then that he would win in Rome, "or die in the attempt".

It was not the empty boast of the self-publicist, because no one was less boastful than Thompson, and his means to an end were comically resourceful. After winning in 1960 he explained: "I realised it was going to be hot in Rome and decided to fix up a steam room in my home in Cranford, Middlesex. For the past few months I have built up the temperature of the bathroom to 100 degrees Fahrenheit, with the aid of a gas boiler, kettles, and an electric fire. Then I performed exercises in a track suit for 45 minutes. It was a rather Heath Robinson affair, but it seems to have worked." Years later he cottoned on to the fact that the dizziness he felt towards the end of these sessions was brought on not by the heat but by the build-up of carbon monoxide from the stove.

Thompson, a mediocre runner, had switched to walking as an 18-year-old after injuring both Achilles tendons. A black training book, first entry March 1951, marked the birth of Team Thompson. Matthews remembers that during races Thompson's father, Laurie, "used to follow him on a bike with a basket on the front. He kept Don's bottles and food and stuff in there." His mother, Doris, outlined the unswerving routine:

> It's a madhouse really, but it seems to have worked. The training has to be done in the family, by the family. Don doesn't do anything else. He comes home from the office – insurance, he's in accounts actually – about 6.30, strips down, looks at the clock, and off he goes. As soon as he hears the gate go, his father rushes

to look at the clock. Don drinks some barley water – his father always mixes his drinks, over the years he's got it just right – goes up, throws off his clothes, and has his bath. Of course, he comes in dripping. His socks are full of grit. I spend hours washing his things. The socks are terrible, wash and soak, wash and soak, because of the dangers of poisoning you see. I do everything to make him feel psychologically right. Athletes are very peculiar, you know. His father looks after his shoes, dubbing them, seeing when they need repair. They mustn't be new, you see, they must be well run in, but not too worn down. He has about eight pairs always on the go. People don't realise there are things like that.

Thompson was utterly dominant in domestic races in the late Fifties, particularly in ultra-distance events; his winning time of 7hr 35min 12 sec for the 53-mile London to Brighton event in 1957 was never beaten. Three weeks before the start of the Rome Games he gave up the hard sweat of the steam room for the tranquillity of the Lake District. He trained hard and found that he could daydream his way into a state of self-hypnosis. Once out in Rome, he was so intent on preserving energy that he refused to shop or sight-see.

On race day, Sept 7, he felt relaxed and ready. The organisers brought forward the start by an hour, but the temperature was well into the eighties when the event began. Thompson, in French legionnaire's hat (his mother sewed on a flap to shield his neck from the sun) and sunglasses, was described by Desmond Hackett in the *Daily Herald* as looking like "a miniature messenger to Dr Livingstone". Fellow athletes, including Matthews, piled into an army jeep which had been assigned to the British team and shadowed Thompson's progress until huge crowds blocked their path.

Harry Carpenter, writing in the *Daily Mail*, provided a vivid commentary on the latter part of the race:

> Now the skyline of Rome beckoned them back from the dry, dusty, country. A mad cavalcade of speed cops, officials in motorised rickshaws, and a fleet of ambulances screeched behind them as the Briton and the Swede attacked the hot tarmac. As the repentant sun began to sink the gap between them continued to shrink, while the huge dome of St Peter's loomed larger. At 30 kilometres [John] Ljunggren was within 34 seconds. At 35 kilometres as they approached the Ponte Marconi

where they re-crossed the Tiber, the gap was down to four seconds. The traffic of Rome had been brought to a choking standstill as bridges and roads were shut one by one. The citizens leaned from their windows, crammed their balconies, and surged against the thin line of soldiers marking the route as this tremendous race came to its climax. At 45 kilometres the two men were matched stride for thrilling stride down the famous long embankment of Michelangelo and the sluggish Tiber was only just keeping pace with them. They came to a feeding station. Both men stopped for a drink. When they stepped off again the spring was still in those short, jerky legs of Thompson; but the Swede's had suddenly turned to paper. Thompson strode away yard by yard.

His winning time was an Olympic record, 4hr 25min 30sec, but he hardly looked dressed for the occasion as he stood on the medal rostrum in vest and pants. "As I didn't consider I had a chance of winning a medal it seemed pointless to pack my track suit," he later explained. He also told reporters that the sight of the 1948 champion, Ljunggren, at his side with five kilometres to go, had inspired him to one last push. "I said to myself, 'I'll never live it down if he beats me – he's almost 41.' " And even in his moment of glory, he had an eye on other challenges, insisting that the Olympic race was "just a warm-up" for the London to Brighton in 10 days' time.

In deference to teetotaller Thompson the intended champagne party in the Olympic village became a water party instead. "Not even a gold medal is going to make me start drinking," he said. Thompson's mother, at home in Cranford, relived her final: "When they said on the radio there'd be no more news till 10 o'clock I couldn't bear it, I was going out for a walk. I had a picture of him walking along in a cool haze, and later I could see that little smile on his face, that smile he has when he's sure. And then the neighbours knocked, saying, 'Congratulations', and we'd missed it."

Thompson's fervent hope, after arriving back in London at lunchtime on Sept 12, was that the fuss would "die down quickly". Five hours later he was closing the garden gate behind him; training beckoned. By 1964, when Thompson defended his Olympic title, he had been usurped as the best Briton over the distance by Paul Nihill. Thompson was three minutes quicker than he had been in Rome and finished 10th; Nihill claimed the silver medal.

Don Thompson presses on relentlessly to win the 50km walk in Rome

Horizons were broadened to an extent by family life – Thompson married in 1967 and had two children – but he was still at his happiest on the open road. He ran in more than 100 marathons (best time 2hr 51min) and remained a slave to his obsession. Thompson broke his collarbone after falling close to the finish of the Thanet Marathon in 1983. He simply got up, finished the race and drove himself home using his one good arm. He still insisted on training the following day, but with his arm strapped up he could not tie his shoelaces. His wife, Maggie, did not fancy getting up at 4am so she tied his laces before he went to bed, and he slept in his running shoes. Maggie admits: "I didn't quite know what I was letting myself in for when I married. Our lives revolved around him and his races for many years. He was a difficult man to live with and he got more cranky."

Thompson taught in west London and Kent but, according to Maggie, "hated it". He lacked the strength of personality to impose classroom discipline with any conviction. A one-man-band gardening business suited him better and he was still working – and training – until the day, in 2006, when he had the first of two strokes which killed him. "After his first stroke he was brain-damaged," recalls Maggie, "and there was no way he was going to be able to carry on as he had done. Basically the best thing that could happen was that he didn't recover because it would have been ghastly for him and everyone else – he would have found it so hard to accept. His body was still trying to get out of bed in hospital at four in the morning. They had to tie him down. Even though he was brain-damaged there was still a message going somewhere telling him it was time to get up."

1964

Oct 14: Long jump, Mary Rand

MARY BIGNAL crumbled under the weight of expectation in Rome. Mary Rand defied atrocious conditions to win the long jump in Tokyo four years later, becoming the first British woman to win a track and field event at the Olympic Games. The wedding ring and motherhood catapulted her to maturity. "Then I was a girl. Now I am a woman," she explained.

Rand was a sportswoman of immense talent, grace and versatility. Her contemporaries – Ann Packer and Mary Peters among them – acclaim her as the most naturally gifted athlete they ever saw. Rand was the 'golden girl' long before it became a default cliché for the tabloids. Peters, who has remained a close friend, said of her: "In life her liking to be the centre of attraction has not brought her complete happiness but during her phenomenal career in sport it was probably her greatest asset of all. It was a concealed arrogance that made her such a natural leader and competitor."

Newspapers loved Rand, and not just for her exploits in track and field. "I was pretty much an open book," she admits, "and I was probably the journalist's dream because I just chatted away and answered whatever they asked." In an era when sportsmen and women were, in general, spared the full-blown celebrity treatment, Rand's elfin-cut beauty and guileless spontaneity made her prey to unsuitable suitors. News desks were kept on high alert and only when she married her second husband, Bill Toomey, and moved to the United States at the end of 1969, was she able to swim clear of the goldfish bowl.

Nothing in Rand's early life prepared her for the attention – she was born and brought up in a council house in England's smallest city, Wells, in Somerset. One of her most vivid childhood memories was of helping her father in his chimney-sweeping and window-cleaning business during school holidays. She was on the verge of leaving Street County Mixed school when she was told that she had been given a sports scholarship to the town's oasis of privilege, Millfield College.

Her English teacher was Robert Bolt, the future Oscar-winning screenwriter, but Rand was rather more at home on the hockey pitch and on the track than in the classroom. Her initial speciality was the high jump and she only lost the British women's title on countback in 1956. Rand began a relationship with a Thai pupil, Jimmy Burakamkovit, but when he went to university she found herself in a battle of wills with the authoritarian founder-headmaster, Jack "Boss" Meyer, who declared their friendship off limits. The stand-off gave Millfield the kind of publicity it did not enjoy; she and Burakamkovit were engaged soon afterwards.

"I am very indignant at the headmaster's action," Burakamkovit told the *Daily Mirror* in February 1958. Meyer responded: "She has reached an age where she wants to flap her wings, but we discourage girls from 'going steady'." Rand remembers that her father backed her to the hilt, telling Meyer, 'Mary complies with all the rules and regulations at the school, but in her free time you can't tell her what to do.'

Despite her abrupt departure from the school, Rand still insists that she relished the experience: "I was mixing with all these people from very wealthy backgrounds. It exposed me to a lot. I was a daygirl for a long time and then I stayed during the week and went home at weekends. I ate different foods that I'd never had. At the same time it was a bit overwhelming for me, because I didn't have the confidence in myself academically. I tried my best, but it was tough for me because I thought everyone was smarter – I was a bit intimidated academically. I look back at it now and think it's a shame that I wasn't pushed a little more when I was younger. I feel I'm pretty smart, but even when I got into the British team there were all these doctors and teachers and I was a bit overawed."

Rand moved to London, joined the London Olympiades club and got a job testing light bulbs for General Electric. The company allowed her time off to prepare for the Commonwealth Games, where she won a silver medal in the long jump, and European Championships, her first experience of a top-class pentathlon competition. Despite a feeble shot putt – at 5ft 8in and nine stone she was hardly built for the job – Rand's excellence in the other four events allowed her to finish seventh.

She also came into contact with the laid-back national coach, John Le Masurier, whose first task was to teach her how to use starting blocks.

Rand began working in the postal department at Guinness, who offered better pay, longer holidays…and a complementary pint a day. In 1959, the year before the Rome Olympics, she announced herself as a potential gold medallist with two outstanding performances in an international against the Soviet Union in Moscow's Lenin Stadium. She followed up a hugely unexpected victory over Irina Press, the world's best sprint hurdler, with a win in the long jump. Rand was chosen as Sportswoman of the Year, an award which she received while ill in bed with flu.

Although Rand had not been beaten in a long jump competition for two years, the favourite's tag did not sit comfortably. She dreamed endlessly of waiting to jump, jumping, but never knowing the outcome. There was an ominous tone to her short contribution to the book *The Road To Rome*, published just before the Games. "I do not mind being beaten in competition, except when I have failed to make a good showing…To have the additional worry of knowing that thousands will be disappointed if I fail is an anxiety of which I would prefer to be free."

Rand was so flustered at the start of the qualifying round that she ruled out her opening jump by walking back through the pit. A leap of 6.33m followed, the third best of all time, seemingly settling her nerves for the final later in the day. Far from it. She over-strode badly on her first two attempts, running through the pit, and jogged down the runway to manage a feeble 6.01m. Six athletes qualified for three more jumps; Rand, predictably, was not one of them, though her failure gave her the unexpected chance to compete in the 80m hurdles final.

She recalls: "I was coming off the field and I was fine until I saw my coach and then I was in tears. He said, 'You're fine, just go out there and win the hurdles.' I said, 'Yeah right.' I literally had to run over. They were all ready to go. I just had to bang my blocks in and get on my marks. Coming fourth in the final was pretty big for me." Not enough, though, to dull the pain of failure in her main event. "I'd come for the long jump and failed," she wrote in her autobiography. "Nothing could completely take away the sick feeling."

The media showed little mercy for Britain's under-performing track and field team. Under the front-page headline, FLOP FLOP FLOP FLOP, the *Daily Mail* carried pictures of Rand, Gordon Pirie (5,000m and 10,000m), Brian Hewson (800m) and Arthur Rowe (shot). Both during and immediately after the Games, Rand discovered that she was as much under scrutiny off the track as she was on it. Shortly before going out to Rome she had broken off her engagement to Burakamkovit, who played the jealous fiancé when he discovered that she had become friendly with the Dutch athlete, Eef Kamerbeek. On the eve of the long jump, the *Daily Herald* reported from Rome: "The Olympic Village here tonight is buzzing with a story that Mary Bignal, star of Britain's women's team, will marry Holland's decathlon champion, Eef Kamerbeek, after the Games." Rand issued a flat denial, but marriage remained on Kamerbeek's agenda, prompting Rand to back away once more. "It was so ghastly, this huge athlete, practically in tears," she reflected.

Next came the 'retirement' story: 'Golden Girl Says, I Quit' ran the headline in the *Daily Mirror*. Rand insisted that a throwaway line was taken too literally; anyway, her beef was more with newspapers than athletics. "I know film stars revel in the glare of publicity but that is part of their job," she complained. "They get paid for it. I am in sport only for the enjoyment of it and I am most miserable about all this probing into my personal life."

She was hardly looking for another relationship when she met Olympic rower Sid Rand in March 1961, but five weeks later they were exchanging vows at Holborn Register Office; the newly-weds delighted the *Daily Express* by giving them a picture exclusive of the low-key ceremony and honeymoon in the Cotswolds…and antagonised the rest of Fleet Street. Sid explained: "We have both had so many romances in the past we thought it would be better not to have any fuss." The couple settled in Henley and when Mary competed in the European Championships the following year – she finished third in the long jump – she was the mother of a four-month-old daughter, Alison. "That was before athletes had babies and came back," says Rand. "Nowadays it's par for the course."

She gave up work and enjoyed juggling maternal duties with training, right down to the "frantic cry of 'wee-wee' " as she pivoted in the shot putt circle. In 1963, she settled on a longer, 19-stride approach in the long jump, designed to make the most of her exceptional sprinting speed. The Russian, Tatiana Shchelkanova, had improved the world record in both 1961 and 1962, but Rand had the better of their head-to-head battles in 1963. Although she was shocked to hear, in July 1964, that Shchelkanova had improved the world mark to 6.70m, Rand was happy to see the pressure piled on to her rival.

She was also delighted that the pentathlon had been included in the Olympics for the first time, promising an almost certain medal. Rand's breadth of ability was so great that she qualified in six different events, but opted out of the hurdles so that she could concentrate on the long jump, pentathlon and sprint relay. Her husband, who would have settled for one event, failed to qualify for his third Olympic appearance, making the trip to Tokyo as a spectator instead. His presence was a source of marital tension during the Games.

Rand roomed with Ann Packer, Mary Peters and hurdler Pat Pryce, "all good muckers". Peters had felt overawed by Rand's style, beauty and self-confidence when she first competed against her in the late Fifties. "She was virtually everything I wanted to be," she wrote in her autobiography. "I had the feeling, there and then, that I was destined to live in this dazzling girl's shadow for the next few years and so it proved to be." A lasting friendship between the two was forged in Tokyo, but Peters soon became aware that Rand was a demanding room-mate. "She was a total fanatic about tidiness and, as the dominant personality in those quarters, she made us live as neat and orderly a life as she did herself."

There was a manic nervousness in the air as the four attempted to get to sleep on the night before Rand's long jump competition. She tried to teach her team-mates *I Used To Have An Old Banjo*, one of her repertoire of bedtime songs for Alison. When she woke at 5am, hailstones were beating against the windows, but this time she insisted that there would be no excuses. Gone were the childish props from Rome: the toy monkey and rubber Bambi.

The *Times* report captured perfectly the day, Oct 14, which, more than any other, defined Mary Rand as one of Britain's greatest all-time athletes:

> No British sportsman or woman has ever won an Olympic gold medal with the consummate grace, precision and authority that Mrs Rand showed here this afternoon as she took both victory and the world record in the women's long jump. This was the perfect championship display.
>
> From the moment at 10.30 this morning, when she led the qualifying competition with 21ft 4¼in, and so beat the Olympic record, until five past five this afternoon, when she knew she had fulfilled all our hopes, Mrs Rand was supreme. She braved the rain she hates, first of all, and then, as the floodlights came on

all around the great bowl, she responded to the challenge of Miss Kirszenstein, of Poland, with the world record of 22ft 2in in the fifth round.

All around her raged the 10,000 metres, stirring the crowd to near delirium as [Billy] Mills, an almost unknown, certainly unconsidered, half-Sioux Indian from the United States team came charging through to the tape first. But Mrs Rand was calmness itself as she paced the grass infield barefoot, a striking figure in white windcheater and blue ski-pants, her short, fair hair shining under the banked arc lights.

Rand was so poised that when the competition was halted to allow the medal ceremony for the men's javelin to take place, she draped a blanket round her shoulders and joined in the applause as the Finn, Pauli Nevala, received his gold medal. "I felt I was a little flat all the way through," she insisted afterwards. "Even the world record, which gave me quite a kick, didn't feel a really good jump. On the other hand I was so consistent that maybe I couldn't tell the difference." For the record, Rand's series, in metric terms, was: 6.59, 6.56, 6.57, 6.63, 6.76, 6.61. Four of the six, including the world record, were into a brisk headwind.

There was a slightly surreal moment during the press conference, when she revealed that during one jump she had thought of two-year-old Alison, who was being looked after by friends in England. A journalist asked: "Which one?" A puzzled Rand replied: "I've only got one." The reporter clarified that he meant jump rather than daughter. Rand said she was not sure, adding: "I've carried her picture and I thought I must do it for her." Le Masurier refused to take credit for the achievement, insisting that it was hard *not* to produce Olympic champions when you worked with athletes of such talent.

Rand had only a day to re-focus before the start of the pentathlon; she felt depressed and lacked motivation, but began the competition itself in a relaxed frame of mind. The gold medal was effectively decided by the second of the five events, the shot, when Irina Press threw 17.16m to Rand's 11.05m. After the first day, Rand was not even in the medal positions – Peters was lying third – but her long jump was almost on a par with her series in the individual competition. She overhauled the Soviet athlete, Galina Bystrova, by running a personal best 24.2sec in the 200m, and had the satisfaction of becoming only the second pentathlete to exceed 5,000 points, finishing with 5,035 to Press's 5,246.

Mary Rand defies the wind and rain to break the world record and win the long jump

Curiously, Rand claimed that the medal ceremony made more impression on her than after the long jump. She said it was "as satisfying as sitting in the cinema with two good friends, and sitting in the middle". Although doubts were voiced about both Irina Press and her shot-putting sister, Tamara, Rand does not allow herself to dwell on the gold medal that got away. "I got to know the Press sisters really well," she says. "They were big women with deep voices, but at that time you never really thought about it. They were very masculine, but they were still women as far as I was concerned." Rand completed her medal set when the British quartet finished third in the 4 x 100m relay and reflected that her success in Tokyo would not have been possible without failure in Rome. Her emotions surfaced in a torrent of tears as she watched Ann Packer win the 800m.

No sooner had she returned to England than Rand was whisked off to Buckingham Palace, where the Queen confided that she had measured out 22ft 2in to demonstrate how far it was to a disbelieving Prince Andrew, then four. There were rapturous receptions in both Henley and Wells, where she perched regally on a vintage car with a 22ft 2in plank held aloft. The procession finished at the town hall, where a sign read: 'We be turrible proud of 'ee'. A pavement plaque in Wells's Market Place still commemorates the achievement.

Offers to appear in advertisements began raining in while Rand was still in Tokyo. A figure of £20,000 was placed on her immediate marketability. Ironically, the person who kept her in the amateur ranks was the pioneering agent, Bagenal Harvey, who negotiated a contract with the *Sunday Mirror*. Rand could not be paid for writing about athletics so she produced a column for housewives instead, going to fashion shows and press conferences. At the Cannes film festival she received an offer to become a female James Bond before deciding that the contractual small print was too constricting.

The fault lines were already starting to appear in Rand's marriage and though she was keen to continue competing until the Mexico Games in 1968, her athletics career drifted. She scraped an unconvincing victory in the long jump at the Commonwealth Games in 1966 and failed to recapture her Tokyo form as she finished fourth in the pentathlon at the European Championships.

Rand was an increasingly reluctant journalist and at weekends Sid, a builder by trade, was working on their plush new home in Henley. She found herself accepting more and more invitations to compete abroad and in 1967, while visiting Los Angeles, she met the decathlete Bill Toomey. As their relationship developed she trained fitfully but still managed to equal her best time for the 80m hurdles, 10.8sec, and broke 24 seconds for the first time in the 200m, at the pre-Olympic meeting in Mexico.

The newspapers were quick to scent blood when the Rand marriage imploded. Alison was made a ward of court by Sid and when Toomey flew to England he was caught up in a media frenzy. In return for an exclusive, the *Sunday Mirror* put the company jet at Rand and Toomey's disposal. They flew to Amsterdam, to Montreal, to Chicago, and finally to Denver, Colorado. Rand was even told to wear a wig to escape detection. Close on their heels were freelance photographers, who then followed them to Toomey's parents' house in Laguna Beach, California.

Rand was in emotional limbo as she and Toomey prepared for the Mexico Games. The conditions at the University of Santa Barbara were ideal, but she missed English coaches, English camaraderie and, most of all, Alison. By the time Rand returned in June 1968 she was being troubled by an Achilles tendon injury and her Olympic hopes were finally extinguished when she broke down in a pentathlon trial at the end of August. Her retirement was announced exclusively on David Coleman's *Sportsnight* programme and a month later she joined Coleman as part of the BBC's commentary team in Mexico. She was rooting for Sheila Sherwood in the long jump, but the Briton finished second to Romania's Viorica Viscopoleanu, who marked the fourth anniversary of Rand's win in Tokyo by stealing her world record.

Remarkably, given his own distracted build-up, Toomey won a gold medal; nine months later he was named as co-respondent when Sid Rand was granted a divorce and custody of Alison. Toomey and Mary Rand married in December 1969 and had their own daughter, Samantha, a year later. After a painfully protracted process of reconciliation, Alison was reunited with her mother in the mid-Seventies.

Mary Toomey admitted, in a newspaper interview in 1980, that she had been "pretty rotten" to her first husband, but she had paid a heavy price. "A lot of people have said a lot of things about me, real nasty things," she said. "I've had it all, snubs, obscene letters. Some people seemed to think I was jumping in and out of bed with anyone. If I wasn't strong enough to know who I am and what I am it would have been very difficult not to have gone under or had a nervous breakdown."

The Toomey marriage broke up in the early Nineties and for almost

20 years Mary has been married to American businessman John Reese. The couple live in the Californian city of Atascadero, midway between Los Angeles and San Francisco. Mary Reese is an infrequent visitor to Britain, though a few days before we spoke – she was already due to visit Millfield in March – she learned, to her great delight,

Mary Rand parades through Wells on a vintage Rolls-Royce BRIAN WALKER that she had been given the freedom of Wells. "It's nice to think that they haven't completely forgotten me," she jokes.

In her seventies she still has the zest of someone half her age, even if her body is proving less co-operative than when she was in her athletic prime. "I've just had both my hips done," she reports. "Two days after Christmas the one that I had operated on two-and-a-half years ago came out of its socket when I was outside gardening. I was lying flat, couldn't move and they had to call the paramedics. I have never experienced pain like that before. So they put it back it and now I'm nursing both of them. People don't give me any sympathy because I look fine."

She still gives her time without expecting reward, even when the BBC take over her home for a day to put together a film about her. "It does make you think," she says, "because I'm sure that there aren't many athletes back home who would have done a whole day for nothing. It's a different era I guess. My attitude has always been that sport has given so much to you and the least you can do is give back a little bit. The one thing I miss about being out here is that I didn't have the chance to give back to the young British athletes."

Oct 15: 20km walk, Ken Matthews

IT started with a whip-round and ended with a joyful embrace in Tokyo's Olympic Stadium. Ken Matthews couldn't match Mary Rand for grace and glamour, but his victory in the 20km walk did give the Games one of its most appealing images when his wife, Sheila, broke through the cordon of trackside officials to share his lap of honour.

"They tried to stop her," Matthews remembers, "but the British supporters pushed her through the middle gate at the front of the stand. She was taller than the Japanese anyhow." Sheila Matthews, a little bewildered by her own brief flirtation with stardom, told reporters: "I lost a shoe and had to stop to pick it up. By the time I reached Ken I was crying so much I could not see properly."

The couple had married in 1962, midway between a crushing setback in the Rome Olympics, when Matthews failed to finish, and his chance for atonement as a 30-year-old in Japan. The press version was that he had refused to travel to Tokyo unless his wife accompanied him. He insists that was not the case, but admits: "The chappies in the power station where I worked started a collection and suggested I'd do better if my wife was there."

They raised £742 – the equivalent of two years' wages for fitter's mate Matthews – to pay for Sheila's flights and accommodation and all was well until the following year. Prompted by the Matthews's move from Birmingham to Wrexham (where he still lives), and a better-paid job, a mean-spirited newspaper article claimed that he had taken the money and run (or walked perhaps). "It didn't look very good," he says, "but it was only a case of my doing what was best for me. There was absolutely no malice in it."

He had followed in his father's race-walking shoes when in his teens. The masochistic long haul favoured by Don Thompson never appealed. Seven miles was his ideal distance, "a good thrash"; 20km required "a bit more stamina". As the Rome Games approached he paid little attention to news of startling times being recorded by Iron Curtain rivals, but the race itself was every bit as demoralising as Thompson's disintegration in Melbourne had been.

Matthews recalls that he was crucially weakened by a recent bout of flu: "I was up with the leaders but by the time I got to 15k my legs had gone weak. It may have been nerves as well, but I just couldn't go on. I was sat by the side of the road when Stan Vickers [his team-mate] came by. He asked me if I was OK, so I just said, 'Go on, go on.' He got the bronze in the end."

The misery was only just beginning for Matthews. "They put three or four of us from different countries in this ambulance. The driver seemed to be going for ages and finally we got chucked in this Catholic hospital. It was midnight before the British officials realised where I was. I'd still got all my kit on and I was soaking wet when I went into the hospital. I'd been

Ken Matthews is joined on the track by his wife Sheila after winning the 20km walk in Tokyo

crying as well because of the disappointment and to make matters worse I caught a chill. The next day I was really ill."

The experience only served to strengthen his resolve and the area round the Hams Hall power station where he worked was an ideal, if unconventional, training environment. Most of the workers, Matthews included, clocked off at 5pm, so he was largely undisturbed as he put in 10-mile stints each evening.

He says that the Tokyo race "went perfectly according to plan". He blew a kiss to his wife as he crossed the line in an Olympic record time of 1hr 29min 34sec, more than a minute and a half ahead of the German, Dieter Lindner, and explained to journalists afterwards: "I had a warning early on, as I did when winning the European title at Belgrade. After that I knew that if anyone was going to be disqualified it would not be me. I put on a sprint speed at two miles to draw the opposition and coax them to run." He deflected questions about his future by joking: "Maybe I will take up running after this. It's the only way I can go faster."

ITV footed the bill for a celebration dinner that night – "though I don't think they were expecting there to be about 30 people" – while the BBC fumed. Matthews explains: "I'd always been with the BBC, radio and TV, but a couple of days before the walk Gordon Pirie [the recently retired distance runner] said, 'Can I have the first interview after the race?' I said OK and never thought any more about it. After I'd finished I was walking from the track when I was approached by the BBC for an interview. I said OK and carried on walking, but suddenly I turned round and had to tell them I'd already promised Gordon. I felt terrible about that afterwards, but it was just the heat of the moment."

He returned to civic receptions in Birmingham and Sutton Coldfield and a more informal show of affection from his workmates. "I was allowed a day off to rest up from all the travelling," he recalls, "but I'm a practical sort of a feller so after that I got the spanners out, put the overalls on and went back to work."

After reflection he did retire from race walking (he has never quite convinced himself that he made the right decision) and found a new passion as a time-trial cyclist. He admits that it was "a bit of a slight" when Lynn Davies, Mary Rand and Ann Packer featured in the New Year's Honours in 1965 and he was forgotten. It took 13 years of patient lobbying by the Race Walking Association before Matthews was made an MBE in 1978. "It didn't bother me that much," he insists. "It was just a blip on the landscape."

Oct 18: Long jump, Lynn Davies

LYNN DAVIES reflects on his Olympic victory in simple terms: "It might have been a different story if it had been warm and sunny, but on that one day every four years you have to expect the unexpected." The observation was as relevant to 1964, when competitive bloody-mindedness won the day for Davies in appalling conditions, as it was four years later, when Bob Beamon put the gold medal out of reach for anyone else with his prodigious world-record leap of 8.90m.

Davies was only 22, still a work in progress, when he went to Tokyo; the realist in him said that third place was the best he could achieve and that 1968 would be his golden year. Both Ralph Boston, the American defending the title he had won in Rome, and Igor Ter-Ovanesyan, the Ukrainian who challenged him for world dominance between 1960 and 1968, were left with the feeling that they had been pick-pocketed of what was rightfully theirs.

Both were professional, full-time athletes in all but name, supported by the collegiate system in Boston's case and by the Soviet state machine in Ter-Ovanesyan's. In examining the blueprint for success, Davies and his coach, Ron Pickering, plumped for a composite of his two main rivals. Boston had "inherent spring and suppleness"; Ter-Ovanesyan was the product of a demanding weightlifting programme and the better model for Davies to copy.

He could have been a footballer – he had a trial for Cardiff City and attracted interest from Aston Villa – and might have made the grade as a rugby player. The selfishness of athletics appealed to him more, even if the facilities available in the late Fifties were at best basic. Davies, brought up in south Wales, did not run on a cinder track, the forerunner of the modern, all-weather surface, until he was 17. Two years later his raw potential was spotted by Pickering, then the national coach for Wales. Davies says of the man who was to become as intrinsic to the BBC's athletics coverage as David Coleman: "Ron Pickering was a great coach. His enthusiasm and love of the sport were infectious and gave me great self-belief and confidence that I could become an Olympic athlete."

Davies was ranked only 42nd in the world in 1963, but made rapid strides the following year. Just before going out to Tokyo he told reporters, with painful precision, that he had lifted "280 tons in weights since last October". He was jumping consistently over 26ft (7.92m), even if his best was a foot (30cm) shy of Boston's newly

Lynn Davies leaps to an unexpected gold medal in Tokyo

achieved world record. He was also a good enough sprinter to be picked for both the 100m and sprint relay in Tokyo, clocking 10.7sec to go out in the first round then helping the relay squad to reach the final.

The Tokyo weather was foul on Oct 18 1964, the day allotted for both the long jump qualifying competition and final. Davies remembers that the run-up was like a quagmire as he first jumped a feeble distance then miscalculated his check mark. A few years later he recalled the build-up to his final qualifying jump as "the worst minute or two of my life". From somewhere he summoned the strength to jump 7.78m, a distance beaten only by Boston.

The American played the prima donna before the final, asking officials if they could jump with the wind into the other sandpit and complaining that Ter-Ovanesyan had illegally scored check marks into the runway itself. Davies revelled in the moment, remembering: "Here were these two great men, in my eyes, behaving just like a couple of children." He also felt much calmer after his brinkmanship in qualifying.

He was third after four rounds, but had drawn great encouragement from a foul where he sailed beyond Boston's Olympic record. As he prepared for his fifth jump, Davies had the composure to check on the flag above the stadium. As it went limp he set off. He knew it was a good jump but had to wait four minutes before confirmation that he had taken the lead with a leap of 26ft 5¾in (8.07m). The *Western Mail* put the performance in parochial context by describing it as "just six-and-a-half inches short of a Cardiff bus". Davies faced the same agonising wait after Boston's last-round jump, initially convinced that he had been overhauled until an eight appeared...followed by a nought...and finally a three. "I went wild," Davies admitted. "It was bloody marvellous." It was also Britain's first gold medal in a field event at the Olympics since 1908; in tribute, he was dubbed Lynn the Leap by local journalist Jim Hill.

Davies's girlfriend, Meriel Griffiths, echoed the feelings of the whole of Wales with a cablegram which read: "Magnificent, fantastic, fabulous. I am speechless." She was equally speechless two weeks later when Davies broke the news of their engagement – they married in 1966 – at a welcome-home function in his home town of Nantymoel. "It is all very well getting publicity on television and in newspapers," he told the 700-strong crowd, "but I thought the best place to announce my engagement was in the town in which I was born." He added: "I thought receptions like this were reserved for the Beatles."

Davies describes Tokyo as "the last of the true amateur Games and devoid of the commercial and financial exploitation which was to follow". Under the strict regulations of the time (in Britain anyway), there was no chance for Davies to exploit anything. He returned to teaching and even at the end of the Sixties he was earning about £1,500 a year as a lecturer in PE at Cardiff College of Education. Rumours of a lucrative switch to rugby league never came to fruition.

'I thought receptions like this were reserved for the Beatles'

He reckons that his peak years as an athlete were between 1966, when he became the first person to hold Olympic, European and Commonwealth titles at the same time, and 1970. In 1968 he joined the elite of 27ft jumpers by leaping 8.23m, which remained a British record for almost 34 years until beaten by Chris Tomlinson in 2002. Davies was understandably confident going into the Mexico Olympics, but the long jump competition was hijacked by the explosive, though previously erratic, Beamon. As Pickering the commentator might have said, 'It was always known that he had a big one in him if he got everything right.'

The effect was all the more startling because Beamon's jump of 8.90m (29ft 2½in) – almost two feet further than Boston's world record – was the first legal jump of the whole competition. According to *The Complete Book of the Olympics*, David Wallechinsky's authoritative guide to the Games, a bemused Beamon still believed that he would be beaten; his rivals knew better. "It's over for me. I can't jump that far,"

Boston told Beamon. "What about the Great Britain dude?" asked Beamon. "And what about the Russian?" The Russian, Ter-Ovanesyan, had turned to Lynn Davies and said, "Compared to this jump, we are as children." Davies told Boston: "I can't go on. What is the point? We'll all look silly." Then he turned to Beamon and said: "You have destroyed this event."

A demoralised Davies's best distance was 7.94m, not even far enough to qualify him for the last three jumps; he finished ninth and was panned for his apparent indifference. "I found it hard to understand that some people were highly critical of my 'only gold' attitude," he says. Forty-four years later he remains unapologetic. "You need an uncompromising attitude to be the best."

There was one more Olympics in Davies, who competed in Munich in 1972 before taking up a position as technical director of Canadian track and field as they prepared for the Montreal Games. He managed the British team at both the Moscow and Los Angeles Olympics and since 2002 he has been much more than a figurehead as president of UK Athletics. Already awarded an MBE in the wake of his victory in Tokyo, he received a CBE in 2006 for a lifetime of service to the sport.

Oct 20: 800m, Ann Packer

ANN PACKER condensed a lifetime's Olympic experience into a single Games. Tokyo was the venue for her unexpected defeat in the 400m and equally surprising victory in the 800m. It was also the place where her fiancé Robbie Brightwell fell short in the 400m. Win or lose, they had decided in advance that they would retire. Brightwell was 24 and Packer, a close rival to Mary Rand for pure ability, was only 22. Athletics may have felt a little short-changed – she admits that if she was competing now she would have committed to at least one more Olympic cycle – but Packer's priorities had changed irreversibly. As teachers she and Brightwell felt that they could not go on milking the goodwill of their employers; they also wanted to start a family.

They married on December 19 1964 and six months before the Mexico Olympics, Packer gave birth to the second of their three sons. She could hardly fail to identify with the disappointment of Lillian Board, another Briton widely touted for 400m success who had to settle for a silver medal. There was no consolation prize for Board and no opportunity to make amends at future Olympics; in 1970, aged 22, she died of cancer.

Ann Packer was born and grew up in the Berkshire village of Mouls-ford; she was a county standard hockey player before unlocking her versatile talent as a sprinter/jumper/hurdler. She started as a high jumper, won the England Schools' 100-yard title as a 17-year-old in 1959 and, in addition to making her international debut as a long jumper the following year, finished second in the schools' 220 yards in Shrewsbury. She received her prize from the Rome-bound Brightwell, whose initial romantic overtures were resisted. He was more successful when they met again at a training camp in the spring of 1961.

Packer's parents, Hector and Lily, had lost their elder child, Robert, in a motorbike accident when he was 18. In the summer of 1961, Lily phoned Brightwell to tell him that Ann was critically ill in hospital in Dartford, where she was studying physical education, after contracting double pneumonia. She remained in a critical condition for almost a week before starting to show improvement.

Dennis Watts, her coach, recognised that she would never be more than a run-of-the-mill sprinter and coaxed her towards the longer distances which were re-integrated into women's athletics in the early Sixties. The 800m had been abruptly removed from the Olympic programme after the 1928 Games in Amsterdam, where the final finished with several runners in a state of collapse. The 200m was the longest event on the women's programme until the 800m was finally reprieved at the Rome Games in 1960. The 400m, curiously, did not make its Olympic debut until 1964.

Most of Packer's communication with Watts – in the absence of a phone at home – was by letter, but she benefited hugely from training with Brightwell and another top-class 400m runner, John Cooper, also a teacher. Packer admits: "Looking back I definitely played around at athletics until I met Robbie, who was an established international athlete, and saw him being sick after he'd done training sessions. I realised that there was a lot more to this than turning up a couple of times a week at Reading Athletic Club." Although naturally slight, Packer built up her strength and stamina by lifting weights and even supplemented track sessions with sand-dune running before going out to Tokyo.

It soon became apparent that the longer distances were Packer's domain: she ran 53.3sec for 400m in 1963, her debut season over the distance, already establishing her as a potential medallist in Tokyo, and in the build-up to the Games she tried to improve her staying power by flirting with the 800m. She only decided to double up after establishing that there was no overlap and that she would not be depriving another athlete of a place; the 800m heats were to be held the day after the 400m final.

Packer was a firm favourite for the shorter distance and Brightwell, the reigning European champion at 400m, looked a good bet for medals in both the individual event and relay. The start of the Games was only two weeks away when, as captain of Britain's track and field team, he became engulfed in a dispute which soon spilled over from the back pages to the front pages of all the national newspapers

The *Times* reported: "On Wednesday evening [Sept 23] several members of the British team, including Brightwell, refused to appear on the BBC television programme, *Sportsview*. They refused because they, and some other members of the International Athletes' Club, have always been against fees for television and radio – which, as amateurs, they cannot accept themselves – being allocated to other bodies than the IAC."

The beneficiaries in this case were the British Amateur Athletic Board, who had negotiated a £1,500 fee with the BBC – also giving them exclusive access to a training camp at Timsbury Manor, near Southampton – without consulting the athletes. Brightwell said: "We have the right to decide as individuals whether we would appear on television or not." The BAAB secretary, Jack Crump (the same Jack Crump who had insisted on the male and female athletes being segregated on the flight to Melbourne in 1956), claimed that without the money the board would be unable to pay the athletes' daily pocket money of 14s 6d (72.5p) in Tokyo.

The plot thickened when the *Daily Sketch* was shown a telegram from Crump, indicating that team manager Tony Sage, previously regarded as a moderate voice of reason by the IAC, would refuse to go to Japan unless Brightwell was replaced. The athletes, Packer included, stood firm in his support and Sage presided over an uneasy truce in Tokyo. "The Timsbury dispute was a storm waiting to happen," wrote Brightwell in his entertaining 2011 e-book, *Robbie Brightwell and his Golden Girl: The Posh and Becks of Yesteryear*. "The butterfly wings that had stirred the revolutionary air in Melbourne 1956 had gathered momentum by Rome 1960, and developed into hurricane force by Timsbury 1964. It marked a turning point whereby the athletic elite signalled that they'd no longer tolerate being treated as vassals. And it heralded the first significant crack in the edifice of amateur athletics."

Ann Packer celebrates with fiancé Robbie Brightwell after winning the 800m in a world record time

Morale was restored by gold medals for Mary Rand and Ken Matthews, and Packer was so impressive in winning her 400m heat and semi-final that a third seemed inevitable. Harold Abrahams, whose 100m triumph at the 1924 Games was immortalised in the film *Chariots of Fire*, wrote in the *Western Mail* that she was "at least five yards faster than all her opponents", adding: "No athlete ever can be regarded as a certainty. Olympic and world record holders fail even to qualify for finals, but barring accidents Ann should get that gold." Even Packer herself was overflowing with confidence after winning her semi-final in 52.7sec. "I am now ready to beat the world," she said. "I hope it doesn't sound big-headed, it's not intended to, but I feel so great nothing can stop me."

By comparison, the Australian Betty Cuthbert had dawdled through the qualifying rounds, but there was no doubting her credentials. As an 18-year-old she had caused a stir of Cathy Freeman proportions by winning both sprints and a relay gold medal in

Melbourne. She was persuaded by "voices" to come out of retirement after the Rome Games to run in the 400m in Tokyo and was also convinced that divine forces guided her every stride in the final. Packer, drawn in the unfavourable lane six, was buffeted by the wind on the back straight but still managed a European record time of 52.20sec to finish a yard and a half behind Cuthbert.

Packer, who was haunted by a recurring dream of quitting 400m races halfway through, still believes that she left nothing in the locker in the Tokyo final. "Betty Cuthbert ran a blinder. She was better than I was; even running faster than I ever had before she still beat me." Years later, Packer was invited to be the special guest when Cuthbert was featured on the Australian version of *This Is Your Life*. By then she had been diagnosed with multiple sclerosis, an illness which strengthened rather than threatened her faith.

Although relaxed going into the 800m, Packer felt de-motivated and soon betrayed her inexperience over the distance. "In the two races I'd done in the UK we'd run off an arc, like the long-distance races do now. That was how I thought it was run. When I came to start the heat we were in lanes. I had to ask somebody whereabouts we were supposed to cut in and start the normal race on the first bend. That's how naïve I was about it."

On the same day Brightwell ran magnificently in grim conditions to win his semi-final in 45.7sec, quicker than any of his rivals. The weather was much improved for the final, but Brightwell's time was exactly the same and only good enough for fourth place. "Robbie really performed below par and that's always been difficult to swallow," admits Packer. He shrugged off the disappointment to run a stirring anchor leg in the 4 x 400m relay which carried Britain into the silver medal position behind the United States.

Packer was, inevitably, dragged into her fiancé's slough of despond, even toying with the idea of missing the final in favour of a shopping trip before being brought to her senses. As it was, she was lucky to be fit for the race after being hit by a cyclist in the Olympic village. In the absence of both the official and unofficial world record holders, the Australian Dixie Willis and North Korean Dan Shin-Geum, Maryvonne Dupureur looked the most likely winner of the 800m. The French woman's front-running tactics brought her the quickest times in both the heats and semi-final and also determined how Packer would run in the final. She was so unflustered by the occasion that she sang Nat King Cole's *When I Fall In Love*, the theme tune of her romance with Brightwell, as she walked down the tunnel into the stadium.

Dupureur, predictably, tried to dominate the race from the start, but Packer remained in touch at the bell. "Going through in under 60 seconds was pretty easy for me," she remembers. "I knew I was strong so, in theory, if I was with them with 150 metres to go I ought to be able to overhaul them. I didn't really know how any of the others ran, so ignorance was bliss."

She was caught on the kerb on the back straight before a space opened up obligingly. The official film of the Tokyo Games captured her untroubled serenity as she cruised past in the final straight to win in a world record time of 2min 1.1sec. She kept on running into Brightwell's arms and explained afterwards: "When Robbie didn't win yesterday I said I would run myself into the ground to get a medal. Before today's race I felt so relaxed I couldn't think too hard about it. That's why I think I did so well. I treated it just like any other race.

"Before the race Robbie told me that he did not expect me to get a medal. Whether or not this was because he had told me the reverse in the 400m and I had ended up with the silver, so he thought a change of tune would spur me on, I don't know. But it certainly helped. I thought, 'I will show him'."

A week later she was being feted at Buckingham Palace, asking Princess Alexandra what it was like to be married and confiding that the Queen had said to her, 'The whole world will be at your wedding – in spirit anyway.' No less memorable was her return to Coombe Hill, the school on the outskirts of London where she taught PE. Miss Packer, gold medallist, was carried shoulder high by pupils into the gym.

There was another Palace invitation in 1965, when the newly married Mr and Mrs Brightwell both received the MBE. Ann acquired "a little nest-egg that carpeted the house" by advertising Bovril; Robbie lectured at Loughborough College before the couple moved to Cheshire in 1971 when he was appointed managing director of Adidas UK. The Brightwells have been Congleton's best-known residents ever since – they even represented the town in *It's A Knockout*. The sporting genes were faithfully passed on to their three sons: Gary was a sub 48-second 400m runner and both Ian and David played for Manchester City.

Ann Brightwell, née Packer, harbours no regrets, though she admits that it would have been nice to have seen how much quicker she could have run over 800m. "It would have been interesting to do a 1500 as well," she says.

1968

Oct 15: 400m hurdles, David Hemery

ALASTAIR MACLEAN'S thriller novel, *Fear Is The Key,* could have been adopted by David Hemery as an apt sub-title for his Olympic adventures. Hemery admits that he was "terrified" before the 400m hurdles final in 1968, and lopped almost a second off the world record. Four years later, in Munich, he felt "absolutely flat" and ran a tactically inept race to finish third.

Hemery's victory provided the defining moment, for the British audience anyway, from the first Olympics to be relayed live around the world by satellite. David Coleman's assertive commentary for the BBC – complete with gaffe – imprinted the moment even more indelibly on viewers' minds. When Hemery came to write his autobiography eight years later he indulged in a little regression therapy, summoning the adrenaline-fuelled thoughts and sensations which had occupied the hour before the Mexico final. He recalls: "I was sitting on the floor in my parents' house in Boston, remembering what it felt like. It was as accurate a recollection from an experiential point of view as I could make it."

Hemery admitted in the book: "I was practically paralytic with fear." He referred to the race as "impending unpleasantness" and was conscious of feeling more nervous than at any other time in his life. Crucially, though, he was prepared to win; in a letter written to him only a week earlier, Hemery's American coach, Billy Smith, had predicted that he would run 48.1 or 48.2sec. His electronic timing was 48.12sec.

The Olympic title was its own motivation, but Hemery's American rivals gave him another tasty bone to chew on. A month before the

David Hemery stretches clear to shatter the world record in the 400m hurdles

Games, Geoff Vanderstock became the first man to go under 49 seconds and predicted that all three medals would be won by Americans. "He was even saying if they could take five athletes they'd take the first five places," remembers Hemery. "I'd beaten him by eight metres in the national collegiate and I hadn't even done any speed work at that stage; I'd run on strength. I said to myself, how can he think I'm not going to be a factor? Over my dead body were they going to get one-two-three. A huge additional motivation was that the Americans were evidently taking steroids at Lake Tahoe and I thought – it shows my ignorance of drugs at the time – that it was some kind of stimulant. The whole idea of winning by cheating was anathema to me."

Hemery gave himself four weeks to acclimatise in Mexico. He turned down the offer of £1,000, a huge amount for a student at the time, from a shoe company who wanted him to wear their spikes. He preferred to stay within the rules, and think about the race rather than his feet when he lined up for the final. Good-luck telegrams began to arrive and letters from both Smith and the British component in Hemery's unconventional two-pronged coaching team, Fred Housden, a former maths teacher at Harrow School. Curiously, the two men met just once, in London. The date – Aug 19 1972 – was not easily forgotten by Hemery.

Smith was the conditioning expert, Housden the technical guru – "his mind's eye was like a movie camera which could break down movement into minute detail, while the athlete was in full-speed motion". Smith's tough-guy attitude to training and Housden's gentler approach seemed, to Hemery, to illustrate the big difference between American and British coaches. Housden was fond of expressing his athletic thoughts in verse. Just before the Mexico Games the 78-year-old wrote to Hemery:

> When others quail
> And Geoff [Vanderstock] looks pale
> And Ronnie's [Whitney] knees are quaking,
> Then is the time
> To heed my rhyme
> And take to record making.
> You know the point
> Where out of joint
> Your chopping may go wonky,
> So don't lose speed
> But keep the lead,
> Each clearance honky-tonky!

Hemery felt moderately nervous for his heat and semi-final, but ran two controlled races to book his place in the final. He was in the mix, but five of his rivals had quicker personal bests. "I went with the process side," he explains, "which was to run the world record which I believed I was capable of and hope it would be good enough to win. I thought I could run 48.4."

The damp and cool conditions suggested that even his target time was optimistic, but as Hemery put ever greater distance between himself and the rest of the field from the fifth hurdle onwards it was clear that he was doing something special. He finished eight metres ahead of the second-placed runner, the German, Gerhard Hennige, and sliced 0.76sec off Vanderstock's short-lived world record.

"Hemery wins for Britain," shouted Coleman as he breasted the tape. "In second place is Hennige. Who cares who's third? It doesn't matter. A new world record if that time is correct. He killed the rest, he paralysed them." The problem was that a lot of people did care who finished third, including 12-year-old Sebastian Coe, watching at home in Sheffield. The bronze medallist was Yorkshireman John Sherwood; it was the first time since 1924 that Britain had won two medals in the same Olympic event. Hemery points out that Sherwood would have been second under the current ruling: "He went in with his chest forward and Hennige went in with his neck down and his head forward. In '68 they counted the neck as part of the torso."

Coleman later explained to Hemery the difficulties he faced in commentating on the final: "He said it was such a margin of win that his eyes raced to the clock, seeing if it was a world record. By the time he got back to the race there were eight guys across the line. Second through sixth were within two feet of each other. Vanderstock was in second with a foot to go and got no medal." Hemery was told when he returned home that the race had already been shown 27 times by the BBC and for years afterwards he found himself replaying it in his mind.

How close was it to perfect? "For the condition I was in it was very close," he says. "I sat a bit over hurdle eight and I didn't run at ten. Billy had said, 'Go at the tenth hurdle as though it's the first in a high hurdle', but as I landed over it I thought, 'I've forgotten to do that. I must get into a sprint now.' It's very hard to initiate a sprint off the last hurdle if you haven't actually gone at it with aggression."

Although he managed to re-focus on the 4 x 400m relay – the British team finished fifth – Hemery admits that he was completely unprepared for the "goldfish bowl" existence which consumed him in the three months after the Games. "It was almost as if I had to say yes to every invitation, to thank the British people for their support. I was doing three or four interviews, dinners, luncheons, receptions, openings a day, all for nothing because it was an amateur era. It had never occurred to me that I'd have to become a public speaker. I don't mind it now but in those early days it was quite traumatic. There'd be a chink, chink on the side of the glass and then…responding on behalf of the guests our new Olympic champion…"

Hemery was also given a sobering insight into the life of the celebrity: the throwaway line which can explode into front-page news.

> I was among a group of athletes invited to a reception for the Miss World contestants. I got talking to Miss Australia, Penny Plummer. Having lived in the US I had no one over here that I knew, so I said to her, 'Would you like to come to a dinner?' I was then stupid enough to say to a press guy, 'I really hope she doesn't win or that'll be the end of my date.' When she did win, there were these reports saying, 'David Hemery's got a date with Miss World'. Because of my profile I'd been asked to host whoever became Miss World, but the organisers had discovered that she'd got a boyfriend back in Australia, so they kept me away

from her. Meanwhile, the Australian press had arranged to fly her boyfriend over so he could rescue her from me. It was ridiculous – we'd had half an hour's conversation. I then saw the wretched press guy who'd written the original story waiting outside the door. I said, 'Please leave us alone, there is nothing to this,' and went back and said to her, 'I really apologise for the situation this has caused you.' In a way it was quite sad because I would have liked to have had the chance to get to know her: she was charming as well as beautiful.

Back in the real world, Hemery needed a fresh challenge, so he began training for the decathlon: "If I'd been good enough at the pole vault and able to put on any weight to throw further I would have stayed with the decathlon. I absolutely loved the event, it had so many challenges. I made the British team but I couldn't get the qualifying mark for the European Championships in '69. If I had I would definitely have gone to the next Olympics as a decathlete." Hemery was a late entry for the high hurdles, finishing second to the Italian Eddie Ottoz. Asked afterwards why he had not shaved, Ottoz quipped: "It is well known that Italian men and Russian women do not shave before competitions."

The death of his friend Lillian Board at the end of 1970 was a critical factor in persuading Hemery to carry on running. Board, the silver medallist in the 400m at Mexico in 1968, was only 22 when she died of cancer. Hemery wrote in his autobiography: "The fact that death had so cruelly taken away her Olympic chances helped to firm my resolve to try while I still had my health and strength, in part on her behalf."

In 1971 he enrolled for a Masters degree at Harvard, which also gave him the chance to resume his coaching relationship with Billy Smith, though his life was obsessively dominated by studying and training. A £400 contribution from Kraft allowed him to live at subsistence level. As the Munich Games approached he was swamped by negative thoughts and became pre-occupied by research suggesting that sprinters peaked at 24 (he was now 28). "Whereas everything was positive in 1968, leading up to Munich I mentally rehearsed over and over again running races where I lost. It took two months to become numb to those pictures."

The contrast between 1968 and 1972 could hardly have been greater. "Where in Mexico I was terrified and ran better because of the adrenaline flow, in '72 I woke up like a zombie, absolutely flat, to the point where I was pressing my nails into my palms to get myself woken up, yelling at myself inside: 'For god's sake there's an Olympic final.'" His race was an object lesson in misjudgment.

"I just went completely flat out. I hit a wall at 300 metres and then John Akii-Bua came past 20 metres later and I realised I'd relaxed nowhere. I thought, just hang on until you get to the line and only because I'd done literally hundreds of hills and sand-dunes did I maintain any sort of strength and stride to the line. And then Ralph Mann came past on the right and in spite of dipping like mad I missed a silver medal by a hundredth of a second. I felt like I'd blown it, one of two Olympic opportunities. It was the second fastest time I'd run but it was nowhere near what I'd prepared." Hemery completed his set of Olympic medals when the British team finished second in the 4 x 400m relay.

He insists to this day that he was capable of matching Akii-Bua's time of 47.82sec (Hemery ran 48.52sec) and cites a race two weeks later, his last in Britain, as proof. "When I got back, they said, you have to say farewell, this is the end of your athletics career. Will you run at Crystal Palace? I said I really didn't want to face another 400 hurdles, but I'd run a 300. I set a world best of 34.6, which was 46.1 pace. I went on round the bend for another 50 metres and thought, I could have gone on at this pace. Obviously I would have slowed a bit but even if I'd lost a second it would still have been 47.1 and the record was 47.8. I just thought I was nowhere near my potential in Munich. I'm not saying I'd have beaten Akii-Bua, but I'd certainly have given him a race."

Hemery had refused to take unofficial payments as an athlete, but picked up an above-board and welcome £4,000 as the first winner of the made-for-television competition, *Sporting Superstars*, in 1973. He relegated the Welsh rugby player, Barry John, to second place, despite giving his rivals a 100-metre start in the final event, a 600m steeplechase.

Much of what Hemery has accomplished in the past 40 years has centred on education, no mean feat for someone who was labelled as "slow" until, at the age of nine, it was discovered that he was dyslexic and so short-sighted that he could not see the blackboard. His family moved from Essex to the United States three years later when his accountant father took a job in Colorado Springs. The bulk of Hemery's schooling was in the Boston area of Massachusetts and it was to Boston he returned in 1975, first to work on his autobiography and then to succeed Billy Smith as head coach. "I had no particular plans for work," he says, "so I thought, sounds good to me."

He was president of UK Athletics from 1999 to 2002 and over the past four years he has dedicated himself to the 2012 Legacy: 'Be the best you can be'. Although Hemery accepts that "sports brings out the best and worst in humanity", he still believes that the Olympics can be a power for good. "I still see youngsters inspired by the ethos. There is something special and unique about every human being. If they can find that and work on it they can contribute to humanity."

Oct 19: Single trap clay pigeon shooting, Bob Braithwaite

DENIS HOWELL, a pathfinder as sports minister in Harold Wilson's government, had good reason to remember his visit to the military camp which staged all the shooting events at the Mexico Games. Howell was introduced to Bob Braithwaite, the Lancastrian who had just completed the first of eight 25-clay barrages in the trap event.

The conversation, Braithwaite recalls, ran something like this:

Howell: How are things going?
Braithwaite: I've missed two.
Howell: Oh, that's not good, is it?
Braithwaite (jokingly): Well I won't miss any more, so it's all right.

The humour eluded Howell, however, and when Braithwaite's 'prediction' came true he was portrayed, with Howell's unwitting connivance, as a true British amateur with a very un-British swagger.

The real Bob Braithwaite was, and remains, unnervingly modest and understated. It is doubtful that anyone in Olympic history has been less impressed by a gold medal, or refused to acknowledge that he was even taking part in a competition. He made a point of ignoring what other shooters were doing. "People find it hard to understand," he says, "but my attitude was that each bird or target that came out was my competitor." Nerves were never a factor, though he admits that he would chain-smoke "madly" between barrages, which were spread over two full days. He compensated for his nicotine addiction by abstaining from alcohol.

Not untypically, for a child brought up on a farm – his family moved from Westmoreland to Lancashire when he was five – the toy gun was soon replaced by the real thing. He became an energetic game shooter and was introduced to trap shooting when a back injury temporarily restricted his mobility. After he had qualified as a veterinary surgeon Braithwaite lost the appetite for shooting live creatures and, in the absence of proper facilities close by, rigged up an oscillating trap beside his father's farm. A local priest, Father Harry Doyle, would feed the contraption as Braithwaite practised as much as his work would allow.

He hit 192 out of 200 targets at the 1964 Olympics in Tokyo, finishing seventh, and learned to put absolute trust in the law of averages. Braithwaite had just celebrated his 43rd birthday when he flew out to Mexico, three weeks before the Games began. "It was the longest time I'd been away doing a lot of shooting," he explains. "My average for 1,600 birds went up to about 98.9 per cent. That became engrained in your mind. You had an average and you shot to it."

The bare essentials of Braithwaite's remarkable (whether he admits it or not) achievement is that he missed with his fifth and 13th shots in

Bob Braithwaite sports his gold medal after hitting 187 straight targets to win the single trap clay pigeon shooting competition in Mexico

misty conditions. He was blameless for the first blip, the clay leaving the trap at such an acute angle that it was outside his field of vision, but admitted at the time that the second error was "bad shooting. I will never forgive myself."

Astonishingly, he and his £560 Belgian rifle hit the last 187 targets, a then unrivalled sequence in the discipline, to finish with a total of 198 which was both an Olympic record and equalled the world best score. The organisers had clearly not factored in the possibility of a British victory and there was an embarrassing delay (not that Braithwaite was greatly bothered) while officials dashed off in search of the National Anthem. The medal ceremony was as low-key as he would have wished.

He was asked to carry the flag at the closing ceremony, but politely declined. Ron Clunie, his partner in the Garstang veterinary practice, was suffering from terminal cancer and Braithwaite felt he had been away for long enough. His return was marked by an emotional welcome in his home village of Scorton, a civic reception in Garstang, filmed for Pathe News, and the promise of a lifetime pass to the ABC Cinema in Lancaster. He explained to his local paper, the *Lancaster Guardian*, that he had rejected an offer to turn professional because it would have involved shooting live pigeons. "As far as I am concerned," he said, "that is just not on."

He appeared on *Desert Island Discs*, having resisted the BBC's initial overtures, and turned down the assorted invitations which came his way. As one of only three individual gold medallists in Mexico, he was considered public property for a few weeks, but soon returned to his chosen life of quiet anonymity. The Braithwaite name returned to prominence as the 1972 Olympics approached, only for the selectors to back-track on their original decision to pick him. Characteristically, he was more disappointed by the lack of clarity than by being deprived of the chance to defend his title; Braithwaite's daughter, Norine, a talented middle-distance runner, lost a run-off for a place in the 800m.

Forty years on, Bob Braithwaite is puzzled by the importance attached to sporting achievement. "There's far too much praise and hallelujah with the modern Olympic people. They're only doing what they have trained to do and which they enjoy doing. The fact that someone can run one yard faster than someone else over two miles I don't see the importance of that. It does nothing for the human race."

There was a simple integrity to his own sporting career; the closest he came to controversy was when, after being given a shooting jacket, he was ordered to remove the logo advertising Eley cartridges. With the principle came freedom. "I didn't want anybody to be able to tell me what to do," he says. "And it was your own choice what you did with your money. I thought it was more important to shoot the odd target than go out and get drunk on a Saturday night."

Oct 21: Team three-day event, Derek Allhusen, Jane Bullen, Ben Jones, Richard Meade

A TELLING blow was struck for equality when 20-year-old Jane Bullen was picked for the three-day event competition in 1968. Bullen had made an unanswerable case for selection when she won the Badminton trials on Our Nobby six months earlier and she became the first woman to be chosen by Britain for the Olympics in a discipline seen for so long as the preserve of hard-bitten Army types.

Bullen could hardly have come from better equestrian stock. Her parents owned a pony stud in Dorset; her brother, Mike, had preceded her as the youngest rider to be picked for Britain's Olympic three-day event team when he competed as a 23-year-old in Rome. He also lined up, alongside two of his sister's Mexico team-mates, Ben Jones and Richard Meade, in Tokyo, dropping out in the cross-country section after breaking his collar-bone and dislocating his shoulder in separate falls. Bullen's sister, Jennie Loriston-Clarke, competed in four Olympics. Although she is the one with the gold medal, Jane Holderness-Roddam (as she became after marrying) insists that she was, is and always will be the third best rider in the family.

There was still a strong military presence in the team: 54-year-old 'Galloping Grandfather' Derek Allhusen, who competed in the pentathlon, a demonstration event at the 1948 Winter Olympics, had been awarded the prestigious Silver Star while attached to the American army in the Second World War. 'Galloping Sergeant' Ben Jones was a career soldier and 'Golden Wonder' Richard Meade had done his National Service in the 11th Hussars before going up to Cambridge. Bullen, two years into her training at the Middlesex Hospital in London, was dubbed the 'Galloping Nurse'.

Britain's success in Mexico was all the more remarkable for the late changes which were forced upon them. Less than a month before the start of the Games, Meade told the *Daily Express*: "You could fill a volume with the disasters that have plagued us. First Foxdor, Ben Jones's mount, dropped dead four weeks ago. Then three short-listed horses went lame, then Barberry had that crashing fall at Burghley and he was out. Then Cornishman, who finished seventh with Ben Jones at Burghley, went lame too, and finally Turnstone did the same. At this stage I stopped worrying any more, and I'm quite certain that when we get to Mexico our troubles will just be starting."

Meade's calmness under pressure was just one of the qualities which underpinned his status as Britain's most successful Olympic equestrian. Another was his professional outlook in a strictly amateur world. After finishing his engineering degree in 1963, Meade focused single-mindedly on making the team for Tokyo. His job as a financial planner for a merchant banking group gave him all the freedom he needed to pursue his sporting ambitions. "It was the summer after the hard winter of 1962-63," he recalls. "I thought, if there was going to be a repeat of that why didn't I go out to Germany where they were used to difficult winters and had the facilities to cope. And I also wanted to work on my dressage. So I went out to Munich for three-and-a-half months, took my horse and Land Rover and trailer. People hadn't done that sort of thing before. We as a nation had been at the very top of the sport through our ability to ride cross country. I felt it was very important to learn the other disciplines and get proficient at them."

The experiment succeeded to the extent that Meade led on Barberry in Tokyo before dropping back to fourth in the show-jumping. He takes a philosophical view: "It was disappointing, but it was also a thrill to lead, if only for 24 hours." Barberry was also Meade's first choice for Mexico and when Turnstone was also ruled out he was fortunate to be lent Mary Gordon-Watson's horse, Cornishman V.

Bought on an inspired hunch by Gordon-Watson's brigadier father in 1963, Cornishman received the star treatment. He was the lone 'civilian' horse to be stabled at Buckingham Palace, where he was given what Gordon-Watson called a two-week "crash course" in dressage by Ben Jones. Her own inexperience showed at Badminton in 1968, when she "made the mistake of going too fast on the cross country, partly due to seeing Ben Jones waving at me as I galloped past. I assumed that he was telling me to go faster when, in fact, he was merely waving encouragement. It all ended in disaster at the coffin fence, three from home, where I fell off and Cornishman was too tired to go on. It was heartbreaking and I would never again ride a horse which wasn't fit enough."

Gordon-Watson was recovering from a broken leg sustained in a fall from Cornishman at Wembley, when her father was "pressurised" into lending the horse to the British team. "It was difficult for us," she admits. "There I was lying in hospital with a broken leg and the thought of Cornishman going all that way was scary. He was our only horse, part of the family almost, and he'd had a pretty sheltered life." Gordon-Watson's plaster was removed just in time for her to be able to fly out to Mexico and she admits to great pride at seeing Cornishman play his part in the gold medal performance. "It was very emotional and exciting," she says.

It was originally planned that the British team would have a doctor with them at Avandaro, the equestrian venue 100 miles north of Mexico City, but he was forced to join the main team because of the altitude problems. Nurse Bullen was entrusted with the pills and potions. Even the horses were left short of puff at altitude. Desmond Hackett reported in the *Daily Express* that the British mounts became addicted to oxygen.

"They get a whiff after every exhausting test, but each morning when it comes to feeding time they make it quite obvious they are more than ready for another sniff. The Poacher, who enjoys a bottle of stout or in Mexico a bottle of ale as well as the next chap, positively sulks unless he gets his daily whiff. Jovial, fighting-fit Ben Jones told me: 'I don't mind having a boozer with me but when I get a hippy thrown in, then it is too much.'"

Bullen remembers being called in for recuperative duties after Meade pulled rib muscles in the swimming pool. "Because of my nursing experience," she wrote in her autobiography, "I was called on to massage Richard, which was always hilarious, since he is so dreadfully ticklish. Ben Jones used to sit in the corner of the room, as chaperon, grinning from ear to ear, while Richard was stretched out on the bed and I massaged him. Understandably, some of the people who came sailing into the room, not knowing that I was acting as Richard's masseur, jumped to quite a different conclusion. One day [chef d'équipe] Bill Lithgow walked in, said, 'Oh, I'm terribly sorry,' and walked straight out, leaving the three of us in absolute convulsions."

When the serious business got under way, the British quartet avoided major disasters to stand fifth after the dressage. Their success was based on a remarkable effort in the cross country. "It was an extraordinary mixture," Bullen remembers. "Some of the fences were very small and others were so tough they wouldn't be passed these days. It made it quite difficult for the horses. Also, the ground was very

Britain's winning quartet in Mexico (from left to right): Derek Allhusen, Jane Bullen, Richard Meade and Ben Jones

false because of these endless downpours and this baking hot sun so you never knew how secure it was."

Allhusen was relatively fortunate in being able to go round early on Lochinvar, when conditions were at their best. Bullen managed to improve her individual position despite falling twice; at one point she heard the watching Prince Philip shout, 'Get back', when Our Nobby lost his bearings. As Bullen picked herself up from the first fall she was shocked to see a dead horse (a heart attack victim). Meade then achieved the near impossible by going clear. Bullen recalls: "It was an amazing performance, riding a horse which he'd never ridden in competition before. The rain was coming down so hard that he could barely see where he was going."

Jones was handed his obligatory lighted cigarette and glass of beer when he and The Poacher came in from the roads and tracks section. As he completed the cross-country course his team-mates were dismayed to see his hat floating downstream towards them; rider and horse appeared soon afterwards. The overall standings filtered through so slowly that it was approaching eleven o'clock at night before the British team knew that they had four fences in hand going into the show-jumping.

Allhusen's clear round earned him the individual silver medal, but Bullen, as the non-scoring member of the team, initially felt that she had not deserved her team gold. She now takes a less self-critical view of her contribution: "If I hadn't got round in the cross country, for instance," she reasons, "the others couldn't have gone for it as they did afterwards." Meade, although he won both team and individual gold medals in Munich, regards the Mexico victory as his most cherished moment in the sport. "We had the most incredible conditions to deal with in the cross country," he says. "It was very dramatic and we had such a good atmosphere within the team. It's great to be able to share it with other people."

Prince Philip, who attended the presentation ceremony, made a point of selecting what he claimed was the pick of the medals for Bullen. A customs official at Heathrow who tried to prevent her bringing it back into the country was less obliging. The highlight of the predictable round of receptions and lunches was a gathering at Buckingham Palace. Again Bullen was singled out for VIP treatment; the Queen, clearly primed by Prince Philip, wanted to know all about the Mexico experience. Princess Anne, at 18 a budding Olympian herself, demanded an even more detailed breakdown of the three-day event experience before being whisked off for a French lesson.

Allhusen, who was a High Sheriff of Norfolk in the 1950s, turned down the offer of an MBE because he felt the whole team deserved recognition; he died in 2000. Jane Holderness-Roddam was made a CBE for her services to equestrian sport in 2004. Jones died of a heart attack while schooling a horse at the Army equitation centre in Melton Mowbray, Leicestershire in 1990.

Oct 21: Flying Dutchman class sailing, Rodney Pattisson, Iain MacDonald-Smith

RODNEY PATTISSON was inducted into the Scottish Sports Hall of Fame in 2002 – an honour, on the face of it, to fit snugly alongside his two Olympic gold medals. The problem is that Pattisson does not, and never has, regarded himself as Scottish. "I think they must have been short of gold medallists when they contacted me," he says. "I told them, 'I'm not Scottish.' 'That doesn't matter,' they said, 'We can still put you in the hall of fame.' I wasn't very pleased about that."

Pattisson was incontestably Scottish-born – in Campbeltown, on the west coast, in 1943 –but only because his father was briefly based at nearby RAF Machrihanish. Two years earlier, Ken Pattisson despatched the torpedo from his Swordfish which is believed to have finished off the German pocket battleship, Bismarck. Pattisson's parents, both English, returned south when he was only a few months old. He was taught to sail at the age of eight and was only 16 when, crewed by his brother, John, he won the Cadets National Championship at Burnham-on-Crouch, Essex. Pattisson went to Pangbourne College, in Berkshire, before joining the Royal Navy training college at Dartmouth.

His eyesight was not good enough to allow him to fly in the Fleet Air Arm, so Pattisson looked for the Naval posting which would be most compatible with his sailing ambitions. He also needed to compete in an Olympic class in order to qualify for leave, so he bought a battered Flying Dutchman and attended trials for the 1964 Games. "It was a disaster," he admitted. "My boat was old, everything was wrong with it, but it was a learning curve and I was determined to buy a new boat and do everything better."

Pattisson was working as a submarine officer and living in Poole, Dorset when, in 1967, he paid local boat builder Bob Hoare £350 for the hull of Supercalifragilisticexpialidocious (after the song from the musical *Mary Poppins*). Pattisson then painted, polished and customised the boat. There was no particular reason for the name but he was already wary in his dealings with the media and admits: "I knew it would annoy the press." Superdocious was soon adapted as a more manageable short form.

Pattisson had the boat. Now he needed the time to prepare and a crewman to help realise his vision. He recalled: "I struck a bargain with Rear Admiral Sir Ian McGeoch, who was a keen sailor and emphasised with me that if I passed my submarine exams I could have all the time off I needed to campaign for Mexico. I was very, very lucky in that respect and because I was on paid leave. That said, we were still campaigning day to day on a shoestring and camping at events." Pattisson's brother, John, was instrumental in recruiting trainee solicitor Iain MacDonald-Smith, a British Universities team-mate, as crewman for Mexico.

MacDonald-Smith, two years younger than Pattisson, needed time to adapt to what the *Daily Mail* called the helmsman's "quick temper under stress". Pattisson outlines what he was looking for in a crewman and admits that he could be a tough employer:

> I wanted a crew who was a good sailor, tactically as well. I knew crews of other boats who weren't tacticians and one realised they were disadvantaged. On the other hand, it was my boat – I owned it – and I could fire the crew if I wanted to. I used to give them hell to be honest. I had a bad reputation and I blamed the crew

sometimes when it was my own fault. I used to say to people who crewed for me, 'I might be dreadful in the boat, I might swear at you and call you everything under the sun, but once we come ashore it's all forgotten.' I said, 'Just bear with me, that's my temperament.'

Pattisson and MacDonald-Smith established themselves as firm favourites for the Olympic title by remaining unbeaten in the preparatory events and, though neither was interested in talking up their prospects beforehand, MacDonald-Smith explained afterwards: "We have got everything worked out so perfectly that we hardly ever talk during a race."

They were fitter than their rivals, Pattisson's attention to detail was on a different plane, and hovering ever resourcefully in the background was team manager Vernon Stratton, who had competed in the 1960 Olympics. Stratton arranged for the team to fly out to Mexico a full month before the Games began so that they could acclimatise to the heat and humidity of Acapulco. David Houghton was recruited from the Met Office to plot tides and winds. Stratton's wife, Pepe, was assistant manager and 'nanny'.

The British pair duly won the first race, only to be disqualified after being held responsible for a collision at the start. MacDonald-Smith

Rodney Pattisson and (right) Iain MacDonald-Smith show maximum respect as the National Anthem is played

recalled: "After the protest I said to a dejected Rodney that we could still win the title but we'd have to win the next five races and make sure the disqualification was our discard. Incredibly, we managed to post five straight firsts but could still have lost it in the last race. That race ended up being the most stressful of my life. To play it 'safe', Rodney started at the wrong end of the line to everyone else, effectively handing them a quarter of a mile advantage. We then had to pass the whole fleet and risk collisions, protests and overlaps at the chaotic mark roundings. We crossed the line second, knowing the gold was ours, but there was no elation, just massive relief."

Pattisson remembers: "I went into the last race knowing all I had to do was finish. To be honest somebody could have knocked my rudder off before the start and I might have tried to seek redress and just been told, that's bad luck. I was determined to finish the race and that first race had taught me just how ruthless the Olympics were. I'd sailed against these guys for two or three years – I knew them all very well. Some of them had even been to train with me in Poole. Everyone was in for the gold medal and anything went. If they could get you out they would. You had no friends in the Olympics and that first race taught me that. I used to tell people like Ben Ainslie to remember that."

Pattisson had given up alcohol before the Games; now he allowed himself a celebratory swig of champagne from a plastic lemonade bottle. As he and MacDonald-Smith were being interviewed for television they were carried off by Canadian and Australian crews and dumped in the bay. They sported old-fashioned yachting caps at the medal ceremony as MacDonald-Smith did his best to match Pattisson's well-practised salute. "When a Mexican brass band sparked up with the National Anthem we were trying not to burst out laughing," MacDonald-Smith admitted. They laughed off accusations that they had worn towelling shirts to soak up water and increase the on-board weight.

MacDonald-Smith stayed on in Mexico for a fortnight, returning to England on the same plane as motor-racing driver Graham Hill, who had just won the Formula One title. A few weeks later, MacDonald-Smith's gold medal was stolen from his London flat, but later recovered by police. The Olympic champions confirmed their dominance in the class by winning the World Championship in 1969 and 1970, but MacDonald-Smith was keen to try his luck as a helmsman. He was a reserve in 1972 and competed, without great distinction, in the Soling class at Montreal.

Superdocious mark one was pensioned off after the Mexico Games, bought for the National Maritime Museum by yachting sponsors Alfred Dunhill in 1973 and is on permanent display at Falmouth. Pattisson had taken the boat to Munich to pace the new model (known as Superdoso) and confessed: "I always dreaded having to race against her. That is why I never sold her."

Oct 26: Middleweight boxing, Chris Finnegan

CHRIS FINNEGAN could have achieved legendary status in the golden age of prize-fighting: a natural-born pugilist who would have been the last man standing in the ring and the last man drinking in the bar. In the modern world of the 1960s and Seventies, his truncated lifespan as a boxer, he achieved about as much as anyone with his lack of single-minded dedication could. But for the misfortune to come up against Bob Foster, one of the all-time greats in the light heavyweight division, he would have joined the exclusive club of Olympic champions who have gone on to win world titles.

Finnegan was a war baby, just, the fourth of eight children and the first to be born in England after his parents moved from Northern Ireland. His mother was from Newry and his father from Liverpool; Finnegan acknowledged the twin loyalties throughout his boxing career by sporting a shamrock on one side of his trunks and the Union flag on the other.

Most successful sportsmen can identify a starting point in their journey to stardom, but Finnegan had little choice in the matter. Fighting was just a part of his upbringing in Iver, on the fringes of west London. His eldest brother, Terence, whom he described as the "godfather" of the Finnegan clan, would organise boxing tournaments in their garden. They soon ran out of neighbourhood opponents, but that didn't stop them fighting among themselves.

Chris Finnegan was only 12 when he was beaten up by his eldest brother in a drink-led fury. He admitted in his autobiography: "The ring has never held anywhere near the sort of fear I experienced that day – I was convinced he would kill me. If someone tied a hand behind my back and sent me to fight Bob Foster again, there's no way I could be hurt as much." The defend-yourself-or-else environment produced two outstanding fighters. Finnegan's younger brother, Kevin, was good enough to win the European middleweight title and loyal enough to earn an 18-month ban for squaring up to the referee when an inexplicable points decision went against Chris at the ABA finals in 1967.

By the age of 15 the elder Finnegan was fighting in the ring as well as out of it, but a promising career was put on hold as he chanced upon a job, as a hod-carrier, which paid well and enhanced his strength and stamina to boot. He also developed a taste for Guinness and coined an apt motto for the fighting Finnegans: 'Win or lose, drink your booze'.

By the time he won the ABA middleweight title in 1966 he had shown himself to be a sound technician who was equally at home in an old-fashioned scrap. He was also prone to cut easily, a weakness which brought his challenge for another ABA title to an abrupt end in 1968 and could easily have cost him his Olympic place. His reprieve came in the shape of a final trial, but he still had to outmanoeuvre one more opponent before getting on the plane: a magistrate demanding £70 in National Insurance arrears. Finnegan dodged that punch…for the time being.

He had quipped that the altitude of Mexico City would be no problem to someone who shimmied up ladders for a living, but found that he did run out of puff in the final round of his opening fight against "a geezer called Titus Simba from Tanzania". Points decisions against West Germans and Yugoslav boxers guaranteed Finnegan a medal and yet another southpaw, the American Al Jones, stood between him and a place in the final.

Finnegan was knocked down twice, but pierced Jones's defences regularly himself to win a 4-1 decision. The crowd, though incensed at the American's perceived misfortune, still favoured Finnegan against the Russian Alexei Kiselyev, who had won a silver medal in the light-heavyweight division four years earlier. After a sluggish start, Finnegan did just enough in the last round to claim the narrowest of split decisions.

He admitted afterwards: "I had a lousy first round and my trainer, David James, told me to put more beef into my jabs and to show more aggression. It was a right good ticking-off which did me good, and by the second round I was more in the fight and thought I just shaded that one. By the third my stamina and speed began to tell, thanks to the new training. Kiselyev kept going into clinches and for the first time I realised I could win the gold medal." When asked what his plans were, he responded: "To go home and increase the family."

The family already consisted of a wife, Cheryl, whom he had married when she was six months pregnant, and a five-year-old

Family and friends greet Chris Finnegan on his return to Iver

daughter, Pearl. The *Guardian*'s Frank Keating, who was working for the ITV at the time, recalled that they had contacted Cheryl a few days earlier. She confessed that her hopes of a ring-side seat in the Mexico Arena rested on a competition entry.

Keating recalled: "She merrily told us: 'The flat is up to 'ere in empty Golden Wonder crisp packets. I can't lose 'cos I 'aven't eaten anything else for the past six weeks.' But Golden Wonder told us, sorry, she hadn't won, by which time it was too late for ITV to fly her to Mexico. So, via the then novelty of satellite, I organised my finest interview ever. As the new gold medallist climbed out of the ring, we clamped earphones on to him to hear his beloved Cheryl squeal: 'Effin 'ell, you 'aven't effin gone and done it 'ave you?' To have Chris, through his cut lips, assure his wife: 'Yes, ol' lady, I effin, effin 'ave.' "

Finnegan arrived back in England to find that his National Insurance demand had been met by promoter Harry Levene. The hard-luck story evoked an instant response from the people of Iver –

everything from small coins to £5 notes and postal orders was slipped through his door. He was still "more or less forced into turning pro" and netted a rumoured £1,000 for his first fight, just six weeks after he had stepped out of the ring in Mexico.

He won the British and Commonwealth light-heavyweight titles in January 1972 and added the European title the following year. Seven months later he was stopped by Foster in the 14th round of an epic world title fight at Wembley. Foster insisted that Finnegan was the toughest of the 11 men who had challenged for his crown over a four-year period. Finnegan went on to lose twice to fellow Briton John Conteh in European title fights, protesting on both occasions that Conteh's head had inflicted more damage than his fists.

Despite drinking prodigiously between fights, Finnegan managed to take to the ring in near-peak condition. His enthusiasm and self-belief were rekindled when he regained his British title from Johnny Frankham at the Royal Albert Hall in 1975, but it was to be his final fight. He started suffering from blurred vision and after a detached retina was diagnosed he needed a delicate operation to save the sight in his right eye.

Relief soon gave way to the realisation that he needed a new source of income. A pub was hardly the most sensible of choices and Finnegan struggled financially for the last 20 years of his life. In October 2008, he was floored by the death of his brother Kevin. Soon afterwards, Chris Finnegan was taken into hospital suffering from pneumonia and he died on March 2 2009.

In his autobiography, published in 1976, he wrote: "What a berk I was – pissing my money away in an effort to enjoy myself, with no thought for the consequences. And, of course, it all proved a dismal failure and now I stand stripped of all pretence."

1972

Sept 1: Individual and team three-day event, Richard Meade; Mary Gordon-Watson, Meade, Bridget Parker, Mark Phillips

BRITAIN won the individual and team title in Munich and still felt short-changed. The disappointment was explained by an IOC edict after the Mexico Games that a single gold medal would now be awarded for "artificial" team events. Richard Meade, who at least had the tangible reward of an individual gold medal for his impeccable display on Laurieston, said: "I suppose they are saving on expenses." The horse's owner, Derek Allhusen, was less diplomatic in his choice of language. "Our team should have a gold medal each, not just one between them," he fumed. "I think it's disgraceful. I will complain through official channels. When we return home the riders are meeting the Queen. She will want to see the medals. What do we do? Swap the medals and go in one at a time. It's ridiculous."

Allhusen did not have to look far or wait long for a sympathetic hearing. Prince Philip, president of the International Equestrian Federation, presented the medals and also arranged for golden spurs to be struck for the team when they got home. The British Equestrian Federation then had copies made of the medal, which were given to the riders in a secondary ceremony.

Preparations ran far more smoothly than they had before Mexico, but in Munich the British management were faced with an eleventh-hour headache when Debbie West's horse, Baccarat, was ruled out by a fitness test as dawn broke on the first morning of the dressage. West's deflation was matched by that of first reserve Lorna Sutherland, a proven winner on Peer Gynt.

The call went out to Bridget Parker instead, on the grounds that her horse, Cornish Gold, would be better suited to the demanding cross-country course. She remembers: "At six o'clock in the morning Colonel Bill Lithgow [the team's chef d'équipe] rang me and said, 'Come to the stables and bring your clothes. You're riding this afternoon.' In a way I was much better off than the others: I hadn't had days of thinking about the cross country, but I had a fearful rush after I'd done my dressage in the afternoon on the first day. Then I had to go round the course again; Bertie Hill was our trainer and he walked round with me. Mark Phillips's father drove me round the roads and tracks and out to the steeplechase course. I'd obviously been round with the others, but when you're not actually going to have to ride it you don't have the same level of concentration."

Parker took her place in a formidable-looking team: Meade's reputation was long established, Mark Phillips had won the last two editions of Badminton on Great Ovation and there was an instinctive chemistry between Mary Gordon-Watson and Cornishman V. Meade's performance on Cornishman in Mexico made invidious comparisons inevitable, but the critical mumblings evaporated as Gordon-Watson won first the individual title at the European Championships in 1969 then the world title at a drenched Punches-town the following year.

Phillips and Great Ovation put together an immaculate dressage test on Great Ovation to lie third, but they were found out by a demanding cross-country section. Suddenly the British team were one more setback away from falling out of contention. Both Gordon-Watson, who suffered an allergic reaction after being stung by a wasp, and Parker were advised to adopt a cautious approach. Despite a stop on the platform at fence 22, effectively costing her a medal, Gordon-Watson was seventh best on the day; Parker was immediately behind her and Meade's faultless performance on Laurieston meant that Britain went into the jumping with a near unassailable lead.

Alan Smith, who covered the Games for *The Daily Telegraph*, recalls: "Munich was the first event to have a precursor to closed circuit TV, in the form of an electronic map of the cross-country course, with a light going on at each fence as it was jumped. Most of the British press were gathered round it while Richard was going round and there were huge cheers each time a light came on."

Gordon-Watson was uncertain how Cornishman might perform in front of 25,000 spectators at the jumping arena beside Munich Airport, but she need not have worried. He went clear, and the team could well afford the one fence which Parker and Cornish Gold, their third counting combination, had down. Meade and Laurieston were faultless in clinching both team and individual golds. Meade explained afterwards: "I didn't take it easy because I remembered Mexico, when riders who were in the lead made mistakes and lost all chance of the gold medal."

He admits that Laurieston proved him wrong in Munich. "I did say that I thought the Olympics had come a year early for Laurieston. He was only eight and not very experienced. It was obvious that he was very talented, but his technique needed a lot of work on it. I found him quite a hairy ride initially – he was a bit chancy with his fences – but he really produced the goods in the end."

The *Daily Mail* columnist, Ian Wooldridge, wrote of Meade: "Tall, blond and apparently haughty, he could be nothing but an Englishman. He's held in much awe here because half the German newspapers say he's going to marry Princess Anne. Meade hit the second fence and he hit the 11th and then, damn me, with the gold medal sewn up he merely patted Laurieston's neck with a white-gloved hand and rode off as though supremely bored with the whole affair."

> **'He's held in much awe here because half the German papers say he's going to marry Princess Anne'**

It was not just the Germans who seemed to regard Princess Anne as an unofficial fifth member of the British team. She could, conceivably, have been competing rather than watching if Doublet had stayed fit, but the British media, and in particular the tabloids, had the Princess permanently in their peripheral vision. As much as the newspapers wanted it to be true, there is little evidence that she and Meade were ever 'an item'. Meade himself reflects: "It annoyed me at the time. Certain things were written which were total rubbish, but there's nothing you can do about it." The press subsequently reported that the age difference – he was 12 years older than the Princess – was too much for Prince Philip to countenance a marriage; history suggests that Meade was an effective decoy for Princess Anne's real beau-in-waiting. She and Mark Phillips married just over a year later.

Bridget Parker recalls that there was a slightly farcical postscript to the Munich triumph, when she was singled out – there were only three female riders competing – for dope-testing. "I had to hand over the horse, then they whisked me off in a car to the doping centre. There were just a load of men standing round, so that caused a fair

Richard Meade and Laurieston on their way to a clear round in the show-jumping phase and gold medals in both the individual and team competition

amount of chaos. They eventually found a lady who was able to accompany me."

Parker, who remains grateful for the British management's faith in her in 1972, has herself been a selector in recent years. Phillips competed in his second Olympics at Seoul in 1988, when Britain won the team silver medal. He was again the non-scoring member of the quartet: his horse, Cartier, pulled a muscle before the cross country. He set up the Gatcombe trials when he and Princess Anne were living there and after their divorce he became chef d'équipe for the American three-day event team. He married the American rider, Sandy Pflueger, in 1997.

Cornishman was retired from competition in 1973 by Gordon-Watson, but he enjoyed a brief career in the film industry, appearing in both *Dead Cert* (1974) and *International Velvet* (1978). Jane Holder-ness-Roddam, part of the gold medal winning team in 1968, doubled for Tatum O'Neal in the riding sequences and the film also featured Holderness-Roddam's actress sister, Sarah Bullen.

Gordon-Watson also made the natural transition from rider to selector. She has written extensively on equestrianism in books, newspapers and magazines, and wonders if she will ever get round to writing a long-intended novel – "there are some great stories from the eventing world if I ever get round to doing it". She became Mary Low when she married in 2006.

Meade again exceeded his own expectations by finishing fourth on Jacob Jones at the 1976 Olympics. He was denied a fifth appearance when the British Equestrian Federation decided not to send a team to the Moscow Games. "I felt very strongly we should have gone," he says, "because I didn't feel it was right for sport to be making a political stand when there were trade delegations going to the Soviet Union. Life was going on as normal in many respects between Britain and the Soviet Union and I thought it was very unfair that sport should be singled out. I always believed that sport should be above politics and perhaps that's an idealistic way of looking at it, but in those days we were idealistic and the Olympics were idealistic."

He stopped competing in 1986 but his name was back in the headlines in 2001, when he was expelled from the RSPCA after urging the society to reconsider its opposition to fox hunting.

Sept 3: Pentathlon, Mary Peters

THE pentathlon was Mary Peters's passport to Olympic glory. Without it, she doubts that she would have been anything more than a "mediocre" shot-putter. With it, she is the closest thing to royalty in residence in Northern Ireland. As lord lieutenant of Belfast, she headed the official welcoming party when Prince William and bride-to-be Kate Middleton visited the city last year.

Peters was born and raised in Liverpool and only moved to her adopted homeland at the age of 11. Her father's job as an insurance agent had taken him to Belfast in 1948 and when he was transferred to Ballymena two years later the family joined him. "Ballymena was the Ulster Scots area," Peters explains. "It was an unusual accent and I found it very difficult to understand. I had to have somebody to sit next to me in school to interpret. Then my father was promoted again and we moved to Portadown. The headmaster there was English and very supportive of all his pupils and he took a liking to me and saw that I had sports talent. While I was at school my mother died and he was very kind to me because my father was grieving and couldn't cope with it."

If Donald Woodman was instrumental in nurturing Peters's sporting talent at Portadown College, her father, too, played a very practical role in securing training facilities for a budding pentathlete (the event itself was not included in the Olympic programme until 1964). How many girls receive two tons of sand as a 15th birthday present? The result was a long jump pit in a neighbour's field. A local foundry shaped a wooden ball so that a shot could be cast of the correct weight and dimensions; Northern Ireland's first concrete shot-putting circle was constructed in the Peters garden.

The teenaged Mary Peters was unsettled by her father's remarriage, six months after the death of his first wife. She was nudged towards a job as a PE teacher, but, perversely, decided to apply for a place at the domestic science college in Belfast instead. In her autobiography, she described Belfast as "a city which made me welcome when I needed love very badly". Peters's father and stepmother moved to England and later followed her brother to Sydney, Australia.

The 1958 Commonwealth Games were pivotal in Peters's career, not so much for her performances in the shot, high jump and sprint relay as for her introduction to the remarkable character, Buster McShane, who was to be her coach, mentor and friend for the next 14 years. Their relationship even survived a mini-crisis in the build-up to the Munich Olympics, when Peters responded badly to criticism and he punched her to the ground. "It was the only time he apologised to me," she said.

McShane was a small man who had raised the bar for himself through body-building (his first weights were adapted from steel which he stole from the shipyards in Belfast). After the Games, Peters was one of the few athletes who responded to a circular from McShane, offering weight-training courses. It was of no great relevance to their relationship but McShane, like Peters, was an atheist.

In 1959, she began teaching at a secondary school. It was a natural environment for her but it did not square with her athletic ambitions; McShane, meanwhile, was keen to convert his third-floor gymnasium into a health club. "I had difficulty getting time off to train," Peters recalls, "so when Buster offered me a secretarial post in his health club I took it." One immediate benefit was that she no longer had to find 10s (50p) out of her teacher's pay packet of £9, to meet the weekly subscription to the club. She also now classed, under the IOC's

Mary Peters shows her delight at a crucial clearance in the high jump

absurdly strict definition at the time, as a professional and cheat. The club went from strength to strength…until a strip joint was opened on the floor below. Six months after they moved to new premises the old building was destroyed by a terrorist bomb.

Even with the greater freedom to train and compete which her new job permitted, Peters's improvement followed a gentle gradient. She finished fourth in the shot at the 1962 Commonwealth Games in Perth and was on the periphery of world record breaking feats from her room-mates, Mary Rand and Ann Packer, in Tokyo. She was content to finish fourth in the pentathlon and, without tipping herself for the ultimate prize, "began to believe that I was capable of more than I thought I was".

She held the thought while sitting out the 1965 season then, at McShane's behest, embarked on what she described as a "nauseating" force-feeding exercise; the sole objective was to win the shot at the 1966 Commonwealth Games in Kingston, Jamaica. "I came very close, literally, to eating my full salary every week," she wrote. "And soon came the problem that I no longer had any clothes at all that would fit me…I suppose I was the only athlete to turn up for the Commonwealth Games in West Indies wearing cast-off maternity clothes." The change in physique – one British coach stated categorically that she was taking drugs – was so marked that she expanded from her usual weight, 10st 6lb, to 13st 4lb.

On the day of the competition she was physically strong but mentally weak, losing the gold medal to the New Zealander, Val Young. McShane stormed out of the stadium in disgust and Peters was in equal disarray when she under-performed at the European Championships later the same year. She was still in recovery in a write-off of a 1967 season and felt weighed down by the demands of captaincy when she competed at the Mexico Olympics in 1968.

Peters also found it hard to come to terms with the implications of Mary Rand's retirement just before the Games. She had felt incapable of beating her and was always aware of being in the shadow of Rand's athletic brilliance and dominating personality. Peters reflected: "I felt that nothing was beyond me but for all that I took no pleasure in her retirement from athletics." She finished ninth in 1968, her performances little improved from four years earlier.

Rand's absence did have an important delayed effect on Peters's career. Again she took time out and when she returned to competition at the start of 1970 she had entered the final lap for most athletes: the thirties. Peters equalled the world record for the 60m indoor hurdles at Cosford and allowed herself to focus on the possibility of winning the pentathlon, which was included for the first time at the Commonwealth Games in Edinburgh later that year. In the event, she followed up a gold medal in the pentathlon, with a Commonwealth record of 5,148 points, by winning the shot as well. "It tasted sweet and I decided I wanted some more," she remembers with a knowing smile.

Northern Ireland was, by now, in the grip of 'the troubles', which had flared up in 1969 and were at their height when Peters competed at Munich in 1972. "It wasn't easy," she admits with huge understatement. "I was lucky enough to get a Churchill Scholarship, which allowed me to go to the States; it was valuable not just because it was away from the troubles but it was also sunny every day. It also meant that I had some tracks to train on. In Belfast our track was full of potholes so I did most of my training in the Queen's University gymnasium, which was the biggest indoor sports hall that had been built at that time. I used to do my shot-putting with a leather shot, then popped over hurdles at the side of the gym. Mike Bull used to pole-vault over one side of the bed and I used to high-jump over the other side. I would go up to the track occasionally, but it was dangerous because of all the potholes. I used to have to travel on two buses, carrying my shot and my starting blocks, and very often bombs would be going off. I don't know why but I always made it to the track. I just kept going."

> **'I used to have to travel on two buses, carrying my shot and my starting blocks, and very often bombs would be going off'**

Dick Fosbury, the American high jumper, played an important, if unwitting, part in Peters's Munich victory. He brought the Fosbury flop to the world's attention when he won the Olympic title in 1968, and three years later Buster McShane persuaded Peters to adopt the technique. "He used to say, 'You'll jump six feet', and I'd just laugh," she remembers. "After all, I was only 5ft 8in tall. In the first session at Crystal Palace I jumped higher than I ever had with my own interpretation of the western roll. That made such a difference with the pentathlon." She would jump 5ft 11½in (1.82m) in Munich.

Nothing less than gold would be good enough for Peters in 1972. "I knew it was my last chance," she explains. "I was 33 and I knew that four years on I wouldn't still be able to compete at that level. I loved training, I loved competing, but I realised that my days were numbered as regards being a performing athlete so I just wanted to make the last competition the most important."

There was a curious dynamic to the event. Peters's best disciplines, the hurdles, shot and high jump, were all on the first day. Her chief rival, Heide Rosendahl, was an outstanding long jumper and sprinter. The drama was extraordinary as the Saturday action in the Olympic Stadium concluded with the men's pole vault and the pentathlon high jump. Peters recalls:

> It was the first time in my whole athletics career that I was centre stage. Everyone else was out in the high jump and I was still there

125

and [East German] Wolfgang Nordwig was pole-vaulting at the other end of the stadium. There were a whole crowd of British supporters down there chanting my name. That had never happened to me before: it was like being on the stage. Every time I cleared the bar they would cheer and then we waited while Wolfgang had a vault. Then he would clear it and the crowd down that end would roar. The people who were there that night certainly helped me over that bar because I'd never jumped that high before.

Did she under-perform in any of the events? "No, but if you hear the BBC commentary you'd think that I did in the long jump because Ron Pickering kept saying, 'She's got to do six metres…this is a mediocre performance,' and I did 5.98. Two centimetres wasn't that bad." Pickering's pessimism was prompted by Rosendahl, who took a huge chunk out of Peters's overnight lead with a jump of 6.83m, further than her winning distance in the individual long jump three days earlier.

McShane had been bombarding Peters with calculations and permutations since the previous night; his last one was that she would have to beat her personal best for the 200m, 24.2sec, if she was going to win the gold medal. Neither had predicted that Rosendahl would run as fast as she did, 22.96sec, but Peters's time, 24.08sec, enabled her to sneak home by just 10 points. "It was my marathon," Peters remembers. "I knew I had to do the best I'd ever done and run the race of my life. I knew if I ran right I could do it, but I ran scared." The icing on the victory cake was a world record total of 4,801 points under the revised system. "You couldn't have written the story any better, could you?" she says with a glint in her eye. "And to win by such a small margin."

In the tunnel afterwards Peters broke away from the sea of microphones for a tearful embrace with McShane. As the athletes waited for the medal ceremony, Rosendahl offered her a cigarette; Peters had worked her way through a packet during the competition and suspected that the German had as well. The ceremony itself was memorable more for a torrent of tears from the bronze medallist, Burglinde Pollak, than for the distracted winner's show of emotion. Peters had already been shocked to the core to hear that her father, whom she had not seen for more than two years, was in the crowd and their reunion took place in the middle of a live BBC interview.

"I had no idea if he had any knowledge of how I'd progressed," Peters admits, "except when I did well at the Commonwealth Games. But he said to my brother that he was going to be there to see me win the gold medal and there he was. I was thrilled. He told my sister-in-law and she rang my brother, who was on a field trip out in the bush. She said, 'Mary's done it.' My brother said, 'Done what?' They were so removed from my life in Northern Ireland, being in Australia."

The breathless climax to the pentathlon was closely followed by the final of the men's 10,000m. Britain's David Bedford had told the world he would win and Prime Minister Ted Heath was there so see him live up to his boast. Bedford finished a demoralised sixth instead and Peters felt like a little-known consolation prize when she was introduced to Heath. She remains humbly aware of what might have been, saying: "I could so easily have gone to obscurity because if a man had won on the track in those Games I don't think I would have been remembered."

Peters later met Rosendahl's husband in a hotel lift. "I said to him, 'I know who you are but you don't know who I am.' He said, 'Indeed I do. How did you beat my wife?' I said, 'I wanted it more.' She won two other gold medals so I think she was content with her silver."

The euphoria of the moment dissipated over the following days: Peters turned down a lunch invitation from Heath when she was told that McShane could not attend and had her triumphant return to Belfast imperilled by a death threat delivered via the BBC. It read: 'Mary Peters is a Protestant and has won a medal for Britain. An attempt will be made on her life and it will be blamed on the IRA. Tell Mary Peters to say something about bringing the people together. I don't want to turn her into a martyr. Her home will be going up in the near future.' Peters insisted that the reception went ahead; it reminded her of the ticker-tape welcome home for American war heroes. The pure joy which her victory brought to the province more than compensated for the odd killjoy moment: the Rev Ian Paisley offered his congratulations before taking her to task for competing on "the Sabbath day".

Peters's place in the public's affections was confirmed when she received the BBC Sports Personality of the Year award from Princess Anne in December 1972. "Hasn't she kept it clean!" she exclaimed. An appearance on *This Is Your Life* ended with her seeing her brother, John, for the first time in 12 years. Peters was a full-time celebrity for four months after the Munich Games, but she was snapped back to reality by two jolting events early the following year.

First, three British soldiers were shot dead in the house bordering on her Belfast flat; a month later Buster McShane died in a car crash (a crowd conservatively estimated at 10,000 stood outside the crematorium). Peters's name was already being used to raise money for the building of the Mary Peters Track and McShane's death persuaded her to take on a final athletic challenge which also won publicity for the fund-raising initiative. Peters and pole-vaulter Mike Bull, another McShane protégé, vowed to honour his memory by winning the pentathlon and decathlon respectively at the 1974 Commonwealth Games in Christchurch, New Zealand.

She was manager of the British women's team at the Moscow and Los Angeles Olympics and felt barely a tinge of jealousy as athletes began to reap huge rewards for their exploits. She had her own health club for 20 years, but it was more a service to the community than an out-and-out business venture. She was upgraded from MBE to CBE in 1990 and in 2000 joined the very exclusive ranks of sporting Dames.

Was your life ever the same after 1972? "Never, happily," she says with a chuckle. "When I started out in athletics I didn't want to be that successful. I just enjoyed the friendship and the travel and the training. People said, if only you'd been competing 10 years later. I suppose I might have had some money in the bank, but it doesn't make you any happier. You can only sleep in one bed at night. I have a little cottage in the country; I've lived there for 35 years.

"If you're lucky you get a running track named after you when you die – I've got it in my lifetime. The Mary Peters Trust helps support young, up-and-coming sports people. That gives me so much joy and pleasure. I just feel very proud that Northern Ireland accepted me as one of them."

Sept 5: Flying Dutchman class sailing, Rodney Pattisson, Chris Davies

RODNEY PATTISSON finally decided in 1971 that "sailing and a life in the Navy weren't compatible". He left the service with a £2,000 gratuity for 10 years' service and a short-term offer to become a director of the Southern Ocean Shipyard in Poole. "I actually did absolutely nothing," Pattisson admits, "although on paper it looked as though I was doing something." Suspicious rivals, unable to beat him on the water, resorted to more underhand tactics.

"The Italians, especially, tried very hard to get me declared a professional," says Pattisson. "At one point Beppe Croce stood up as chairman of the IYRU and declared that I'd been to some regatta in Italy and been paid too much. We were able to prove that it wasn't true, and that the yacht club had kept most of the money and just paid over a small fraction for my travel expenses, which was all I was claiming."

After his victory in Mexico, Pattisson was inevitably seen as one of Britain's brightest prospects for gold in Munich, but he was no more co-operative with the press than he had been in 1968. "A year before the Games," he recalls, "Chris Brasher was doing a piece about potential gold medallists in the *Observer* and he rang me, 'I want to interview you,' he said 'Oh yes,' I said, 'I'm not interested in being featured or interviewed.' He said, 'You owe it to the public.' I said, 'I don't owe it to anybody, least of all the public.' He never forgave me."

Brasher had to make do with marine engineer Chris Davies who, at the suggestion of Britain's first Olympic team coach, David Robinson, replaced MacDonald-Smith as crewman. "Chris was less argumentative than Iain," says Pattisson. "He was a softer character and took all the bad language I gave and didn't grumble. He was going to get married and postponed that for a year, which was very good of him. Amazingly, his eyesight wasn't very good and seeing the windward mark was very important and the RYA paid for his contact lenses and gave him extra long sight. Only now, having tried to wear contact lenses myself, do I realise how hard that was. That showed his determination."

The new partnership found it harder to win the trials where, according to Pattisson, "everything broke", than the Olympic regatta. They even had the luxury of sitting out the last day's racing after winning four of the first six races at Kiel. The medal presentation was on the same day, Sept 6, that terrorists killed nine Israeli athletes whom they had earlier taken hostage. Pattisson sounded a suitably sombre note: "Of course I am satisfied with my second gold medal, but what is victory worth when people kill each other during the Olympics?"

As a helmsman, Pattisson was more autocrat than democrat, but he was also fiercely loyal, as proved by his lengthy campaign to win recognition for Davies. Pattisson and MacDonald-Smith had been awarded MBEs in the 1969 New Year's Honours list; Davies was mysteriously overlooked. It was even suggested (and strenuously denied) that he may have offended Prime Minister Ted Heath by tipsily blurting out, 'Hello Teddy' at a reception shortly after the Munich Games. Pattisson threatened to return his own gong before Davies was finally honoured in 2001.

Pattisson was, in a sense, the victim of his exploits on the water. "The more successful you were the harder it was to stay an amateur and the harder it was to get a job," he says wistfully. After the Munich Games, he began importing 470s, the new Olympic class, from Spain. "I used to bring back seven at a time, two on the car and five on a trailer," he recalls. "I got offered a job by Equinox, a French clothing manufacturer who wanted to start up an office in England. They asked me to be a technical adviser and wear their gear. I wrote to the RYA and they said, 'That will make you a professional.' "

He largely disappeared off the competitive radar screen, rowing with officials over travel grants before finally confirming a renewal of his partnership with Julian Brooke-Houghton, his crewman when he won the world title in 1971. There was a tone of weary resignation in John Nicholls's eve-of-Montreal article for the *Times*: "He is, so far as one can tell, determined to win another [gold medal]. I have to say 'as far as one can tell' because Pattisson is not telling anything. He makes no effort to conceal his dislike of the press and is rarely, if ever, interviewed." An unidentified American journalist described Pattisson as "still an unlovely son of a bitch".

The British media were relieved to discover that Brooke-Houghton was more approachable. Two months before the Games he gave a little insight into the Pattisson methodology: "Rodney is one of those guys who says, 'This is the way I do it, take or leave it.' I've won a world championship with him five years ago, and my immediate reaction was to say, 'I don't want to go through all that again.' But here I am. The point is that Rodney Pattisson is a superb and single-minded sailor and you have to go along with him in his attitudes. Because of the demands he makes on himself and his crew, I have delayed right until this point getting together with him again."

Pattisson himself reflects: "Julian said I was obsessed with winning. He wasn't obsessed enough, that was the trouble. I never said that to him, but women were more important to him. I'm sure he realises it now, but there was one occasion when he went on strike and said, 'We've done enough practising for the day.' I said, 'No we haven't. We've still got to test this sail.' He said, no, and I had to sail back to the harbour. You don't win gold medals that way."

They might have won in Montreal but for some cynical revenge-seeking by the Dutchman, Erik Vollebregt, who was disqualified from the fourth race after a protest from Pattisson, and the intransigent Beppo Croce's insistence, as president of the jury of appeal, that the results of what Pattisson calls "a ridiculously fluky race" should be allowed to stand. The British pair were leading the regatta with three races remaining, but Vollebregt concentrated all his efforts on hampering Pattisson and Brooke-Houghton in the next two races before, finally, being warned off by the jury and other competitors. The Britons had to settle for a silver medal behind the German brothers, Jorg and Eckart Diesch.

The more abrasive edges to Pattisson's personality were smoothed out by his involvement in a variety of team projects. In 1983, he co-skippered Victory, Peter de Savary's America's Cup boat, and ran out of time in his effort to qualify for the 1984 Olympics (the RYA had opted out of the 1980 Games). "The boat builder made some gross errors," he says, "and it hit the water on the eve of the first race in the trials." Lack of boat speed left him with an impossible task to make the British team in 1988.

Pattisson, a late recruit to married life in 2003, has enjoyed racing trimarans and schooners in recent years and has developed a huge admiration for long-distance sailors. After the Frenchman, Francis Joyon, broke the solo non-stop round-the-world record in 2004, Pattisson presented him with one of his gold medals. He asked Ellen MacArthur to hand over the other after Joyon had shattered her record in 2008. "The French press were very pleased by the gesture," says Pattisson, though both medals were later returned. "I'll be custodian for a few months, but I can't keep them," Joyon told Pattisson.

He was nominated as a torchbearer for the 2012 Games by Parkstone Yacht Club, but learned just before Christmas last year that the application had been turned down. He described the decision as "a bit extraordinary", adding: "I like to think that my carrying the torch a few yards might have inspired a few people." Pattisson was equally unimpressed by what he describes as a "curt" explanatory email from Lord Coe and insists: "I'm glad now. As far as I can see it's a mickey-mouse operation."

1976

July 20: 200m breaststroke, David Wilkie

DAVID WILKIE'S early life could be described, in geographical shorthand, as 'born in Sri Lanka, schooled in Scotland, made in America'. The moody, morose teenager was transformed by his stint in Miami into the mature swimmer who obliterated the field in the final of the 200m breaststroke in Montreal. It was not just the most impressive performance in the pool at the 1976 Games, and the one blip in an arrogant display of dominance by the American men, but an emphatic final word in the rivalry between Wilkie and John Hencken. Their relationship had been one of few words; this brief exchange after the 200m final ranked with their longest ever conversations.

Wilkie: "John, it has been four good years – thanks a lot."
Hencken: "It certainly has."

Rewind to March 1954 and a birth notice in the *Aberdeen Weekly Journal*: "WILKIE – On March 8 in Colombo, Ceylon, to Jean (née McDonald) and Harry Wilkie, a son, David Andrew, a brother for Caroline." David Wilkie's parents were Aberdonians; his father was lured to post-independence Ceylon – the name was formally changed to Sri Lanka in 1972 – by an engineering job. The island was still comfortable with its colonial past and David enjoyed an idyllic early childhood, mostly spent outdoors. "I swam almost before I walked," he recalled. He competed from the age of eight, but the word 'training' was absent from his vocabulary until, very reluctantly, he was enrolled as a boarder at Daniel Stewart's College in Edinburgh in the autumn of 1965.

The first two years were "sheer hell" and Wilkie found no solace at the Warrender Baths Club. Swimming was now a chore against the backdrop of leaden skies rather than the expression of freedom it had been in Colombo. He became painfully shy and uncommunicative, channelling his energy into excuses for skipping training. An exasperated Frank Thomas, the club's coach and president, threw Wilkie out of the club then reinstated him. The latent talent was enormous and Thomas became aware that when Wilkie deigned to put in an appearance he was a quick learner.

He began to specialise in the breaststroke in 1969, and improved so rapidly that he broke the 200m British record the following year and, though still only 16, won the bronze medal at the Commonwealth Games in Edinburgh. Even when confronted with such clear evidence of his potential, Wilkie remained at best indifferent towards the sport and at the start of Olympic year, 1972, there was no guarantee that he would try to make the British team for Munich. He even told Thomas that he was thinking of giving up swimming.

The Games were only three months away when he finally agreed to commit himself unreservedly. The setting up of an elite training centre in York seemed to herald a more professional approach, even if allegations of marijuana smoking between training sessions threw the preparations into chaos. Three swimmers were chucked off the team; others went unpunished. In the pool it was the same old story: only three Britons reached finals in Munich.

One of them was Wilkie who, despite the distractions of the lurid headlines and questions in Parliament, revelled in the environment of competitive camaraderie which the York training camp fostered. He exceeded most expectations by reaching the 100m final and was disappointed to finish last in a race won by Japan's Nobutaka Taguchi in a world record time of 1min 4.94sec. "The only mistake I made was not turning well," said Wilkie afterwards.

He qualified for the 200m final as the second fastest swimmer behind Taguchi, but the outcome of the final itself was determined by Hencken's blistering first 50 metres, at which point he was already almost two seconds ahead of Wilkie. Hencken maintained the gap to break the world record and Wilkie held off Taguchi to finish in 2min 23.67sec, a European and Commonwealth record. It was to be Wilkie's last defeat in his premier event and an important tactical lesson.

Four years later he reflected: "I did not have enough confidence in myself in Munich to swim the race the way Hencken swam his, to go out hard and hold on."

Wilkie's performances in Munich advertised his potential to a host of American universities and in January 1973 he took up a full scholarship at the University of Miami. The guaranteed warmth and sunshine, the closest equivalent on offer to the Sri Lankan climate, were the clinching factors. Initially, he studied marine biology but later switched to a less time-consuming course in broadcasting and communications. He described Miami as the place where he "grew up and found myself".

The benefits of the new arrangement were soon apparent – Wilkie became the first man to break 2min 20sec when he won the 200m breaststroke at the 1973 World Championships in Belgrade. He received the MBE in the New Year's Honours and showed his versatility at the European Championships in Vienna by winning both his banker event and the 200m medley; his time of 2min 6.32sec was a world record. Wilkie also chose this as the moment to pre-announce his retirement after the Montreal Games. "I want to quit at the top," he explained, "because pretty soon I'll be getting to the stage where all sorts of people will start beating me, and I don't want that."

Hencken opted out of the 1975 World Championships, held at altitude in Cali, Colombia, allowing Wilkie a relatively untroubled path to a breaststroke double, and his dedication was absolute as Montreal loomed. The training emphasis was more on stamina than speed; Wilkie averaged 12,000 metres a day in the nine months leading up to the Games, which one newspaper helpfully equated to a transatlantic swim. As hostilities got under way, he predicted, with admirable prescience and implied self-confidence, that the world record could be lowered by as much as three seconds.

He announced that he would shave off his beard…but the trademark moustache would stay. "I'll do this because I like the feel of fresh water against my face on an important swim," he explained. "But I won't shave off my moustache – it has not restricted me before." Swimming watchers were used by now to Wilkie's other calling cards: the ever-present goggles (which helped to offset his allergy to chlorine) and cap to contain his long hair. The tartan cap which he wore before races complemented the slightly bohemian image.

He liked the "quiet water" of the Montreal pool and insisted that there was no ill feeling between him and Hencken, just the guardedness of two greats coveting the same slice of cake. "It may make a good story for newspapers that I'm not fond of John Hencken but it is also untrue," he said. "You could say that the only thing we have in common is that we don't speak to each other." The *Daily Mirror* dubbed it the "Silent Duel of the Deep".

The shorter and more powerfully built Hencken – the arm man to Wilkie's leg man – maintained his superiority over 100m, but needed another world record, 63.11sec, to deny Wilkie. The Scot was also inside Hencken's previous record and insisted that he had not given the event his full attention. "I was deliberately doing bad things in the heats and semi-finals," he said. "In the heat I didn't even do a grab start. In the semi-final I hadn't even shaved my arms and upper body."

David Wilkie on course for victory in the 200m breaststroke final

After the race, there was the air of two boxers trying to land psychological blows before a rematch. Sydney Hulls wrote in the *Daily Express*: "David Wilkie looked at the 100 metres breaststroke gold medal hanging around the neck of his deadly rival, American John Hencken. Then he murmured in his transatlantic accent: 'John Hencken, you've had your day. I hope you enjoyed it.' Hencken responded: 'You'll have to take away my world record if you want to take away my title.' " Wilkie, wearying of the volley of questions directed exclusively at Hencken, made a low-key exit from the press conference.

He was only fractionally outside Hencken's record in qualifying for the 200m final four days later and knew that he had plenty in reserve. Hencken's only chance was to claim a telling lead in the first 50 metres, but he was already behind Wilkie, who simply got quicker and quicker to win in an extraordinary time of 2min 15.11sec, 3.1sec faster than Hencken's world record. He was the first British male swimmer for 68 years to win an Olympic title – Fred Holman had taken almost a minute longer to win the same event in 1908.

Anita Lonsbrough, the winner of the women's equivalent event in 1960, did her best to stifle a tear as she analysed proceedings for BBC Radio. The television coverage was beset by technical problems so commentator Alan Weeks had to use a combination of microphone and telephone to accompany the historic pictures. He admitted afterwards: "David's victory gave me my proudest moment in 25 years of television broadcasting."

Dave Haller, the British coach, had almost as much belief in Wilkie's ability as the swimmer had in himself. He said recently that he regarded the Montreal swim as "probably the greatest individual performance I have witnessed". At the time he made the telling observation: "David probably only swims really well for about 15 minutes a year: when it matters."

Ian Wooldridge, the *Daily Mail*'s perceptive columnist, warmed to Wilkie; the same could not be said of Hencken. "With his beard off but his moustache still on, he has the classic looks and bearing of an Edwardian Coldstream subaltern," Wooldridge wrote. "These, however, conceal an alert brain, a surprisingly pronounced American accent and much charm…Hencken, who reminds you of one of Scott Fitzgerald's more insufferable society young bloods, has a pomposity quite unsuited to his 22 years."

Wilkie celebrated with champagne, his first drink for three months, and admitted that Miami had kept him in the pool. "If I'd stayed in the UK I would have given up swimming by now. There are so many problems to overcome back home, not the least of which is finding bath space in which to train at reasonable hours. I am really grateful to America for having given me the chance to win this gold."

He has subsequently admitted that if he had been able to make a living out of the sport he would have carried on competing, at least until the Moscow Games, but Wilkie has continued to promote the sport, particularly in Scotland, and carved out a highly successful career in commerce after founding the nutrition company Health Perception in 1989. The business was sold for almost £8 million in 2004.

July 22: Team modern pentathlon, Jim Fox, Danny Nightingale, Adrian Parker

IN an ideal world – the kind of world the Olympics used to believe in – Jim Fox and Boris Onischenko would have retired with a salute and a handshake borne of huge mutual respect. Instead, Fox found himself

Boris Onischenko has his épée inspected after being accused of cheating in Montreal

cast as the reluctant whistleblower when Onischenko was exposed as a hapless cheat.

Fox had been carrying the flag for more than 10 years, the lone Briton of international standard in a sport dominated by east European soldiers. He competed in Tokyo as a 23-year-old and though he turned his back on the Army – and modern pentathlon – after the Mexico Games, to take up a poorly paid managerial job in Jersey, he missed the regimental spirit, signed on again with the Royal Electrical and Mechanical Engineers and set his sights on Munich.

Britain still lacked the strength in depth to challenge for a team medal, but Fox came fourth in the individual standings. He admits that he was "both very pleased but very disappointed not to finish that one place higher". He would almost certainly have claimed a medal if the International Modern Pentathlon Union had adopted a more princi-pled stance against 14 unnamed competitors who were found to have taken the sedatives Valium and Librium before the shooting discipline.

"We all thought the names would come out and they would be disqualified," remembers Fox, "but as far as we could understand the authorities thought it would bring the sport into disrepute and nothing was done about it." Neither of the drugs was on the IOC's banned list at the time.

The emergence in the mid-Seventies of two highly promising and driven young pentathletes, Adrian Parker and Danny Nightingale, began to convince Fox that a podium place might be possible in his fourth and swansong Olympics. Parker, an outstanding runner-swimmer, recalls that he had only to negotiate the riding course unscathed in his first competition to become part of the unofficial Great Britain B squad. After completing his degree he had joined the family business, a music shop in London's West End which specialised in brass instruments. "I worked four days a week for a year, but I wasn't getting better quickly enough so my parents agreed that as long as I was available as cover I would run the business on a Thursday morning, which was a half day then."

Nightingale, a doctor's son from Somerset, was reading engineering at the University of Sussex. He, too, bought into the low-budget lifestyle as he, Fox and Parker trained together in Surrey in the 18 months leading up to the Montreal Games. Fox won the individual bronze medal at the World Championships and Parker was second at the Europa Cup, a prestigious club event which attracted a greater volume of top-class entrants than the Olympics themselves.

The *Daily Mail* reported during the Montreal Games that the British team received £1,000 from the Sports Aid Foundation, £500 from the Olympic Preparation Fund and the same amount from the Sports Council. These figures fail to strike any particular chord with the supposed recipients, though Fox remembers that they were given a derisory £8.50 in expenses when they used the 50-metre pool at Crystal Palace. The nerve centre of the British Federation was poky offices above an estate agents' business in nearby Purley.

Despite a lack of support and specialist coaching – Parker's sister, Sarah, a swimmer of near international class, assisted with pool sessions – the British trio remained on course for Montreal until Parker damaged an Achilles tendon at the start of the season and needed intensive physiotherapy to get fit in time. "I was one of those awful patients who tries to chat up their physio," he jokes, adding: "I wouldn't have got to the Games without her." Physio Jane became wife Jane the following year.

Parker and Fox both managed clear rounds in the riding, the first of the five disciplines, but Parker still felt inhibited by his Achilles when he fenced on the second day of the competition. All three Britons struggled and in normal circumstances would have seen their chances of the team gold vanish there and then; Onischenko's antics changed everything. Parker, the first of the Britons to face him, recalls:

Danny Nightingale hugs his wife-to-be, Liz, after confirmation that Britain have won the modern pentathlon gold medal

When the light went on I knew I hadn't been hit. I'd done enough fencing at a good level to be fairly aware and he'd just been waving his weapon about. It never got closer than probably a couple of feet when he theoretically hit me. I kicked up a real fuss and it was only when they threatened to disqualify me if I didn't get off the piste that I gave up. I would think I was up there arguing and getting equipment tested for 15 to 20 minutes. It seemed like forever and I got no back-up from the team officials. Jim said he was sure I hadn't been hit, but he was obviously trying to psych himself up for his next fight so he didn't want to get involved. The team officials' view was more or less: you must have been hit, the light went on, get off and take it like a man, which I was very disappointed about.

As soon as it happened with Jim, he went over, grabbed his weapon and said, 'I want this tested.' So it was taken away and a couple of hours later they came back and said there was something wrong; the whole thing brewed up over the day. I don't think it affected me, but Jim was very upset by it all.

The subject was declared off limits by Fox when we spoke, but he could hardly avoid commenting at the time. He confided to the *Guardian*'s John Rodda: "I'm sickened. The game's gone." Rodda wrote: "His fencing went to pieces and a brush with a judge was no help; by the end of the day Fox's last chance for an individual gold medal had been lost in his depression: the stab, deep and wounding to his pride, that one of his friends could bring such disgrace to the sport."

Onischenko's instinctive response, when collared, was to disassociate himself from the rogue weapon and try to fight on with a replacement. Fox said: "It was a silly thing to do and I'm very sorry because we are such good friends. He was a Master of Sport, he was due to be promoted to lieutenant-colonel and he was a hero back home. I'm just surprised that he thought he could get away with it." The official explanation was that Onischenko's épée handle had been hollowed out and an instrument inserted which was covered with chamois leather. He was then able to trigger the light without scoring a hit.

Doubt was inevitably cast on Onischenko's past exploits on the piste – he had won the fencing in Munich en route to the individual silver and team gold – but Parker believes his incompetence in using the device suggests it was a new toy. "My suspicion was that if he'd been cleverer and practised with it no one would have been able to tell."

Onischenko, guaranteed prominence in sport's all-time rogues' gallery if nothing else, was sent home to Kiev. The official Soviet news agency, Tass, commented sternly: "Onischenko's action aroused the just condemnation of Soviet sportsmen." The competition, with the gold medal suddenly up for grabs, went on, though the British team struggled to stay in touch. They were off the pace in the shooting and, despite Parker's seventh place in the swimming, trailed leaders Czechoslovakia by 537 points going into the final day's running. They were also behind Poland, Hungary and the United States.

Fox did not believe that the gold medal was within reach, but Parker reasoned that if Nightingale and Fox could take a minute each out of the two quicker Czechs he could go round the demanding 4,000-metre course two minutes faster than the lumbering Jiri Adam – "brilliant fencer, expert shot but rubbish at running compared with his other abilities".

Parker also felt, as the fastest runner, that he should have been allowed to start last, but when that was vetoed he insisted on being first out. It gave Britain what proved to be a critical advantage because the draw dictated that he would be the first runner of all to set off (the rest followed at minute intervals). "Parts of the course were very easy," Parker recalls, "but you went out of the stadium, straight up a great big hill to the golf course and park area. There was probably half a mile of climb in the first 1,000 metres and in the third 1,000 they put you through a couple of bunkers and tight bends, so it was a bit ugly."

His time, 12min 9.5sec, was 17 seconds quicker than anyone else and "psyched out a lot of the runners coming after me". It also lifted him to fifth place in the final individual standings. Nightingale was fourth fastest and the last Briton to set out, Fox, compensated for what he admitted was a "terrible" competition overall by recording the sixth quickest time. They had to wait 40 minutes for the official verdict, but trusted their own sums enough to know that they had made history as the first British team to win the most exacting test of cross-sport ability. The Queen, too, recognised that they had achieved something special, singling them out for a detailed chat at the end of a reception on the royal yacht Britannia.

Fox now reflects: "Being in the first five or six for all those years, you're always hopeful that you'll make that breakthrough, but there always seems to be someone to finish ahead of you." The irony was that he made the breakthrough, in his final competition, despite performing way below the standards he had come to expect of himself. His immediate reaction was: "Think of me, the most experienced member of the team, having to rely on my team-mates to win me a gold medal at my time of life. Adrian and Danny ran like maniacs. I was supposed to carry them through the skill sports and leave them to make up in the swimming and running, but they never faltered all the way."

The British team were asked what they would do with their lone gold medal. "Hang it in the loo," was the flip response. A month later, Fox, Parker, Nightingale and reserve Andy Archibald were slightly embarrassed participants in a shameless publicity exercise at the Waldorf hotel in London. The double glazing firm, Alpine (the record-breaking summer of 1976 was not helping business) handed out unofficial gold medals and promised to help promote the sport. Nightingale was already aware that the real thing guaranteed nothing but prestige. "It hasn't done me any good," he admitted. "I am out of work but I won't accept the dole."

Parker, though only 25 at the time, bowed out of top-level modern pentathlon when he married and started a family. Nightingale was also 25 when he prompted the *Daily Mirror* headline, 'Danny Rocks

Russia', by becoming the first west European to win the prestigious Spartakiad in Moscow in 1979; he could finish only 15th in the following year's Olympics at the same venue. He coached the British team to the bronze medal at the 1988 Games in Seoul and became a PE teacher in Redcar, north Yorkshire. In February 2012 he was granted the freedom of the Somerset city of Wells.

Fox, a swashbuckler of a ladies' man throughout his modern pentathlon career, finally adapted to marriage and parenthood. Successively honoured with the MBE and CBE, he left the Army to carve out a new career as a hands-on property dealer in Wiltshire, only to be stopped in his tracks by the onset of Parkinson's disease in the late Nineties.

On a relatively optimistic note he says: "I was lucky enough to be prescribed this new drug, which has made a huge difference, though it does have side-effects. Before I was given it for the first time I did a test in hospital. With a male nurse either side to prop me up, it took me about a minute and three quarters to cover 10 metres. They gave me this stuff and I did it in about six-and-a-half seconds, so we knew we were onto a good thing."

Fox regrets that the camaraderie of the old-style modern pentathlon, decided over five days, has gone, but it was only by condensing the five disciplines into a single day that it kept its place in the Olympic programme. The team event was struck off in 1992. Despite the Games' lost soul, Fox also remains a huge fan of the Olympics. "It's still the finest medium for people to meet and understand each other," he insists. "I don't think there'll ever be anything to replace it."

July 27: Tornado class sailing, Reg White, John Osborn

TAKE away the dead body and the man overboard and Britain's victory in the Tornado class in Montreal was a routine effort: a triumph for solid family virtues. Reg White built the boat and his brother-in-law John Osborn was the crewman. Two weeks earlier they could have been forgiven for thinking the omens were conspiring against them. White's son, Rob, was at the helm when Tunnel collided with an unidentified object on Lake Ontario; the initial diagnosis was that a semi-submerged log was the culprit but it later emerged that the obstacle was a drowning victim from an earlier accident. All-night work was needed to repair the boat's hull.

The competition itself was dominated by the Britons until, that was, the fifth of seven scheduled races. White and Osborn were steaming ahead when misfortune struck. Journalist Bob Fisher, a lifelong friend of White, wrote in the *Guardian*: "Halfway down the reach, the hook broke off Osborn's trapeze harness and he was left swimming. White brought the boat up into the wind as quickly as he could but it still meant a swim of some 150 yards for his crew. Five boats went past while Osborn got back on to the boat."

They recovered to finish fourth, a result which, according to Rob White, was even more dispiriting for the rest than the British pair's previous victories. "I think the others thought then, if we can't beat them in those circumstances then we're never going to beat them," he says.

The foundations had been laid more than 30 years earlier, when Reg White was growing up in the Essex coastal town of Brightlingsea. His father, Bert, was an oyster merchant and Reg was entrusted with bringing the oysters ashore on a rowing skiff which he soon customised with a home-made spar and sails made from bedsheets. When he was 15 he left school to join a local firm of boat-builders; the loft in his father's shop was the makeshift workshop in which he constructed his first Hornet dinghy. White's first taste of competitive success was aboard a Brightlingsea One-Design boat, named Tiller Girl after the high-kicking dance troupe of which his sister, Pamela, was a member.

White was married at 18 and his own boss by the age of 21. The business initially catered for the dinghy market but later, in the guise of Sail Craft, branched out into the more exotic world of multihull boats: catamarans and trimarans. When Osborn began crewing as a 10-year-old he was just the kid brother of White's new bride, Lyn, but the half-generation gap was rapidly broken down by their rapport at sea. Twenty years later White explained: "We don't say a lot to each other when we are racing, but we understand each other so well." Osborn was still only 16 when he and White combined forces to win the Hornet World Championships in 1962.

Sail Craft flourished in the lucrative slipstream of the Little America's Cup, a match-racing event for catamarans which was set up in 1961. White was either at the helm or crewed for British boats which won the trophy on six successive occasions between 1963 and 1968. In 1967, designer Rodney March had approached White with the blueprint for what he hoped would be adopted as the first Olympic-class catamaran. Sail Craft had sole manufacturing rights for the Tornado, which was put through its competitive paces by March and White in a race from London to New York in 1969. They returned to Britain with more than £30,000 in orders and had even greater cause for celebration when the boat was included in the Olympic programme for 1976.

Despite their intimate knowledge of the boat, White and Osborn were not automatic kings of the class. The Tornado they sailed was, and had to be, fundamentally the same craft which their rivals could buy for about £2,000 in the mid-Seventies. There was a three-year hiatus in White and Osborn's partnership before they combined again in 1974 for an all-out assault on the Olympic title. The accent was almost as much on fitness off the boat as competence on it. White would run three miles a day, lift weights and play regular games of squash. He shed two stone in the process and in tests conducted just before the Montreal Games, Osborn was found to be the fittest of all the competing British yachtsmen.

The anxiety of three successive runners-up positions in World Championships was allayed when White and Osborn won the 1976 title in Sydney with a day to spare; four months later they were setting out for Montreal, ensuring that they gave themselves a full three weeks to familiarise themselves with the conditions at Kingston. Newspapers had scented an unusual angle as the trials loomed – 'son denies father Olympic place' – but 20-year-old Rob knew that it was a Games too early for him. He was still asked to helm the support boat against which his father and Osborn tuned up Tunnel, "because of all the sailing we'd done against each other".

The British pair imposed themselves on the rest of the fleet by winning the first two races. On day two they also met the Queen when she visited the yachting centre at the eastern end of Lake Ontario. They trailed in fifth in the third race, but normal service was resumed on the fourth day of the regatta. Even when disaster threatened, White felt sufficiently relaxed to shout out to his partner, "Get a move on, Wilkie", as he tried to swim back towards Tunnel. A clearcut victory in the sixth race – White described the brisk south-westerly as "lovely, like a British summer day" – meant that he and Osborn had clinched the gold medal with a day to spare. They were able to play half-interested spectators as the rest battled it out for the minor medals. John Nicholls, writing in the *Times*, described White and Osborn as "easily the best crew in any class".

The people of Brightlingsea turn out in their thousands to greet the returning heroes, John Osborn and (right) Reg White
ESSEX COUNTY STANDARD

There was an extra poignancy to the victory as the Games marked the end of their sailing partnership. They returned to an emotional victory parade in Brightlingsea before Osborn and his family headed back out to Montreal, where he started working for Sail Craft Canada, a sister company to the British concern.

Rob White believes they were close to being the perfect helmsman-crew combination. "Dad was the one with tunnel vision," he says. "He was an incredibly generous man, but he could also be selfish because that gave him the drive to do what he wanted to do. He was the more aggressive of the two, whereas John was more tacit and wanted to make sure that everything was right with the boat."

After five Tornado-centric months leading up to the 1976 Games, Reg White needed a breather. "You tend to get snarled up when you do the same thing all the time," he explained. The competitive hunger was restored when he and his new crewman, 18-year-old Steve Olle, won the World Championship in 1979, but the rivalry between father and son was intensifying year on year. Reg sounded a diplomatic note: "As a team, I think we stand a very good chance in the Olympics. Which of us actually competes there next year doesn't really matter – we're all in it together."

The easy interpretation of the Royal Yachting Association's decision not to send a team to Moscow in 1980 is that it cost Reg

White the chance to defend his title. In reality, Rob, having beaten his father in the European Championships three months before the Olympics, might have been picked instead. The year was not a memorable one for the White family. Reg had always defended his lengthy absences from Sail Craft with the observation that the business would not suffer if he was winning on the water, but the company was sunk in 1980 by a hike in VAT to 25 per cent and a £1.2 million order (more than the annual turnover) which failed to materialise. The Whites found a new business partner in the French sailor/designer Yves Loday, who won the Tornado gold medal in 1992. Loday White, based in Brightlingsea, is now one of the leading producers of the latest generation of catamarans.

The sporting attention shifted to White jnr during the Eighties: he won a world title but could only finish sixth and eighth in the 1984 and 1988 Olympics. Reg White never quite exhausted the competitive bug and when he died of a heart attack in May 2010 he was recapturing the buzz of his youth, aboard a newly built Brightlingsea One-Design, White Spirit, with his long-time crewman, Olle, and grandson Fred. The predictable 'it's-how-he-would-have-wanted-to-go' line appeared in tributes and obituaries, but Rob White asks, rhetorically: "Does anyone really want to go without saying goodbye?"

Reg White's memorial service recreated the route taken when he and John Osborn came back with their gold medals in 1976. The crowds were every bit as big for Brightlingsea's favourite son. Last May a £9,000 statue, dubbed 'Reg's Rock' by the family, was unveiled in the town.

When asked for the key to his father's sporting success, Rob White settles for "bloody-mindedness". The family's random, snapshot memories are of his yellow socks, bright-coloured shirts and Brightlingsea accent known as 'Reginese'. Osborn, still living in Canada, remembers him as "everybody's pal".

1980

July 22: 100m breaststroke, Duncan Goodhew

DUNCAN GOODHEW carved out a little bit of history for himself when he stood on the medal podium in Moscow: he was the first Briton to see the Olympic flag raised in recognition of his gold medal. In place of *God Save The Queen* was a less-than-note-perfect rendition of the Olympic anthem.

Goodhew, in common with Britain's other four gold medallists in 1980, missed the emotional connection, but regarded it as a small price to pay for the right to compete. Margaret Thatcher's Tory government supported the American-led boycott – in protest at the Soviet invasion of Afghanistan – but stopped short of imposing a blanket ban. The British Olympic Association decided to send a team, though governing bodies for equestrianism, hockey, sailing and shooting opted out.

Two of the British winners in Moscow, Goodhew and Seb Coe, headed the athlete lobbyists who argued in favour of participation. The other chief activist was Colin Moynihan, cox for the rowing eight who won a silver medal in 1980, a future Minister for Sport and now chairman of the British Olympic Association. The common purpose launched a lasting friendship between Goodhew and Moynihan.

Goodhew later reflected: "At the time there were only two things the world freely communicated on. One was the weather, the other was sport. I feel that while you're talking there's a chance you may reconcile differences, that communication and being together is the best way to break barriers and melt ice. My agent said at the time: 'If you have a Stradivarius played by an ogre, do you destroy the violin?' It seemed to Colin and me that the Olympics should have been the last thing to be picked on, not the first. With hindsight, we were absolutely right."

There are no easy journeys to Olympic glory, but Goodhew's triumph over adversity has made him a particularly inspirational figure in the 30 years since he retired from competitive swimming. His early childhood in Sussex had been privileged and idyllic; the family firm, later bought by Whitbread, owned a chain of 60 hotels and restaurants. There were holiday homes in Alderney and Corfu to enjoy. Goodhew's father, Donald, hired a JCB to dig up the family tennis court and installed a swimming pool in its place – from the age of five Duncan was hooked.

The first big test of Goodhew's character and resilience came when he was 10: he fell 18 feet from a tree during a PE lesson, landing on an exposed root. The swollen lip and black eyes healed, but the lasting legacy of the fall was the loss of his hair. Then it was discovered that he was dyslexic, though only after years of unexplained reading difficulties and 'Duncan the Dunce' jibes. Goodhew described dyslexia as "like somebody stabbing you in your self-esteem".

Swimming was his one outlet for excellence and Millfield School in Somerset was the ideal environment for him to nurture the talent. He was 14 when he announced with complete conviction to housemates that he would compete in the Olympics. The bold declaration was to come true in Montreal four years later, by which time he had taken up a scholarship at North Carolina State University. He even managed to beat David Wilkie at the start of Olympic year, but at the Games themselves he could not convince himself that he belonged in the company of Wilkie and John Hencken. "Deep down inside myself, I questioned my right to be there," he admitted.

Seventh place in the final reflected his lack of self-belief, but the American experience gave Goodhew a tighter technique and greater mental strength. The merciless criticism of his coach, Don Easterling – 'get your legs together, chrome dome, I can see the green fields up your arse' – was a powerful incentive to improve. Even so, it was doubtful, on the evidence of results from major championships between Montreal and Moscow, that Goodhew would be capable of winning a gold medal. In 1978 he came away from the Commonwealth Games in Edmonton, Canada, with three silvers. Graham Smith, inspired by competing in front of his home crowd, beat him in both the 100m and 200m breaststroke. At the start of 1980 Goodhew returned to Britain and prepared under Dave Haller, "the best breaststroke coach in the world" according to the swimmer. Haller also coached Peter Evans, the Australian who won the bronze medal in Moscow.

The swimming events at the Games were undeniably weakened by the Americans' absence and the 100m breaststroke, Goodhew's speciality, was no exception. There was no Steve Lundquist, who boasted the quickest time in the world that year. Also missing were the multi-talented Smith, who had won six gold medals in Edmonton two years earlier, and the world record holder, Gerald Morken, from West Germany.

Goodhew still predicted at a pre-Games press conference that the winner would have to break the world record and, by implication, believed that he was capable of improving Morken's time of 1min 2.86sec, set at the European Championships in 1977. Goodhew, who finished fourth in that race, argued: "I've been consistently turning in 63-second swims over the past year and nobody else has done that. The world record isn't that far away…Now I know it's about being mentally right on the day."

Despite an untidy turn in the heats, Goodhew still posted the quickest time. He looked forward to the following day's final with a sense of destiny: "Just pondering about breaking the world record brings goose bumps to my skin," he admitted. "I have this romantic notion of looking back when I'm 85, at having achieved something like going faster than any other human being before me." He strode out for the final wearing the flat cap owned by his father, who had died eight years earlier. Goodhew's mother, Perle, was in the second row of the stands, but his stepfather, Bill Crawford-Compton, a retired air vice-marshal, was absent on principle. "If you go to Moscow," he had told his stepson, "I won't be coming."

The race itself did not go quite according to plan; Goodhew was unexpectedly trailing at halfway. "I knew I had gone out too slowly," he explained afterwards, "and I quickened my stroke immediately after the turn." A lone Union flag fluttered defiantly as Goodhew took the lead with 20 metres to go and won in 1min 3.34sec. He finished almost half a second ahead of the Latvian, Arsens Miskarovs. His mother said: "It certainly matches the moment when I held him in my arms for the first time. I have never seen anyone look so happy."

As Goodhew stood on the podium, he doffed his cap to the crowd. "I felt my father was at my side as I swam," he admitted, adding later: "Losing him at that age really spurred me on to achieve everything I could. It made me evaluate my own life. I made a commitment at that stage to work really hard at swimming." His verdict on the muted medal ceremony was: "If that is the sacrifice we must make to keep politics out of sport, I am happy to make it. I am still British and strongly believe in my country. I believe I swam tonight for Britain."

Goodhew added a bronze medal in the 4 x 100m medley relay and went in search of new challenges: he was brakeman for the British bobsleigh team at the European Championships in 1981. Alongside his work as a motivational speaker he has had a longstanding involvement with Swimathon, the charity fund-raiser which has raised £35 million since its launch in 1986.

July 25: 100m, Allan Wells

THE immediate shot from Moscow's Lenin Stadium was of Allan Wells's balletic leap and pirouette after discovering that he had stolen the verdict in the 100m final; the morning-after image was of his wife, Margot, screeching, 'C'mon on, Allan!' as he tore down the track.

Neither was aware, until hauled into the BBC's makeshift studios, that a camera had been trained on Margot during the race. A device which is now overused seemed engagingly novel 30 years ago and all the more impactful because of her multi-faceted role in his success. Having strapped herself in for the bumpy ride when the pair married six years earlier, Margot Wells was partner, coach, consultant, manager, sounding board and second pair of eyes rolled into one.

Allan remembers being deeply moved: "It hit me, on a very personal level. It was the reaction of someone who cared as much as I did." At the time Margot described it as "the worst 10 seconds of my life", before paying tribute to her husband's incredible dedication: "I have seen him train in rain, snow and everything, but now it's all worthwhile." She said, only partially in gest, in a recent interview: "I think monks had a better lifestyle."

Although Wells, at 28, became the oldest runner to win the Olympic 100m title, the journey from mediocrity – as a club-class long jumper – to sprinting magnificence was remarkably short. "Deep inside I always felt I was a quick runner," he says. "What you've got to realise as well is that for the first 22 years of my life I lived 100 metres from the track at Edinburgh Southern Harriers. From my bedroom window you could see the last 30 metres up to the finishing line."

Wells enrolled as a boy in the Charles Atlas correspondence course for bodybuilding (foreshadowing the impressive physique of his peak years as an athlete). After leaving school, he began working for Brown Brothers, the marine engineering firm, but was treading water as an athlete until the "crossing point" of watching an indoor meeting at RAF Cosford on television. He was "gobsmacked" to see a former training partner, Drew Hislop, winning the 60m and within 24 hours had made contact with the man behind Hislop's transformation, Wilson Young, a former professional sprinter. Young, in turn, was a disciple of Jim Bradley, who in the 1950s had evolved a pioneering method based on repetition work with the speed ball, more commonly used then and subsequently by boxers.

Both the method and the camaraderie of working with a disciplined group appealed to Wells. He made huge strides, metaphorically and actually, finessing and endlessly analysing his training with the help of an engineer's eye for bio-mechanical detail. By 1976, the year after he joined the group, Wells would probably have been included in the sprint relay squad if Britain had taken one to the Montreal Games.

At the start of the following year, he equalled the British 60m record at Cosford, receiving his award from Harold Abrahams, the last Briton to win the Olympic 100m title, in 1924. Abrahams was not alive to witness Wells's emergence as a sprinter of world class in 1978, when he first equalled Peter Radford's 100m British record of 10.29sec, which had stood for 20 years, and claimed the record for himself with a run of 10.15sec in difficult conditions at Meadowbank Stadium in Edinburgh. In between the two races Wells and Young parted company, and Wells believes that anger made him run faster. "There was a lot of aggression there because of what had happened. I think I utilised that and it probably gave me half a yard."

He recognises his debt to Wilson and admits: "We're our own worst enemies sometimes. It was just two bloody-minded people. I'm not saying I regretted it and it would have happened at some point, but it made life very difficult because suddenly I didn't have the same people to train with."

The highly respected sports journalist, David Miller, wrote in the *Daily Express*: "Allan Wells, almost without anyone noticing, has emerged as probably the greatest British sprinter of all time." Wells himself told the paper: "Maybe the greatest satisfaction that I ever get is coming out of a gym on a winter's night after working with a speed ball and knowing that I have worked as hard as I could and that I have got a bit stronger."

In August 1978 he recorded his fastest times over both 100m and 200m (10.07 and 20.12), though both were heavily wind-assisted, to win silver and gold medals respectively for Scotland at the

Commonwealth Games in Edmonton, Canada. In January he swapped the rain and snow of Edinburgh for the sun and sand of Australasia – his employers gave him six months' paid leave to help him prepare for the Olympics.

By now Wells's progress could be measured in hundredths rather than tenths of seconds. At the start of Olympic year he was back in New Zealand, this time with a documentary team in tow. *No Easy Way* was a faithful account of the final leg in his journey to Moscow. Lynn Davies, the 1964 gold medallist who managed the British team at the 1980 Games, offered an interesting insight into what set Wells apart from the rest. Interviewed at the British team's spring training camp on the Côte d'Azur in France, Davies described Wells as a "fanatic" and a man apart. "I'm not saying that the other athletes are not committed, but Allan is totally committed," he added. Wells is not about to dispute Davies's view. "I trained very hard for Moscow," he says. "I was in good shape. Margot was the eyes: she was motivated by the fact that I was motivated."

Suddenly a jolting speed bump appeared on the road to Moscow. Wells recalls:

> About two-and-a-half weeks before we were due to fly out I felt something go in my lower back. I wasn't really that worried about it, but when I tried to get up in the morning my back was solid. I had to roll out of bed sideways. I said to my doctor, 'I don't think I'm going to the Olympics.' I was put on to three different treatments, ice, mobilisation and ultrasonics, and that was four times a day for a whole week. That just about killed me psychologically. I didn't do any training. Then it was reduced to twice a day for a week and the day before I left I did a very tentative start and it was fine.

The last thing Wells did before setting out from home for Moscow was visit the attic. "I was looking for something which would make me feel a wee bit different, a wee bit special, and there was a red, white and blue hat right in front of me. I think God was placing my hand on this damn thing. It had a label for Amoco, the oil company, on it, so I took that off, put the hat in my bag and off I went. I thought it would convey a different aura to people and I was wearing the hat as I walked out every time in Moscow." Wells is also convinced that there was a higher presence behind his injury. "We do have somebody watching over us, no matter what anyone says. He was telling me, 'You've trained enough, you've got to stop now.' The back problem was his way of doing that."

Although Wells had only begun using blocks when they were made obligatory for the Moscow Games, his first, tentative starts, as he eased his way back to full throttle after the injury, were impressively smooth. He was ready for action. The absence of the Americans certainly reduced the overall strength of the sprints – Stanley Floyd boasted the fastest 100m time in 1980 – but nothing which happened afterwards, or the following year, suggested that they would have denied Wells his golden moment.

Even if it meant expending more energy than was strictly necessary, Wells was determined to impose himself in each round – four races over two days for the finalists. Before the first round, he told his wife: "I've got to stamp my authority or I'll do nothing." He beat the top Jamaican, Don Quarrie, and also won a quarter-final suspiciously featuring four heat winners and Hasely Crawford, the defending champion, in a British record of 10.11sec. There was a bizarre prelude when Crawford, unaware that Wells was in the same race, asked if he could borrow his spikes. Silvio Leonard, the Cuban who in 1997 had become only the second athlete to dip under 10 seconds, remained the title favourite, but only just.

"The semi was a bit of an anti-climax because it wasn't as tough as I thought it would be," Wells admits. Even with the final looming, Margot was struck by her husband's relaxed demeanour. He tucked into his current reading matter, *Forty Years of Murder*, the autobiography of pathologist Keith Simpson, and refused to let a disconcerting prelude to the final disturb his tunnel vision.

"I was lying down in the report room and there was a bit of a commotion and the Russian, Aleksandr Aksinin, came in about five minutes late. All he had on was a pair of socks and underpants. Just under the pants there was a trickle of blood in the area of his glutes. And I thought, what the hell's going on here? Is he doing something here deliberately? Marian Woronin [the Pole] came over to me and said, 'Do you see that?' And I said, 'Marian, the one thing you've got to ensure is that he does not beat you.' That's to a guy I'm competing against!"

Once again the lane draw was perverse, though at least this time it appeared to be equally unfavourable for both the main protagonists: Leonard was in lane one, Wells in lane eight. The Scot was drawn next to Osvaldo Lara, the second Cuban, and on the strength of seeing practice starts between Leonard and Lara he estimated that he would need to be clear of Lara after 30 metres. There was a distracted air to the crowd as the finalists were called to their marks – the outstanding Georgian triple jumper, Viktor Saneyev, was making an ultimately unsuccessful attempt to win the event for the fourth successive time (he finished second).

The tension was heightened by a false start; again Wells may have thought he was being smiled on from above, as he went unpunished for his own "pathetic" start. The gun went off again. "It wasn't quite as good a start as I wanted to have, but better than the one before," he recalls. "It took me to about 60 metres to get past Lara. I didn't see anybody there, but maybe with about 20 to go I had a slight squint to my left and there was Leonard. I thought, keep going, and then I dived for the tape at the last split second."

Leonard, seemingly unaware that he was under threat, did not lunge for the tape. He and Wells were given the same time, a modest 10.25sec in a swirling wind. The cameramen, instinctively, focused on Leonard and it was only when a slow-motion replay was shown on the giant screen that Wells was confirmed as the narrowest of winners. When he looks back at the pictures of the medal ceremony he sees a man who has shed 10 years in 10 seconds. "I've got no lines on my face. I look as though I've had a facelift because the burden had just been taken off my shoulders."

Although, arguably, Wells was a better 200m runner than over the shorter distance, he did not have quite enough fuel in the reserve tank to complete the double. He led Pietro Mennea for most of the race, but four-and-a-half hours' sleep a night caught up on him as the Italian drifted past in the final 20 metres. Wells was only two hundredths of a second slower than Mennea's winning time, 20.19sec, and had the consolation of a British record. He remains convinced that if he had not won the 100m the 200m would have been his. "The edge comes from just wanting it that bit more," he reasons.

Newspaper reports on Wells's victory in the 100m predicted fame and fortune – the first bricks were being chipped out of the previously impregnable walls of amateurism – but Wells could not quite match Seb Coe, Steve Ovett or Daley Thompson for fame, and the fortune remained a theoretical pot of gold. "I didn't do my athletics for the money," he insists. "The money was there, whether it be under the table or whatever, but if I'd taken the attitude that I was running because I wanted to make money I don't think I would have achieved what I did.

I wasn't influenced by the financial gains I might have made. On one occasion I was asked to run at Crystal Palace and I said no because I'd got a slight injury. I got a phone call back saying, 'How about if we double the money?' I said, 'Look. I'm not running.' "

The defence of his Olympic title ended with injury and last place in his semi-final in Los Angeles, but he remained competitive well into his thirties. He held off Canada's Ben Johnson to win the Commonwealth Games 100m in 1982 and dead-heated with Mike McFarlane in the 200m (he was also the first top athlete to compete in cycling shorts). By then he and Margot had settled in Guildford, Surrey. He admits that the move south was not beneficial for his athletics career, but it gave him and his family a better standard of living. Wells works as a systems engineer at the University of Surrey ("I needed something to keep myself occupied") and also assists his wife with the running of Wellfast, the Margot Wells School of Speed.

July 26: Decathlon, Daley Thompson

AWAY from the track, the sandpit and the throwing circle, Daley Thompson could be a PR nightmare: he dispersed autograph-hunters with expletives, he antagonised the press and he ridiculed fellow athletes. In his chosen domain, Thompson was a sporting showman of multi-gifted brilliance. He is one of only two athletes to retain the Olympic decathlon title.

Thompson's early years could hardly be described as a model of stability. He was six when his Nigerian father left home and 12 when his mother, Lydia, phoned his boarding school in Sussex to break the news that his father had been murdered while working as a mini-cab driver in Streatham, south-east London. In his early teens, Thompson could not see beyond a career as a professional footballer. Although he ran 11.9sec for the 100m when he was 14, athletics did little more than fill the gap between the end of one football season and the start of the next; he played for Chelsea and Fulham boys' teams. Gradually, however, he felt drawn towards a sport in which the plaudits for victory did not have to be shared. Equally, there was no one else to blame if you failed.

He dabbled with sprints and jumping events in 1974, joining the Essex Eagles club, and was persuaded by his first coach, Bob Mortimore, to branch out the following year. Thompson felt that he had as much latent sprinting talent as Allan Wells but never discovered how far he might have gone as a 100m runner. He was just short of his 17th birthday when he competed in his first decathlon, at Cwmbran, in south Wales, in June 1975.

Thompson's mother, who hailed from Dundee, refused to accept that athletics was "a proper career" – the sport clung stubbornly to its amateur ethos in the mid-Seventies – and Thompson responded by quitting the family home in Ladbroke Grove, west London and moving to the Maida Vale flat of Doreen Rayment, his mother's best friend, unofficial aunt and number one supporter.

He had completed O Levels at Hammersmith College, but made another great leap into the unknown when he decided to become a full-time athlete. The first stage of Thompson's career was masterminded by Bruce Longden, decathlon coach for the South of England. Thompson moved to Crawley, where he lived with Longden and his wife, Sue, who was the leading British pentathlete at the time. Longden's five-year plan was geared around the Moscow Olympics, but Thompson exceeded expectations by scoring 7,684 points in the AAA Championships in Cwmbran and qualifying for the Montreal Games in 1976. It was the highest ever score by a 17-year-old.

The experience was everything for Thompson, who celebrated his 18th birthday on the second day of the competition. He also came 18th, with a relatively modest 7,434 points, but he had seen the Olympics up close and wanted more. "I was out of my league at the time," he admitted. "It just seemed to me that there was nothing I had seen there that I couldn't beat one day, given enough hard work. I thought I might be in the top six by 1980, maybe among the medals, and that by 1984 I could win it."

Thompson was being unduly cautious in his predictions: he set a world junior record a few weeks later, topped 8,000 points for the first time in 1977 – he described it as the decathlete's equivalent of the four-minute mile – and had just turned 20 when he won the Commonwealth title in Edmonton, Canada, with an exceptional total of 8,467 points. His wind-assisted long jump of 8.11m was second only to Lynn Davies on Britain's all-time list.

On a less positive note, Edmonton was the setting for the first of many tiffs between Thompson and the British press. He opted out of the traditional press conference after the medal ceremony, saying he had agreed to meet his 'aunt', Doreen, for a meal instead. The media, predictably, were unwilling to forgive easily when a reluctant Thompson submitted to their questions the following day. He gained a reputation for being even less accessible between competitions: Longden deflected most inquiries and Thompson's answering machine dealt with the rest. His on-going complaint was that the sporting press had no real interest in multi-event competitions; he once promised a journalist an interview...if he could name the decathlon's 10 events in their correct order. He couldn't.

Thompson was unable to retain his competitive edge, finishing second in the European Championships in Prague a few weeks later. He now classed as an unemployed, full-time athlete, though the financial strains were eased to an extent when Sports Aid Foundation funding began to trickle through. Guido Kratschmer, who went to Prague as the favourite, pulled out injured in the first event, the 100m. Thompson regarded the West German as his greatest rival in the late Seventies and but for the German boycott in 1980 he might also have been the biggest obstacle between Thompson and the gold medal in Moscow. In the absence of face-to-face competition in the Lenin Stadium, Thompson and Kratschmer vied for supremacy on less exalted stages.

On the face of it, Thompson was not in the best mental state to break world records. At the start of 1980 he decided that his relationship with Bruce Longden had run its natural course. "Bruce was a good coach, but he was never a motivator," Thompson wrote in his athletic memoirs, *The Last Ten Years.* "He couldn't inspire me. Not that I needed it really but it would have been nice once in a while. He did fine by me, helped me a lot. He was there when I needed him most in those early days. Now I needed something else."

The little Austrian town of Gotzis, which had begun hosting annual decathlons in 1975, was the setting for Thompson's first world record. The feat left him more confused than elated – he was expecting to peak in Moscow. He needed to run the 1500m in 4min 26.1sec to beat the record set by the American, Bruce Jenner, when he won the Olympic title in 1976. Thompson finished in 4min 25.49sec and raised the mark to 8,622 points. When he got home there was a congratulatory cable awaiting him from Jenner. "My Wheaties contract is up in a year: I'll give them your name," he joked.

Kratschmer, well beaten in Gotzis, delivered his riposte a month later when he added 27 points to Thompson's total, but the Briton was unconcerned and so was his coach. Longden assured the world that the competition was for second and third place in Moscow; the gold was already won. Thompson felt relaxed and completely prepared when he arrived at the stadium and quickly imposed himself by running 10.62sec for the 100m, despite a swirling wind, and jumping exactly eight metres in the long jump – into a head wind. After that, the accent was on avoiding injury in cold, damp conditions. Thompson was able to jog home in the 1500m and still record a total of 8,495 points, 164 clear of the Russian Yuri Kutsenko. Dignified restraint was not Thompson's style: at the medal ceremony he wielded an imaginary baton to conduct the 250 British supporters in an impromptu version of the National Anthem.

He was asked to do a little crystal-ball gazing at the press conference: "I'm 21 now, I'll be 25 in Los Angeles," he mused. "I won't even be 30 at the 1988 Games. Why stop doing something that's fun? Of course I'd like to make a million. But I'm an athlete first and foremost. I want to get the best out of myself at that before I try anything else."

Thompson was photographed with fellow gold medallist Duncan Goodhew and couldn't resist the opportunity to score a point at Steve Ovett's expense after he dismissed the decathlon as "a string of Mickey Mouse events" followed by a 1500m in which no one was any good. Ovett was pointedly absent from the photoshoot, prompting Thompson to say: "Shame. It would have been the good, the bald and the ugly."

The offers had begun trickling in from American universities in 1978; now it was quicker to name the institutions who didn't want to subsidise Thompson's athletics career. He took it all in his sardonic stride: "If somebody came up to me and said, 'Here is your chance to make a million dollars', I would be tempted to take it. Instead, all I've had is about 30 scholarship offers from American colleges. What do they give you? Enough money to pay for education, books and laundry. It would not help me as a decathlon athlete. I prefer to stay with my sport until one of those fabulous offers comes along. In America, in discussing money, they talk telephone numbers. In England, we speak in single digits."

July 26 and Aug 1: 800m and 1500m, Steve Ovett and Sebastian Coe

SEBASTIAN COE and Steve Ovett were united by age and talent. They were kept apart by promoters and their own pickiness (they competed against each other only seven times). Together they gave the

Olympics one of its most compelling stories, turning the conventional plot on its head in Moscow.

They were caricatured as the fiercest of rivals – the natural (Ovett) versus the manufactured athlete (Coe), the media-friendly diplomat (Coe) versus the silent street-fighter (Ovett). While Coe built bridges and brought the Olympic Games back to London, Ovett burned them, falling out with his mother, Gay, his race manager, Andy Norman, and his trusty pacemaker, Bob Benn. But when the dust had settled on the three Olympic gold medals and 12 individual world records, Coe and Ovett found a kinship in their shared experience.

Ovett's upbringing could hardly be termed conventional: his mother was only 16 when he was born in Brighton in October 1956. Home was her parents' house and, in an instinctive rebellion against the cramped surroundings, five-year-old Steve turned a Sunday visit to his paternal grandparents into a five-year stay. About the same time, Ovett recalled, he had his first taste of unfettered speed – a fear-inspired dash for home after he had hit a boy over the head with a milk bottle.

Both his father and grandfather were market traders, dealing in poultry, eggs and meats, and Ovett helped out on the family stall from the age of eight. He passed his 11-plus (an exam which Coe failed a year later) and went to Varndean Grammar School, though his exceptional ability as an athlete was only nurtured when he joined Brighton and Hove Athletic Club. Ovett set a host of age group records, winning his first English Schools title, in the 400m, when he was 14. At the same age he leapt 20ft 6in in the long jump.

The precocious improvement was maintained when, a year later, he broke 50 seconds for the 400m and ran the fastest ever 800m by a British 16-year-old, 1min 52.5sec. Ovett was already capable of running any distance from 200m to 1500m and in 1973 he came under the wing of the dogmatic Harry Wilson, the national middle-distance coach, who introduced him to a more flexible training programme. Ovett was still two months shy of his 18th birthday when he won the 800m at the European Junior Championships in 1min 47.5sec, a world best for a 17-year-old and a performance which did not go unnoticed in America.

Ovett was immediately bombarded with scholarship offers, but opted for the home routine (and unemployment) instead. Despite a bout of glandular fever which interrupted his winter training, he made even bigger strides towards greatness in 1974, his first season in the senior ranks. He became the youngest British athlete to run a four-minute mile and his expectations were already so high that he was disappointed with the excellent time of 1min 45.77sec which earned him the 800m silver medal at the European Championships in Rome.

The Ovett family made a powerful enemy when they severed relations with the press in July 1975. In his autobiography, Ovett referred to the media coverage as "a distortion, a misrepresentation of what Steve Ovett was doing in the sport". He was tired, he said, of being asked banal, repetitive questions, the answers to which could have been gleaned with a modicum of homework. The vow of silence was sealed when Ovett said he would be going to watch his girlfriend at the time, Lesley Kiernan, take part in the European Junior Championships rather than compete himself in the European Cup final. The press, predictably, accused him of being unpatriotic.

Arrogance was the charge, not for the first or last time in his career, when Ovett premiered his victory salute en route to winning the 1500m at the Olympic trials in 1976. He did not enjoy the claustrophobic security in Montreal but in Games remembered for Britain's lack of success – Brendan Foster won the only track and field medal, a bronze in the 10,000m – Ovett at least offered hope of future success. He failed to come to terms with being drawn in the outside lane in the 800m final, finishing fifth in a race notable for a world record from the powerful Cuban, Alberto Juantorena, and was eliminated in the semi-finals of the 1500m.

In 1977, Ovett showed both his appetite for competition and extraordinary versatility. One day he would be running a 4 x 400m relay leg for his club in the National League; the next he would be taking on the great Ethiopian, Miruts Yifter, over 5,000m. Three weeks after that, he was winning the Dartford half-marathon in one hour five minutes. The speed work and the stamina combined to produce British records in both the mile, where he clocked 3min 54.7sec to beat John Walker, the Olympic champion over 1500m the previous year, and the 1500m (3min 34.5sec in the World Cup).

Sebastian Coe's journey to the top followed a shallower gradient; he was only a year younger than Ovett but, up until 1978 anyway, the gap always appeared to be much bigger. Ovett was taller, stronger, more confident and more combative. Although Coe's determination to succeed was every bit as intense, he was more of a work in progress than the finished product.

Coe was born in Chiswick, west London, in September 1956, the son of a ceaselessly inquisitive engineer father, Peter, who had been inured against petty obstacles by his wartime experiences – he was being transported to an internment camp when he escaped by jumping off a train. Coe's half-Indian mother, Angela, had acted in repertory before meeting her husband-to-be. The family moved to Sheffield when Peter become a design engineer for a firm of cutlery manufacturers and it was there, in frustration at the lack of guidance which his son was receiving at the Hallamshire Harriers club, that he took on the job himself of moulding a promising 13-year-old into a world-beater.

The competitive streak was innate, but Coe was also a hyper-sensitive child who suffered from nervous eczema and pollen asthma. Although his father was casually portrayed as a remorseless Svengali who drove his son to tears, it was plainly a joint operation. Peter Coe's genius was in sifting through all the evidence, written and oral, with scientific rigour, before coming up with a master plan. Seb bought into the concept, in the same way that he redoubled his efforts to succeed academically after failing his 11-plus. He was rewarded with eight O Levels and went on to do an economics degree at Loughborough University.

He referred to his father as Peter; to sceptics it was confirmation that the parent-athlete relationship was unconventional at best. For them it was a necessary device, establishing Peter's authority in the training environment. He also adopted the habit of referring publicly to Seb as 'my athlete'.

As an early point of comparison, Coe ran 1min 56sec for the 800m when he was 16, three-and-a-half seconds slower than Ovett at the same age. They had competed against each other for the first time at the English Schools' Cross-Country Championships in 1972, Ovett finishing second and Coe 10th. The winner, Kirk Dumpleton, went on to become a school teacher and occasional interviewee for 'when I beat a sporting great' features. Although Ovett and Coe did not line up on the same track for another six years, Coe was fully aware of the giant strides being made by his rival. He could talk a mature game, insisting at the age of 14 that if he continued to progress at the same rate he would be a potential Olympic gold medallist in 1980, but he was still fighting childish insecurity. He once went out for an extra training session on Christmas Day, in the fervent hope that Ovett would be staying indoors.

Coe's attempts to bridge the gap were hardly helped when he missed the whole of the 1974 season because of a stress fracture, but in 1976 he ran his first sub-four-minute mile and, the following March, won the European indoor title over 800m. A mark of Coe's improvement was his first outdoors timing under 1min 45sec, just before his 21st birthday; a year earlier his best time over the distance was almost three seconds slower.

The much-trumpeted convergence of Coe and Ovett's careers finally happened in 1978 at the European Championships in Prague. Coe, fresh from a British record of 1min 44.25sec in Brussels, was the favourite to win the 800m and fully expected Ovett to be his main opposition. Ovett, who doubled up, appeared to have no credible rival over 1500m. Coe was still recovering from a stomach bug when he lined up for the 800m final, but faithfully stuck to his father's experimental race plan: run like crazy for the first lap then try to hang on. The effort required to reach the bell in 49.3sec left Coe running on empty in the last 200 metres, when first Ovett caught him, then the muscular East German, Olaf Beyer, surged past to win in 1min 43.8sec. As Ovett placed an arm of commiseration on Coe's shoulder, he blurted out: 'Who the **** was that?' It was a fair question – Beyer's previous best time was two seconds slower. Ovett played the waiting game to perfection in the 1500m final, accelerating away from the field to win in 3min 35.6sec, and ran a world best for the two miles less than two weeks later.

He was told that he was a contender for the BBC Sports Personality of the Year award, but made it plain (or his mother did on his behalf) that he would only attend the ceremony to pick up the winner's trophy. Despite the breach of protocol, unofficial word of his victory was relayed to Brighton, where Ovett hastily went in search of a suit. He enjoyed the occasion, but still concluded that it must have been a "thin year" for British sport.

Ovett's successor was Coe, a more gracious recipient of the award, who put together a remarkable sequence of three world records in 41 days in 1979. The first two were at the atmospheric Bislet Stadium in Oslo. He sliced over a second from Juantorena's 800m record with a startling time of 1min 42.33sec then ran 3min 48.95sec to undercut John Walker's mark for the mile by half a second (Ovett refused to run, claiming that the race should have been held in Britain, and insisted, with an egotistical flourish, that his absence make the achievement a hollow one). The final leg in Coe's record-breaking orgy was in Zurich, where he ran 3min 32.03sec to beat Filbert Bayi's world best for the 1500m, which had stood since 1974. The promoter, Andreas Brugger, had wanted to include Ovett in the line-up, but Coe's hard-nosed stance – 'you can have a record or a race, you can't have both', was the gist of it – persuaded him to preserve the status quo.

Races rather than records were top of the agenda in 1980, when Coe honed his political skills by lobbying his future employers, the Conservative government, for the right to compete in Moscow. He rounded off his preparations for the Games by running a series of ever-quicker 800m races, then proved his stamina with a 1,000m world record in Oslo. On the same night, Ovett made an even more articulate statement of intent, beating Coe's mile world record in a time of 3min 48.8sec, and equalled the 1500m record barely a week before the 800m heats in Moscow. In a rare public utterance, Ovett said cryptically: "I discovered that my body would obey my will."

He emphasised his maverick approach by flying out to Moscow two days after the rest of the team. By the time he arrived, the media-friendly Coe had already made the right noises in a press conference attended by close on 500 journalists and broadcasters. They did their best to sound neutral but, almost to a man, they were rooting for Coe and knew that win or lose the quotes would all be his. Coe's sense of inferiority to Ovett – extraordinary, on the face of it, for a 23-year-old multi world record holder – remained a matter of personal turmoil rather than soundbite material. In David Miller's book, *Born To Run*, published in 1992, Coe admitted: "The sense of inferiority was on account of what I saw him to be: mentally and physically arrogant."

Miller, a journalist not given to empty hyperbole, was covering the 1980 Games for the *Daily Express*. In the build-up to the 800m final – Coe and Ovett came through their

> **'A 700 million TV audience awaits the meeting of Sebastian Coe and Steve Ovett with all the expectation of the first moon shot'**

heat and semi-final in efficient style – he wrote: "A 700 million TV audience awaits the meeting of Sebastian Coe and Steve Ovett with all the expectation of the first moon shot." Ian Wooldridge steered clear of a confident prediction in the *Daily Mail*: "If you had to pick a son-in-law you'd probably choose Coe. If you wanted a helping hand in a rough house you might well go for Ovett. Over 800m in Moscow you'd do well to sit there and let them settle it at last themselves."

Wooldridge's 'rough house' allusion was apt: whereas Coe ran a timid, non-committal race from lane eight, Ovett bounced off and barged through his rivals as though he were a human Dodgem. Somehow he manoeuvred himself into the ideal attacking position as the Belarusian, Nikolai Kirov, made the first assertive move and powered clear in the final straight to win by three metres. Coe's response was far too late, allowing him to do nothing more than overhaul Kirov just before the line. The winner reserved his thoughts for ITV, describing him and Coe as "associates in the running business", and his exclusive column in the *Sunday People*.

Coe was left to account for the unaccountable at the press conference. "I choose this day of all days to run the worst race of my life," he said. "And I cannot even explain why. I made a tactical mistake. I did not have the speed of thought or movement necessary." Twenty years later, interviewed for Pat Butcher's book, *The Perfect Distance*, Coe put his tentative performance in earthier perspective. "It was just a ****-up from beginning to end," he said. Peter Coe fumed: "There's no joy in that silver medal. We'll put it in a bottom drawer at home – if we don't throw it away."

Ovett was used by now to the negative press, but even he was taken aback by the stunned expressions on the faces of journalists – "as though they had lost money on a horse," he later wrote – and fellow athletes. As he had done after his heat and semi-final, he sky-painted the letters ILY, an 'I Love You' message to his girlfriend, Rachel, who was at home in Maidstone, Kent, suffering from a kidney complaint. The gesture led indirectly to a row between Coe and his mother in Moscow, on the eve of the 1500m final. Rachel was predictably tracked down and when her photograph appeared in newspapers, Gay Ovett flew into a possessive rage; the schism was never healed.

The Coes were going through their own mini-crisis. Peter said publicly that Seb had run like "a chump" and "a novice". He was heard to use a rather stronger word to 'his athlete' – beginning with c and ending with t – as Coe entered the room where the press conference was held. Miller later saw evidence that Peter could still play the consoling parent, putting his arm around Seb in a taxi which drove them away from the stadium.

In the immediate aftermath of the 800m, Miller wrote that the 1500m was a formality for Ovett. Statistically it was hard to argue otherwise – Ovett's victory in the semi-final extended his three-year winning sequence over 1500m and a mile to 45 races; he waved to the crowd before he had even hit the front. By now, Miller was giving Coe a fighting chance…if he ran a smart race. Coe himself did nothing to dilute the hype, saying: "It's going to be the race of my life. I must win it. I have to. Nothing else will do." Britain came to a near standstill: 20 million viewers tuned in to see if he could pass the ultimate test of character.

Coe and Ovett, facing each other for the very first time over the distance, were joined in the final by a third British great in the making, 19-year-old Steve Cram. Predictably, he was never a factor in a race led tentatively for two laps by the powerful East German, Jürgen Straub, whose sudden acceleration with 700 metres to go convinced Peter Coe that 'his athlete' would win. Seb had extricated himself from more than one tight spot in his semi-final; here Straub was like an acquiescent pace-maker in a record attempt. Ever aware of Ovett's lurking threat, Coe held second place before easing past Straub in the final straight to win by three metres in 3min 38.40sec.

> **'I had a weep and then had a whisky'**
> Angela Coe after 800m final

> **'When he asked me to send him some wellies and a brain, I knew he was back to his old self'**
> Angela Coe after 1500m final

He sunk to the ground – joy and relief merging – before embarking on a slightly dazed lap of honour. He could hardly blurt out a coherent word as, still breathless, he was interviewed at trackside by the BBC's Ron Pickering, but Coe's modest poise had returned by the time he faced the press. "It was nice to climb a mountain," he said. "It was an absolute must to win. I felt very much more relaxed than just before the 800m, possibly because that was the one I was expected to win. I just felt a completely different person today. It was a very smooth race: that was the key to it. I was able to do what I'm best at – running freely and uncluttered."

Media objectivity was put on hold that day. The *Daily Mail*'s Ian Wooldridge admitted as much: "The British press were beside themselves. By and large, they don't like Ovett for his high-handed prima donnishness, his refusal even to pass the time of day. Cheering in the press box is like spitting in church, but we rose in our dozens to roar Coe home, with Ovett irrecoverably beaten." Wooldridge added of Coe: "He lifted the soul, he ennobled his art, he dignified his country, and he emerged a very great man…His conduct in triumph matched his humility in disaster."

David Miller, closer to the Coes than any other journalist, wrote in his book *Born To Run* that the 1500m final in Moscow was "the single most captivating *individual* event in the history of British sport. It was the making of Coe as an athlete of legend, possibly the making of him as a person in adult life."

Ovett's mother took the defeat worse than he did. She was still fuming over the publicity for Rachel Waller and saw the Moscow Games remembered more for Coe's brave riposte in the 1500m than for her son's swaggering win in the 800m. Much was made of the fact that Coe and Ovett had, in effect, won each other's events, but both accepted that the script could have been reversed. Ovett lacked the necessary edge of intensity going into the 1500m, but still wrote in his autobiography: "The one feeling I have no doubt about is that had Straub not been in the race I would have beaten Seb."

As 1980 drew to a close, the Coes reflected on a "poor year" which had been salvaged by one great result and a significant win two weeks later over New Zealander John Walker and the American, Steve Scott, in Zurich. Both were absent from the Olympics because of the US-led boycott. Coe narrowly missed the world record that night; a fortnight after that, Ovett beat it by almost a second in Koblenz, West Germany, running 3min 31.36sec.

Ovett's medals went on temporary display at the family stall on Brighton Market, but the simmering row with his mother finally boiled over when his girlfriend was excluded from the top table at a function to mark the re-opening of the local Withdean Stadium. Ovett quit the family home and never returned, later reflecting that his parents were unable to stop living their lives through him. He and Rachel Waller were married the following September. Coe was an athlete/student in contented transition, dividing his time between postgraduate studies at Loughborough and London. He was starting to become more independent in thought and deed from his father.

1984

Aug 1: Small-bore rifle three positions, Malcolm Cooper

MALCOLM COOPER was responsible for one of the less passionate victory quotes in Olympic history when he pronounced himself "quite pleased" to have become Britain's first rifle shooting gold medallist for 72 years. Cooper was more in tune with the hyperbole required after successfully defending his title four years later. "I am in the clouds – let me get down," he said as he raised his arms aloft.

There may have been a touch of flamboyance about Cooper's appearance – the beard, the sweatshirt with 'Cooperman' (a nickname of which he was immensely proud) emblazoned on the front, and the red, white and blue headband – but he was as relentless in his pursuit of perfection as another double gold medallist, yachtsman Rodney Pattisson. His widow, Sarah (Cooper died in 2001), recalls:

> Malcolm was single-minded, dedicated, had belief in his abilities, paid immense attention to detail, planned meticulously, prepared for 'what ifs?...', researched techniques and technicalities and wasn't afraid to ask folk (Americans, Germans, Russians, Romanians, etc) about their training regimes. He tried new ideas, thought things through – even some ideas which seemed outlandish at the time. His (and therefore our) lives were so dedicated to shooting they excluded 'normal' activities, attending family weddings for instance. We lived for the sport.

There were no children, no pets and no television at the Coopers' house on Hayling Island, but there was a practice range, converted from a coal bunker, under their garden. In a previous home their indoor practice facilities involved shooting from the kitchen, through two other rooms, to a target on the back of the front door.

Although his name meant little to anyone outside the shooting community prior to 1984, Cooper was no overnight sensation. Most small boys contented themselves with firing imaginary guns, or at best toy weapons; Cooper demanded the real thing. He remembered: "I wanted to shoot since I was nine years old, but I was so small at the naval school which I attended that the gunnery officer told me to 'sod off'. It took me two years to talk him into it and when he gave in I missed the target every time."

Cooper's success rate improved in New Zealand, where his family lived for three years during his father's posting with the Royal Navy. When they returned to England in 1964, 16-year-old Malcolm worked as a shipwright's apprentice in Portsmouth and qualified as a naval architect, specialising in submarines.

In 1970 he won the British title in what was to become his speciality event, the small-bore rifle three positions (prone, standing and kneeling over a 50-metre distance) and made his Olympic debut in Munich in 1972, finishing 18th. He recognised the need for extreme measures, taking a year out from work to prepare for the Montreal Games, and still came 18th.

Sarah, whom he married in 1974, remembered: "He was really fuming after putting in so much work. In fact, he was so wild that we both went to night school. I took offshore navigation and Malcolm studied astro navigation. We were going to sell up and move to New Zealand." In the event they remained in Hampshire and in 1978 Cooper founded Accuracy International, a rifle manufacturing company which now claims to produce the "best sniper rifle in the world".

"Because of negative publicity in the media where shooting was concerned," explains Sarah Cooper, "we kept AI as separate as possible from shooting as a sport. In interviews Malc was 'an engineer' and had 'an engineering firm'. We didn't want any future shooters to suffer from the possibility of bad publicity because of something we had said. Several years after Malc had retired from competitive sport AI produced a Cooperman rifle for 300 metres shooting."

Malcolm Cooper never forgave the National Small-Bore Rifle Association for falling in line with the Thatcher government's call for a boycott in 1980. Armed with the clout of a gold medal in 1984, he accused the organisers of treating competitors like children. "We were just pawns for them to make a lot of money with," he said.

Although his wife, an ex Wren, shot internationally herself, she could not quite match her husband for obsessive dedication to the sport. In an effort to improve his cardiovascular system he would swim 30 lengths a day in his local pool at Havant…and then go out running. He studied yoga and Zen Buddhism, reasoning: "When you start to think positively almost anything in life is possible. The difference between us and the Americans is that they know they are going to win and discuss who is going to come second."

By the time of the Los Angeles Olympics, Sarah could hardly recognise him from the shuffling reticence of their courting days. "He has

> **'When you start to think positively almost anything is possible'**

certainly changed," she said in 1984. "It took him ages to ask me out in the first place. It's not that he's knowingly cocky now. He just can't see why people are not as good as he is."

On the domestic stage, Cooper was as good as unbeatable in the three positions discipline and when he won gold medals at both the Commonwealth Games and World Championships in 1982 it became clear that he was ready to challenge for glory in the Olympic Games. As if in recognition of what he was about to achieve, Cooper was made an MBE in the Queen's Birthday Honours in 1984.

There was an eve-of-competition scare when his rifle disintegrated, but Cooper's skills as an amateur gunsmith enabled him to rebuild it in three hours. The event itself, held at the Prado Range in the Los Angeles suburb of Chino, could not have gone much better for Cooper. A gusty wind made conditions tricky in the afternoon, accounting for a couple of misses, but he still managed a score of 1,173 (out of a possible 1,200) to equal the world record. "Every little thing I tried worked," he admitted. "I am just pleased that I didn't run out of steam: I have been ready for three weeks, like a cat on a hot tin roof." His wife, who confessed that she had been "shaking like a leaf" as she watched, finished 10th in the women's equivalent the following day.

Cooper's rifle club, Worthing PSK, arranged for a bus to meet him on his return to Heathrow Airport. Sarah Cooper recalls that the other British gold medallists were promised sports cars, adding: "We were not surprised that Malc didn't get one – shooting very non-PC – so one of the other shooters later presented Malc with a Dinky Toy model of one."

Aug 5: Coxed fours, Martin Cross, Richard Budgett, Andy Holmes, Steve Redgrave, Adrian Ellison (cox)

STEVE REDGRAVE'S local paper, the *Bucks Free Press*, predicted that his coxed four would win in Los Angeles; the national media were less convinced. British rowing, without an Olympic gold medal since 1948, was still factional and under-funded. The crew itself was, from any standpoint, a motley outfit.

Redgrave, then 22, was unemployed, receiving £35 a week in dole money and a princely £5.76 from the Sports Aid Foundation. He thought he should be competing in the single sculls instead. Andy Holmes, regarded as all potential but no performance, worked as a hod-carrier after completing a French degree. Martin Cross was a left-leaning history teacher with a bronze medal from the coxless fours in Moscow. Richard Budgett, who had failed to win a Blue at Cambridge, and cox Adrian Ellison were both medics. The four were propelled from competence to brilliance by the injection of Redgrave's raw power three months before the Games.

As someone born and brought up in the Thames-side town of Marlow, Redgrave felt the lure of the river from an early age. He was held back by dyslexia – a CSE grade one in woodwork was the summit of his academic achievements – but immersed himself in sport. He was 13 and already over six feet when he was identified as a potential rower at his comprehensive school, Great Marlow. Redgrave was the teenage powerhouse in the crew who ruffled public school feathers at junior regattas in the mid-Seventies.

Taking his lead from his father, Geoff, who opened a garden centre, Redgrave began his own landscaping company. He left school when he was 16, in 1978, and by the following year he had established himself as the best junior oarsman in the country. Despite opposition from national selectors, he also began to explore his potential as a single sculler and came under the wing of the former international coach, Mike Spracklen. Redgrave had high hopes of competing in the Moscow Olympics as part of a quadruple scull, but they were the one men's crew to be left behind when the BOA, under-funded in the wake of the American boycott, imposed a quota system. "I was extremely bitter," Redgrave admitted. The selectors toyed with drafting him into the eight, who won a silver medal in Moscow, before deciding to send Redgrave and Adam Clift to the World Junior Championships instead; they, too, finished second.

There was on-going tension between Redgrave and Clift – they almost came to blows on more than one occasion – and Redgrave had a new target for his youthful disgruntlement when Martin Cross joined the quad. He was unimpressed with Cross as stroke, even after the British crew had reached the World Championship final in 1982. Redgrave, as the most talented member of the boat, came under increasing pressure to revert to rowing, but though his enthusiasm for the quad had been exhausted he was still intent on making his mark in the single sculls. Redgrave, in common with the whole British team, performed dismally at the 1983 World Championships. The only finalists were the coxed four, including Cross and Budgett.

The domineering Penny Chuter, director of coaching and rowing's intransigent answer to Margaret Thatcher, tinkered endlessly before the line-up for Los Angeles was finalised. Redgrave was hauled up before her at the ARA offices in London and told, according to Redgrave, 'If you don't do as I say, if you don't row, then you're out. You won't be going to the Olympics.' Redgrave walked out and it was only thanks to diplomatic intervention from Spracklen that a compromise was reached. Redgrave was allowed to scull at the season-opening Mannheim regatta in Germany on the understanding that he rowed in the coxed four the following day. He finished a distant third in the single sculls, but a practice paddle with Redgrave at stroke (taking John Beattie's place in the boat) was enough to settle the issue.

Cross recalled: "It was an incredible sensation. The four with Steven in was dynamite. I could hardly keep up with the pace that he was setting in the two practice starts which we did. There was a brutality about the attack we now had on the catches which I had never experienced before. I thought, 'My God, this is what it feels like to row in a gold medal boat.' " The initial impressions were underlined the following day when the four won in imperious fashion. Cross was quickly aware of the impact which Redgrave's introduction had on his other crewmates. "Behind Steven, Andy needed no urging to show him that he could match his power. 'Budge' was crazy enough to follow any lead and row flat out until he dropped."

The British four's Olympic prospects brightened still further when the gold medal favourites, from East Germany, were ruled out by the Eastern Bloc boycott. On the evidence of the Lucerne regatta, where the Redgrave-inspired crew sliced five seconds off the unofficial world record to beat the East Germans, they were capable of beating all-comers anyway. The fifth man who flew out to Los Angeles, three weeks before their first race, was cox Adrian Ellison, who had competed at the previous three World Championships.

The *Sunday Times* rowing correspondent, Richard Burnell, who had won a gold medal in the double sculls at the 1948 Games, labelled the British crew "the unlikely lads"; Redgrave described the four as "an extremely diverse group". He was as aloof, especially in the early stages of his rowing career, as Cross was sociable. "We used to call him 'Mr Have-a-chat'," Redgrave recalled. "At regattas, we'd be rigging the boat and he'd be off talking and gossiping to people from all different countries." No sooner had the team arrived in the United States than Holmes, a Cadillac enthusiast, went off in search of California registration plates.

Mindful of the fact that racing at Lake Casitas would begin at 7am each day, before a gathering sea breeze made the course unrowable, the British team settled into a routine of getting up at 3.45am. The depleted field for the event – there were only eight entries – meant that the heat winners went straight into the final. The British crew had three seconds in hand on the American four, but faced a nervous week's wait before the final. A heavy mist lifted just in time for racing to go ahead as scheduled. A 16,000 crowd, the majority interested only in seeing a home victory, came into view. The Americans invested everything in burning off the opposition in the first 1,000 metres, but the British crew were still within a length and they surged through in the last 250 metres to win by 1.64 seconds. Redgrave, surprised by the Americans' speed in the middle of the race, confessed that he felt no elation, only relief. As they paddled back up the course, he was sick over the side of the boat.

Holmes reflected afterwards: "During those last five strokes I could see the finishing line and knew we could not be caught. It was a fabulous feeling. They went out so fast we were forced to bide our time. They were trying to crack us early but we held them always within a canvas. Going for the winning line we raised our striking rate. They tried to resist, but we knew we had the beating of them." Burnell told Redgrave: "You're world champion for one year; you're Olympic champion for life."

He returned home to muted celebrations and financial realities which, apart from the offer of free meat from a local butcher and money for a boat and equipment from DAF Trucks, were as grim as before. Redgrave still believed that he had unfinished business in the single sculls and immediately adjusted his focus to Seoul. The remaining members of the Los Angeles crew were also re-assessing their priorities.

Budgett, who had recently qualified at St Mary's Hospital, Paddington, retired from competitive rowing to concentrate on his medical career. He went on to specialise in sports medicine and worked with the British team at every winter Olympics between 1992 and 2006. In 2007 he was made chief medical officer for the 2012 summer Games. Holmes, who was about to get married, took a year out to consider his options; Ellison went back to his job as a radiographer at Charing Cross Hospital.

Cross reverted to his teaching job at Hampton School and admitted his sense of resentment when his name was omitted from the New Year's Honours in 1985 (he relished the thought of turning down an MBE in a very public snub to Margaret Thatcher's Conservative government). None of the Los Angeles five received immediate recognition, though Redgrave was honoured in 1987, Holmes was made an MBE after winning his second Olympic gold medal and Budgett's work for the BOA eventually earned him an OBE.

In his entertainingly discursive book, *Olympic Obsession*, Cross admitted to a more general sense of grievance. He soon discovered that the gold medal meant very little in terms of funding. Cross would compete in two more Olympics, but he was unsettled by the experience of going to the Atlanta Games as a spectator and descended into deep depression the following winter. One of the first people he sought out for help was Budgett. After recovering, Cross became an assertive rowing commentator for both BBC radio and television.

Aug 6: Javelin, Tessa Sanderson

THE Olympics were like a four-yearly fix for Tessa Sanderson. Five of her six appearances ended in varying degrees of disappointment; the other, in 1984, brought her the first ever gold medal for a British woman in a throwing event at the Games. When Sanderson competed as a 40-year-old in 1996 – billed as "the oldest slinger in town" – she equalled the record for the most Olympics by a Briton. She now shares the accolade with fencer Bill Hoskyns, whose last Games coincided with Sanderson's first.

Sanderson's childhood followed a pattern which was not untypical for West Indian families who settled in Britain in the 1950s. While her parents laid down roots for a new life in Wolverhampton, Sanderson was brought up in Jamaica by her grandmother. The family was reunited when she was eight and she threw herself into sports with more enthusiasm than she could muster for school lessons. She was still a couple of months shy of her 18th birthday when she competed in the javelin at the 1974 Commonwealth Games in Christchurch, New Zealand. Sanderson's performance was modest, but she made such an impression on the Tanzanian, Filbert Bayi, who won the 1500m in a world record time, that he proposed in the middle of a sheep-shearing contest; he was politely rebuffed.

There were no obvious signs that Sanderson was built for the job: when she competed in Montreal in 1976 one of her rivals, the American Karin Smith, mistook her for a sprinter and pointed her in the direction of the track. "No one, it appeared, had seen a five feet six inch, nine-stone javelin thrower before," she remembered. "I said, 'Am I hell!' and, snap, I was in the proper, aggressive state of mind." Sanderson threw a British record distance of 57.18m to qualify for the final, where she finished 10th.

The winner was the world record holder, Ruth Fuchs, but Sanderson made a spectacular breakthrough, statistical and psychological, when she threw 67.20m to beat the East German in Dublin in 1977; only Fuchs herself had thrown further at the time. Sanderson was still working as a copy typist and told the *Daily Mirror*: "I earn about £40 a week, but by the time the taxman has finished with it there is not much left." She was tempted by the offer of a sports scholarship in the United States, but her gold medal potential was also spotted closer to home. Six members of the Variety Club of Great Britain pitched in with £1,000 apiece in a three-year deal designed to lighten Sanderson's financial worries in the build-up to Moscow. "All they ever asked was that I should write them the occasional postcard telling them what I was doing and where," she explained. At much the same time she was "adopted" by Telford Development Corporation, who gave her rented accommodation in the new town and a job as a sports assistant.

Towards the end of 1978, Sanderson began working with the Yorkshire-based coach Wilf Paish, a relationship which, according to Sanderson, developed into a "father-daughter" bond. He described her in 1979 as "a delightful simple lass who is a very talented athlete in the Greek sense of the word". He also saw her as a top-class multi-eventer in the making, especially if the javelin was incorporated. This duly happened when the heptathlon replaced the pentathlon for the 1984 Olympics.

Fellow javelin thrower Mick Hill, who was only 14 when he joined Paish's group in 1979, remembers: "It was inspirational for a young lad to be training with someone who was on the telly and winning things. She was a bubbly character and one hell of an athlete. We used to have great banter – she could give it and take it as well."

Sanderson had underlined her championship credentials in 1978 by winning the Commonwealth title and finishing second to Fuchs in the European Championships. At the same time a domestic rivalry, one which would give the women's javelin considerably higher profile in Britain for the next 10 years, was starting to brew between Sanderson and Fatima Whitbread, five years her junior. The initial rapport which Sanderson felt soon evaporated as Whitbread and her adoptive mother, Margaret, who would later become national javelin coach, distanced themselves from the British team at championships.

Fatima Whitbread was too young and experienced to be a factor in Moscow, but Sanderson was now in her prime. Less than two months before the Games, she upped the ante with "a magical sky searcher" of a throw, 69.70m, which only a few weeks earlier would have been good enough to break the world record. With the benefit of hindsight, Sanderson described it as her "Moscow throw exactly seven weeks too early". She was consumed by negative thoughts when she visited the Lenin Stadium on the eve of qualifying and could not even manage a 50-metre throw. As she made a tearful exit from the arena she heard Andy Norman, the promoter who later married Whitbread, exclaim, 'Oh s***, she hasn't qualified.' Sanderson brushed aside reporters immediately afterwards, reflecting later from the sanctuary of the Olympic village: "I just don't know what went wrong. I have no excuses. I've been training for this for four years and I guess I just blew it. I was just the unlucky athlete who blew it on the day. I died out there."

Sanderson returned home to a barrage of criticism, and not just from the press. One consoling note from a nine-year-old was drowned by shoals of hate mail and racist abuse. There was precious little encouragement elsewhere: Unigate withdrew their sponsorship and demanded the return of the car they had provided; the winding-up of the Telford Development Corporation left her unemployed. In a curious marriage of humiliation and recognition she would be asked for her autograph as she stood in the dole queue.

She began to explore her potential in the heptathlon and was convinced, but for tendon injuries which kept her out of action for almost two years between Moscow and Los Angeles, that she could have won an Olympic title in that event. As it was, she could only watch from the sidelines as Whitbread threatened her status as Britain's premier javelin thrower. In 1983 Sanderson moved to Yorkshire – Paish was based in Leeds – and was offered a training-friendly job with a television promotion company, Telvista. Despite continuing discomfort from her Achilles and throwing arm, Sanderson threw in excess of 70 metres for the first time, then a mighty 73.68m in Birmingham.

She finally went under the knife towards the end of 1983 and was only able to resume serious training in the spring of 1984. Paish's coaching input was now crucially supplemented by the specialist knowledge of Miklos Nemeth, the Hungarian who had won the javelin gold medal in Montreal. Sanderson spent time in Budapest, leading to wild accusations that she was bulking up with anabolic steroids. Just prior to the Los Angeles Games, Sanderson was astonished to see herself cast as the baddest of the bad girls in an extraordinary 'exclusive' by Marea Hartman, the school-ma'am-like secretary of the Women's AAA, in the *News of the World*. Hartman alleged that Sanderson had been caught in bra and pants by a startled monk while at a training camp near San Diego (and that was when she wasn't cavorting around in the nude). Sanderson later received an apology for Hartman's groundless accusations.

Paish had to employ native cunning to be at Sanderson's side in Los Angeles. One apologies-for-absence fax to the media accreditation centre was all he needed. As Sanderson described it: "For the duration of the Olympic Games he had become one Matias Prats, a Spanish television commentator who, peculiarly, spoke only West Country English." Paish's view that Sanderson should reduce her run-up was endorsed by Daley Thompson, and this time there was no mistake in qualifying: her first throw booked her place in the final.

The competition, which began at 2.15am British time, was effectively decided in the first two rounds. Sanderson, who had already seen Whitbread throw just under 65 metres, responded with a distance of 69.56m, an Olympic record. The world champion, Tiina Lillak, was already struggling with an ankle injury and poured all her remaining energy into her second-round throw, which measured exactly 69 metres. Whitbread moved up to claim the bronze medal and suggested that she and Sanderson embark on a joint lap of honour. They shrugged aside an official who tried to bar their path on the grounds that Carl Lewis was on the long jump runway.

"This is just the greatest moment in my life," Sanderson gushed afterwards. "I couldn't believe I was watching the Union Jack and hearing the National Anthem all for me. I'm going to call my mum and when I've stopped crying I'm going to tell her to stop crying." When she did ring home she discovered that her father had slept through the competition.

For four years she had felt unfairly characterised by her meltdown in 1980 and said pointedly: "I hope Moscow is buried now." In a coded thank you to Barrie Whitford, the managing director of Telvista, she said in a television interview: "The eagle has landed." The reflected glory could not prevent the company going into liquidation soon afterwards and once again Sanderson was left jobless and almost penniless.

Triumph and trauma seemed to go hand in hand for Sanderson, most notably when a proposed appearance on *This Is Your Life* in March 1985 was aborted. A series of defamatory letters were sent to the programme's producers and Sanderson's home, culminating in a suggestion that just before the show was broadcast a national newspaper would be shown a document which proved Sanderson had used anabolic steroids. She insisted that any purported evidence of this kind would be a fake. Sanderson had a clear idea of who she thought the "guttersnipe" was – an athletics insider who knew from the early planning stages that she was to be featured on *This Is Your Life* – but the police drew a blank.

More cheering were civic receptions in Leeds and Wednesfield, the town on the outskirts of Wolverhampton where Sanderson's parents lived. A Wednesfield housing estate, Sanderson Park, was later named after her. She also had two Buckingham Palace dates to fulfil, one a small lunch hosted by the Queen and the Duke of Edinburgh, the other to receive her MBE.

Athletics was a sport hurtling towards professionalism between the 1984 and 1988 Olympics, but Sanderson felt like the poor relation beside Seb Coe and Daley Thompson, Britain's other track and field gold medallists from Los Angeles. At Coe's suggestion, she signed up with Mark McCormack's International Management Group, only to ask to be released from her contract after they had generated less than £2,000 for her in the first year.

By the time the Seoul Olympics came around, Fatima Whitbread had the swagger of someone who believed – with the European and world titles in her pocket – that she was ready to usurp the East German, Petra Felke, as the queen bee of javelin throwing. She dismissed Sanderson as "not mentally strong enough to win". In the event a legacy of injuries caught up with both Britons: Whitbread did well to finish second and Sanderson could not even muster the strength to qualify for the final. "The last 10 days I've been to hell and back," she sobbed. "This whole time I've been here has been a disaster. I've either been stuck in my room or visiting doctors or physiotherapists."

Sanderson was taken on by Sky Sports as a presenter in 1988 – television seemed like an ideal medium for someone with her cheery brand of self-confidence – but was sacked after two years in the job. Early in 1990 she was awarded £30,000 in libel damages against Mirror Group Newspapers after a High Court jury decided that she had been unfairly accused of "stealing" Derrick Evans, better known as GMTV's Mr Motivator, from his wife.

TESSA TIMES SIX

1976: 'There was just no buzz at all – no razzamatazz. The thing I remember most was being mistaken for a sprinter'

1980: 'I was just the unlucky athlete who blew it on the day. I died out there'

1984: 'Whatever else happens in my life, this was the greatest moment, the time I felt immortal'

1988: 'The last 10 days I've been to hell and back'

1992: 'I'm 99 per cent certain this will be the last time'

1996: 'That's it. This is absolutely the end. The curtain comes down'

The final part of Sanderson's athletics was like an eternal sunset. Whitbread was forced to retire at the start of 1992 – the head-to-head tally finished 27-18 in Sanderson's favour – but her rival soldiered on. The sense of struggle and sacrifice was as strong as it had ever been: Sanderson spent the previous winter training in the gym of a sixth form college in Walthamstow, east London. "I'm 99 per cent certain this will be the last time," she said before the Barcelona Games. "I could be going in on crutches if I go for a sixth Games."

Sanderson came through a gruelling qualifying competition in Barcelona and finished a very creditable fourth in the final. She was no longer the single-minded athlete she had been in the early part of her career, but still she found it impossible to close the door and the farewell features had to be dusted off and recycled for Atlanta in 1996. Sanderson was pictured with her 40th birthday present to herself, a Mercedes C180 with the registration plate 5 TES. She gave a bizarre example of how her two lives could overlap: "The last time I was tested [for drugs] was two years ago when they turned up at a theatre in Bournemouth where I was in pantomime. There I was in my fairy godmother's costume trying to wee into a bottle."

There was no fairytale ending in Atlanta – Sanderson failed to qualify for the final – but an understandable pride in her sheer resilience. "That's it," she said. "This is absolutely the end. The curtain comes down." She reflected wistfully: "There have been too many tears, a lot of injustice – and not enough money along the way. Athletics hasn't made me a fortune, far from it. But it's brought happiness and heartache, and my mum has lived them both with me."

Mick Hill regards her as "an unbelievable athlete", adding: "She could have been a world-class heptathlete had she put her mind to it. The Achilles thing kept flaring up, but that just showed the character of the lady. That kind of thing is inspirational, to see someone like that on a day-by-day basis, keeping their enthusiasm for something which is very repetitive. And it does put you in hospital from time to time. There aren't that many athletes with that kind of dedication."

Pay-the-bills media appearances (remember *Celebrity Wife Swap* with former football manager Ron Atkinson?) and charitable work have been the staples of Sanderson's life since she retired from athletics. She set up the Tessa Sanderson Foundation and Academy in 2009 and in 2010 married her long-term boyfriend, Densign White, judo player and former Olympian, at St Paul's Cathedral. The couple, whose star-studded nuptials were captured by *Hello!* magazine, were qualified to hold the service at the cathedral by virtue of the CBE awarded to Sanderson in 2004.

Aug 9: Decathlon, Daley Thompson

DALEY THOMPSON was an increasingly reluctant celebrity in the aftermath of his win in Moscow. Although there was no major championship to focus on the following year, he was happiest in his close-knit training group. In 1982, Thompson was back at Gotzis, this time accompanied by a healthy contingent of British reporters.

Showing un-Thompsonlike sincerity, he thanked them for coming and rewarded their commitment with another world record. His first-day score, 4,629 points, had never been matched, and he kept his foot down to record a total of 8,707. He was asked how he compared to Seb Coe and Steve Ovett. "I'm better at their event than they are at theirs," he insisted, "because they have rivals very close to them and nobody can get close to me."

Two months later it became apparent that Thompson did have a genuine rival (in record terms anyway). The 6ft 7in West German, Jürgen Hingsen, had been a fairly distant runner-up in Gotzis, but he stole Thompson's record in a domestic decathlon to raise the stakes before the upcoming European Championships in hot and humid Athens. Hingsen's challenge disintegrated during the second day's events and Thompson had the odd experience of being cheered on by Hingsen's compatriot, Guido Kratschmer, as he fought exhaustion in the 1500m. The result: 8,744 points and another world record.

Thompson's aversion to opening ceremonies was established long before he was subjected to a barrage of criticism for turning down an invitation to carry the English flag at the opening ceremony for the 1982 Commonwealth Games in Brisbane. "What does England want: a flag carrier or a gold medallist?" he said, pointing out that the decathlon was getting under way two days later. He won without the need for over-exertion and treated millions of television viewers to an unscripted 'oh s***' when he was announced as the BBC's Sports Personality of the Year.

Unusually, for a multi-event athlete, Thompson had avoided serious injury, but as the inaugural World Championships approached he was laid low twice, first by a back injury then, freakishly, by a torn abductor muscle when he slipped on the floor of a clothing shop in Crawley. Hingsen, fresh from regaining the world record, launched a pre-Helsinki charm offensive; a fractious Thompson shunned publicity. In the heat of battle there was only one winner. Thompson was the quick-witted ringmaster (the king of quips, Muhammad Ali, was Thompson's sporting idol) to Hingsen's ponderous patsy. The Briton had the luxury of being able to slope in eight seconds behind Hingsen in the 1500m and still have 20 seconds to spare.

Coe described Thompson as 'a Stalinist', on the grounds that he needed not only to win but to destroy his opponents mentally as well. Hingsen knew the sensation. In May 1984, he added a few more points to his world record score and desperately tried to convince himself that he had Thompson's measure off the track as well. "He can't kid me anymore," Hingsen said. "I know he's as scared as I am. Now I know that I am as good as he is…The only thing he does better than me is tell jokes."

Thompson was in his irreverent element in Los Angeles. He sported a self-deprecating cap with the words, 'This Space For Rent' on the front; he seemed to have a cupboard load of T-shirts, all designed to amuse, taunt or infuriate. He also had the capacity to snap back from comedian to competitor in an instant. After two throws in the discus, the sixth of the 10 disciplines, he was 66 points behind Hingsen (in seven decathlons he had never trailed the German). After the third throw Thompson was 34 points to the good. Crisis averted.

"It was the best and worst moment of my life," Thompson later reflected. "Some people shy from the high-pressure moments. It was what I had been looking for, a culmination of all I had trained for. Just to be faced with the situation in an Olympics, the feeling was incredible. And I'd faced it and overcome it in the thing I'm least competent in, the discus. I'd really hit the s*** out of that discus."

Hingsen, conversely, wilted under similar pressure in the pole vault. Thompson did a back flip of delight after one clearance; the German was sick in the stadium tunnel. The competition was over and Hingsen's world record was there for the taking. Perversely, the motivation was not enough for Thompson, who finished a single point adrift of the record. He went back to the top of the all-time list when the points system was finessed at the start of 1985.

As Thompson embarked on his lap of honour he wore a T-shirt with the message, 'Thanks America for a good games and a great time', on the front. On the back were the words, 'But what about the TV coverage?' There was a change of top and a cheekily cryptic message on display at the press conference: 'Is the world's second greatest athlete gay?' Could he *possibly* mean Carl Lewis?

Thompson had been congratulated at trackside by Princess Anne and, inevitably, he was asked what she had said to him. "She says I'm a damn good-looking guy. I told her she was telling the truth," he quipped. In typically throwaway fashion, he announced that he would allow himself a rest…and maybe even start a family. Who might the mother be? "You've just named the lady," he shot back, adding that the Princess hoped the children would be white.

The British press, while far from hoodwinked, suggested that Thompson might have crossed the line. Buckingham Palace rushed out a mollifying statement from the Queen's press secretary, Michael Shea: "Princess Anne wants to make it quite clear that she finds it totally and absolutely absurd that anyone should think anything said by Daley Thompson after his outstandingly brilliant achievement was offensive in any way."

Another voice of influence leapt to Thompson's defence in Los Angeles: Bob Mathias, the only man previously to have retained the Olympic decathlon title. Asked to compare Thompson to Lewis, who won four gold medals at the Games, Mathias responded: "Daley gives it everything he has in the spirit of competition. He's a nice guy, a funny guy. He brags a little bit, but that's just his personality. He doesn't mean it in a serious way. He's the complete opposite of Carl Lewis, who has been so cold and calculating."

'Princess Anne wants to make it quite clear that she finds it totally and absolutely absurd that anyone should think anything said by Daley Thompson after his outstandingly brilliant achievement was offensive in any way'

Thompson was still only 26, but injuries restricted him to a last glorious summer – in 1986. Even the combined might of a partisan crowd and local heroes Hingsen and Siggi Wentz could not prevent Thompson from winning the European Championship decathlon in Stuttgart. He also completed a hat-trick of Commonwealth Games titles in Edinburgh, sending the main sponsors, Guinness, into an alleged lather of outrage by crossing out their name on his England vest. Teetotaller Thompson pointed out, irrelevantly, that he did not like Guinness, but relented when told that the whole £2 million deal was under threat. He was happier to be seen (and paid handsomely for) promoting Lucozade in a campaign which revitalised the brand in the mid-Eighties. In anticipation of a life after athletics, Thompson tried out for the Los Angeles Raiders American football team; he did a screen test for a projected police series; Daley's Decathlon joined the ranks of computer games.

An unbeaten record stretching back to 1979 finally ended at the World Championships in 1987, when he was patently hampered by a groin injury. "I was the defending champion and had to see it through to the end," he said. "I feel bad at the moment, but I would have felt a lot worse if I'd stayed at home and watched it on TV." All hopes of a successful title defence in Seoul vanished when he injured his left thigh a week before the competition; there was a symbolic air to the pole which snapped as he made his first attempt in the vault.

Bowing out gracefully was not Thompson's style. He even made an abortive last-ditch attempt to qualify for the Barcelona Games when a place was left open for him. With the deadline approaching, a special competition was arranged at Crystal Palace, but he was unable even to complete the 100m.

Five children and 20 years later, Thompson is an ambassador (but never a diplomat) for this, a spokesman for that, a corporate motivator. He does his bit for the Laureus Sport for Good Foundation, but admits: "The reason I do the Laureus thing is I get to hang out with some of the greatest sportsmen the world has known."

Aug 11: 1500m, Sebastian Coe

SEB COE and Steve Ovett, as the chief architects of the explosion of interest in athletics, were expected to be in the vanguard of high earners when the sport went open in 1982. In anticipation of the new opportunities, Coe had signed with Mark McCormack's International Management Group. Both he and Ovett insisted that athletic integrity came before money. Ovett became a consultant for U-Bix Copiers and set up a sportswear business; Coe said yes to a television commercial for Horlicks and no to a £100,000 offer from Brut.

The 1981 season had lacked the obvious focus of a major championship (and, inevitably, hand-to-hand combat between Coe and Ovett), but in racing terms neither had, nor would, run better. Coe surprised even himself by clipping six tenths of a second off his own 800m record, running an astonishing time of 1min 41.73sec in Florence; the record lasted 16 years before being beaten by Denmark's Wilson Kipketer. A month later, he took more than a second off his 1,000m record, clocking 2min 12.18sec in Oslo, and attempted to beat both Ovett's 1500m and mile records in the same race, in Zurich. "It wasn't a particularly good night," Coe later reflected. He was two seconds outside Ovett's time when he passed 1500m, but speeded up so markedly that he still claimed the mile record in a time of 3min 48.53sec.

A week later, Ovett was back in possession thanks to a 3min 48.40sec run in Koblenz. His friend and pacemaker, Bob Benn, a moderate half-miler, became a well-known aide in record-breaking attempts, though he and Ovett later fell out. At that point it was still believed that Coe and Ovett would meet in the IAAF Golden Mile in Brussels, two days later, but Ovett was not in the high-class line-up. Although Coe regarded it as a race more than a record attempt, he felt "unbeatable" and so confident that he even contemplated leading from the gun. Although he was half a second outside Ovett's Koblenz split at the bell, a majestic last lap enabled Coe to take more than a second off the record. The time, 3min 47.33sec, remained intact until beaten by Steve Cram four years later.

Ovett fully expected to be better and stronger the following year, but his whole career was on the line when his right knee collided with church railings during a training run in Brighton in December 1981. Perversely, for someone so protective of his privacy, Ovett's recuperation was captured in an ITV documentary which tracked his progress (or lack of it) over a nine-month period.

IMG and Andy Norman, the increasingly influential Mr Fixit of British athletics, brokered a three-race deal in which Coe and Ovett would meet over 3,000m, 800m and a mile. The protagonists got as far as sharing the stage at a London press conference, in May, to announce dates and places (they even conversed amicably during light training runs in Hyde Park). Ovett, however, was not alone in suffering health issues in 1982, and the races went ahead without one or both of the main attractions. Coe suffered a stress fracture then contracted glandular fever; Ovett's slow recovery from his railings mishap was followed by a torn hamstring which ruled him out of the European Championships in Athens. He commentated instead for the BBC, confidently predicting a Coe win in the 800m, and admitted on air that he was flabbergasted when the West German, Hans-Peter Ferner, took the title instead.

Coe did figure in a ninth world record, anchoring a British team in the rarely run 4 x 800m at Crystal Palace, but he was a peripheral figure in 1983. Although Steve Ovett finished the season on a high note, running 3min 30.77sec to break the 1500m world record in Rieti, Italy, he, too, was overshadowed by Cram's emergence as the 'third man' in British middle-distance running. Cram, who had also claimed the European and Commonwealth titles the previous summer, won the 1500m at the World Championships in Helsinki (Ovett could only finish fourth) to underline his threat to Coe's Olympic defence. Coe himself, unhappy at the furore over his pre-selection for the 1500m, said he no longer wanted to be considered over the longer distance and was ruled out of the whole championships when he contracted the parasitic disease toxoplasmosis.

Ovett had warmed to more than the Australian weather when he visited the country in 1981 and based himself there for seven weeks at the start of 1984. His overall verdict – "Australia is my kind of country and Australians my kind of people" – more than hinted that he would return permanently when his athletics career finished. His build-up to Los Angeles was hampered by illness and predictions of a British one-two-three, realistic if Coe, Ovett and Cram had all been fit, looked increasingly far-fetched. Even Cram's preparations were interrupted by a series of injuries.

Coe came under pressure and criticism from Peter Elliott, a Yorkshireman by birth rather than by residence, who beat him over 800m in the trial. He believed he had earned the right to double up, at Coe's expense when, on the eve of the squad announcement, he defeated him again over 1500m at the AAA Championships. The selectors seesawed in Elliott's favour before siding with Coe, whose halo had not so much slipped as gone missing. In an attempt to dodge the flak, Coe based himself in Chicago before heading out west. When Ovett confronted the heat, smog and pollution of Los Angeles he knew that he would struggle to compete effectively.

The 800m, in particular, had grown up over the past four years. There were three Americans capable of running under one minute 44 seconds and a Brazilian, Joaquim Cruz, with the potential to go considerably faster. Coe and Ovett both qualified for the final, though Ovett was already in distress, stumbling over the line to take fourth place in his semi-final. The fast-run final played into

'I think we're a bit too old to be playing at this'

the hands of Cruz, who had almost five metres to spare on Coe at the end. "I think we're a bit too old to be playing at this," Coe told Ovett afterwards. Ovett twice collapsed in the tunnel and spent two nights in hospital before deciding, against his wife's wishes, that he would make a token appearance in the 1500m. He was to pull out during the final.

Coe still had to discover if four competitive 800m races in successive days had sharpened him or depleted scarce resources, but one obstacle to a successful defence was removed when Cruz pulled out ill before the semi-finals. Coe concentrated on preserving energy and was the tactical master in the final, covering injections of pace by

Steve Scott and the Spaniard, Jose Abascal, before accelerating away from Cram in the straight. His winning time, 3min 32.53sec, was an Olympic record; he was also the first 1500m champion to make a successful defence.

In a very un-Coe-like show of anger, "bordering on hatred", he later admitted, he pointed accusingly in the direction of the press box and shouted: "Who says I'm finished now!" He has insisted since that the target of his displeasure was not just the media, but the wider athletics community, who had called into question his father's credibility and humanity as a coach. Coe took no lasting pride in his belligerent outburst and even on the day he was able to put a more diplomatic slant on his victory: "It's been a bit of a dream come true," he said. "This day last year I had been out of hospital for four days and I wasn't able to run again until after Christmas. It was a battle to catch up until three or four weeks ago. This year has been a mental battle as much as anything. To come back at all in Olympic year is very satisfying and I'm elated it's ended this way."

COE v OVETT: HEAD-TO-HEAD

March 25 1972	English Schools Cross-Country Championships	Hillingdon	Coe 10th	Ovett 2nd
Aug 31 1978	European Championships, 800m final	Prague	Coe 3rd	Ovett 2nd
July 26 1980	Olympic Games, 800m final	Moscow	Coe 2nd	Ovett 1st
Aug 1 1980	Olympic Games, 1500m final	Moscow	Coe 1st	Ovett 3rd
Aug 6 1984	Olympic Games, 800m final	Los Angeles	Coe 2nd	Ovett 8th
Aug 11 1984	Olympic Games, 1500m final	Los Angeles	Coe 1st	Ovett DNF
Aug 13 1989	AAA Championships, 1500m final	Birmingham	Coe 1st	Ovett 10th

After the 800m, Coe resigned himself to the probability that he would never win a major title over the distance. The gap in the trophy cabinet was filled when Coe headed a British 1-2-3 (with Tom McKean and Cram in his wake) at the 1986 European Championships in Stuttgart. A week later, Coe threatened Said Aouita's 1500m world record, running a personal best of 3min 29.77sec in Rieti. Ovett was more obviously past his best, though 1986 was also to provide him with his last golden memory: the 5,000m title at the Commonwealth Games in Edinburgh.

Coe could no longer guarantee continuity, but when he was fit he was still competitive and, despite what he had said four years earlier, he wanted to defend his title in Seoul. He failed to qualify by right and was forced to rely on the sympathy vote. Juan Antonio Samaranch, the IOC president, went as far as calling for a unique wildcard before backing down under a barrage of criticism. The immediate effect was that Coe decided to carry on competing.

On Aug 13 1989, Coe and Ovett, 32 and 33 respectively, met for the first and last time on a British track; at stake were places in the England team for the Commonwealth Games the following January. The Ovett of old would have been in his element, barging and boring his way through the 1500m field at the AAA Championships, but this was not the Ovett of old. He crunched into the back of Coe, almost putting both of them out of the race. Coe danced his way out of the trouble to win; Ovett finished 10th and broke down in tears afterwards. It was effectively the end of the road for both, though an ailing Coe did take his place at the Commonwealth Games in Auckland.

Ovett was a straight-from-the-hip commentator for the ITV and he has continued to contribute to athletics coverage in Canada and Australia, where he, Rachel and their four children settled after a spell on the Scottish borders. The couple separated in 2005. Coe, single-minded and single for the bulk of his athletics career, married three-day-eventer Nicky McIrvine in 1990, the same year in which she won the Badminton Trials. They, too, had four children before divorcing. Coe married his long-term girlfriend, magazine journalist Carole Annett, last summer.

More than any other gold medallist featured in this book, Coe has left his imprint on the wider world. He won the Falmouth and Camborne parliamentary seat for the Conservatives in 1992 before being voted out in 1997. He was William Hague's chief of staff and judo partner when he led the Tories in opposition and was made a life peer in 2000. Coe also proved to be the perfect advocate for London's 2012 Olympic bid, after replacing Barbara Cassani as head of the bid team, and has been the high-profile front man for LOCOG, the organising committee, in the build-up to the Games.

1988

Sept 19: 100m breaststroke, Adrian Moorhouse

ADRIAN MOORHOUSE not only extended Britain's modern-day lineage of Olympic champion breaststrokers by winning the 100m title in Seoul; he also championed a swimming revolution. Moorhouse told the Amateur Swimming Association in 1986 that he had signed two commercial contracts and unless they introduced trust funds immediately he would be competing illegally. Two months after his Olympic victory, Moorhouse wrote in a column for the *Times*: "Swimming in Britain is breaking free from amateurism."

The negotiating skills, the golden memories and character-building championship setbacks were all successfully channelled into Moorhouse's subsequent business life. In 1995, he set up the consultancy firm Lane 4 – the lane in which the fastest qualifier swims and his route to success in 1988. The company, a haven for ex-sportsmen, has been an ever-present in the *Sunday Times*'s annual list of best small companies over the past few years.

Moorhouse's road to competitive fulfilment started when he was six and took instantly to swimming in his home town, Bradford. As he began to compete seriously in his teens, exam results suffered, obscuring an intellect keen enough to qualify him for Mensa. Moorhouse's father, Clifford, a wool merchant, backed him both verbally and financially: to the tune of an estimated £100,000. After seeing his son swim to glory in Seoul, he described it as "the best money I have ever spent".

Adrian was part of the British junior team when he was 15 and was a natural successor to Duncan Goodhew when he retired after winning in Moscow in 1980. Both Goodhew and David Wilkie had benefited from time in America; not so Moorhouse. He had never been to the

United States before taking up a scholarship at the University of California, in Berkeley, when he left school in 1982. A year later he was back in England. Simon Barnes, who interviewed Moorhouse for the *Times* in 1992, wrote: "He became perhaps the first athlete in the history of American college sports to drop out because he was spending too much time in the lecture theatre [Moorhouse was reading philosophy and psychology]. He was cutting training in order to go to more lectures."

Moorhouse won the Commonwealth 100m title in 1982, scoring the first psychological blow in a lengthy rivalry with the Canadian, Victor Davis. He also took first place in the 200m at the European Championships but, like Goodhew, he was essentially a sprinter and the shorter distance was his main focus in Los Angeles in 1984. Fourth place in the final – the American, Steve Lundquist, won in a world record time of 1min 1.65sec – was a crushing blow to the 20-year-old Moorhouse.

He later reflected: "In L.A. I put too much pressure on myself and paid the penalty. I built the Olympics up as the only thing in my life and that and the media pressure proved too much for me to handle. The worst moment was waiting to give a urine sample in the dope-testing room with the three who had won medals. They all had something to be happy about and there was me sitting in the same room feeling like it was the end of the world."

The depression lingered…all the way through to New Year's Eve in 1984. "Everyone else was out enjoying themselves but I stayed in alone and moped. I then decided that I could not throw everything away and gave myself four months to get right back to the top." He was reassured by victory over 100m at the European Championships in 1985 and thought he had won the world title the following year, waving his arms in triumph before discovering that he had been disqualified for a faulty turn and his European record instantly annulled. Davis, who was already receiving an estimated £40,000 a year in endorsements, was handed the title. "I almost packed in swimming there and then," Moorhouse reflected, "but after two days in which I was in almost perpetual shock, I decided I was going to show them. After all, you cannot just sit down and let everything get on top of you."

Moorhouse carved a little bit of history for himself when, in February 1987, he became the first swimmer to beat the minute barrier for the 100m breaststroke, recording a time of 59.75sec at a short-course meeting in the German city of Bonn. He set out for Seoul with a calmer, more mature perspective; his father, mother, Kath, and brother, Stephen, headed the supporters' club. Moorhouse also had with him a telegram from his former Sunday school teacher, Geoff Carter, who had offered prophetic consolation in Los Angeles with the words, 'Very bad luck. All proud of you. There will be a next time'.

Predictably, Moorhouse and Davis were the quickest qualifiers for the final, but the race itself was anything but predictable. The Russian, Dmitri Volkov, set such a fierce pace that he was 1.3 seconds ahead of the sixth-placed Moorhouse at the turn. Moorhouse's coach, Terry Dennison, said afterwards: "Adrian has never been that far behind before." Volkov admitted that he was "washed out" halfway down the second length – Moorhouse overhauled him with 10 metres to go – but the Hungarian, Karoly Guttler, was putting in an even stronger finish. Moorhouse's margin of victory over Guttler was a hundredth of a second; the time, 1min 2.04sec, was disappointing, but it hardly mattered.

Moorhouse was asked if he had thought at any stage that victory was beyond him. "I'm not that kind of person," he responded. "I'm a Tyke – we never give up." He added: "When I looked up at the scoreboard at the finish I could not believe I had won. I knew Volkov would die in the final 25 metres, when I'm at my strongest, but I had to work like a beaver to catch him. As for Guttler, I never saw him coming." Moorhouse also reflected back to his disqualification in Madrid: "If I had retired after the worlds, I would never have known what I could do and I would never have experienced such a fantastic moment as today."

David Wilkie, who had fired the 12-year-old Moorhouse's Olympic ambitions when he won in Montreal, said cryptically: "The British breaststroke ark is beginning to get a little crowded." Peter Ackroyd, Moorhouse's coach at school in Bradford, had an even more unconventional take on the victory, alluding to his former charge's intuitive, Buddhist-like concentration in the final stages of the race. Ackroyd's pool-side seat was a competition prize in a Hong Kong newspaper. His winning tie-breaker, chosen ahead of 2,000 rival claims, read: "I want to go to the Olympics because I was Adrian Moorhouse's coach and I want to see him win the gold."

It was widely expected that Moorhouse would retire, especially after breaking a bone in his left hand while competing in a pro-celebrity saloon car race at Brands Hatch a few weeks later, but swimming was a powerful drug. He admitted just before competing in the Barcelona Olympics: "I couldn't wait to get back into the water. I was like a kid with his security blanket. I feel sometimes that I will find it hard to let go when I do. I'm trying to wean myself off it."

Moorhouse ticked off another ambition when he returned to familiar surroundings, Bonn, and broke the long-course world record for the 100m breaststroke at the European Championships in 1989. Remarkably, he recorded the same time, 1min 1.49sec, twice more over the following 12 months, including at the Commonwealth Games in Auckland. It was a strange occasion; Victor Davis had retired the previous July and died in a hit-and-run accident four months later. Moorhouse was asked to join a small group of Davis's family and friends on a boat as his ashes were scattered in Auckland Harbour.

Another Hungarian, Norbert Rozsa, emerged to challenge Moorhouse, and a fellow Briton, Nick Gillingham, became the latest breaststroker off the domestic production line. He and Moorhouse were even promoted, fancifully, as swimming's answer to Coe and Ovett. Gillingham won the silver medal in the 200m, but he and Moorhouse were seventh and eighth in a highly competitive 100m final. "Perhaps I stayed one year too many," Moorhouse admitted as he announced his retirement immediately after the race.

He was engaged at the time to the pole vaulter, Kate Staples, whom he met on *Jim'll Fix It*. Staples gained a little fame of her own as Zodiac on the ITV show *Gladiators* in the 1990s. The couple split up two years later and Moorhouse is now married with four children. After retiring, he assisted with the ASA's youth development programme before launching Lane 4 with sports psychologist Graham Jones. He supplements his business commitments with commentating work for the BBC.

Sept 22: Small-bore rifle three positions, Malcolm Cooper

MALCOLM COOPER was so dominant in his chosen sport that he won all five individual disciplines at the European Championships in 1985 and set five world records at the World Championships the following year. The lure of becoming the first person to retain an Olympic rifle title ensured that there was no let-up in Cooper's punishing practice regime, but he hinted strongly that, win or lose, he would quit after Seoul.

Just before setting out, he admitted: "I don't want to train any more. I like competing, but I have had enough of all the training. I have been going through the hard routine for around 20 years. I have been up at six, on the range at seven, off to work at 10.30 and back home at eight. Then you grab something to eat and go off to bed. Next morning it starts all over again. You just feel pretty pooped after all that, and there is still six or seven hours' shooting to get through at the weekends. It is just too much. You become so tired and there is no leisure time left. You have to keep an edge. If the enthusiasm goes, then it becomes a real slog."

A week before the start of the competition, Cooper was left speechless by the clumsiness of a BBC employee who knocked over the £1,200 rifle which had been specially adapted for use in the standing position. "This is pretty grim news," his wife, Sarah, said in the immediate aftermath of the accident. "I think I'll keep my head down." Team manager Tony Clark admitted: "He's upset at the moment. Who wouldn't be if you had a £1,000 rifle dropped on the deck? I think it's best if he's left alone. It will be OK, I'm sure. Malcolm has the approach and the temperament not to let it affect him when it comes to the competition."

This time the repair was beyond Cooper himself, but a Russian armourer ensured that the drama did not develop into a crisis. As the revamped competition began, Cooper was the picture of *sang froid*. "When it is time to shoot, my blood pressure and my pulse rate drop automatically," he explained.

It was soon apparent that the greatest challenge to Cooper's quest for a historic second gold would come from his friend and team-mate, Alister "Jock" Allan. They were portrayed as shooting's answer to Coe and Ovett. Allan, an Anglo-Scot who had first competed at the Mexico Games in 1968 and claimed the bronze medal behind Cooper in Los Angeles, was well placed to win the prone title in Seoul before missing twice in fading light to fall out of the medal places.

His form in the three positions, however, was outstanding, and if the competition had taken the same form as in 1984 Allan would have won the gold medal instead of the silver. His total after 1,200 shots was 1,181, one more than Cooper, but organisers had introduced a media-friendly shoot-out for the top eight. Sarah Cooper, who had absent-mindedly shot at a fellow competitor's target in finishing next to last the day before, likened it to a 100m race at the end of a five-hour marathon. Allan wilted under the pressure, but Cooper, despite the time limit of 75 seconds for each of 10 shots, was in his element. "There's a fine edge between holding still and another wobble. That's

Duncan Goodhew stretches out for victory in the 100m breaststroke in Moscow

Allan Wells (on the far side) dips to beat Cuba's Silvio Leonard (near side) to the line in the 100m final in 1980

Steve Ovett on his way to victory in the 800m in Moscow

Sebastian Coe atones for his 800m disappointment in Moscow by winning the 1500m in brilliant style

Daley Thompson celebrates the final-round throw in the discus which was critical to his decathlon triumph in 1984

Sebastian Coe gestures angrily towards the press after winning the 1500m in Los Angeles

A beaming Tessa Sanderson shows off her gold medal after winning the javelin in Los Angeles

Malcolm Cooper is flanked by fellow medallists (left) Alister Allan and the USSR's Kirill Ivanov in Seoul after retaining the small-bore rifle three positions title

Adrian Moorhouse is congratulated by his arch rival, Canada's Victor Davis, after winning the 100m breaststroke in 1988

Bryn Vaile (in goggles) and Mike McIntyre sailing to victory in Seoul GETTY IMAGES

Sean Kerly sweeps home the late winner for Britain in their thrilling semi-final against Australia in Seoul

Steve Redgrave and (right) Andy Holmes celebrate their coxless pairs victory in Seoul

Linford Christie raises his arms in triumph as he claims the 100m gold medal in Barcelona

Sally Gunnell puts the pressure on (left) Sandra Farmer-Patrick during the 400m hurdles final in 1992

Greg and (centre) Jonny Searle celebrate with cox Garry Herbert after receiving their gold medals in Barcelona

Chris Boardman and his innovative Lotus Sport bike form an unbeatable combination in Barcelona

Steve Redgrave hugs daughters Natalie and Sophie after partnering Matthew Pinsent to victory in Atlanta

A remarkable run enables Steph Cook to claim the modern pentathlon gold medal in Sydney

Jonathan Edwards sets the seal on a brilliant career by winning the triple jump in Sydney

Denise Lewis puts maximum effort into the long jump as she shrugs off aches and pains to win the heptathlon in Sydney

The British eight celebrate after coming ashore in Sydney

Ben Ainslie in gold medal winning action in 2000

Shirley Robertson puts previous disappointments behind her to win the Europe class sailing in Sydney

Audley Harrison takes the initiative during his gold medal bout against Mukhtarkhan Dildabekov, of Kazakhstan

Richard Faulds shows off his gold medal after winning a dramatic shoot-off in the double trap event in 2000

Jason Queally on his lap of honour after winning the kilometre time trial in Sydney

Leslie Law and Shear L'Eau negotiate an obstacle during the cross-country section in Athens

Ed Coode hugs a tearful Matthew Pinsent after the British four's narrow victory in Athens

Bradley Wiggins negotiates a bend on his way to victory in the individual pursuit in Athens

Chris Hoy celebrates his first Olympic gold medal, the kilometre time trial in Athens

Britain's garlanded quartet, (from left) Mark Lewis-Francis, Marlon Devonish, Darren Campbell and Jason Gardener, enjoy their golden moment in Athens

Kelly Holmes can scarcely believe it after following up her 800m triumph with victory in the 1500m

why I take so long," he explained. Simon Barnes, writing in the *Times*, captured the frenetic mood of the shoot-out:

> In an extraordinary afternoon, more reminiscent of darts at Jollees than the Queen's Prize at Bisley, Cooper shot with unimaginable calm...After each shot, the scores are announced, rather as a darts announcer calls his hundred-and-eighties. There were around 100 cameramen, fighting for places behind the shooters. Spectators elbowed furiously for a view of the television monitors that showed each individual target...It was mayhem. Not good for the nerves.

Cooper was the top dog on a day of six medals for Britain: the biggest one-day haul since 1928. He was mobbed by photographers and reporters, and several minutes elapsed before his wife could force her way through to give him a hug. He announced, cryptically, that he would celebrate by being "in the wagon tonight", explaining: "I have been on the wagon for two long months. It is the night for getting into it." He recovered in time to carry the British flag at the closing ceremony.

The competitive juices were finally exhausted for Malcolm Cooper in 1991 when, after suffering severe headaches for almost a year, he had a necrotic pituitary gland removed. Faced with taking pills for the rest of his life and fiercely opposed to drugs in sport, he had no option but to retire. His career embraced an extraordinary 149 medals, 61 of them in Olympic, world or European competition. A new 50-metre range at Bisley, built for the 2002 Commonwealth Games, was named after him.

The Coopers applied for New Zealand residency when Malcolm turned 50 in 1997 – he had always wanted to return to the country where he lived as a child – but he died of skin cancer in 2001, just before the application was granted. Sarah's initial instinct was to abandon the idea, but she eventually went through with the move herself.

Sept 25: Coxless pairs, Andy Holmes, Steve Redgrave

STEVE REDGRAVE had demons to confront in 1985, on and off the water. His back seized up during the World Championships in Hazewinkel, Belgium, forcing him to pull out during his single sculls semi-final. A slipped disc and curvature of the spine were both manageable conditions but there was no easy cure for a disintegrating relationship with his long-time girlfriend, Belinda Holmes, and the couple separated in the autumn of 1985.

Redgrave toyed briefly with giving up the sport, but found a welcome diversion by competing as a brakeman at the British Bobsleigh Championships in Winterberg, Germany. He was in the winning four-man bob in 1989 and even competed in a World Cup event. Although Redgrave continued to scull, he was persuaded to divide his energies between sculling and rowing. Crucially, too, Holmes was back on the scene in 1986, intent on winning gold medals at both the World Championships and Commonwealth Games. He was also keen to form a pair with Redgrave. Much has been made of the tension between the two, but they did share some common ground. Both were introverts and their family backgrounds were similar. Redgrave recalled that the only time they came close to blows was while playing five-a-side football in 1983.

Redgrave's whole career was based around the complementary qualities of technical precision, power and competitive drive; the only doubts surfaced when he was sculling. Martin Cross cited the example of the Diamond Sculls at Henley in 1986, when Redgrave stopped racing as he came under pressure in the final from the lightweight Dane, Bjarne Eltang. He was heard to say, 'What have I done?' before setting off again. According to Cross, Holmes enjoyed the moment. "The result had confirmed Andy's view that Steven had

'It was not one of my proudest moments'

a soft centre, and that when he was on his own in a sculling boat his physique was not enough to see him through. But with Andy behind him in the bows of a pair, Steven would feel his tough, unrelenting presence and push through his own fear of performing flat out."

Redgrave himself called it "one of the most humiliating defeats of my career". He wrote in his autobiography: "It was not one of my proudest moments, and it hurt badly. Afterwards I felt thoroughly ashamed. I shouldn't have stopped, of course, but I just felt embarrassed rowing past the enclosure packed with people expecting me to win." The legacy for Redgrave was the realisation that he would never match the standard he expected of himself as a single sculler. He bowed out of the event by winning the Commonwealth title at Strathclyde.

Ellison was jettisoned as cox just before the World Championships in 1986 and replaced by Pat Sweeney. Redgrave never believed that coxes added much value to a boat and he and Holmes were united in their antipathy to Ellison; Redgrave did not warm to his "condescending manner" and self-aggrandising analogy to Formula One motor racing. Ellison, he said, regarded himself as the driver; the rowers were just his engine. With Sweeney on board, Redgrave and Holmes beat the formidable Abbagnale brothers to win a hugely satisfying gold medal. Redgrave also began to find personal contentment in 1986 with Ann Callaway, a member of the women's eight at Los Angeles, who had just split up with her long-time boyfriend…Martin Cross. Redgrave exercised his right as an MBE holder to marry Ann in the crypt of St Paul's Cathedral in March 1988. She later became the chief medical officer for GB Rowing.

Redgrave and Holmes were given the chance to double up in Seoul, competing in both the coxed and coxless pairs, when it was agreed that the finals would be held over two days. They also took part in both events at the World Championships in 1987, winning the coxless pairs before being edged out by the Abbagnales the following day. Their commitment in training was unstinting: Holmes would, on a regular basis, cycle the 35 miles from Guildford to Marlow, train for three hours with Redgrave and then ride home again.

Media indifference prior to the 1984 Games was replaced by feverish interest in the build-up to Seoul. The suggestion that Redgrave and Holmes loathed each other was sewn by a lengthy article in the *Sunday Times* magazine by Peter Gillman, who was given almost daily access to the pair over a three-month period. Holmes was quoted as saying he wished he had become a drummer in a rock band instead. Although Redgrave has been consistent in his denials ever since – "if we had a fault it was simply that Andy and I very rarely spoke to each other" – the mud has stuck.

Holmes and Redgrave tuned up for Seoul at a training camp in Chuncheon. Holmes's older brother, Simon, was accredited as the team's official psychologist and introduced Redgrave to hypnotherapy; they focused on the exacting challenge of rowing six races in as many days and managed to engineer an easier semi-final in the coxed pairs by deliberately finishing second to the Abbagnales in their heat. The semi-finals were held on the same day, but Redgrave and Holmes were up to the task, winning one race and claiming second place in the other.

Although the coxless event was their clear priority, they were able to preserve a little energy in what Redgrave rated as their best race in partnership – a supremely controlled piece of rowing. In reflecting on their third place in the coxed pairs final the following day, Redgrave saw a clear parallel with the 800m and 1500m on the track in Moscow, where Seb Coe's greater appetite for victory gave him the edge over the longer distance.

Sept 27: Star class sailing, Mike McIntyre, Bryn Vaile

BRITAIN'S victory in the Star class sailing in 1988 was endearingly amateur in its conception and utterly professional in its execution – right down to the 'fat is fast' diet of hamburgers and Mars bars which left Mike McIntyre and Bryn Vaile begging for mercy. Drawn together by chance 10 months before the Seoul Games, they leapt from fourth to first on a final day of 30-knot winds and rare drama.

The triumph was attributed to a combination of skill and luck, but Vaile insists that it was "bad preparation" which cost the champions elect, Mark Reynolds and Hal Haenel, a broken mast. McIntyre points out that the Americans, failing to factor in the possibility of a British victory, were not even in gold medal position when disaster struck. "We were really sorted for the conditions," says Vaile, "whereas most of the other teams weren't up for it. We knew we had to win. Coming second would make no difference to the score at all."

McIntyre, born in Glasgow, was a talented swimmer before the victory of Rodney Pattisson and Iain MacDonald-Smith in 1968, when he was 12, planted a fierce ambition to become an Olympic champion himself. McIntyre's motivation for moving to England when he left university in 1977 was "to find the best job that I could close to the south coast so that I could sail Finns". In the next few years he established himself as one of Britain's foremost dinghy racers and announced his medal credentials for Los Angeles by finishing in the top three in all five lead-up regattas, culminating in victory at the Finn European Championship. A capsize in the first race, in which he finished 13th, jolted McIntyre's confidence and he was seventh overall. "It was disappointing to say the least, awful," he admits.

He quit his job with Racal Electronics to take his place on the British boat, White Challenger, which tried to qualify for the America's Cup in Australia at the end of 1986. McIntyre's priorities switched to home and hospital – he had by now moved to Wiltshire – when his two-year-old son, Angus, was diagnosed with a brain tumour in the summer of 1987 before making a full recovery.

Vaile, too, was on the operating table early in 1987 after contracting an infection which robbed him of sight in his left eye for three months. "It was pretty hairy," he says with stoic understatement. He needed a corneal graft and during the Olympics wore goggles to prevent the salt water getting in his eye; he also required drops to prevent rejection. "The joke was that I was legally on steroids," he says.

McIntyre and Vaile had known each other since 1982, but Vaile was still crewing a Star for former Olympian Peter Erzberger. In the autumn of 1987, the Swiss Brazilian announced that business commitments would prevent him from competing in Seoul, but he had two boats available and effectively said to Vaile, 'Go and find a helmsman.' McIntyre remembers that it took him "three milliseconds" to say yes. They were plunged into a race against time both to forge an on-board understanding and come to terms with the extreme demands of a keelboat. "Because our campaign was so short it forced us to concentrate on the priorities," says McIntyre. "Rod Carr, the team manager at the time, put it very simply. He said we were doing more work in two days at the weekend than the guys who were sailing full time were doing in a week. We were actually achieving more because we were focused all the time." McIntyre was working as a sales manager for a car phone company, Vaile was in Mobil's marketing department.

Eating (a lot) was not just considered an optional extra; it was a critical factor in balancing the mainsail on the Star as well as being the engine for maximum power and speed. For the sake of the team, the 5ft 11in Vaile inflated to 16st 7lb. He explains:

> This was in the era where crew weight was unlimited. Basically fat was fast. We'd been sailing in the 90-95 kilo band. For the Olympics we pumped it right up to 108 kilos. Plus about 20 kilos of wet clothing, which is probably why I've had to have four back operations since. I was eating like a pig: hamburgers and lots of Mars bars. It took me seven years to eat another Mars bar after that. We were still reasonably fit, but we had to be. We knew what the conditions were probably going to be like and we trained for those conditions.

Organisers had plumped for Pusan, Seoul's second city, as the venue for the sailing events, partly because it was reported to be an area of light winds. Less than a year before the Games it was discovered that the readings had been taken from the city's heavily sheltered airport. "We were fortunate to have really detailed information," McIntyre recalls. "There was a complicated tidal system off Pusan. Some of the time there was one tide a day and other times two tides. At certain points in the cycle there was a huge eddy in the bay, almost like a whirlpool."

Vaile adds: "We were the only team that really recognised that there would be at least two races in 20-knot-plus winds. We'd done our preparations for those conditions very thoroughly and we were absolutely in tune with the conditions. We knew we could do it, we just had to put the series together. We didn't talk ourselves up, but we believed we were in the medal zone. We certainly weren't just there for the T-shirts, even though we were both working and had had to give up an awful lot."

In analysing the performance blueprint for an Olympic champion, McIntyre and Vaile had discovered that the gold medallist normally won at least two races. They were comforted to have one first place under their belts as early as the second day, when McIntyre played an inspired hunch to separate from the rest of the main contenders. They crossed the finish line half a boat length ahead of the Italians. Keith Wheatley, writing in the *Sunday Times*, emphasised the brawn and subtlety demanded by the Star: "The huge mainsail and the spidery, bending mast need to be played like a powerful salmon on light tackle."

'I was sailing semi-concussed and there was blood all over the deck'

The fifth race, or the preliminaries, all but ended the Britons' challenge. Was it courage or lunacy which kept them afloat? Vaile recalls: "Just before the start the boom landed on my head during a tack. I was sailing semi-concussed and there was blood all over the deck – I don't remember the race at all. The first thing I could recall was sitting in the treatment room in the team hotel with the surgeon putting in half-a-dozen stitches."

They were able to discard the result, but the prognosis was not promising going into the final race. Reynolds and Haenel only needed to finish in the top six to win the gold medal. The British pair led off the start line and though the Dutch were in front at the weather mark they reached out for the wrong buoy; McIntyre and Vaile ploughed on through nine-foot waves and had 11 seconds in hand on the fast-finishing Australian Colin Beashel. Wheatley put the achievement in context: "Mike McIntyre and Bryn Vaile did more than win a gold medal at Pusan. They cracked a myth. A belief had solidified in international sailing that the Brits were fine in the little 470 dinghies and maybe the Flying Dutchman, but that keelboats were for the macho men of North America and the maestros of mainland Europe."

McIntyre revealed afterwards that his resolve had been strengthened by soundings among rival coaches before the race: "None thought I had a chance," he said, "and that made me so angry I was determined to prove them wrong." He added: "I won't forget September 27, ever." The Britons' misfortune was that Sept 27 1988 is more widely remembered as the day on which Canadian sprinter Ben Johnson was stripped of his 100m gold medal; every other news line from the Games was downgraded. McIntyre also believes that they have never been given due credit. "It's slightly annoying that still, after 24 years, you see reports that we only won it because the Americans lost their mast, as though we were handed it on a plate. Everybody's able to do it, but we're Brits, aren't we, so we like a good blow."

He promised to retire from Olympic competition, but his wife, Caroline, who learned of the victory as dawn broke in England, responded: "I'll believe that when it actually happens. Sailing is a huge part of his life." McIntyre returned to a party of Olympic proportions at his local pub; 200 people, including friends from his sailing club in Scotland, Helensburgh, attended. The kinship of the global sailing community was shown when Hal Haenel flew from Los Angeles to attend Vaile's wedding in February 1989. McIntyre and Vaile have an on-going commitment – to meet on Sept 27 each year – and last summer they sailed together for the first time in 18 years.

Despite his spur-of-the-moment vow, McIntyre was keen to reunite with Vaile for a title defence in 1992, but reflects sadly: "We were in the middle of another damn big recession and no one would give us any money." He agreed to become chairman of the Royal Yachting Association's Olympic steering committee instead. "One of the reasons for doing it," he explains, "was to try to make sure that sailors got the support which they needed to compete and not be left high and dry like we were."

Both his daughters are keen sailors. The younger of the two, Eilidh, is in the Olympic development squad. Gemma crewed her father to second place in the Flying 15 World Championships at their home club, Hayling Island, last summer – "quite good for an old guy and his daughter". Vaile has worked for the sports marketing company, Matchtight, since 1994 and, in his capacity as president of Bob Skeleton, watched with pride as Amy Williams won a rare winter Olympics gold medal for Britain in 2010.

Oct 1: Men's hockey, Ian Taylor, Veryan Pappin, Paul Barber, David Faulkner, Steve Martin, Jon Potter, Martyn Grimley, Russell Garcia, Richard Dodds, Robert Clift, Richard Leman, Jimmy Kirkwood, Imran Sherwani, Sean Kerly, Steve Batchelor, Kulbir Bhaura

THEY could be forgiven for what midfield player Richard Leman described as "probably the worst ever rendition of the National Anthem". They could also be forgiven for polishing off the Hyatt Regency's entire champagne supply – 187 bottles – that night. The British hockey team's victory in Seoul was one of the last great success stories of the amateur era.

Leman was one of nine players in the 16-man squad who had tasted the possibilities by bringing home bronze medals from the Los Angeles Games in 1984. Only three months earlier, they were wondering if a British hockey team would ever participate in the Olympics again, yet alone finish on the podium: they had not taken part since 1972. In 1976, the squad got as far as Heathrow Airport before discovering that they would not, after all, be drafted into the tournament when Kenya joined the African boycott. In 1980, the hockey authorities cow-towed to the Government by opting out of the Moscow Games.

Britain were in familiar territory in 1984, the first reserves in an untidy qualification process before the USSR's tit-for-tat boycott gave them a reprieve. They inherited the Soviets' seeding, seventh, and had just three months to prepare. Two relatively simple matches eased them into the tournament and they won all five group games before losing to West Germany in the semi-final.

Leman recalls that team manager Roger Self, "the Brian Clough of hockey", had an unconventional way of stirring the passions before the third-place play-off match against Australia, which they won 3-2. "You were never quite sure the way the wind was going to be blowing with Roger," says Leman. "In the team meeting before the bronze medal game, he did a character assassination of every member of the team, taking us all down a peg. Mark Precious got up before the end of the meeting and said, 'Blow you, Mr Self, we're going out there.' It was exactly the way he wanted it. He didn't do it by the book, he did it his own way." Self, an insurance broker by profession, was destined to be a star performer in Seoul, as prickly and unpredictable with the press as he was with the players.

The foundations for Seoul were now laid and the players who had shone in Los Angeles formed the nucleus of the England team who finished as runners-up to Australia in the 1986 World Cup, which was held in London to mark the centenary of the Hockey Association. "It reinforced what had happened in Los Angeles," says Leman. "We were seeded second for Seoul, which shows just how far we'd gone in the four years, from being 13th and not even going to the Olympics to a side ranked second in the world. The Seoul Games were completely different in the way we approached them and the pressures were different as well. From being no-hopers, now we were expected to win the silver medal."

The average age of the British squad in Seoul was 27 – at 18, Russell Garcia was six years younger than any of his team-mates. They could not afford the luxury of a three-month training camp to prepare; most had to fit in solitary weekday training sessions around their jobs. The captain, Richard Dodds, had delayed taking up a new position as a surgeon, while striker Sean Kerly quit his job as a sports equipment buyer for Next when they refused to allow him five months' unpaid leave.

Out of adversity came a shared sense of purpose and boundless solidarity. "If you were to write down the 16 names on a piece of paper," says Leman, "you'd see that each of us was in a different place. Having to make individual arrangements in our own lives, putting various things on pause, taking the financial sacrifice or just saying, I'm not going to do this until next year. We all got on so well as a group, on and off the field. There was such camaraderie that it didn't feel like a sacrifice. We were enjoying it so much."

Two weeks before the Games began, the British squad set off for Hong Kong, leaving behind family, media commitments and what Leman calls "the whole Olympic bubble". He remembers that there was an intense nervous energy just below the surface. "We were practically hitting each other on the practice field. We'd been waiting and waiting and waiting and now everyone just wanted to get on and play. It was like a corked bottle."

After settling in the athletes' village and enjoying goalkeeper Ian Taylor's appearance as flag-bearer at the opening ceremony, they became aware that their Olympic adventure was attracting unparalleled media interest. The handful of specialist hockey writers was supplemented by rank-and-file reporters, as well as Fleet Street heavyweights like the *Daily Mail*'s Ian Wooldridge. If they didn't know before, they were soon aware that Roger Self was 'good copy'.

He was quickly into his provocative stride after the British team had let slip a 2-0 lead in their opening match to draw 2-2 against a Korean team who had been put together from scratch when the Games were awarded to Seoul. It could have been even worse: the Koreans had a goal disallowed just before the end when an umpire ruled that the ball had not been stopped dead, as the rules then demanded, at a short corner. A spat between Kerly and Self hardly added to the sense of well-being in the British camp.

> **'Our game isn't about cash. Hockey isn't ready for that sort of thing yet'**

Afterwards, Self was asked if he had heard that the Soviet players would pick up bonuses of £12,000 each if they won the gold medal. He looked shocked, said it was news to him and added: "What the hell. If I could have guaranteed Britain's players £12,000 for winning that match alone they couldn't have played their guts out any harder. Our game isn't about cash. Hockey isn't ready for that sort of thing yet." So, what about the result, Roger? "We're not happy about it, but my players aren't happy about having microphones shoved under their noses all the time either. We're all voluntary performers, you know. We're in the game for the love of it. Just leave us alone for a bit."

The press were there for the long haul, however, gripped by a story which began on the second day of the Games and ended on the penultimate day. The theme was one of gathering momentum, though a 2-1 defeat by West Germany in the third match, when they felt aggrieved to have a penalty stroke awarded against them, was not part of the game plan. Paul Barber, Britain's penalty corner specialist, scored in all five group games, including one in the 3-0 win over India which clinched their place in the semi-finals.

They were watched by Princess Anne, whose presence gave coach David Whitaker a Self-style opportunity to jab the press in the ribs. "The great thing about having that lady here," he said, "is that she doesn't ask any damned stupid questions. She's been through it all herself. She knows the pressures. We really appreciate that." The British team were also grateful for the support of a lively throng of flag-waving supporters who bantered with the players after matches.

The semi-final against Australia, who won all their group matches, was a rousing affair described by Leman as the best game he ever played in. A 2-0 lead, courtesy of goals from Kerly, was wiped out by Australia, who then pressed hard for the winner. Kerly remembered the "dreadful prospect" of extra time in sapping heat before, with less than a minute and a half left, he played a one-two with Imran Sherwani to net the winner. "I was too exhausted to reach it with an authentic shot," said Kerly, "so I lunged at the ball. It was half a dive and half a belly flop." Leman recalls: "It was a brilliant moment. When you come away from a game like that, you think that's what all the training has been for."

Britain were able to put out their all-English, first-choice team in the final. The West Germans, critically, were without their centre forward, Stefan Blöcher, who was hit between the eyes by a goalbound shot in the semi-final win over Holland. Self, varying his motivational tactics, had challenged the British players to admit that they had achieved nothing simply by reaching the final. They responded with a performance, in front of a crowd of 12,000 in the Seongnam Stadium, which made the Germans look ponderous and predictable.

Kerly set up Sherwani for the opening goal, midway through the first half, then added a second himself after the break. The pacy Steve Batchelor, who was also of near international standard as a tennis player, eluded a tackle on the right before sending over a cross which Sherwani converted to prompt Barry Davies's memorably dismissive line, "Where were the Germans but, frankly, who cares?" on the BBC commentary.

Germany pulled a goal back 10 minutes from the end, but in the final few seconds Britain were able to bring on the two players previously unused in the tournament, reserve goalkeeper Veryan Pappin and Steve Martin, ensuring that they, too, received gold medals. It was the first time since 1920 that Britain had won the title. There was barely time for the players to gather breath before the medal ceremony. Leman remembers the "pickle of emotions" as he stood on the rostrum. "We all set goals in our lives, but you never know whether you're going to get there."

As ever, Roger Self had the antidote for any overdose of romanti-cism: "We're amateur," he said. "We're so amateur that the first people

I'd like to thank are the employers of so many players who backed their men and gave them time off to train. They were our true sponsors at the Olympics." He was asked, inevitably, whether they might do it differently in the future. "Why, because we have done well here, should people start talking about hockey as an industry? Why should we start thinking about setting up professional circuses which could collapse in a couple of years?"

Euphoria merged into an alcoholic haze – most of the players had been on the wagon for the previous three months – as the champagne flowed in downtown Seoul. The party atmosphere continued on the flight back to London, where the players finally appreciated how their success had grabbed the nation's attention. They were chosen as team of the year at the BBC's Sports Personality awards and the captain, Richard Dodds, was made an MBE in the New Year's Honours.

Kerly flirted with wider celebrity for a few months, but he and British hockey were destined to resume their place among the sporting have-nots. He was one of six players from the 1988 squad who were picked again in 1992, when Britain finished sixth; they have been no

WHERE ARE THEY NOW

1	Ian Taylor	GK	Somerset	Sports stadium consultant
2	Veryan Pappin	GK	Oman	Runs activity company
3	Paul Barber	Defender	Bath	Works in construction business
4	David Faulkner	Defender	Hampshire	Performance director England/GB Hockey
5	Steve Martin	Defender	Belfast	CEO Irish Olympic Committee
6	Jon Potter	Defender	Connecticut, USA	Partner in consultancy
7	Martyn Grimley	Defender	Cheshire	Partner in wealth management company
8	Russell Garcia	Defender	Germany	Hockey coach
9	Richard Dodds	Midfield	Berkshire	Surgeon
10	Robert Clift	Midfield	Hertfordshire	Banker
11	Richard Leman	Midfield	Sussex	President GB hockey, Owner of recruitment companies
12	Jimmy Kirkwood	Midfield	Belfast	Banker
13	Imran Sherwani	Forward	Birmingham	Teacher
14	Sean Kerly	Forward	Kent	Owner of marketing consultancy
15	Steve Batchelor	Forward	Surrey	Teacher/Coach
16	Kulbir Bhaura	Forward	Middlesex	Sports shop owner

higher than fifth since. There were brief hopes that the newly launched National League might attract significant crowds – 3,000 turned up for Southgate's opening match – but the interest soon dwindled.

Richard Leman, who succeeded Roger Self as president of Great Britain Hockey in 2007, admits that he still hears accusations of 'missed opportunity', but is adamant that the sport can plead not guilty. "The National League came off the back of it, which was good for the sport," he says, "but there wasn't much else you could do." He remembers the 1988 side as "a group of very good players who happened to come together at the same time. It wasn't about any particular system, it was about a combination of expertise, commitment and skill. The starting eleven were all brilliant at doing something."

Reunions have been held every five years and Leman was reminded last autumn, when 13 of the 16 players attended the BOA's fund-raising ball, that the bond of shared experience and achievement is unbreakable. "We were straight back taking the mickey out of each other as though it were 25 years ago," he says.

1992

July 29: Individual pursuit cycling, Chris Boardman

TALENT and technology have rarely combined to more telling effect. When Chris Boardman sped to victory on his revolutionary Lotus bike in the 4,000m individual pursuit in Barcelona, the sporting world looked on in astonishment. It was like some dreamy merger between science fiction and reality.

It is easy to down-play Boardman's part in the enterprise. He was 23; the career high points prior to Barcelona were three bronze medals from team events at the Commonwealth Games. He was 5ft 8in and weighed 10 stone, significantly shorter and slighter than the typical pursuiter. Crucially, though, Boardman was a man with a plan and the determination to see it through. His forensic attention to detail, which earned him the nickname 'the professor', guaranteed that everything which could be monitored was monitored. His coach, Peter Keen, who became British Cycling's first performance director after the Atlanta Games, was similarly driven and meticulous.

The accelerator pedal was provided by Mike Burrows, a maverick designer whose idea of a 60th birthday celebration was to cycle from London to Manchester and back in a day. Burrows dreamt up the concept for the Windcheetah in the mid-Eighties (by complete coincidence, Boardman tried out the prototype as a 16-year-old in 1985), but the indifference of British manufacturers and a competition ban on monocoque bikes persuaded him to shelve the project in 1987. The world governing body, the UCI, relaxed their regulations in 1991 and, in Lotus Engineering, Burrows found willing partners based only a few miles from his Norwich home.

Lotus acquired the rights in February 1992 and their own, longer-distance time trial – the five months available before the start of the

Olympic Games – was under way. Boardman put the bike through its paces for the first time in April, when it was being tested extensively in wind tunnels. Theory was translated into confirmatory practice when Bryan Steel, who rode in the team pursuit in Barcelona, took five seconds off his best time for two kilometres at the Saffron Lane track in Leicester. It appeared to bear out Burrows's contention that the Lotus Sport 108 was worth as much as 10 seconds over five kilometres, though Boardman estimated, on reflection, that the advantage was no more than three seconds. He adapted his riding technique to the 'superman' position, his lower arms resting on the handlebars, and dipped under the world best time for 4,000m in training.

The body specifications of the new bike were described as "advanced composite monocoque with minimum-drag aerodynamic cross-sections, formed with unidirectional and stitched high-strength carbon fibre in an epoxy resin matrix". On a less prosaic level, the black and gold bike presented to Boardman on the eve of the British team's departure for Barcelona was a sleekly splendid piece of engineering. Richard Hill, the head of design, said every part of the Lotus Sport was like an aircraft wing, working "with the wind rather than against it".

"I knew the bike had potential," Boardman said, "but I didn't know what the rest of the world was going to do." He did know that three days in the Horta Velodrome would shape the rest of his life and, with or without a technological leg-up, he had given himself the best chance to succeed. "I had to know if I was good enough. Not knowing would have been awful," he reflected later. Boardman, whose telephone engineer father, Keith, came close to selection for the Tokyo Olympics as a time trialist, gave up work as a cabinet maker to become a full-time sportsman. Since he was ineligible for the dole he relied on his wife, Sally, to claim benefit for him. At the time of the Barcelona Games, the couple had two children, aged three and one, and lived in a terraced house in Hoylake, on the Wirral. "The family gives me incentive," Boardman said. "When the kids start crying I'm on my bike."

The Proto III was completed and flown out to Barcelona only three days before the start of the individual pursuit; it was clear, from his first ride, that Boardman and the Lotus were an unbeatable combination. He lopped more than three-and-a-half seconds off the world record in the qualifying round and went three seconds quicker again to reach the semi-finals. There was a day's gap before the last two rounds, enough time for Boardman (and bike) to achieve overnight celebrity and for his rivals to come to terms with the new order. His wife made a spur-of-the-moment decision to fly out to Barcelona and had to pay a tout £30 for a ticket to get into the cycling arena. "It's the most important day of our lives and you don't fly all this way and quibble over a few extra pounds," she said.

Boardman eased through his semi-final and into a gold medal match with the German, Jens Lehmann, who had won the world title the previous year on a specially developed carbon fibre bike. There was only an hour and a half between the two races and, while Lehmann limbered up on the track, Boardman was tucked away in the bike shed, listening to Tears for Fears' *Greatest Hits* and quiet words of encouragement from Peter Keen and team psychologist John Syer. Lehmann was demolished and demoralised in the final as Boardman built such a lead that he caught the German with a lap remaining. Lehmann charitably conceded that he had been beaten by the man rather than the machine. Boardman could afford to take a more realistic view. "The bike was ob-viously a significant advantage, otherwise I wouldn't be using it," he said. "It could have made the difference between a gold and a bronze."

> **'It's the most important day of our lives and you don't fly all this way and quibble over a few extra pounds'**

He admitted that much had changed since the 1991 World Champ-ionships. "I did a time there that I thought would win but someone moved the goalposts," Boardman reflected, in clear reference to the technological advances made by the German team. "I wondered whether to carry on because of my young family. But now I have moved the goalposts." He also contrasted his tiredness in Stuttgart the previous year to his vitality in Barcelona (the result, in part, of enforced recuperation after a bad fall in France, when he dislocated a bone in his shoulder). In 1990 he had undergone a five-and-a-half hour operation on a twisted bowel.

Sally confessed afterwards that she had been so nervous she thought she would faint. Her husband knew the feeling. "From the point of view of nerves it was the worst three days of my life," he said later. "I was almost physically sick on the day of the final. Cycling is a very sick sport." He also revealed that he had suffered panic attacks between the qualifying round and final. Four months on, Boardman was still dipping his toes tentatively into the celebrity pool; he invested in a mobile phone and had 'Olympic gold medallist' business cards printed up. He joked: "The bike's got a busier diary than I have." The two had been reunited a few weeks after the Olympics, slicing eight seconds off the world amateur record for five kilometres.

Lotus, who ploughed an estimated £500,000 into developing the Olympic pursuit bike, were criticised for failing to exploit all the commercial possibilities. A handful of replicas were sold for £15,000 apiece and the gold medal winning bike fetched a record £27,000 at auction in 1997. At the start of 1993, Lotus began work on a time trials model, the 110, which was used for the first time by the Dutch rider, Erik Breukink, in the Tour de France prologue. Shortly after his Olympic victory, Boardman had described the Tour as "absolutely hideous", adding: "Physically I'm suited to the Tour de France. Mentally I'm not." He began to revise his opinion when he set a prologue record at the start of the Tour in 1994, beating the legendary Miguel Indurain by 15 seconds and becoming the first Briton since Tommy Simpson in 1962 to wear the race leader's yellow jersey. Boardman matched the feat in 1997 and again in 1998, when the Tour began in the Republic of Ireland, though he crashed out on the second stage after careering into a stone wall.

Boardman, who had taken advantage of the new liberalism in cycling by turning professional in 1993 (and winning his debut race) was determined to diversify. He and the Scot, Graeme Obree, both beat the world hour record – Boardman maximised publicity for his attempt in Bordeaux by synchronising it to the arrival of the Tour de France – and in 1994 Boardman won the individual pursuit and time trial at the World Championships in Sicily. He was a victim of his own priorities in 1996, putting the Tour de France before his pursuit defence in Atlanta and falling short of his own expectations in both. Boardman was 39th in the overall classifications for the Tour, which finished only three days before the start of the Olympic pursuit. He competed in the individual time trial instead, fading in the heat to take the bronze medal behind Indurain.

The frustrations were taken out on his rivals in the World Championships in Manchester a month later, when Boardman reduced the world record to a scarcely believable 4min 11.114sec. The rider he beat in the final, Italy's Andrea Collinelli, had recorded a time almost 10 seconds slower to win in Atlanta. The 'superman' position was outlawed soon after Boardman's Manchester masterclass ride and his record remained intact until beaten by the Australian, Jack Bobridge, early last year.

Boardman's Manchester encore was to break the hour record again, but in 1998 he was diagnosed with a form of osteoporosis. He delayed receiving drug-based treatment until he had competed in one last Olympic Games, finishing 11th in the time trial before making a final assault on the hour record for a traditional bike, set by Eddy Merckx in 1972. Boardman's distance of 49.444 kilometres was just 10 metres further than that managed by the great Belgian.

There has been no let-up in Boardman's post-competitive schedule: he has commentated for the BBC, ITV and Eurosport and set up a manufacturing company, Boardman Bikes, in 2004. He has also played a mentoring role in helping to bring through the next generation of Olympic cyclists, most notably the multiple gold medallist, Bradley Wiggins, who has admitted that there were "considerable teething problems" in their relationship. Boardman, he wrote, "is very organised and disciplined and has an objective and remorseless approach to dealing with a problem".

Boardman's victory in Barcelona may have inspired Wiggins but, according to Peter Keen, lessons had still to be learned. Keen said: "He was just another one-off success. Leave no ropes. Leave no trail. There was no system so there was no legacy."

Aug 1: Coxless pairs, Steve Redgrave, Matthew Pinsent

STEVE REDGRAVE made his first 'retirement' speech after finishing third in the coxed pairs at the Seoul Games; it was really just a cry for help. Reports contrasted the poverty of Redgrave and Andy Holmes with the Abbagnale brothers' reward from the Italian federation – £20,000 apiece – for winning the coxed event. "This defeat might drive me on," said Redgrave, "but I doubt it. My life has been devoted to rowing for more than 10 years. But now I am married it is about time to start a career. I already have some business ideas to develop. To succeed at the top level you must devote yourself full time." Cox Pat Sweeney lent his endorsement, saying: "Holmes and Redgrave have had to make unreasonable financial sacrifices to win medals for Britain."

On reflection, Redgrave decided that he did not want to do anything else and committed to another four-year cycle. He insisted that his decision to recruit a new partner was purely based on Holmes's indication that he would only row for one more year before retiring. Redgrave broke the news to Holmes at the Motor Show in

Birmingham; they never spoke again. Early in 1989, when Redgrave had begun rowing with Simon Berrisford, Holmes tried to recruit 18-year-old Matthew Pinsent as his new pairs partner. He got as far as leaving a brief message on the answering machine at Pinsent's home. Sensing the question that Holmes wanted to ask, Pinsent delayed returning the call and discovered soon afterwards that Holmes had teamed up with the stroke of the Olympic eight, Nick Burfitt, in a short-lived partnership.

Holmes turned his back on rowing soon afterwards. The medals, trophies and mementoes were thrown into a suitcase which was then consigned to the loft. He set up a furniture removal company, bought a drum kit and renovated a house in Banyoles, the venue for the rowing events at the 1992 Olympics in Barcelona. He was in residence (oblivious to the result) when Redgrave and Pinsent won the pairs gold medal. In 1996 Holmes refused to appear when Redgrave was featured on *This Is Your Life*, but eventually he forgave rowing, if not his former partner. Holmes contracted Weil's disease, a water-borne infection, while competing in a sculling marathon in Boston, Lincolnshire, and died in October 2010, aged 51. His fifth child had been born only a month earlier.

Pinsent, who described Holmes as "one of the few things Steve and I didn't talk about", had his own view of the divorce. "In future years I held the position that it is inexcusable to fall out with someone with whom you have won an Olympic gold medal. You don't have to like them, you can disagree with them on lots of things. But the bond that is created in competition at that level is like a family one – whatever happens you are part of a team. But obviously Steve felt differently and I didn't see it as part of my job to educate him on this."

Redgrave struggled for motivation in 1989 and he and Berrisford were beaten into second place at the World Championships. The door of opportunity opened for Pinsent when Berrisford was hit by a sculling boat in training, injuring his back. Pinsent, the son of a vicar, was following the classical route into rowing – Eton and Oxford – and had teamed up with Tim Foster, another future Olympic crewmate, to win the coxless pairs at the Junior World Championships in 1988. Pinsent and Redgrave made their regatta debut together in an eight at Lucerne and, despite an eight-year age gap, quickly struck up a rapport which had been so obviously missing from Redgrave's relationship with Holmes. They also shared a fiercely competitive streak which manifested itself in anything from amusement arcade games to golf.

Steve and Ann Redgrave asked Pinsent to be godfather of their first child, Natalie, who was born in 1991. "You don't do that if you feel the other person is just passing through your life," Redgrave wrote in 2001. "I felt that whatever happened to our futures in rowing, we'd still be friends after we retired. I'm still sure that will be the case."

Alchemy in a rowing boat took longer to achieve. Redgrave and Pinsent were confirmed as the pair for the World Championships but finished third and dispirited. Redgrave, in particular, was grateful to be given a fresh perspective on the sport by the arrival of the East German coach, Jürgen Grobler, at the start of 1991. Women's crews coached by Grobler had claimed five Olympic gold medals, and though his command of English was initially almost non-existent he quickly imposed his quiet authority. Grobler introduced weight-training and to Redgrave's consternation, initially anyway, swapped the pair over so that Pinsent was stroking the boat.

They dominated the major regattas in 1991 and also won at the World Championships in Vienna, where they not only broke the world record but were a second quicker than the time which Grobler had already predicted would be needed to win in Barcelona. The sense of well-being was shattered early in the New Year when Redgrave picked up a debilitating stomach bug on a training camp in South Africa. As the start of the season approached he was still suffering from persistent diarrhoea and he and Pinsent were unexpectedly defeated by Jonny and Greg Searle at the Easter trials in Nottingham. Stomach cramps simply added to Redgrave's discomfort. He underwent a series of tests before discovering that he had ulcerative colitis, inflammation of the colon.

Redgrave continued to train through the discomfort while medication took effect and was back at maximum efficiency when the British team set out for their pre-Barcelona training camps in the Austrian Alps and Italy. He was asked to carry the British flag at the opening ceremony and, inspired by the example of a Soviet weightlifter in Moscow, insisted on holding the flag in one hand as he paraded in front of 85,000 people.

On the eve of the Games, Redgrave was asked, in obvious cryptic reference to Andy Holmes, whether better relations produced better results. "You can hate each other or you can be quite fond of each other. It does not make any difference," he insisted. The outcome was certainly the same in Barcelona, where he and Pinsent put together three immaculate performances to win the gold medal. They led the final for all but the first 200 metres and were almost five seconds clear of the German pair at the end.

Redgrave's place in the pantheon of great Olympic achievers was confirmed. He joined water polo players Paul Radmilovic and Charles Smith as the only Britons to win gold medals at three successive Games and became the first British rower since Jack Beresford to win titles at three Olympics. Pinsent, who had taken a year's sabbatical from Oxford to prepare for the Games, was no longer Redgrave's junior partner; it was now a marriage of equals. He celebrated his new-found status with a trip to the launderette in the Olympic village.

Money, as ever, was mentioned at the press conference. Alan Fraser wrote in the *Daily Mail*: "Steve Redgrave, by virtue of his record in such a physically demanding sport, deserves to be considered one of the greatest athletes in Britain. Yet, Redgrave will not be in Atlanta, never mind wherever in 2000, if a sponsor does not come riding over the horizon. This day, four years ago, in the aftermath of victory in Seoul, sponsorship was in place for Barcelona. A £35,000 per year agreement is about to end with nothing ready to take its place. 'We basically need to get money or we can't afford to do the training or get the equipment to stay out there with the other countries.'"

Grobler let his charges off the leash for a few weeks after Barcelona. He and Pinsent joined Redgrave on the open-topped bus which paraded through Marlow, while Pinsent felt that he had joined the ranks of true sporting celebrities when he was asked to appear on *Question of Sport*. On a more mundane level, there were geography finals to prepare for at St Catherine's College. As Oxford president, Pinsent suffered one of his less memorable days in a boat when Cambridge inflicted an ignominious Boat Race defeat in 1993.

Redgrave was reminded of his good fortune, in being able to compete in Barcelona, when colitis symptoms returned soon afterwards. Financial worries eased in 1993 when he and Pinsent were offered £25,000 a year by the insurance company ManuLife. The deal kept them afloat, though not much more, through to Atlanta. By a quirk of the system, the personal sponsorship made them ineligible for Lottery funding.

Aug 1: 100m, Linford Christie

HOW does Linford Christie deserve to be remembered? As the athlete who re-defined sprinting durability – he won the Olympic 100m title at the age of 32 and broke 10 seconds for the last time when he was 35 – or for the stigma of failed drugs tests?

He will maintain his innocence until his dying breath, but the records show that he tested positive for pseudoephedrine during the Seoul Olympics in 1988. Christie blamed ginseng tea and was given the benefit of the doubt. He was 39 and in semi-retirement when he was up before the beaks again. This time the steroid nandrolone was detected when he was tested at an indoor meeting in Dortmund, Germany. Christie was cleared of wrongdoing by UK Athletics but the world governing body, the IAAF, confirmed their original two-year ban.

Accept both verdicts and you still have someone who was both very proficient at passing drug tests for the majority of his career and happy to go the extra evangelical mile, sporting T-shirts emblazoned with '100 per cent natural'. Christie's transformation from journeyman athlete to Britain's greatest ever sprinter *was* dramatically quick, but he was 24 before he knuckled down to his first winter of serious training.

Seventeen years earlier he had been reunited with his parents, who moved from Jamaica to England soon after his birth in 1960. Christie was initially brought up by his grandmother in Kingston and found it difficult to come to terms with the lack of discipline and respect which he found in his new home, west London. Respect, in all its forms, continued to preoccupy Christie; the point was driven home when he gave his management company the name Nuff Respect.

Christie's parents, James and Mabel, viewed sport as the refuge of the idle, but Linford enjoyed competing, if not yet training (an evening of dominoes at the local café was his drug of choice). He ran the 200m in the England Schools Championships in 1979 and, after moving into the senior ranks, twice broke the British indoor record over the same distance. Even when he moved from London Irish to Thames Valley Harriers, and came under the scrutiny of his long-time coach, Ron Roddan, Christie's half-hearted approach to athletics persisted. He felt he deserved a relay place at the Los Angeles Olympics but was not selected. Soon afterwards he received an ultimatum letter from Roddan: train properly or stop wasting my time.

Christie, who had done a series of clerical jobs after leaving school, finally decided to become a full-time athlete. He and his girlfriend, Mandy Miller, had moved into a rented one-bedroom flat the previous year and her receptionist's income just about sustained them. Christie's new-found dedication to athletics began to translate into performances: he won his first title of note, the 200m at the European

Indoor Championships in Madrid, in February 1986. Four months later he was back in Madrid to run an extraordinary British record of 10.04sec in the 100m; Christie had arrived and so had the cynics (how could anyone improve that much without…?) Marginally slower times earned him the silver medal behind Ben Johnson in the 1986 Commonwealth Games and, a few weeks later, the gold at the European Championships.

In 1987, Christie nicked a hundredth of a second from his British record, but Johnson appeared to have taken the 100m to a new level when he won the World Championships in 9.83sec. Christie, already wary of the press, grew another protective skin when he arrived in Seoul the following September to discover that he was being falsely accused of having an affair with the reigning Olympic javelin champion, Tessa Sanderson.

Christie eased through the rounds in the 100m and in a final dominated by Johnson became the first European to run below 10 seconds. He was promoted from third to second when Johnson was disqualified in the highest-profile drugs scandal to hit the Olympics. Christie confessed that he cried when he heard the news and he was in tears again a few days later when his own positive test, taken after a heat in the 200m, was revealed. He ran another British record, 20.09sec, to finish fourth in the final and also anchored the relay team to a silver medal, just nine hundredths of a second behind the Soviet Union.

The 'lunch box' references were another stick with which to beat the press, but Christie was happy enough to showcase his impressive physique in a flamboyant array of body suits in the early Nineties. He wrote in his autobiography: "The crowd no longer saw eight black guys who looked the same. Now they knew which one was Linford Christie. I became more and more outrageous. I would wear cutouts – suits with big holes in the side – penguin suits, anything."

The media also bought into a posturing rivalry between Christie and the emerging American sprinter, Leroy Burrell, who claimed the world record for the 100m when he ran 9.90sec in June 1991. Christie had won both the Commonwealth and European titles the previous year, but he was forced to re-assess his place in the world order when, despite lowering his British record to 9.92sec, he finished fourth in the Tokyo World Championships. He took umbrage at negative press coverage and threatened to retire; Roddan persuaded him to keep going, until Barcelona at least.

Christie's prospects brightened considerably when Carl Lewis, the winner in Tokyo, failed to qualify for the American team in the 100m, and he shrugged off the grim facilities – "the village was terrible and the accommodation even worse" – to improve round by round. Another American threat, in the shape of Mark Witherspoon, was removed when he snapped an Achilles tendon in the semi-finals. Burrell, who had edged Christie to reach the final, was inhibited after a false start, but the Briton showed statue-like composure as he waited for the gun; he imagined his lane was a tunnel, "with everything on either side a blur". He made a good start and knew at 60 metres that the gold medal was his; the winning time was 9.96sec. Christie replaced Allan Wells as the oldest winner of the Olympic title and even cheered up the Wembley crowd who had just been told that Michael Jackson was cancelling his London concert that evening because of a virus. Ian Wooldridge wrote in the *Daily Mail*:

> There are ways and ways of getting your own back on a stifling summer's night. One is to go out and beat up an inner city. Another is to go to the Olympic Games and smash the world in the 100m. Thank God that Linford Christie chose the latter. It is no secret that as a young black man from the Caribbean he did not find London's streets paved with equality. Hopefully his riposte will prove inspirational to others who feel similarly crushed. It was a run powered as much by maniacal determination as muscle and finely tuned technique. The face was contorted, the concentration so intense that I don't think he once blinked.

Christie and hurdler Colin Jackson set up the management company, Nuff Respect, immediately after returning from Barcelona. The company continues to flourish, but the friendship and business arrangement fractured. In 1993 the West London Stadium was renamed in Christie's honour and the what-might-have-been debate sparked by Lewis's absence in Barcelona finally resulted in a lucrative July showdown at Gateshead; Christie won and was rewarded with a kiss from Lewis. The outcome was the same a few weeks later when Christie completed his full set of major titles by winning the World Championship 100m in Stuttgart. His time, 9.87sec, was only a hundredth of a second slower than Lewis's world record and remains the best by a Briton.

He picked up the BBC Sports Personality of the Year award just before Christmas and was still running well enough at the start of 1995 to set a world indoor record for the 200m of 20.25sec in Liévin, France. Christie had enjoyed remarkable luck with injuries, but a hamstring strain troubled him both before and during the World Championships in Gothenburg that summer. He also had to deal with questions about his son, Merric, one of three children outside his relationship with Mandy Miller. Merric had just become a father, and Christie a 35-year-old grandfather.

He posted impressively quick times to reach the Olympic final in Atlanta, but Christie's title defence ended in high controversy when he was disqualified for two false starts. He claimed that the second infringement was a false reading and refused to leave the track; seven minutes passed before the race could begin. Christie still demanded his share of the limelight, saluting the crowd like a champion when the real winner, Donovan Bailey, was pulling up after setting a world record of 9.84sec. "I don't stop being the world's best athlete because I lost one race," claimed Christie. "You saw the reaction of the crowd: they booed the judges. They knew they'd been robbed of a better race than the one they saw. I'm still the people's champion so I did my little bit down the home straight." The *Daily Telegraph* columnist, Robert Philip, described Christie's bare-chested 'victory' parade as "the most cringingly embarrassing moment of the highly embarrassing Olympiad for the once-great British team". American sprinter Mike Marsh called Christie "grossly immature".

Christie was denied a last hurrah in the sprint relay after a fumbled handover between Darren Braithwaite and Darren Campbell. For the first time in his career Christie had come away from a major championship without a medal. He stopped competing the following year, but coached both Campbell and Katharine Merry to Olympic medals in Sydney (he was dropped from the BBC's commentary team in 2000 after the IAAF's ban was upheld). Over the past few years Christie has branched out into more diverse projects, including gardening columns and an appearance on *I'm A Celebrity: Get Me Out Of Here*.

He has seen no reason to alter the view expressed in his 1996 autobiography: "If you are black and complain the first thing they say is that you have a chip on your shoulder." Derek Redmond, also black, and a former-teammate, lampooned the opinion with this observation of Christie: "He is a perfectly balanced athlete: he has a chip on both shoulders."

Aug 2: Coxed pairs, Jonny Searle, Greg Searle, Garry Herbert (cox)

NO ONE applauded more loudly than 15-year-old Jonny Searle when his history master, Martin Cross, stood up in assembly to show the coxed fours gold medal he had won in Los Angeles. "I felt this intense pride," Searle later recalled, "that I actually knew somebody who had won the highest honour in sport and I suppose, from that moment on, I had a desire to do the same."

The ambition was fulfilled in 1992, when Searle and his younger brother, Greg, both products of Hampton School, in south west London, trampled on the victory parade of rather more exalted siblings, Giuseppe and Carmine Abbagnale. The Italians had established themselves as one of rowing's all-time great combinations, winning the Olympic title in 1984 and 1988 and seven World Championship gold medals. They had not been beaten since 1986.

The day was brimful of emotions for Cross, who watched with almost paternal anxiety, knowing that two hours later he would be lining up in the eights final, his fourth and last Olympic appearance. Cross set the scene for the Searles' race in his book, *Olympic Obsession*. He wrote of Jonny: "I'd known him for 11 years and watched him grow from the cocky little schoolboy who sat at the front of my history classes, through his first awkward strokes in a boat, to a potential Olympic champion." As early as 1988, Greg Searle, bigger and stronger than his brother, had been touted as the next Steve Redgrave; he assured Cross that he would be *better* than Redgrave. Even the Searles' cox, Garry Herbert, had been inspired by Cross's example. He, too, had been a pupil at Cardinal Vaughan School in Kensington, and was drawn to rowing by a picture of the winning four in Los Angeles which hung in the school lobby.

The three-year age gap between the Searle brothers meant that their junior careers unfolded separately. Jonny figured in three successive winning Oxford crews in the Boat Race (the last in company with Matthew Pinsent) between 1988 and 1990. Greg was such a precocious talent that he joined his brother in the British eight which finished fourth in the 1990 World Championships. He also became the first British rower to compete in the senior and junior World Championships in the same year. The eight, featuring not just the Searles but also Cross, and coxed by Herbert, improved to a bronze in Vienna in 1991.

An Olympic gold medal was, realistically, out of the reach for the British eight, and the Searles were paired up for Olympic year, bringing them into direct competition with the greats-in-waiting. To give himself a daily reminder of what they were up against, Jonny stuck an unflattering picture of Redgrave and Pinsent on his fridge. The brothers also put their faith in Steve Gunn, their coach at Hampton, who took a sabbatical from his teaching duties.

Jonny admits to a "fierce rivalry" which extended well beyond two men in a boat. Redgrave and Pinsent represented Leander and its elitist traditions; the Searles were attached to the newer, hipper Molesey club. Redgrave and Pinsent were Grobler men; the Searle brothers were independent-minded. Jonny elaborates: "We were the challenger brand. We liked to do things a bit differently. They tended to do a lot of long-distance, low-intensity training and we were a bit more into punchy, racing stuff. We thought that was more useful for us. There was a genuine difference to how we approached things. If they were doing 40 to 50 kilometres a day of low intensity we were probably doing 30. It was more about achieving the level of fitness and the mental state you needed to race. The Molesey guys thought we were good racers; the Leander guys were good trainers."

They duly beat Redgrave and Pinsent at the April trials in Nottingham, but victory came at the cost of a rib injury for Jonny. "I was shouting at them for the last 100 metres," he remembers, "and something got stirred up. Within about a week I had a stress fracture, though at that stage I didn't realise what it was so I carried on racing. It didn't get diagnosed for six weeks."

By the time he was restored to full fitness, the senior pair had been preferred for Barcelona, leaving the Searles to team up once more with Herbert. The latent talent was obvious, but half-a-dozen competitive outings hardly stacked up against the Abbagnales' medal-laden CV. Cross knew, however, that Jonny was a supreme orchestrator. "On the big occasion, like the Olympics," he wrote, "during racing he somehow seemed to come alive. When the pressure was on, he'd become like a demon, an aggressive racing brain combined with an innate ability to motivate his crewmates. This was especially the case in the second half of the races when his crew needed to produce something extra. Jon's gift allowed him to be the catalyst for some incredible performances. Usually the person that Jon was inspiring was his brother, Greg."

They posted Olympic best times to win both their heat and semi-final, and the final unfolded as widely predicted. On the previous evening,

Herbert had told Cross that as long as the British boat was within five seconds of the Abbagnales at 1,000 metres they could make up the gap in the second half of the race. Their advantage was 4.4 seconds and the Searles' acceleration so pronounced that they actually rowed the last 500 metres 4.5 seconds quicker than the Italians.

Herbert, described by Alan Fraser in the *Daily Mail* as "like some floating John the Baptist but with his urgings audible across the Banyoles Lake", screamed his way through the full repertoire of cox-speak: "Do you want to make a little bit of magic for ourselves? Do you want to make a little bit of history? If not now, when? If not you, who?" Jonny Searle also revealed afterwards that they had been inspired by an image planted in their minds by team psychologist Brian Miller: "He told us about a Spanish-American runner who used to imagine he and his opponents sitting round a table, each holding a hand in the flame. He knew he would be the last to pull his out."

Fraser wrote: "The Searles put their hands into the Olympic flame and kept them there longer than any of the opposition." The Abbagnales, who still had a length's advantage going into the last 100 metres, were so stunned that they stopped rowing for the last five strokes. Still on adrenaline overload, Herbert said afterwards: "I wanted them to be prepared to die for us…and they nearly did." Greg Searle admitted: "Everything was going black at the end, but being brothers we both switched into the same autopilot and got moving. There is no one I would rather row with and no one I would trust more than Jonny. We have always been competitive with each other and now it's brilliant to be on the same side." Steve Rider, who was anchoring the BBC's coverage, was heard to say off-mike: "That was unbelievable."

Jonny Searle reflects: "We always knew that they would lead and we would try to catch them. What we didn't know was whether we would be fast enough to catch them or how far away they would get. When I watched the video I was quite surprised at how far behind we got. I remember thinking the night before, I don't know if we're going to win. I knew we might win. I did know that it would be a fantastic race and that we would do our best. I can say that at about 1250 I looked across and they were a long way ahead and I started to get a bit worried. And then Garry was very positive, saying, 'We can catch them all, we can beat them all.' People say, what does a cox do in a race? For a period there he was quite crucial in keeping us engaged in the plan to beat the Abbagnales. It's quite a rush as you see you're catching. We made a massive push at 1250 with a view to stopping them moving away. I would say we won the race at that stage. Instead of moving ahead they were hanging on from about 1250 to 1750 and then they really had nothing left. They just died."

The achievement was put in wider context by Redgrave, who had won his third Olympic gold medal the previous day: "Our race had been all about dominance and control," he said, "but you couldn't beat the Searles' brilliantly judged surge for the line to claim the prize for sheer excitement." Hugh Matheson, who had been in Britain's silver medal winning eight in Montreal, wrote in the *Independent*: "It was as striking a reversal of the old order as any in rowing."

The Searles beamed and Herbert blubbed at the medal ceremony – a cox has rarely stepped so memorably into the limelight. The encore was a repeat victory over the Abbagnales at the 1993 World Championships, but Jonny Searle admits that the Olympic gold medal redefined his relationship with Greg. "The dynamic definitely changed and we started arguing quite a lot. I still had the older brother, I'm always right attitude. He'd had 20 years of me conditioning him to the notion that I was always right. After 1992, when we were both gold medal-

> **'We got in a row one day in training and he jumped out of the boat and swam away. I thought it was quite funny; Garry didn't'**

lists, the relationship was a lot more even. Physically, he was very powerful, so from a rowing point of view he was at least my equal. It was quite tense rowing together. We knew we were annoying each other. We got in a row one day in training and he jumped out of the boat and swam away. I thought it was quite funny; Garry didn't. We had to get the boat back, so our coach jumped in. Steve was an OK rower, but we were all over the place."

Any plans for an Olympic defence were wrecked when the International Rowing Federation, in an effort to accommodate light-weight rowers, cut the coxed pairs from the programme for Atlanta. The Searles were still able to attract a £250,000 sponsorship deal from Andersen Consulting and they formed a coxless four with Rupert Obholzer and Tim Foster. Obholzer was a near contemporary of Jonny Searle at Hampton, a minor public school with a reputation not just for rowing but for fostering an underdog mentality. Herbert trained as a barrister, coxed the eight in Atlanta and tried to keep his emotions in check as a BBC commentator.

The four improved from third at the 1994 World Championships to second the following year, but it was not just Redgrave and Pinsent who were feeling the pressure as the British crews prepared for the start of racing in Atlanta. Pinsent wrote in his excellent book, *A Lifetime In A Race*:

> Tensions were rising all round. That night, Steve wandered over to the four in the garden and mentioned that there was lots of post in the village for them. Jonny Searle replied that it might have been nice if he had brought it back with him and got a fairly tense reply about how Steve wasn't going to be their effing postman. Within seconds they were facing off to each other and Greg Searle and I were trying to calm our respective team-mates, although I certainly wasn't going to step in between the two biggest sets of arms in the rowing world and get my nose broken. Sure enough, it all ended without violence, but the tension between the two boats (never good to begin with) ramped up even further. Not that it made much difference to either of us, but there would be precious little encouragement between the boats on finals day.

Once again the Searles figured in the race of the regatta, but this time (they were last after 500 metres) they left themselves with too much ground to make up in the final stages. Jonny Searle admitted: "We've no one to blame but ourselves. With five strokes to go we knew the gold just wasn't ours and second or third just isn't good enough." In *Olympic Obsession*, Martin Cross likened Searle's "very public display of annoyance on the medal rostrum at Atlanta" to the behaviour of a petulant child.

Greg Searle, mindful of the one discipline which Redgrave had not mastered, sculling, began working with the inspirational New Zealander, Harry Mahon. The four-year plan was geared to winning the single sculls gold medal in Sydney, but early improvement was not maintained and he was eventually paired with Ed Coode in 2000, finishing 0.12sec behind the bronze medal winning Australians in yet another outstanding final. Jonny Searle's chances of competing in a third Olympics had disappeared when he broke an arm in a motorcycle accident earlier in the year.

The younger Searle, who works for Lane 4, the company set up by swimmer Adrian Moorhouse in the mid-Nineties, was employed as a grinder in the America's Cup Challenger Series in 2002. He came out of rowing retirement in 2009, consumed by the ambition of marking the 20th anniversary of the Barcelona win by competing in 2012. Jonny Searle works as legal counsel for the Swedish media company, Modern Times Group.

Aug 5: 400m hurdles, Sally Gunnell

BRUCE LONGDEN framed the suggestion with the care of someone under the critical scrutiny of libel lawyers: "There are ladies from the Eastern European countries you are going to chase forever," he said. "Let's not ask why. Let's change to 400 metres hurdles."

The year was 1988, the Seoul Olympics were looming. Longden was completing a four-year contract as head coach for the Norwegian federation and the athlete he had guided from her school days, Sally Gunnell, had reached a plateau of competence as a sprint hurdler. She had capitalised on a boycott from the African countries to win the Commonwealth title in 1986, three days after her 20th birthday, but her lack of progress was shown the following summer when she clocked 13.01sec on five different occasions. "I always think Bruce had a bigger plan," she reflects. "From quite a young age he knew where I was destined to go."

In the European Championships, Gunnell allowed herself to be spooked in the heats by the "beefy-looking" Bulgarian, Yordanka Donkova. She wrote in her autobiography: "As we settled down on the starting blocks I noticed her hands. They were mutilated: the tips of two of the fingers on each hand were missing. I imagined a dreadful accident, involving some kind of industrial implement in a distant Iron Curtain country. She grunted as she settled on the blocks, a great and terrifying champion beside me." The actual explanation was not quite as alarming – Donkova had lost two fingers on her right hand in an accident when she was five – but she certainly proved the wisdom of Gunnell's change of events. In 1988 Donkova set a world record of 12.21sec, which is still intact, and won the Olympic title.

Gunnell, who was born on the eve of England's World Cup victory in 1966 and grew up on a 300-acre farm in Chigwell, Essex, had shown her adaptability before. Her speciality was the long jump when she joined Essex Ladies and became part of Longden's training group at Crystal Palace. He advised her to take up the pentathlon, which introduced her to hurdling, and she graduated to the heptathlon when it was added to the Olympic programme in 1984. Gunnell finished an agonising seven points short of the qualifying mark for Los Angeles.

She decided to concentrate on the hurdles, which was easily her strongest suit in the pentathlon, and felt liberated. "Once the decision had been made," she wrote, "the heptathlon lifted off me like an old weight that had been holding me down. No more javelin and shot. Best of all, no more high jump!"

Gunnell met her husband-to-be, Jon Bigg, on a trip with the junior England team to Australia at the start of 1985. Bigg was a middle-distance runner and training partner to Steve Ovett; he was also responsible for giving Gunnell a new perspective on training. She believed, initially, that he was pushing himself too hard. His half-joking message to her was: 'Is that all you have to do to be number one hurdler in the country? You could do so much more.' The couple had been going out for three-and-a-half years when, just before the Seoul Olympics, they bought a house together in Brighton.

During the 1988 season Gunnell trained for and competed in both the 100m and 400m hurdles; she also found that the longer distance had a beneficial effect on her performance in the sprint hurdles. She ran a British record of 12.82sec, which would have been good enough for fifth place in the Olympic final, but her rapid improvement over 400m convinced both her and Longden that she had made the right call. She broke the British record six times in the build-up to Seoul and lowered the mark again in her heat, semi-final and final, clocking 54.03sec to finish fifth behind the Australian, Debbie Flintoff-King. Gunnell was less pleased to go out in the semi-finals of the 100m hurdles, but she illustrated that she was no slouch on the flat by helping the British team to sixth place in the 4 x 400m relay final.

Gunnell tasted victory and defeat at the Commonwealth Games in Auckland at the start of 1990. She failed to defend her 100m hurdles title but had the satisfaction of beating Flintoff-King in a relatively slow 400m hurdles final. She was regarded as a clear medal contender for the World Championships in Tokyo the following year, along with the American, Sandra Farmer-Patrick, and the Belarusian, Tatyana Ledovskaya. Despite stuttering badly on her approach to the last hurdle in the final, Gunnell almost managed to overhaul Ledovskaya on the run-in and set a Commonwealth record of 53.16sec.

Influenced by the detailed mental preparation which David Hemery had used to win in Mexico, Gunnell learned to pre-visualise races. She also managed to put a positive slant on her indifferent form in the build-up to Barcelona in 1992, reasoning that Farmer-Patrick had emerged as the obvious favourite to win the gold medal. Gunnell lost twice to the American and had her preparations hampered by a thigh injury. Two weeks of speed work in the most un-exotic of locations, Portsmouth, convinced Gunnell that all was well.

She ran so convincingly in her heat and semi-final, clocking the quickest times in both rounds, that she assumed the mantle of favourite. The final was scheduled for 6.30pm the following day. Gunnell wiled away the hours in the equally hyper company of her room-mate, Jenny Stoute, who had qualified for the semi-finals of the 200m. "Jenny and I were both as high as kites," Gunnell remembered, "and we spent a lot of time laughing, singing silly songs, and shouting at people through the windows. None of this was behaviour which becomes the British team captain, but neither would have been the alternative. We were so nervous that if we hadn't been giggling we would have been crying."

Gunnell was delighted to be drawn in lane three for the final, with both Farmer-Patrick and Ledovskaya outside her. The Belarusian false-started then went off at a manic lick when the race did get under way; Farmer-Patrick was not far behind. Gunnell's greater strength and hurdling fluency brought her level on the final bend. This time she maintained her rhythm and she had three metres in hand on Farmer-Patrick when she crossed the line. "The sound was so loud it was almost a physical presence," she said. "I glanced to the side, where there was a sea of Union Jacks waving crazily. Everyone seemed to be jumping up and down. Everyone was smiling, hurling their arms around. Everyone was looking at me."

Jon Bigg had followed the normal routine by staying at home; he was at work in London on the day before the final when he made a spur-of-the-moment decision to fly out to Barcelona. He was able to watch the race, in company with Gunnell's brother, Paul, from a prime vantage point adjacent to the finish. Her parents, attending major championships for the first time, were by the first bend. Gunnell managed quick embraces as she did her lap of honour and later that night she was properly reunited with Bigg as Des Lynam interviewed her for the BBC.

Gunnell recovered her competitive focus in time to help the British team to a bronze medal in the 4 x 400m relay, but she admits that she found it hard to come to terms with her new-found celebrity. "I became very careful about judging people and their character," she said some years later. "You begin to realise that a lot of people do not have your best interests at heart. They offer you things – right, left and centre. You wonder why they are doing it. Why would someone want to give me a car?"

An early casualty was her part-time job as a research assistant with the London accountancy firm, Pannell Kerr and Forster. As a comparative newcomer to Brighton, Gunnell turned down the offer of an open-topped bus tour through the city, but there was one immediate perk: *Hello!* magazine's pictorial exclusive subsidised her marriage to Jon Bigg in Florida in October 1992. The ceremony had to be delayed when Linford Christie's hire car failed to start.

Still eager for improvement, Gunnell began working with a nutritionist at the start of 1993 (complete with cold showers and six pints of water a day). Her early-season form was better than the previous year and another ambition was ticked off when she broke the world record at the World Championships in Stuttgart, clocking 52.74sec. Not for the first time the self-obsessed Farmer-Patrick did her best to hijack the occasion. After the 1991 race in Tokyo she accused Gunnell of bumping into her; after the Olympic final, as they waited for the medal ceremony, she subjected Gunnell to an "excruciating" 10-minute description of *her* race; now she was only interested in stressing that she, too, had beaten the world record.

"We had such a rivalry," Gunnell reflects. "We didn't communicate much during our athletic careers, but afterwards, when I was working for the BBC and she was with the American team, we met up and we just sat chatting for about four hours. We were like long-lost friends."

Gunnell completed the full set of major titles when she won at the European Championships in 1994, and for the third successive year was in the top three in the BBC Sports Personality of the Year awards. Injuries brought her career to a frustrating and premature close; she was working as a trackside interviewer for the BBC the following year and had the curious experience of congratulating the American, Kim Batten, for breaking her record at the World Championships. "I was very polite," she says. After 18 months out with a heel injury, Gunnell eased her way back into the indoor circuit at the start of 1996, only to break down in her semi-final in Atlanta (it was also her 30th birthday). She made her last competitive appearance at Gateshead in 1997.

"Once you get to the point when you've got all these thoughts about retiring in your head it's really hard to motivate yourself," Gunnell admits. "I wasn't one of these people who wanted to stay in my sport for as long as I could. Just thinking, right I'm going to go there and get another Olympic medal wasn't giving me the drive I needed. In some ways I think I should have done another event, maybe the 800m, or retired a year earlier."

Gunnell never looked completely suited to her interviewing role for the BBC, but she insists that she enjoyed the challenge: "I loved what I did – being the first person to interview Kelly Holmes after she won her gold medals in Athens was an amazing feeling. It was brilliant, but I had three young kids. It got to that point where you'd go off on a Friday, get back on the Monday morning and they'd started school and I'd missed them. I thought, there's more to life." Gunnell put down the microphone in 2006 and over the past few years she has juggled media work and mentoring with family life.

1996

July 27: Coxless pairs, Steve Redgrave, Matthew Pinsent

THE ripples were still settling from their victory in Barcelona when Steve Redgrave and Matthew Pinsent predicted a repeat performance in Atlanta. Nothing happened in the intervening four years to raise serious doubts about their ability to deliver (the worst they could be accused of was arrogance). They had yet another world title under their belts and Redgrave admitted on the eve of the Games that it was all or nothing. "Everything we've done over the last three-and-a-half years is meaningless if we don't win gold in Atlanta. If we don't win everything we've done will be tarnished. We'll be known as the crew that didn't win this Olympic Games."

The pair had gradually built momentum. The 1993 season was one of low-key endeavour and they were stretched to near breaking point in retaining their World Championship title in Roundice, near Prague. The following year brought the seeds of a serious challenge to their supremacy from the German pair, Peter Höltzenbein and Thorsten Streppelhoff, who were recruited by Cambridge for the 1994 Boat Race. They pushed Redgrave and Pinsent so hard in Lucerne that the British pair had to take three seconds off the world record to win, but the defeat deflated the Germans so badly that after losing to Redgrave and Pinsent at the World Championships they announced that they were going in search of another event.

Redgrave again carried the flag at the opening ceremony in Athens, a shambolic affair in keeping with the whole Games. A few days later Redgrave and Pinsent quit the Olympic village and moved into a hotel, concerned, among other things, that they might go down with a virus. Both were astonished by the level of media interest – about 200 journalists attended the press conference held after they had won their heat – though the British interest was understandable, given Redgrave's proximity to another piece of history and the scarcity of gold medal prospects in other sports. Pinsent articulated the unique appeal of the Olympics:

> I can make a comfortable living, but I'm not in it for whatever fame and fortune there is in rowing. It is the way it makes me feel. It is the way it changes me inside my head. It is laying yourself on the line, spending four years of your life working your socks off to achieve something. And you get here under all the pressure and you stick your neck out and say I'm going to do it. Success in that situation is like something else. It is a drug. It is enticing. You raise your expectations to a level where you think that just by entering a race you are going to win it. That's how we feel. I said before that it would be interesting to see who wins silver. That is not as arrogant as it sounds. It is confidence. But you have to be arrogant. And why not? We have won everything for the last four years. You can't be all British and polite about it.

There was no let-up after a semi-final which Redgrave and Pinsent won after being led at halfway by a pumped-up American combination. Redgrave, annoyed by the repetitive line of questioning, walked out. Pinsent described it as "the only time I ever saw him lose his cool at the Olympics". On the day of the final, they woke to the news that a bomb had gone off in Atlanta's Centennial Park, killing two people and injuring more than 100. The Games went on regardless.

Redgrave's family were out in force to support him; it was the way he always liked it. Just before the final he was inspired by hearing his five-year-old daughter, Natalie, shout out, "Come on, dad." The parting words from Grobler, familiar but still reassuring, were: "You are so strong, I am sure no one can beat you." Redgrave and Pinsent surged to the front in the opening 500 metres and had just enough in hand to protect their lead, winning by a second from the Australians, David Weightman and Robert Scott. Redgrave became Britain's most successful Olympian.

The inevitable question was: would he carry on? Redgrave was suspended between euphoria and fatigue when he was intercepted by Dan Topolski. "I hereby give permission to anybody who catches me in a boat again to shoot me," he spluttered. The memorable line – even the Queen mentioned it at a Buckingham Palace reception – ensured that his equally live reference to Pinsent as an "effing powerhouse" was less widely diffused. Redgrave stuck to his line, though in less emotive terms, at the press conference. "I don't ever want to go through the hell that I have these past few weeks," he said. "It is the commitment I want to get away from."

His wife, Ann, still needed convincing. "I'm quite relieved that it might be the end," she said, "but I have yet to be convinced. I would certainly not be astounded if, in about a year, he decided to give it another go." Pinsent confessed that he was in a state of limbo, referring to "this big hole of emptiness".

The Games were still at their halfway point when Redgrave and Pinsent won what was to be Britain's only gold medal in Atlanta. The knives of condemnation were already being sharpened and even the silver medallists – five individuals, two pairs and the 4 x 400m relay team – were made to feel like failures. They included two future gold medallists, Ben Ainslie and Jonathan Edwards. Roger Black, who finished a full second behind Michael Johnson in the 400m, insisted: "The silver behind Michael is worth the gold in front of anybody else." The Republic of Ireland, or specifically swimmer Michelle Smith, won three gold medals; Kazakhstan, Nigeria and North Korea all finished above Britain in the medal table.

Redgrave admitted in an interview with *The Daily Telegraph* two years ago that he and Pinsent expected a heroes' welcome when they returned home. "We thought, ah well, it's bad for British sport; at least it will be good for us, we'll get all the attention. We got nothing. Because the Games had been such a disappointment, it rubbed off even on the gold medallists. I thought I'd be mobbed going down Marlow High Street. But nobody knew me from Adam."

By the time Redgrave appeared on *This Is Your Life* (he was nabbed while guesting on the National Lottery draw), he had decided, but not yet announced, that he would carry on to Sydney. His wife said she was still hoping that he would give up, though she, too, sensed that he was prepared to put his ageing body through four more years of punishment. On the recommendation of the BBC presenter, Steve Rider, the insurance company Lombard invested £1 million over four years in the Redgrave brand, at least guaranteeing that he would suffer in greater comfort. The formal announcement, much to Lombard's delight, coincided with Redgrave's high-profile confirmation that he would row on. As Pinsent pointed out, there was a clear message in the photoshoot, which featured him at one end and Redgrave at the other end of a four-man boat.

1996: THE VERDICT

"This Olympics has not been an embarrassment for us….By the next Olympics I hope there will be big changes in Olympic sport."
Iain Sproat, Sports minister

"We have reached a watershed, a moment of truth. We cannot bluff it. We have to get our act together. We need more funding."
Dick Palmer, BOA secretary

"Old attitudes, which formerly provided British success, are outmoded. Britain will cease to be successful in the field of international sport unless there are radical changes."
Malcolm Arnold, Head coach to British athletics team

"We admire people who are gallant in defeat almost more than we admire our winners. Some of our winners get slated. If we are serious about the Olympics we have to realise that there a lot of other people around the world who are very serious, too."
Matthew Pinsent, Coxless pairs gold medallist

"I have a message for John Major. We need money. If the government want a feel-good factor, they must provide it."
Paul Palmer, 400m freestyle silver medallist

"We are a nation that has become second-rate at sport."
Nigel Clarke, *Daily Mirror*

"One big question ought to be asked out here. And it is not whether Britain's Olympic reputation is ever likely to be salvaged and restored. Everyone from the United States to Uzbekistan should wonder whether the Games themselves are worth saving. It is hard to be nationalistic because failure goes far deeper than mere ineptitude by our struggling team. The major problem stems from the Olympic movement itself."
John Sadler, *Sun*

"The reason for Britain's disappearing act in Atlanta is far more fundamental than perhaps poor administration or lack of funding. It is about a generation of children who've been allowed to slurp Rice Krispies while watching *Neighbours*. It is about an era of barmy local authorities and teachers who have decreed that fierce competition is distasteful and unfair. It is about the word elitism being expunged from the dictionary of political correctness. It is about already weary school-leavers complaining about the lack of opportunity and immediately heading for the welfare queue instead of the Job Centre. It is about the womb-to-tomb safety net for the idle. And it is about the implanting of the attitude that the world owes you a living from your date of birth."
Ian Wooldridge, *Daily Mail*

2000

Sept 16: 1km time trial cycling, Jason Queally

JASON QUEALLY did more than win a gold medal for himself when he flew round the track to win the kilometre time trial on the opening day of the Sydney Games. He opened up a treasure trove of possibility for the whole British team. The media contingent may have been caught unawares – only four British journalists were at the Dunc Gray Velodrome that night – but his fellow athletes watched, gripped, in the Olympic village as 30-year-old Queally swapped anonymity for instant celebrity. He became a reference point for all the rowers and runners who sought their own slice of glory in the ensuing fortnight.

When the British team came home from Sydney, clutching their grand haul of 11 gold medals, chef d'équipe Simon Clegg described Queally's win as "the defining moment for the success of the team. It inspired everyone, lifted the pressure off the team. After that, there were only two days in the whole Olympics when we did not win a medal."

Curiously, though, Queally found himself sucked back into obscurity by the gold rush. Even at the coming-home press conference, fellow medallists struggled to put a name to the face. Three months down the road, he had launched a Lancashire edition of *Monopoly* and turned on the Christmas lights in Chorley, but was still without a sponsor. A year later, in an effort to increase his public profile, he was lying on his back, competing in the World Human Powered Speed Challenge in Nevada.

Queally has been game for a challenge ever since. He competed again in the Athens Games, retired after missing the cut for the team in Beijing, but was lured back into the sport as the tandem partner for the partially sighted Anthony Kappes, who had won two gold medals at the 2008 Paralympics. That, in turn, led to an invitation to train with the able-bodied team pursuit squad and finally the beguiling prospect of making the sprint team in 2012: as a 42-year-old.

There were no Olympic appearances, let alone gold medals, on the horizon when Queally was growing up in Lancashire. He was bright, winning a place at Lancaster University to study biological science – he stayed on afterwards as a laboratory technician – and making gentle waves as a sportsman. "I came from a swimming and water polo background, and I wanted to do some triathlon," he explained, "but I never actually got round to doing one. I got hold of a bike and started to race on it and found I had an aptitude for it." With minimal training, he recorded a time only two seconds off the national record. "At last I'd found something in life I enjoyed and was quite good at. It needn't necessarily have been sporting, it might have been academic, but it turned out to be cycling. Then I wanted to know how good I could be at it."

His parents and girlfriend, Vikki Pike, a clinical psychologist, subsidised Queally in the early stages of his cycling career, which was not short of setbacks. He was knocked off his bike in a freakish 35mph collision with Chris Hoy on the Meadowbank track in Edinburgh, in 1996. As he landed, an 18-inch splinter ripped out of the ageing wooden boards and lodged in Queally's back. "I've got half the effing track in my back!" he screamed. Although Hoy was also hurt, his mother, Carol, who was on first-aid duty, concentrated all her attention on Queally and took him to hospital after on-the-spot treatment. Queally later admitted that he had been lucky to survive. "The doctors said that if it had pierced the thoracic cavity I'd probably have been killed," he said. He needed 70 stitches and was so traumatised that he was unable to cycle in groups for years afterwards. In Sydney the resulting scar was compared to the work of a local shark.

In the same year, Queally showed his lack of preparedness for top-level competition when his shoe fixings gave way during the team sprint at the World Championships in Manchester. There were no such problems when the trio joined forces to win the silver medal in Sydney.

The injection of Lottery funding in 1998 gave Queally licence to become a full-time cyclist, but he regarded himself as nothing more than an outside bet for an Olympic bronze medal in an event regarded as the sport's most concentrated test of pure power and speed: all lactic acid and oxygen debt and black spots before the eyes on the final lap.

"You have to train your body to cope with it," said Queally, "but, bizarrely, the fitter you get the more you can hurt yourself."

The 16 cyclists went off in reverse seeding order in Sydney; the gold medal favourite, France's Arnaud Tournant, rode last. Queally, starting 13th, drew strength from team-mate Rob Hayles, who had just posted the second quickest qualifying time in the 4,000m individual pursuit. Watched by his parents, girlfriend and an assortment of aunts and uncles, and riding a Hotta bike which had been put together by freelance designer Chris Field in his garage in rural Devon, Queally put in what he admitted was a "ridiculously quick" kilometre, 1min 01.609sec, a second and a half faster than his previous best. "Oh my god, where did that come from?" he gasped to himself after crossing the line. Queally suggested, charitably, that Tournant "just got caught up in the craziness of a big sporting event", setting off at a suicidal pace before fading on the final lap to finish fourth.

The victory was much more than a bolt from the starting blocks for the British team; it was also a priceless vindication for Lottery funding. On day two, Queally became the first Briton since Sebastian Coe in 1984 to win gold and silver medals at the same Games when the sprint team finished as runners-up to France. He was immediately recruited to endorse the Labour government's announcement that £1 billion was to be ploughed into sports facilities in schools.

Queally was not remotely interested in fame; he would have settled for a little slice of fortune instead. He knew, as Steve Redgrave and Jonathan Edwards purred away from Heathrow in plush limousines and he got on the Tube, that he was lower division to their Champions League life styles. In the absence of backers, he had a new battalion of fans who wrote to him from Germany, Finland and Sweden. While preparing for the World Championships in Manchester at the end of October 2000 – he finished third behind Tournant – Queally received a pair of black ladies' knickers through the post, and an accompanying note reading, 'I've been watching your progress in Sydney and look forward to meeting you in Manchester.'

After competing in the lucrative keirin series in Japan at the start of 2001, Queally piloted the £100,000 Blueyonder Challenger to a European record of 64.34mph for HPVs (human-powered vehicles); the winner exceeded 80mph. Back in his more familiar upright position, he was restricted to minor medals in both World Champ- ionships and Commonwealth Games before finishing fifth in the team sprint in Athens, where Hoy succeeded him as winner of the kilometre event. Queally never stopped insisting that he was "just an ordinary bloke who happens to be good at something".

Sept 20: Double trap clay pigeon shooting, Richard Faulds

LITTLE things can make a big difference when Olympic gold medals are on the line. Richard Faulds maintained his concentration in Sydney by focusing on a blue-dot sticker in the centre of his watch and transforming himself into 'the Iceman'. He won not only the double trap gold medal but a $10 side-bet with the Australian he beat in the shoot-off, Russell Mark.

Faulds had also been in medal contention as a precocious 19-year-old in Atlanta, but lost the plot in the final round to finish fifth overall. "My problem," he explained, "was that in between shooting pairs of clays, I thought about silly things like what I was going to have for tea. Irrelevant stuff, but it put me off. I was struggling to keep a one-track mind." Two years later, he turned to Peter Terry, a sports psychologist who had previously worked with the England cricket team, the Welsh rugby side and snooker player Jimmy White.

Deep breathing didn't do the trick, but the alter ago seemed to work. Terry, who described Faulds as "just a normal guy struggling to get the best out of himself", decided to keep the imagery simple as well. "The Iceman idea gave him an anchor to fix all his effort on during tournaments. In competition, he'd been more of a nervous child than an Iceman, but he underwent psychological growth."

At the suggestion of Faulds's mother, Sue, Terry and coach Ian Coley kept him happy in Sydney by administering to his every need (bar hitting targets). They also played him the Whitney Houston song, *One Moment in Time*, to implant a sense that he was destined to win. Faulds was certainly not short of confidence – he had just won the world sporting title in Findon, Sussex – and he shot consistently in the Olympic competition to tie Mark, the defending champion, after a final round for which only the top six qualified. They both hit 187 targets out of a possible 200. "I remember looking at the scoreboard for probably 30 seconds," says Faulds. "I was thinking, god almighty, I've won a medal. I didn't know whether it was going to be silver or gold, but I could hardly believe it was really me in that situation. I remember looking at my coach and he was going absolutely berserk."

Faulds and Mark barely had time to gather their senses before the shoot-off began. Both hit one and missed one target with their first two shots and when Mark was off target again with his third clay, Faulds had only to record two hits to become the first Briton to win an Olympic trap event since Bob Braithwaite in 1968.

He admitted afterwards: "My heart was beating so fast it was almost coming out of my ears as I fired the final shots." His mother, watching on the family farm in Hampshire, described it as "the most exciting 15 minutes of my life. I was screaming at the television like a small child." Faulds reflects now: "You wouldn't have expected him to miss twice like that, but the situation we were in, with him being defending champion and in front of a home crowd, put immense pressure on him. Similarly with me. I didn't really realise what had happened for some time. It all went so fast. I felt as though I was in a daze. When I watch the video, and I still look at it now occasionally, I still see things which I had no idea happened at the time. When you're competing you're in such a zone."

'I was screaming at the television like a small child'

Faulds was instantly adopted as a priceless propaganda weapon in the fight to preserve recreational shooting, which had been forced on the defensive after the Dunblane killings in 1996. Kate Hoey, the sports minister and gun sports supporter, gave Faulds a congratulatory hug and said: "I am particularly pleased for shooters and shooting in general." James Mair, the British team's assistant coach, picked up the theme: "You can't describe what this win will do for the image of the sport. The people in shooting were as devastated as anyone else about what happened at Dunblane. The guy was one lunatic who, had he had a car instead of a gun, would have mowed down a bus queue."

The victory was not just a personal triumph but a reward for the Faulds family's investment and a stinging retort to the PE teacher who had written Richard off because of his poor hand-eye co-ordination. His father, Bruce, bought him shooting lessons as a 10th birthday present, and he took to the sport so readily that he made his international debut when he was 13 and won his first world title at junior level when he was 16. Bruce Faulds had a private range built at the family's 300-acre Owls Lodge farm just before the Atlanta Games.

Richard's success and celebrity did nothing to appease neighbours who had complained about noise from the range from the word go. He was blocked in his efforts to renew the licence in November 2000, forcing Faulds to make a temporary 150-mile round trip to Yeovil to practise, and the dispute was only resolved after almost 15 years of wrangling. Faulds held Test Valley Borough Council partially responsible when he finished only ninth in the World Championships in 2001. Results improved a little – Faulds was seventh in the Olympic test event in Athens – but the opposition was getting stronger as well.

Any hopes of a successful defence vanished when Faulds missed nine times in his first 50 shots; he finished in a tie for 13th place and cut a miserable, disillusioned figure afterwards, saying: "Maybe I'll be back but I'm not making any promises." He was at a loss to explain why he had fallen so short of his normal standard in the opening round: "Perhaps it was nerves, perhaps I put too much pressure on myself," he said. John Leighton-Dyson, the performance director for Team GB shooting, could only offer the sport's equivalent of they-scored-more-goals-than-we-did, saying: "Others have just shot straighter than him."

Faulds's appetite was restored in time for the Beijing Games and, judging by his performance at the World Cup in Suhl, Germany, the previous month, his aim was true. En route to victory, Faulds equalled the world record of 147 (out of 150) for the preliminary round, and there seemed to be a new maturity to his outlook, befitting someone who now had a wife, Tanya (also an international class shooter), and nine-month-old baby to occupy his thoughts. He was unable to match his World Cup score, but 137 hits were at least enough to take him into the final round, where he finished last of the six qualifiers.

The use throughout the competition of flash targets, which emit a puff of dust when hit, led to confusion and, Faulds believes, cost him a medal. "With the Chinese, every time they missed a target it seemed to be given as a hit," he claims. "Everyone else had targets taken away, including me. I hit two targets which didn't count and that took me back from the bronze medal position to sixth."

The lure of London was too much for Faulds to contemplate retirement, but he laid down business roots for his life after competitive shooting by opening the Owls Lodge Shooting School, near Winchester, in 2009. He booked his place for 2012 as early as March last year and followed up with an individual silver medal in the double trap at the European Championships and team gold.

Sept 23: Coxless fours, James Cracknell, Steve Redgrave, Tim Foster, Matthew Pinsent

STEVE REDGRAVE did not take much persuading from Matthew Pinsent to consign their pair to history. At a press conference announcing that their Sydney focus would be on a four, Redgrave said that it would give them "more variety, enthusiasm and drive". The initial selection process was reasonably simple: James Cracknell, Tim Foster and Greg Searle were the prime contenders from the British team in Atlanta and Searle had already indicated that he would throw his energies into the single scull. The new combination bedded down impressively in 1997, their first competitive season, culminating in victory in the World Championships; the final at Lac d'Aiguebelette was on the same day as the funeral of Diana, Princess of Wales.

A few weeks later, Redgrave discovered that he was diabetic and inevitably questioned whether the condition would end his rowing career. "The problem," he wrote, "was trying to get enough energy inside me to feed the demands that I have without it dangerously affecting my sugar levels." In time, he found that he could control his blood sugar levels without a drastic change to his diet, but only by giving himself insulin injections six times a day. The uncertainty and stress brought on a recurrence of colitis and Redgrave felt so low that, without even notifying Jürgen Grobler, he disappeared on a two-week skiing holiday with his wife.

Grobler's past came back to haunt him in 1998 when Stasi files were made public, suggesting that the Leipzig College for Physical Culture, where Grobler had been based, had used hormone-doping to aid performance. "I am not a doping coach," Grobler insisted. "I am not a chemist. I had to live with a system which I knew was wrong." In rowing, he claimed, doping had never been the "number one priority" in East Germany. The ARA backed Grobler to the hilt, stating with confidence that rowing in Britain was clean.

Foster and Cracknell had both been keen to assert themselves, challenging the routines that Redgrave and Pinsent had established during their six years together, as well as Grobler's low-intensity training regime. Cracknell was the product of Kingston Grammar School and Reading University, where he briefly swapped rowing for rugby – at the expense of a broken shoulder which prevented him from being picked for the Barcelona Games – before completing a degree in human geography in 1993. He was denied the chance to compete in the double sculls in Atlanta when he contracted tonsillitis the day before his first race and later admitted: "I was distraught. I couldn't believe I'd trained so hard for four years and was not going to race."

While at Bedford Modern School, Foster became the first British rower to win gold medals at successive Junior World Championships

(1987 and 1988). After tasting the world outside academia for two years – Foster worked behind the Safeways fish counter in Bedford – he did an economics degree at the University of London. Both there and at Oxford, where Foster did postgraduate studies (allowing him to compete in the 1997 Boat Race), he threw himself into student life with reckless abandon. The consequences were almost catastrophic: in April 1998, a well-oiled Foster put his hand through a plate glass window at a party in Oxford, severing tendons in his little finger and lacerating an artery; he lost two pints of blood. Pinsent recalled his reaction in his book *A Lifetime In A Race*: "I was furious, boiling with an indignant, selfish anger that was worried less about Tim and his hand and more about what the stupid accident would do to the four."

Foster's apologies were accepted and his absence actually served to confirm his value to the boat – he was the least powerful of the four but a brilliant technical rower. The Croatian-born Luka Grubor, who had recently become a British citizen, subbed for his friend. The mix did not work and the British four could only finish fourth in a World Cup race in Munich; it was the first time that Redgrave had been involved in a championship defeat for three years. He said at the time: "It's a feeling I'm not used to, and one I hope I'm not going to get used to."

Normal service was resumed when the four, with Foster restored to the boat, won the Stewards' Cup at Henley, beating the Australians, who had been dubbed the 'oarsome foursome' after winning in Atlanta. They went on to win at the World Championships in Cologne, only to suffer another, longer-term setback when Foster tore a disc in his lower back; he had surgery just before Christmas 1998 and was unable to resume rowing until the middle of the following March. Another replacement was needed and in Ed Coode, the strongest rower in the British eight at the time, they found someone capable of doing more than keeping Foster's seat warm.

Coode retained his place throughout the 1999 season, which culminated in victory at the World Championships at St Catharines in Canada. Foster was a reluctant member of the British eight who also won a world title. His feelings were laid bare in a video diary, commissioned by the BBC, which featured in the documentary *Gold Fever*. "I don't really see the eight as a long-term option," Foster confided. "If I'm not rowing in the four I don't know whether I want to do it."

The issue was still far from resolved at the start of the 2000 season and, on the face of it anyway, the selection poser for Grobler extended beyond a simple choice between Foster and Coode. Redgrave acknowledged that Pinsent had assumed his once untouchable status as "the prime mover of the boat" and that health and age (he was now 38) had forced him to compromise in training. The unthinkable question had to be asked: was Redgrave still worth his place? Foster and Coode both rowed on the same side of the boat as Redgrave so, as Pinsent put it: "If he wasn't at his best, it wasn't a choice so much between Ed and Tim, but more Tim, Ed and Steve." Redgrave even got to the point of telling Grobler that he should stand down; the German ridiculed the idea.

Pinsent described the Easter trials, in which he and Redgrave, Cracknell and Foster, and Coode and Greg Searle, paired up under the scrutiny of not just Grobler but the press, as "a disaster". Cracknell and Foster won; the legends were third. The obvious loser, however, was Coode, who put a brave face on the formal announcement in mid-April. Coode's new Olympic focus was in a pair with Greg Searle.

The British four secured the World Cup by winning the first two events, but rowed lethargically to be beaten both in the semi-final and final (where they finished an unthinkable fourth) in Lucerne. Grobler was more upset by the Redgrave obituaries which began to appear than by the significance of the results. It was not just a case of rewriting history to suggest that they had over-trained in the week before the Lucerne regatta. Equanimity was restored by the time they set out for Australia at the end of August.

> **'Don't judge his whole career on Sydney. It doesn't make him a success or failure if he wins or loses there. He is already an icon '**

Despite Pinsent's top-dog status in the boat, public interest rested solely on whether Redgrave could turn four gold medals into five. He may as well have been teaming up with three cardboard cut-outs. Pinsent, as ever, played the part of selfless cheerleader. "Steve deserves to be recognised as the finest Olympian we have ever produced," he said on the eve of the Sydney Games. "I don't care whether you compare him with Coe or Ovett, Daley or Linford. I don't care if you line up Liddell or Abrahams. Whatever happens in Sydney, Steve is head and shoulders above any of them. To be able to perform at this level for 20 years is extraordinary. This is certainly his crowning moment, his finest hour. But don't judge his whole career on Sydney. It doesn't make him a success or failure if he wins or loses there. He is already an icon."

They settled into a routine of 4.30am starts to the day, a *modus operandi* which suited all but the laid-back Foster. Pinsent brought a little more personality to the flag-carrying role at the opening ceremony than Redgrave had done – he was feeling less in control of his emotions when he was sick during a warm-up paddle before the heats. The British quartet were seeded fourth, a harsh punishment for their lowly finish in Lucerne, but issued a powerful statement of intent by winning their first race. They also muted a raucous crowd of more than 20,000 by beating the Australian four and remained on course for the gold medal with another dominant row in the semi-final.

The final was scheduled for 10.30am local time, which translated into an inhospitable 12.30am on Saturday morning back in Britain. Newspapers had no option but to pack their early editions with filler material which was then stripped out to accommodate Redgrave's moment of glory or despair. A television audience of seven million in Britain prepared to witness history. Cracknell, intense at the best of times, was welling up with emotion as the race approached; Redgrave had achieved a state of calm.

The conditions, too, were benign for the coxless fours final. Redgrave, as he had done hundreds of times before, 'called' the race, keeping an eye on the computerised pace coach – an innovation proposed by Foster early in the life of the four – which measured the boat's speed. They carved out a lead of almost a second over the Australians in the first 500 metres and just about held off a quickening Italian challenge before pressing for a decisive push between 1,000 and 1,500 metres. "Gold medal catches," was Redgrave's low-key cue for a redoubling of effort which repelled the Italians…just. To the untutored eye, the race was unbearably close. Redgrave, both in real time and in subsequent analysis, believed that the British four remained in control, even though their victory margin was an unpleasantly tight 0.38sec. Pinsent recalled Redgrave's final call, the last words he would utter in competition, "In the water!" A cliché under cold analysis was Shakespearean in the heat of battle.

Redgrave, Foster and Cracknell were too exhausted to do anything more than rest limply in the boat; from somewhere Pinsent conjured the energy to clamber over Foster – "it's not quite how I want to remember the Olympic Games, having a sweaty crotch over the top of my head," he reflected – and embrace Redgrave. The "blubbery whale", as Redgrave affectionately described his friend, disappeared over the side of the boat and almost took Redgrave with him.

Redgrave joined two Hungarian fencers as the only Olympians to have won gold medals at five consecutive summer Games; German canoeist Birgit Fischer-Schmidt was welcomed into the exclusive club in Athens. Part of him expected the fawning attention, but Redgrave was still embarrassed and a far from docile interviewee for the BBC's Steve Rider immediately after the race. "Do you get that sense of history?" Rider asked. "No," Redgrave shot back. "Every day's history, isn't it?" Rider tried another tack. When did he know that the race was won? "After 250 metres," said Redgrave. Rider gave him the chance to correct himself. Surely he meant with 250 metres to go? No, Redgrave insisted, he didn't.

If Redgrave wanted to be regarded as one of a team, the IOC wanted to highlight a remarkable achievement. The normal protocol of presenting medals according to rowers' position in the boat was abandoned so that the Princess Royal could congratulate Redgrave first; he also received an IOC pin from the president, Juan Antonio Samaranch. There were an estimated 150 journalists at the press conference and there was no let-up when he returned home.

Photographers jostled for the definitive shot of Redgrave easing away from Heathrow Airport in his dream car, a Jaguar XJR, a surprise present from his wife, Ann. A crowd of 25,000 turned out to greet him on an open-topped bus parade through Marlow and he was predictably showered with awards at the end of the year – not just BBC Sports Personality of Year but also *Smash Hits*' Hero of the Year. The widely predicted knighthood was confirmed in the New Year's Honours list.

Foster returned to a life of relative anonymity after retiring from the sport in 2001, becoming head coach to the Swiss squad in 2007. Redgrave has learned to embrace his celebrity, picking up five-figure fees for motivational speaking and preaching a you-can-do-it-too message through various books. He has also written regular columns for *The Daily Telegraph* and enhanced the BBC's rowing coverage with his unparalleled insight into what it takes to succeed at the highest level. The Steve Redgrave Fund, set up in 2001, raised more than £5 million for youth sports projects before joining forces with Sports Relief in 2008.

Sept 24: Eights rowing, Andrew Lindsay, Ben Hunt-Davis, Simon Dennis, Louis Attrill, Luka Grubor, Kieran West, Fred Scarlett, Steve Trapmore, Rowley Douglas (cox)

THE imagery before the eights final was all of charging bulls; the talk was of 'kill or be killed'; the mantra was, 'today's a good day because I'm going to make it a good day'. The inspiration was the British crew's assistant coach, Harry Mahon, who had already lived two years longer than doctors predicted when he was diagnosed with colon cancer in 1997.

Mahon had established his coaching credentials in the early Eighties, when he guided his native New Zealand to back-to-back eights world titles. In the 1990s, he was the ultimate rowing guru, a have-megaphone-will-travel genius who preached technique over brute force. One avid disciple was Martin McElroy, an engineering graduate from the University of Dublin who went full time with the British national squad in 1997, only two years after he had started coaching at Imperial College in London.

McElroy had no hesitation in recruiting Mahon, a move which Ben Hunt-Davis, at 28 the oldest man in the crew, describes as critical to the success in Sydney. "A lot of people would think that bringing in someone who is potentially better than you was a weakness," says Hunt-Davis, "but actually Harry was fantastic in certain areas and poor in other areas and Martin was brilliant at managing the whole thing. He used Harry for what he was best at: he got him in to help him technically, but what he also got was somebody who had a much calmer personality and was able to be a steadying hand in the World Championships in 1999 and the Olympics in 2000. Martin was fiery and hadn't been in those positions before, whereas Harry had and was able to steer and guide Martin and keep him sane."

The eight, essentially, were the best of the rest after the elite had been creamed off into pairs and fours. McElroy was fortunate in being able to pick from a talented and committed group – 16 different rowers took their place in the boat at one stage or another between 1998 and the Sydney Games. The World Championship results were respectable in 1997 and 1998 – they finished fourth and seventh – but the breakthrough came with a silver medal in St Catharines, Ontario, in 1999. The class act in the crew was Tim Foster, still trying to force his way back into the Redgrave four.

Mahon was so committed to the cause that he timed chemotherapy sessions to avoid clashes with races and key training sessions. "Harry came out to St Catharines against all medical advice," says Hunt-Davis. "He wasn't allowed within about 10 metres of us. While we were on the water that was fine and then for post-outing discussions he would sit in the van with a megaphone and talk to us like that. His immune systems were so weak that he couldn't risk getting an infection."

A mark of the squad's strength in depth was the quality of the nearly men: the coxed four won the gold medal at the World Championships in 2000. There were bound to be grievances and no one felt his omission more keenly than Bobby Thatcher, whose ambitions of

WHERE ARE THEY NOW

Andrew Lindsay	London	CEO utility warehouse
Ben Hunt-Davis	London	Owner, Point8 Coaching
Simon Dennis	Wiltshire	Teacher
Louis Attrill	Isle of Wight	Manager engineering company
Luka Grubor	Croatia	Sail Croatia
Kieran West	London	Management consultant, McKinsey
Fred Scarlett	Hampshire	Super yacht broker
Steve Trapmore	Cambridge	Head coach CUBC
Rowley Douglas	Bath	Olympic ambassador, GE

double sculls success in Atlanta had vanished when James Cracknell went down with tonsillitis. Thatcher, a member of the crew in St Catharines, was made the scapegoat for a defeat by the Australians at Henley, and in his resentful state refused even to travel to Sydney as spare man. Andrew Lindsay, a bagpipe-playing Old Etonian, took Thatcher's place as the British crew completed their pre-Olympic race programme with a victory at the Lucerne regatta. Simon Dennis, one of three members of the eight who had been coached by McElroy at Imperial (the others were the Croatian-born Luka Grubor and Louis Attrill), had already come in for Foster.

Although Australia were regarded as potential gold medallists, the British crew had not bargained on losing to them in their heat. "I have never been angrier in my life," said Dennis. He was still seething when Britain lined up alongside the Australians in the final six days later.

Mahon pointed to the horizon, saying cryptically: "Boys, the dressage event is over there." Grubor understood the message: "What Harry meant was that we were just a bunch of little soft kids, that we were too well brought up, too concentrated on the technique and not enough on, 'Who needs this most?' We had the speed but not the heroics. We didn't believe in heroic performances. Then we saw it on the video. We weren't racing, we were just rowing along. That was the catalyst. We had to say out loud, 'We're here to kill everyone.'"

The British crew took advantage of their back-door route to the final, the repechage, and their new-found intensity spilled over into training. Rival coaches were amazed to see six men rowing and the others, Ben Hunt-Davis and Andrew Lindsay, fighting during one session. Hunt-Davis points out that the object of his anger was actually cox Rowley Douglas.

> We were out doing our first training session after losing the heat. I was absolutely knackered, incredibly pissed off that we'd let ourselves down so badly and Rowley was pushing us really hard, and he was suddenly giving me a whole load of feedback which would have been more helpful before we'd lost. I got to the stage halfway through the outing when I decided that the best thing to do was to kill Rowley, so I was trying to get out of the boat so I could swim down and drown him. Andrew grabbed me and stopped me and we had a bit of a ruckus. Tensions were incredibly high. It was a complete over-reaction, but that's what happened. Martin and Harry thought it was brilliant. They'd accused us of being too well brought up, so they actually thought that us trying to take each other out was quite a good thing.

Hunt-Davis was on emotional overload in the 24 hours leading up to the final. He roared home the Redgrave four then wept as Greg Searle and Ed Coode missed a medal in the coxless pairs. "I was worried the guys might think I'd cracked," he later admitted, "but I wanted it so much I could taste it. We devised this crazy race plan to give it everything we'd got and then keep adding to it. I was sure if we got it right, nobody could beat us. But how brave were we?"

On the eve of the race, Mahon said he would never speak to any of the crew again if they were able to stand up to receive silver medals; he told them to come out like a bull after the gate is opened; Steve Trapmore, the stroke, audibly growled in anticipation of five-and-a-half minutes of pure pain and endeavour. He set a storming rate from the start. The Britons were ahead after a dozen strokes, 0.6sec clear of Croatia after 500 metres, a second to the good at 1,000 metres and had an advantage of more than two seconds at 1,500 metres. Finally, the Australians began to make up ground; the noise from the stands was so great that the British cox, Rowley Douglas, could barely be heard above the tumult. "We were there and the Australians were there," Grubor recalled. "We looked into their eyes and they looked into our eyes, and they blinked. It was a matter of total self-belief." The British crew were fourth fastest over the last 500 metres, but their high-risk strategy paid off – they finished 0.8sec ahead of Australia.

All quotes led back to Mahon. "I always hated him," said Lindsay afterwards. "He coached Cambridge to victory three times when I was in the Oxford boat. But I got to know him this year. His attitude is brilliant. He is given a week to live and he says, make it a month; he is given a month and he insists on a year. He tells us to live our lives and not worry about small things."

Four of the crew rowed their last competitive stroke in Sydney. Only one, Kieran West, was part of Britain's team in Athens. Three weeks after the triumph, Britain's first in the eights since 1912, Hunt-Davis got married in Italy. Although he delayed issuing wedding invitations until after the final, all but one of his team-mates attended. Mahon died in May 2001, a full three years later than predicted; McElroy went on to become performance director for Irish Rowing; the winning crew have the date Sept 24 permanently ringed in their diaries as a reminder of their annual reunion.

Sept 24: Heptathlon, Denise Lewis

TWO days after winning the heptathlon title in Sydney, Denise Lewis dissected a "horrible" competition and "terrible" score; she still dreamt of the definitive performance. "I escaped with a first gold medal," Lewis wrote in *The Daily Telegraph*, "but I have this vision of an Olympic Games where I'm really on song, where everything is poetry in motion. I want to break through the 7,000-point barrier for the seven events. When I go I don't want to be remembered as just another athlete who scraped a gold."

An Achilles injury prior to the Games and a searing pain which shot through her foot during the long jump were the mitigating factors. Although Lewis's score of 6,584 points was the lowest winning total since 1984, her coach, Charles van Commenee, said it simply told the "story of all the injuries". Van Commenee was less understanding of the delayed medal ceremony. By the time Lewis climbed on to the podium there were barely 10,000 spectators (mostly British supporters) remaining in the 110,000-capacity stadium; an hour earlier it had been packed. "Do you think they'd have done it for the 100m final?" Van Commenee fumed.

In the immediate aftermath, Lewis admitted: "It's been a battlefield for me out there. Every event has been uphill. I said at the beginning it would be about who could survive, and that the fittest would survive. I have to say I nearly didn't make it, but here I am." She thanked supporters, physiotherapist Kevin Lidlow, coaches and, above all, her mother, Joan, who had moved from Jamaica to Wolverhampton in 1966, given birth to Denise in 1972 and raised her alone – her father jumped ship for good when she was six months old.

Lewis was wedded to athletics from the day, as an eight-year-old, she visited Aldersley Stadium for the first time. She joined the Wolverhampton and Bilston club and it was soon clear that she had the breadth of natural ability to become a top-class multi-eventer. Initially, Lewis specialised as a long jumper, winning the England Schools' title at Under 14 level and a National Dairy Council scholarship which paid for clothing and training fees.

Bill Hand, the girls' coach at Wolverhampton and Bilston, feared the three B's – 'boobs, boys and Birchfield'. Lewis did not let him down on the first two counts, but she was lured away by Birchfield Harriers, based at the Alexander Stadium in Birmingham, and began working with Darrell Bunn, a selector for the West Midlands squad. During her teens, Lewis found it easier to communicate with Bunn than with her mother.

She was already strikingly attractive and imagined herself as the next Whitney Houston; she confessed to having a crush on Steve Cram and enjoyed the post-competition camaraderie with contemporaries like sprinter Donna Fraser. Lewis did not yet possess the stern self-discipline of an Olympic champion in the making. She and her equally outgoing circle of friends were nightclub addicts with a weakness for odd combinations of drinks.

Lewis still imagined that her athletic future lay with the long jump, but Bunn encouraged her to diversify. She showed immediate aptitude in the javelin, tolerated the shot and detested the 800m. Lewis wrote in her autobiography: "I soon realised that heptathlon is as much about overcoming and surviving the events as it is about beating your opponents."

She competed in her first heptathlon in 1988, but a serious knee injury the following summer put her career on hold. Finally, in 1991, she was fit enough to compete in the European Junior Championships and had high hopes of qualifying for the Barcelona Olympics in 1992. She was still unable to put together a consistent competition, however, and failed to reach the qualifying mark. The 1993 World Championships also bypassed her, but Lewis made her breakthrough at the 1994 Commonwealth Games in Victoria, Canada.

The pivotal discipline was the penultimate event of the seven, the javelin. Lewis sought out Steve Backley, the leading British javelin thrower, for advice and was told: "Give it some welly, mate." The tip, however basic, obviously worked. Lewis threw 53.68m, six metres further than she had managed before, to take a lead which she defended with another personal best in the 800m, finishing with a points total of 6,325.

Lewis was overwhelmed by media interest on a level she had never experienced before, though the superstar lifestyle was some way off. She had started working part time for Birmingham City Council's community development office in 1992; the job was enjoyable but the lengthy bus-train-bus journey from home was a chore. She switched to sports development then, in 1995, became a full-time athlete. Other changes were phased in: she overhauled her diet to become a 'grazer', eating smaller meals more regularly; she started taking power naps and re-assessed her goals with the help of a sports psychologist. Lewis also featured in *Britain's Girls of Sport* calendar for 1996. She was pleased with the results, her mother less so. "Did you have to stick your chest out?" she said. Joan was even less impressed two years later, when her daughter appeared, in all her body-painted glory, in *Total Sport* magazine.

The Atlanta Olympics were only two months away when Lewis broke Judy Simpson's longstanding British record, at the Gotzis meeting in Austria, amassing 6,645 points. The eventual outcome in Atlanta was satisfactory – she finished five points ahead of the Pole, Urszula Wlodarczyk, to win the bronze medal – but she was down on her Gotzis total and had performed with frustrating inconsistency. A below-par long jump was offset by a personal best in the javelin.

Tension had crept into Lewis's relationship with Bunn and she relished the chance to work with the Dutch coach, Charles van

Commenee, at a training camp in Tallahassee, Florida, in 1997. A stricter regime suited Lewis, who was still mulling over her 'new direction' speech to Bunn when she returned to Gotzis. She added another 91 points to her British record and the World Championships in Athens developed into the predicted battle between Lewis and the German, Sabine Braun, for the gold medal. Lewis managed a personal best of 1.84m in the high jump, but Braun went even higher and had an unbridgeable six seconds in hand on Lewis going into the 800m.

Van Commenee told Lewis that she was 'soft' before agreeing to coach her in the autumn of 1997; a year later they had negotiated the first two stepping stones to Sydney, winning the European title in Budapest and Commonwealth Games in Kuala Lumpur. A fresh threat to her Olympic ambitions emerged in 1999: the Sierra Leone-born Eunice Barber, who was now competing for France. Lewis's preparations were hampered by injury, but she was reasonably content to be a point behind Barber going into the second day and still in with a chance of catching her until a sub-standard javelin.

Lewis began Olympic year on crutches, the legacy of a leg operation, and preoccupied with Barber's all-round strengths as an athlete. The anxieties were heightened by Barber's form in Gotzis, where she finished with 6,842 points, only 19 fewer than her total in Seville, and eased marginally by Lewis's riposte in Talence, France. She managed four personal bests to lift her British and Commonwealth record to 6,831 points, which was to remain her lifetime best score.

Less than two months before the Sydney Games, Lewis picked up an Achilles injury which threatened her very participation. Only after intensive physiotherapy was she given the all-clear to start jogging and felt more optimistic as she (and her faithful teddy-bear, Egbert) upgraded to business class for the flight out to Brisbane. Three days before the start of the heptathlon, she took up residence in Sydney.

The competition started on a positive note for Lewis, who ran a championship best 13.23sec in the 100m hurdles. She then cleared 1.75m with ease in the high jump, opted out at 1.78m (Van Commenee described it as the misguided confidence of a novice) and failed at 1.81m. If Lewis was faltering, it was becoming increasingly clear that Barber was unfit. At the end of the first day, Lewis was in a medal position and Barber was seventh.

One tentative long jump was enough to convince Barber that it was futile to continue. Lewis, who had already posted a respectable 6.48m, gestured sympathetically, shook Barber's hand and tried to re-focus on her own final jump. Suddenly, she felt a jolting pain across her foot and agonised before deciding to jump through the discomfort. There was a six-hour gap before the start of the javelin, but despite intensive manipulation, strapping and padding by physiotherapist Kevin Lidlow, the pain refused to ease significantly. Concentrating solely on technique, and given much the same advice by Backley that he had offered in Victoria six years earlier, Lewis exceeded her own expectations by throwing 50.19m to move into the gold medal position.

Quick calculations before the 800m showed that she had 10 seconds in hand on the Russian, Yelena Prokhorova, who opened up a 2.3-second gap by the end of the first lap and steadily increased her advantage over the second 400 metres. As Lewis crossed the line she thought she had won, but did not know for sure; confirmation came when the German, Sabine Braun, asked her what it felt like to be Olympic champion.

Injuries were a recurring theme for the rest of Lewis's career, denying her the chance to join the elite 7,000-point club (members: Jackie Joyner-Kersee, Carolina Kluft and Larisa Turchinskaya). She missed the World Championships in 2001 and was out of action for the whole of 2002 after giving birth to her daughter Lauryn, the product of a relationship with the Belgian sprinter, Patrick Stevens.

Lewis did compete in the World Championships in 2003, but only after a build-up punctuated by injury and illness. She finished fifth and was in even worse shape for her Olympic title defence in Athens, pulling out with two disciplines remaining. "I'm physically and emotionally devastated," she said. "I am completely empty at this moment and unable to continue and would do myself even less justice going through the motions when all my hopes have gone. I have put my heart and soul into this year with only one goal and one mission in mind – to come away from the Olympic Games with a medal."

She vowed to "put herself back together again", and re-set her sights on finishing her career at the 2006 Commonwealth Games in Melbourne. Her body would not co-operate, however, and Lewis announced her retirement in June 2005. She married property developer Steve Finan, the son of comedian Tom O'Connor, in 2006, and had two more children, Ryan and Kane. Since she gave up competing, Lewis has been a regular voice and face on the BBC's athletics coverage.

Sept 25: Triple jump, Jonathan Edwards

THE surprise was not so much that Jonathan Edwards won an Olympic gold medal, but that it took him so long to rubber-stamp his greatness as a triple jumper. The title was the counterpoint to one of the stand-out performances in athletics history – his world record leap of 18.29m at the World Championships in 1995.

The Brazilian, Joao Carlos de Oliveira, had re-defined possibilities in the event by adding 45 centimetres to the world record in 1975, but his jump of 17.89m was a Bob Beamon style bolt from the blue. There was much more substance to Edwards's serial record-breaking in 1995. A month before the championships in Gothenburg he had leapt even further, a wind-assisted 18.43m in Lille, northern France. Seventeen years on, Edwards's world mark remains intact and he still boasts five of the best six jumps of all time.

Although his faith has dissolved in recent years, Edwards was bible-led for the duration of his sporting career. He was seen as a latter-day Eric Liddell, refusing, initially anyway, to compete on Sundays. Edwards's father, Andy, had joined the clergy after starting work as an insurance clerk. Jonathan was born in Windsor, educated initially in Blackpool, then at West Buckland School, near Barnstaple, in Devon. He was, by his own admission, "a swot and a Christian".

Edwards was too slight and unassuming to be taken seriously as a schoolboy sportsman; his younger, brother, Tim, on the other hand, was a brilliant sprinter and rugby player in the making. Tim lost interest as Jonathan blossomed as a gifted all-rounder. Despite a reluctance to train he made rapid strides as a triple jumper, winning the English Schools' title in 1984, when he was 18, with a leap of 15.01m.

After being turned down by Oxford University, Edwards went to Durham, where he invested more effort in his physics course – eventually graduating with a respectable 2:1 degree – than in his athletics career.

His father, fortunately, took a more proactive approach, writing to Malcolm Arnold, the national coach for Wales, before being referred to Carl Johnson, who had responsibility for the North East. By the time he left Durham, Edwards had decided that his faith and an athletics career – albeit alongside a paid job – were not incompatible. He also elected to stay in the North East and found a job in a genetic research laboratory.

Edwards's first experience of blanket press coverage came in 1988, when he refused to compete in the Olympic trials because they were held on a Sunday. He would also give the Europa Cup the miss the following year and opt out of the World Championships in Tokyo in 1991. The British selectors had enough faith in Edwards's ability to give him the discretionary third triple jump place in Seoul, but he was almost a metre down on his personal best in failing to qualify for the final. He promised to do better in future. "I thought, next time I come to an Olympics I want to have a chance of competing for a medal and not be an also-ran."

Towards the end of the 1989 season, Edwards emerged as a genuine contender by jumping 17.28m at the World Cup final in Barcelona. A similar distance would have earned him his first major title the following February, but he had to settle for a silver medal at the Commonwealth Games in Auckland. Later that year his father performed the service as Edwards married Alison Briggs, the daughter of a Hebridean evangelist.

Edwards had reconciled himself to the likelihood that either the qualifying round or final in the Barcelona Games would be held on a Sunday, and was delighted to discover that the allocated days were a Saturday and Monday. The qualifying coincided with Linford Christie's victory in the 100m final, but the vibes of British success did not reach across the Montjuic Stadium to inspire Edwards. His wife and parents could barely look as he ran through the pit with his first attempt, lost critical momentum between the second and third phases with his second jump and performed even worse on his final effort. "I was devastated from moment one," he admitted. "I didn't even have the energy to make an effort to somehow hide the fact."

Although he felt that he was subject to divine governance, Edwards also had to face the practical reality that all the significant triple jump competitions in 1993 were to be held on Sundays. Encouraged by a friend's dream, in which Edwards appeared, symbolically anyway, to compete on the Sabbath, he announced the relaxation of his principle through the *Christians in Sport* magazine. Although the decision attracted media cynicism, there was little direct criticism in the mainstream press.

At this stage in his career, Edwards was earning no more than £5,000 a year from athletics. He was still working part time at the cyto-genetics laboratory and became the sole bread-winner when Alison gave birth to their first child, Sam, just before the World Championships in Stuttgart. A personal best of 17.44m brought him the bronze medal; soon afterwards a grant from the Great North Run Trust gave him the freedom to become a full-time athlete.

Edwards was laid low by a virus in 1994, again finishing second in the Commonwealth Games, but 1995 brought a change of environment, a change of coach, a change of technique and instant benefit. At the start of the year Edwards trained in Tallahassee, Florida; he then began working with Peter Stanley, the father of a triple jumper and, prompted by video footage of Mike Conley – "it was like a light bulb had been switched on," said Edwards – adopted the unified arm action on the jump phase which had carried the American to a marginally wind-assisted jump of 18.17m in Barcelona. Edwards was ready to take triple jumping into rarefied territory.

As an appetiser, he broke Keith Conner's British record, which had stood since 1982. Then came the "surreal, dream-like" experience of jumping 18.43m at Villeneuve d'Ascq. Malcolm Folley wrote in his biography of Edwards that he "had not simply moved the goalposts; he had uprooted the pitch". Two weeks later, a legitimate jump of 17.98m tacked a centimetre on to Willie Banks's world record, set 10 years earlier, and there was no bursting his bubble of excellence. Edwards's first two jumps in the World Championships were 18.16m and 18.29 (a fraction over 60ft); the competition was over.

Suddenly Edwards was in athletics' big league. There was a Mercedes (the bonus prize for all the gold medallists) in the garage; he won the BBC's Sports Personality of the Year award and became an MBE in the New Year's Honours. The accumulation of wealth was hardly Edwards's top priority, but he signed with Jonathan Marks's management company MTC and did not feel too compromised by endorsing soft contact lenses. Edwards did, however, attract criticism for his loyalty to Andy Norman, the brusque policeman turned promoter.

As Olympic year dawned, Edwards's doubts and insecurities resurfaced. He did not know whether he was destined to maintain his world-beating form of 1995 or rejoin the mere mortals. One thing was certain: everybody else expected him to win in Atlanta (he had not been beaten for 18 months). Worryingly, however, the new technique was threatening to unravel; the double arm shift felt alien rather than natural. The American, Kenny Harrison, jumped a wind-assisted 18.01m to win the US trials and pile more pressure on Edwards.

Harrison was much more impressive than Edwards in qualifying and the final itself was shaped by the two men's opening jumps.

Edwards, going second, fouled by a fraction; Harrison, jumping 10th of the 12 finalists, soared to 17.99m, sending the crowd into patriotic rapture; then, responding to Edwards's first respectable jump, 17.88m, in the fourth round, he found another 10 centimetres. In a curious echo of the Barcelona Games, Linford Christie was again centre stage, this time refusing to accept his disqualification from the 100m final. Edwards interpreted it as a sign that it was his turn to win, recapturing the missing rhythm to put in a majestic jump in the final round. Momentarily convinced that he had overtaken Harrison, he turned to see the judge's red flag raised.

Edwards did not regard a silver medal as failure, but others did, and his reputation for faltering under the bright lights of top-level competition was underlined when he finished second to the Cuban, Yoelbi Quesada, at the 1997 World Championships in Athens. There was no self-forgiveness on this occasion, only a very public show of emotion as he was interviewed by the BBC's Paul Dickenson. When he returned to the room he shared with 400m runner Roger Black, Edwards flung his medal away in disgust. For a few months he was a Porsche owner, though the love affair soon ended in a guilt-ridden divorce.

He was back over 18 metres in 1998 and, though he was preoccupied with thoughts of injury when he went to the European Championships in Budapest, he jumped impressively to win with a distance of 17.99m. Edwards was now working with the innovative Czech coach, Jan Pospisil, who impressed on him the need to put athletics before family in the 16-month period embracing the World Championships in Seville and the Olympic Games in Sydney. The plan was rapidly revised when his mother-in-law was diagnosed with a brain tumour.

After finishing third in Seville, he felt that he let down both his mother-in-law and wife, explaining: "I did not want them to deal with any more disappointment." In a painfully public show of emotion, he collapsed in Alison's arms at trackside. Edwards was more up-beat after another tonic trip to Tallahassee in the new year. He was lifting greater weights than at any stage in his career and he was capable of running quicker than 10.5sec for the 100m. The 34th birthday which he celebrated in Florida was just another statistic.

The storm clouds gathered again as soon as he arrived in Australia. On a relatively trivial level, he was under fire for quotes attributed to him on the Sky Sports website which painted the British swimming team as an "awful" rabble of "party animals". Although he apologised, he was adamant that he had said nothing of the kind. More importantly, he learned that his mother-in-law had died in a Glasgow hospice.

The scenario had already been confronted in the Edwards household and there was never any serious likelihood that he would return home. Andy Norman had said repeatedly, in the build-up to the Games, that 'only Jonathan Edwards could beat Jonathan Edwards'. The view was given added credence when Edwards ambled dreamily through the qualifying competition. Alison Edwards, watching at home, said he looked like "Andy Pandy out to play".

He was shaken out of his seeming indifference in an intense conversation with his close friend, Phil Wall, and felt alert when he woke on the day of the final. Whatever happened to Edwards in the Olympic Stadium, he, and everyone else competing, would just be extras in the Cathy Freeman Show; a record crowd of 112,524 watched her win the 400m. As Edwards had shown himself, and seen confirmed when Kenny Harrison beat him in Atlanta, the triple jump had a boundless capacity to throw up surprises. There were no wild detours from the predicted script in Sydney: a second-round jump of 17.37m left Edwards second behind the Russian, Denis Kapustin, and a season's best distance of 17.71 in the next round gave him a lead which was never seriously challenged subsequently.

Edwards said afterwards: "I've become used to carrying the expectation of the nation. Every year since I won the 1995 world title, I've been seen as our main hope for a medal. I haven't had much success since then, so it's great to finally win something again. We were a bit of a sideshow tonight, there's no doubt about that, but I was prepared for the commotion I might have to walk into. I was overwhelmed at the end. I was on the point of crying a number of times and I had to choke back the tears. I couldn't believe I was in this stadium, at the Games and that I was the Olympic champion. It was almost too much."

The victory gave Edwards the springboard for an impressive finale to his international career. He jumped 17.92m to win the world title in Edmonton, Canada, in 1991 and plugged the one remaining gap in his major trophy collection when he won at the Commonwealth Games the following year. He bowed out of competitive athletics at the 2003 World Championships in Paris, finishing last of the 12 finalists.

With retirement came re-evaluation and finally, in 2007, the admission that he now doubted the existence of God. In an interview with Sky, Edwards said the almighty was too glibly adopted as "a lucky charm" by sportsmen. "They believe that if they believe in God, He will give them the strength to win. That has to be a nonsense – why would God be concerned with the outcome of a sporting contest?"

Edwards's involvement with *Songs of Praise* was an obvious casualty of his new-found scepticism, but he remains an integral part of the BBC's athletics coverage, presenting as well as commentating.

Sept 29: Laser class sailing, Ben Ainslie

VENGEANCE was high on the agenda when Ben Ainslie lined up for the race to decide the Laser class gold medal in Sydney. Four years earlier, the Brazilian-German, Robert Scheidt, had hood-winked 19-year-old Ainslie into disqualification to steal the verdict in Atlanta. This was payback time.

Ainslie's pre-race discussions with coach John Derbyshire floated the attacking and the defensive option. He could win the gold medal by finishing at least 10 places higher than Scheidt or he could concentrate on blocking his rival. If Ainslie prevented Scheidt from finishing no higher than 21st, he would have to make it one of his two discards, again handing the title to Ainslie. The capricious conditions settled the argument. Ainslie told Derbyshire: "The only way I can make sure I win is by sailing him down the fleet."

He likened the confrontation to "a boxing match, with two heavyweights eyeball to eyeball". Scheidt had to take two penalty turns after brushing against Ainslie's boat at the start. He tacked and tacked again, screaming at Ainslie in Portuguese as jury boats watched for any infraction. Ainslie almost fell overboard at one point. The rival boats collided again, leaving Scheidt in the clear, and he picked up a favourable wind on the penultimate leg to improve to 22nd before being held off by the Singaporean, Stanley Tan. Ainslie's provisional win was confirmed when protests and counter-protests brought Scheidt's disqualification for the second collision.

Alan Fraser, writing in the *Daily Mail*, described it as "the most poetical and symmetrical of revenges". Ainslie said after the race: "What goes around comes around. It's a shame it had to come down to that. I would rather have won with a race to spare but I did what I had to do, just as he did what he had to do in 1996." He admitted that he had been "younger and naïve" in Atlanta. Scheidt made his own silent statement by boycotting the press conference.

Not everyone accepted that the end justified the means. Sir Roger Bannister, the first man to break the four-minute mile, made his disapproval known (to Ainslie's clear annoyance). Brazilians were also unhappy: effigies of Ainslie were burned on the streets of Sao Paulo and emailed death threats were intercepted by Australian police. Nothing could prick his elation, however, when the protest hearings ended and he was free to celebrate with his parents, Roddy and Sue.

After Ainslie had won the silver medal in Atlanta, Roddy admitted that he had ploughed £25,000 into his son's campaign. He described it as "money well spent" and insisted: "He will win in Sydney. No question." Ainslie snr was both benefactor and experienced sailor in his own right – he skippered a boat in the Whitbread Round the World Race in 1973. He sold the family business, which made wooden utensils, and the Ainslies moved from Cheshire to Cornwall when Ben was seven. His love affair with sailing began when his parents bought him an Optimist dinghy as a Christmas present.

Ainslie's sporting idols were not the predictable footballers but giants of the America's Cup like New Zealanders Russell Coutts and Chris Dickson. His desire to compete in the cup ran alongside his small-boat ambitions. Ainslie was an under-motivated pupil at Truro School and was bullied because of a photosensitivity which caused blistering and rashes. He was more at home on the water, competing in the Optimist World Championships in Japan when he was only 12 and, as a 16-year-old, won both the European and World Championships for Laser Radials in 1993.

The Lasers were adopted as an Olympic class in 1996, prompting Ainslie to put his A Level studies on hold – his long-time friend, Iain Percy, was a contemporary at Peter Symonds College in Winchester – to concentrate full-time on securing a place in Atlanta. The move was justified when he won a highly competitive qualifying regatta in August 1995, becoming the youngest British sailor to compete in the Olympics. Three other future Olympic champions, Percy, Andrew Simpson and Paul Goodison, were among the opposition. Ainslie was already so committed to his sport that on the odd occasion he went out drinking he would punish himself with a midnight run.

Ainslie was already well aware of Scheidt's reputation and the Brazilian underlined his dominance in the class by winning the world title in Cape Town in March 1996; Ainslie finished third, a huge improvement on the previous two years' results. He admired Scheidt for his professionalism, fitness and, initially anyway, friendly tips. The advice dried up once Scheidt began to see Ainslie as a rival and the Briton's threat rating increased when he won the European title in 1996.

If Scheidt was a tough competitor, the French sailor, Guillaume Florent, was a candidate for the psychiatrist's couch. He shouted out, 'You're effing cheating', as Ainslie passed him in a training series. On the first day of the competition proper, Ainslie almost passed out with heat exhaustion as he finished 28th then weathered a fatuous protest from Florent to claim a fourth place. Ainslie put together an impressive sequence of two first places and three seconds – including one in which he and Scheidt collided – to claim the overall lead with three races remaining.

Ainslie's challenge in the last race, if he was to win the gold medal, was to finish five places ahead of Scheidt. The Brazilian, without any of his rivals being aware, drifted over the start line to be disqualified. In a cleverly cynical manoeuvre, he set off just before the gun sounded, triggering a group of boats to follow suit – including Ainslie. All were disqualified, giving Scheidt the gold medal. Ainslie discovered later that his parents had watched the racing from the spectator boat…accompanied by Scheidt's parents.

Ainslie completed his A Levels at a tutorial college before turning his attentions back to sailing and, more specifically, the goal of turning silver into gold in Sydney. He made his first reconnoitring mission in 1997, won test events in Sydney in both 1998 and 1999 and wrested the world title away from Scheidt in the same years. Scheidt regained the crown in 2000, and though Ainslie was disappointed to finish third his consolation was to be spared the need to qualify for the Olympics through national trials. Goodison finished fifth in the World Championships and agreed to be Ainslie's training partner in Sydney.

The results in the regatta itself fluctuated like the wind and the currents in Sydney Harbour; Ainslie described it as "a bit like sailing on a giant version of the Thames". Scheidt led after the first day, Ainslie won twice to steal the advantage and maintained the lead until "a bad tactical error" allowed Scheidt to sneak back in front. He dominated again in the first race on the final day; Ainslie was relieved just to haul himself up the fleet in the latter stages to finish fourth.

He insisted that his game plan in the last race was the only one available to him. "People make out that I just took the guy out of the race. But to stop one of the best sailors in the world finishing in the top 20 in a race is a huge ask. That's probably the biggest challenge you'll ever face in a yacht race. It's not as though I just ran into the guy and pulled him backwards. I had to do it within the rules, with pinpoint positioning, boat-handling, aggression, tactics, under that much pressure."

Sept 29: Europe class sailing, Shirley Robertson

SHIRLEY ROBERTSON remembers all too clearly the feeling of emptiness when she came home from the Atlanta Olympics in 1996. "I got in the car at Gatwick Airport," she says, "and just sat there for a very long time, not really knowing if I put the car in gear where I would go, what I would do."

In objective terms, fourth place in the Europe class event represented clear progress from Barcelona, where she had finished ninth, but Robertson struggled to put a positive spin on the campaign; she looks back on it as the lowest point in her sailing career. "I'd really worked hard and it meant everything. I hadn't really had much life between, apart from trying to win a gold medal in Atlanta, so it was pretty tough to be so close. I went into the last race in medal contention. It's just so difficult to leave empty-handed. You've nothing to vindicate any of your decision-making or any of the people who've gone out on a limb to help you. Fourth is a really funny position. They don't phone you up or anything – it's strange, like a bereavement."

The inadequacies of British sport were painfully dissected in the wake of the lone gold medal in Atlanta, and Robertson took the criticism personally. "Whatever the results, everyone was trying their best," she says. "It was awful, a real winter of depression for everyone."

This was not the sport she had taken to joyfully as a six-year-old on Loch Ard after her father, Iain, invested £400 in a kit boat which he pieced together in the family's garage in Menstrie, near Stirling. Five years later, he came back from the Boat Show in London with an official Olympic envelope, complete with a message from Rodney Pattisson, the Scottish-born sailor (though avowedly English) who had won his first gold medal in 1968, when Robertson was three months old.

She remembers being "awestruck" when she finally met Pattisson, but for now he was an inspiration – to train longer than anyone else and test more equipment than anyone else. It was said that Pattisson would almost sail to France in his quest for perfection and Robertson identifies with that level of dedication. She watched, enthralled, as a *bona fide* Scot, Mike McIntyre, won in Seoul, and dared to dream of her own golden moment when a women's single-handed dinghy class, the Europe, was incorporated into the Barcelona programme in 1992.

Robertson decided in 1990 that she could only compete effectively if she went full-time and based herself in the south of England. "I'd done my degree at Heriot Watt and I went back to do post grad. I'd been there two weeks and I suddenly thought, if I'm going to go to the Olympics and actually do something while I'm there I need to get on with it. And I left. It was quite a sharp decision – I didn't actually have any money – but I just knew that staying in Edinburgh wasn't the way to do it."

She earned her place in Barcelona by winning the trials and naively expected to be in medal contention. "Everyone thinks they're going to be standing on the podium, but it isn't quite that simple. I still have this vivid image of watching the medal ceremony. I thought, I actually do want to do this. I want to be the one seeing my flag hoisted up the pole. In many ways I wanted it too much, but I worked as hard as I could, not always perhaps in the right direction. I was at the gym twice a day; I had the bike in the garage; I'd seen how the winners won."

The funding picture was still bleak – Robertson recalls receiving a £250 grant which was swallowed up by the cost of driving from Scotland to the south of England and back four times for qualifiers – but the Sports Aid Foundation eased the load. She also admitted, in an interview just before the Atlanta Games, that she was not above a little eyelash-fluttering when sponsorship was at stake. "I've become especially good at flirting with

> 'In Atlanta, I came off the start line and my back leg was shaking so much I couldn't balance the boat'

people with money," she said, adding: "I've no job. I don't own a great deal, just two boats and 20 suits of sails. I've become completely one-dimensional. I've arranged my whole life to achieve a goal. Will I change when it's all over? I hope so."

The desperation to succeed made Robertson emotionally frail – she had a reputation for bursting into tears at the least setback – and anxious. "In Atlanta, I came off the start line and my back leg was shaking so much that I couldn't balance the boat," she recalls. "It might work in the 100m, but not in sailing. Often the boat feels your tension." Despite taking third place in the final race, she finished two points adrift of the bronze medallist, the American Courtenay Becker-Dey.

Robertson turned 30 in 1998, the same year when Lottery funding began to ease the pressure on Olympic sportsmen. With age came a more relaxed outlook. "After Atlanta, I felt that I'd invested so much and I didn't know what else I could do. I did some match racing, sailed with other people and I just knew I couldn't do it the same way. I couldn't approach it with the same level of intensity; I had to spread my wings. I was in much better shape, mentally, physically and technically, by the time we got to Sydney. I was a completely different person when I stepped off the plane to how I had been four years before in Atlanta." Second place in the 1998 World Championships had simply strengthened her resolve.

Sydney Harbour in spring was tricky: a test of technical ability, patience and stoicism. Robertson was equal to the challenge, even when Argentina's Serena Amato led the fleet with three races remaining. "I knew that there would be ups and downs and I just rolled with it. We got to the last day and two races and I had the first blip of the week. I remember approaching Mark Littlejohn, who was my coach, and it was the first time I'd been emotional and the first time I'd thought, 'It won't happen, maybe I'll choke under pressure.' You think of all those other athletes who have...Maybe I can't pull it off on the big occasion. He said, 'Congratulations.' And I said, 'What do you mean congratulations?' He said, 'You came here to win a medal and you have. It's amazing. Take a moment to think about that.' So I thought, let's try to make it gold."

This time, third place was enough; Robertson, Ben Ainslie and Iain Percy received their gold medals on the same night, on the steps of the Opera House. "As we were waiting for the ceremony," Robertson recalls, "Ian Walker [silver medallist in the Star class] said, 'This may never ever happen again. Make sure you enjoy every second.' " Robertson already knew that if there was going to be a repeat performance it would not be in the Europe. She never set foot again in the boat, which is on display in a museum on the Isle of Wight, but says half-jokingly: "I might retrieve it one day and sail it because it was a lovely boat to sail."

In the after-glow of victory – she was the first Scottish woman to win an Olympic gold medal since 1912 – Robertson did a lap of honour before a rugby international at Murrayfield; she was spotted in the Royal Box at Wimbledon. In an interview before the Athens Games, she reflected: "Life was hectic: loads of opportunities, a lot of parties – an awful lot of parties, two or three nights a week. It was a bit mad for a while, opening supermarkets and all that." Robertson's new-found celebrity had another side benefit: *Hello!* magazine bought the exclusive rights for pictures from her wedding to Jamie Boag in June 2001. "My husband hated all that," she admitted. "My attitude was to take the money and have a really good party. The cash meant we were able to invite everyone. It was quite fun, really."

Sept 30: Finn class sailing, Iain Percy

IAIN PERCY found himself swept along on a wave of patriotic pride as Britain finally identified a formula for success in Sydney. "We kicked every other country's behinds," he said after winning the Finn class with a race to spare. "It's nice to see that we can do it in some sports. We have the best organisation and the best-supported team here. The whole scene of British yachting is looking good."

Ben Ainslie and Shirley Robertson, Britain's other sailing gold medallists in 2000, were able to draw on their previous Olympic experiences; Percy was in uncharted waters. Only a year earlier, he had felt torn between persevering as a full-time sailor – he was still uncertain about his status within the sport – and putting his economics degree to lucrative use in the City. The win in Sydney made the decision for him.

Although he was still only 24, sailing had been part of Percy's life for 20 years. His general practitioner father, David, and physiotherapist mother, Gillian, wanted a sport which they could enjoy with their four small children, all of whom would go on either to win or finish second in national youth championships. They joined the Weston Sailing Club in Southampton and Percy had already tasted victory, in an Optimists race for under eights, when a fiercely competitive streak revealed itself for the first time. He was so distraught at being beaten by his sister, Katrina, that he lay down in his boat and was still in a rage when he was picked up by a rescue boat.

As a teenager, Percy competed with and against Ainslie, a year his junior, at Hayling Island Sailing Club. On one occasion, they lost control in lively seas and had to be rescued by a lifeboat. Percy twice won national titles in the Laser class and also finished fifth in the Laser World Championships before outgrowing the smaller boat and switching to Finns in 1996, by which time he was a year into his degree at Bristol University.

He graduated with a 2:1 in 1998 and, with the benefit of Lottery funding – the basic allowance for sailors was then in the region of £20,000 a year – he was able to commit full time through to Sydney. Beyond that, he was keeping his options open and, according to the *Sunday Times'* Keith Wheatley, "fond of saying that economics was just as exciting as sailing and more intellectually challenging than charging round in dinghies".

Results began to pick up in 1999 for Percy, who also now had British Aerospace on board, financing the development and building of carbon fibre masts. He had a reputation for sailing aggressively and maintained that the sport was not quite as complicated as was made out. "You just go flat out upwind and then fast downwind," was the game plan. The physically demanding Finn class was a test of strength and endurance, so Percy devoted three hours a day to aerobic work and weight-training.

He finished a single point ahead of Poland's Mateusz Kuszniere-wicz, the reigning Olympic champion, to win the European Championship and, equally significantly, came out on top at the pre-Olympic regatta in Sydney. Percy was so dominant in Britain's Olympic trials the following April that he won eight out of nine races to secure his place for Sydney with a day to spare. The only setback of note came when he was disqualified three times in five races as he finished 18th at the World Championships in Weymouth.

When he arrived in Sydney, Percy declared himself happy with his preparation, relaxed and desperate to get started. Kusznierewicz had no hesitation in nominating Percy as his main rival; the other contender of obvious pedigree and experience was the Swede, Fredrik Loof. He and Kusznierewicz had both won the World Championship twice over the past four years.

Percy was master of the fleet and the tricky conditions almost from gun to finishing line. He led after adding a win to his second place in the first race and was never lower than ninth before putting himself in a near impregnable position with victories in races seven and nine. The tension told in the normally affable Percy's clipped response to media inquiries, but he went into the final day's two races with a 20-point cushion over Loof. A Machiavellian approach was called for.

"It looked simple on paper but it certainly didn't feel it," said Percy afterwards. "I was very nervous before the first race. The Swede was the only other person who could win, so I had two options. One was to try and win myself, which is always risky. The second was just to sit on top of Loof and make sure he didn't have a good race. I just had to make sure he didn't finish in a high position rather than go out for the lead and maybe see it go wrong on a wind shift or someone getting lucky. It's not my natural style but I knew what I had to do and about halfway through the race I knew it was going to happen right and I started to relax."

Loof was 11th, Percy 14th (his worst result of the regatta) and gold was his with a race to spare. "I was a comfortable winner in the end," he admitted. "A few people have made mistakes but I didn't. I just set up every morning and tried to do the best I could on the water." He deflected credit to his coach, David Howlett, saying: "David has been the biggest single factor in my improvement over the past 12 months. Having him around while I'm racing and using his knowledge to do better the next day rather than next month has been so important." Howlett, a former Olympian himself, responded: "He's got stamina, tactical ability and everything else you need. He can be as good as he wants to. There are no limits."

Oct 1: Super heavyweight boxing, Audley Harrison

AUDLEY HARRISON had "a full bucket of self-belief" when he was growing up and not much else. His mother walked out on the family when he was four and by the age of 17 his temporary home (for 18 months) was the Feltham Young Offenders' Institution in north-west London. He contemplated a life as a professional criminal. The salvation of a boxing career was still some way off, but he worked on adding fitness to his already impressive physique. He also began to realise that his boredom and pent-up aggression could be channelled more usefully than by train-surfing (riding on the top then climbing back in as tunnels approached), street robbery and graffiti.

Harrison made his debut in the ring in 1991, when he was 19, though he remembered his first significant 'bout' as a street fight with a local thug which established him as "someone not to be messed with". It was somehow appropriate that his first boxing match under Queensberry rules, on May 14 1992, should be against a policeman. He won and the adrenaline buzz was much the same as it had been when he was making mischief in Harlesden High Street.

Although Harrison had left school without a single qualification, there was a sharp brain waiting to be activated. He took night courses in community sport and recreational management, delved into sports psychology and, in an effort to put his fledgling boxing career back on track after a series of defeats, joined the famous Repton Boys' Club, in Bethnal Green. The first of three hernia operations prevented Harrison from fighting in 1996, but he started a sports studies and leisure management degree at Brunel University which concluded with a 10,000-word thesis, 'A Sociological Perspective on the Justification of Amateur Boxing'. Backing words with deeds, he set up a boxing club at the university and claimed in his autobiography that he was "living ten people's lives at once".

His own boxing career took precedence in 1997, and he earned a trip to the 1998 Commonwealth Games (and £700 a month in Lottery funding) by winning back-to-back ABA titles in front of the television cameras. Short-term loss for long-term gain was Harrison's bargain with himself. He was deeply in debt, and couldn't even afford to run a car, but decided that he would resist any overtures to turn professional after the Kuala Lumpur Games.

Harrison was the unofficial spokesman for team discontent – mostly aimed at manager Brian Pollard – both before and during the Commonwealth Games. He was shop steward, court jester and camp commander rolled into one. The super heavyweight division was so under-represented that Harrison needed to win only three fights to claim the gold medal. He made himself more visible in the shop window by sporting gold streaks in his hair.

The final against the Mauritian, Michael Macague, lasted 63 seconds; four punches from Harrison were enough. The harder part was afterwards, when Brand Harrison took over, handing out signed photographs to Malaysian children and rapping for the benefit of the television cameras. "I wanted to make a public exhibition of myself in Kuala Lumpur," he admitted. The press, too, were subjected to both barrels from the Harrison hype gun: "I'm going to win the Olympic crown," he promised. "Then I'm going to be professional heavyweight champion of the world."

Harrison was more concerned with taking on the world of perceived injustice when he got home. The funding dried up and there appeared to be a genuine prospect that no British boxer would compete in Sydney; he decided to champion the cause by setting up the Amateur Boxing Union of England. The BOA stepped in with assistance and Harrison, fresh from securing his BSc, was finally able to focus on the World Championships in Houston. Promoter Frank Warren dangled a £100,000 signing-on fee for him to turn professional, but Harrison resisted overtures, only to lose his second fight in Houston.

The road to Sydney was no smoother than it had been to Kuala Lumpur. Harrison, one of only two British boxers to compete at the 2000 Games (light heavyweight Courtney Fry was the other), fell out with his trainer Terry Edwards. Even though Edwards went out to Sydney, Harrison refused to speak to him and, after intervention from Simon Clegg, the British team's chef d'équipe, Kelvin Travis was drafted in as trainer. Once again, Harrison was determined to emphasise the product. T-shirts sporting slogans like, 'H-Bomb. The Time For Talking Has Stopped', were distributed to British fans; Donna Fraser, the 400m runner, became his unofficial hair stylist during the Games.

Harrison had to beat a former world champion, the Russian, Aleksei Lyozin, in his first fight, and when he outpointed the Ukrainian, Oleksei Mazikin, he was already guaranteed at least a bronze medal. In the semi-final, Harrison was inspired by a capacity crowd of 10,000 to produce what he rated his best ever performance as an amateur. He overpowered Paolo Vidoz, a resilient Italian, and saw the biggest obstacle to a gold medal as the knuckle on his left hand which swelled up alarmingly after each fight. He was already insisting that he was "destined" to win the title, adding: "I know that it's Mount Everest that I'm on and that climbing is very dangerous. But I know that I'm climbing the right mountain, the rewards are at the top and I'm happy to be going up."

> 'I know it's Mount Everest that I'm on, but I'm climbing the right mountain'

A painkilling injection reduced the knuckle pain before Harrison's final against Mukhtarkhan Dildabekov, of Kazakhstan. If he needed any more motivation it came with the suggestion that the difference between gold and silver could be £50 million. Harrison opened up after a cagy first round to build a points lead which Dildabekov could not recover. The final margin was a decisive 30-16 in Harrison's favour. He felt nothing but exhaustion in the first few minutes after the fight, but treated journalists to another rap before outlining his vision for the future.

"People turn pro too soon in Britain," he said (Harrison was now 29). "They are all hype and no substance. It is important for me to turn pro as a genuine contender. It's important from a marketing point of view that Audley Harrison the product is right. If I'm fighting for a British title I expect to sell the place out. I'm not going to get involved in anything that leaves me feeling marginalised. I won't be happy if I don't have some control. I put my neck on the line and, in the professional game, it will mean a good lawyer and a lot of negotiation."

Chris Finnegan, the last British boxer to win an Olympic title before Harrison (in 1968), commented: "He seems a bright young guy – very different from the way so many of us were in my day. So maybe, 32 years from now, he might still have more of what he makes than I've ended up with."

Harrison was famous, but not so famous that everyone could get his name right. As the British team filed through the Heathrow arrivals' hall, a photographer shouted out: "Audrey, over here!" At a Buckingham Palace reception, he was accorded more respect by the Princess Royal who, according to Harrison anyway, said to the Queen: "Mummy, this is the boxer Audley Harrison I was telling you about." She allegedly replied: "Of course, I know all about you."

The dialogue with television companies and promoters on both sides of the Atlantic began almost immediately. Harrison wanted to stay in Britain and was swayed by the greater reach of terrestrial TV when A-Force Promotions, the purpose-built company he set up, agreed a 10-fight deal with the BBC worth £1 million. The cynics were circling from the moment Harrison despatched his first opponent, the journeyman American Michael Middleton, in the opening round of a fight which attracted six million viewers. The standard of the opposition did not improve markedly and Harrison attracted more publicity for action outside the ring after he had beaten Matt Ellis at York Hall, Bethnal Green, in May 2003. A war of words between Harrison and Herbie Hide sparked a near riot and hastened Harrison's relocation to the United States. He claimed that the BBC's decision not to renew the deal amounted to institutional racism.

Harrison was still at base camp in his assault on Everest, but he was given one last glimpse of the summit when he took on WBA champion David Haye at the M.E.N. Arena in Manchester, in December 2010. Harrison landed one punch before being stopped in the third round and initially had part of his purse withheld by the British Boxing Board of Control.

Oct 1: Modern pentathlon, Stephanie Cook

STEPH COOK and her modern pentathlon team-mate, Kate Allenby, were joined for their 5.15am breakfast by boxer Audley Harrison. He

267

tucked into a fry-up; they settled for muesli and banana. Both were recipes for British success on the final day of the Sydney Olympics, though Cook and Allenby had to work rather harder for their taste of glory. Harrison was in the ring for nine minutes; they were at it for 13 hours.

Cook's gold medal, her reward for making up a 49-second gap on the American, Emily DeRiel, in the cross country, the final discipline, was the last to be won at the Games. It was also, according to the *Daily Mail*'s Neil Wilson, one which deserved to stick in the memory. "Sight of her run was restricted to 18,000 in the Baseball Stadium," he wrote, "but it deserved nothing less than the full house of the Olympic Stadium. Nothing seen there on the track in the previous nine days could have surpassed it for excitement."

Although Cook, 28, had put her medical career on hold to prepare for the 2000 Games, tapping into the sport's centre of excellence at the University of Bath, her sense of priority was unswervingly consistent. Medicine was her calling; modern pentathlon was her hobby (albeit one for which she trained with a professional athlete's dedication).

Cook's mother was a university administrator and there was never any doubt that Steph would make full use of the education system. Her family moved from Irvine, in Ayrshire, to Bedford when she was two. She was a keen member of the Pony Club (useful grounding for the modern pentathlon), swam strongly and was a good enough runner to finish seventh in the national cross-country championships in 1997. Cook's schooling ended in Cambridge, where she also attended university, adding another string to her sporting bow as a lightweight rower. A rib stress fracture forced her to give up the sport and while completing her clinical training at Oxford she turned her attention to modern pentathlon. One of her team-mates was DeRiel and both lobbied hard in 2002 for the sport's retention in the Olympics when, only two years after women were included for the first time, it was threatened with expulsion. The men's team event, won by Britain in 1976, was thrown out in 1996 and the individual competition was condensed into a single day.

After qualifying as a doctor in 1997, Cook struggled to fit in training around house jobs in Poole and Oxford before taking up a research position in Guildford which gave her greater flexibility. Her results at the 1998 World Championships – she finished eighth in the individual event and helped the British team to a silver medal – earned Cook full subsistence funding and she moved to Bath in 1999 to train full time at the new national training centre for modern pentathlon. Cook recalled that before she came under the expert tuition of the Slovakian coach, Fridrich Foldes, her fencing instruction amounted to, 'Just stick your arm out and get her before she gets you.'

Cook was now more comfortable with foil in hand, though fencing was still her weakest link. She lost 13 of her 23 bouts, including the first five, to finish joint 18th out of 24 competitors. Significantly, though, she managed to beat Allenby, who later became national champion as a fencer. If the result had been reversed, Allenby would have won the gold medal instead. Even after a personal best in the third event, the swimming, Cook appeared to be off the radar of potential medallists. She was then 14th and still only eighth after a riding competition won by DeRiel.

British interest focused on Allenby, who was second at this stage, 20 points behind DeRiel and 178 ahead of Cook. The only person who did not accept that her chance had gone was Cook. "I've made up bigger deficits before, so I always knew that I could do it," she said afterwards. "It was just a case of keeping my head and not going out too fast." The time-delayed starts just added to the drama – Cook hauled in Allenby with 400 metres to go and passed DeRiel 250 metres from the finish.

"Once I was past Emily," she said, "I knew then that no pentathlete was capable of coming back to me." Allenby was as gracious in defeat (she regarded the bronze medal as a genuine consolation) as Cook was euphoric in victory. "I'm thrilled to bits," said Allenby. "What a way for Britain to finish the Games. Steph's a demon trainer. She's trained so hard she's deserved everything she got out there."

For a few months, Cook was happy to tread the boards as a celebrity. She co-presented the People's Awards at the Royal Albert Hall with Matthew Pinsent; she was the face of British Smile Week; she pressed the button on the National Lottery Show, modelled a dress at an ITV charity auction and even spent an hour lying in the window of Selfridges to advertise British Airways' flat-out first-class seat. "That's up there with the most ridiculous things I've done since Sydney," she admitted in an interview in 2001.

Cook also managed to keep her eye on the ball, losing four times to her heiress apparent as Britain's top modern pentathlete, Georgina Harland, but winning the European title, the final World Cup event and her emotion-charged farewell to the sport, the World Championship, at Millfield School in Somerset. "I know I'm going to miss it incredibly," she reflected, "but I know that I'm doing the right thing."

Steph Cook's two lives, as sportswoman and medic, were bridged by a week-long stint as an aid worker for the medical relief agency, Merlin, in the earthquake-hit Indian state of Gujarat. Her sporting idol, Eric Liddell, the 400m winner at the 1924 Olympics who subsequently devoted himself to missionary work in China, would have approved. "It is not easy to become an Olympic champion," she said at the time. "But it is even harder to rebuild your life after you've lost everything in a disaster such as this."

Cook flew out to India two days after her victory at Millfield. She flew back the day before taking up her appointment as a senior house officer in the accident and emergency department at the Royal United Hospital in Bath. In a diary for the *Times* – her fee went to Merlin – Cook described her first night: "We had everything from dislocated fingers, broken toes, head injuries and sprained ankles to an acute asthma attack and a heroin overdose. Quite a lot of the staff know me and what my name is, so I feel as if I ought to know theirs too. People are pleased that I've returned to medicine, and none more so than me. I feel that, in a way, I'm back in the world I belong in – although at 3.30 this morning I started to wonder why I'd given up the luxury of being able to sleep through the night."

She married Daniel Carroll, a vet, in 2005, suffering no more than bruises to body and pride when she fell from a horse while riding side-saddle to the reception. She now has two children and works as a GP in Sussex. Cook was part of the BBC's commentary team when Harland matched her first place in the cross country to win a bronze medal in Athens.

2004

Aug 18: Individual three-day event, Leslie Law

LESLIE LAW was competing in novice horse trials at Solihull, in Warwickshire, when he discovered that he had won three-day eventing's ultimate prize: the individual Olympic title. The news was broken to Law in a phone call from Yogi Breisner, his friend, mentor and the British team manager in Athens. "You're not going to believe this but you've got the gold," Breisner said breathlessly. There was silence at the other end of the line. "Hello. Leslie, are you there?"

Law, who had left Athens with his fate resting in the hands of the Court of Arbitration for Sport, knew that a verdict was imminent but he was still lost for words. "Oh my God," he eventually responded. "I was gobsmacked," he admitted to reporters afterwards. "But I can tell you it feels pretty good. Now I intend to hold another party." He withdrew his two horses from the competition and went home to the Gloucestershire village of Naunton.

The complex farce had been set in motion three days earlier, when television evidence showed that the German rider, Bettina Hoy, had crossed the start line twice on Ringwood Cockatoo in her first show-jumping round. A 14-point time penalty was overturned on appeal and she went on to clinch the gold medal. Cue for a barrage of counter-protests from the British, French and American teams, who all had a vested interest. The chief beneficiary, when the Court of Arbitration ruled that the appeals committee had exceeded their powers, was Law; his individual silver was upgraded to gold and the British team were promoted to second place behind France.

Law was denied the instant thrill of receiving his reward, but the compensation package was almost as memorable. In mid-October, all the British medallists were paraded on an open-topped bus tour of

London. When Law admitted to the BBC's Sue Barker that he had missed hearing the National Anthem in Athens, the accompanying band struck up in his belated honour. Later, at a Buckingham Palace reception, Princess Anne presented him with his gold medal, to a torrent of applause from the other medallists.

The recognition, for what would have been Britain's first victory in Athens, was diluted by the delay, but the achievement – Law was council house raised and comprehensive school educated – was in no way devalued. At 39, he was approaching veteran status; he had never won a top-class title as an individual; Law and Shear L'Eau were regarded as solid back-up for the true stars in the British team, Pippa Funnell and William Fox-Pitt.

Law was brought up in Herefordshire; his father, Lawson, was a lorry driver with the instincts of an entrepreneur. He spruced up second-hand mobile homes and caravans before selling them on and employed Leslie and his younger brother, Graham, to break in ponies which were then sold at a tidy profit. Leslie left Lady Hawkins School with four GCSEs and advanced his equine education by spending two years in the United States. He then worked for the documentary maker, Revel Guest, at her Cabalva House stud near Hay-on-Wye in Herefordshire.

In the early Nineties, Law was briefly married to fellow eventer Harriet Harrison, the granddaughter of actor Rex Harrison; Law was only able to meet the divorce settlement by selling a horse in which he had a part share. His riding career was interrupted when he snapped a cruciate ligament while jumping off a haystack and although he eventually got back in the saddle he then managed to knock himself unconscious by riding into a tree.

Law was the top British finisher on New Flavour at the Badminton trials in 1996, earning selection for the Atlanta Olympics, but New Flavour was ruled out by a bruised foot at the first horse inspection. Law was stripped of his accreditation and admitted in his auto-biography: "I felt as though I'd been found guilty of a crime and sent to jail." The following year, his horse Capitano dropped dead while competing at Gatcombe, but Law's longer-term prospects improved immeasurably with the purchase of the Irish-bred full brothers, Shear H20 (aka Solo) and Shear L'Eau (Stan), named after owner Jeremy Lawson's insurance company Shearwater. Shear H20 partnered Law to win the Bramham trials in 1999 and they booked their passage to Sydney by finishing second at Badminton in 2000.

The British team – Law did not compete as an individual – claimed silver medals behind Australia, but felt that they had let a chance slip. Ian Stark's horse, Jaybee, had failed the final inspection after the cross country, leaving Law, Pippa Funnell and Jeanette Brakewell to carry the flag. All had fences down, while both Funnell and Brakewell incurred time penalties. The Australians were not made to pay fully for their own errors on the final day.

In 2001, Law was part of the winning British team at the European Championships in Pau, France, though his own score did not count. Rider error accounted for the 20 jumping penalties imposed on Shear H20 during the cross-country section at the 2002 World Equestrian Games in Jerez, Spain. Again Law was the discard, but Britain's bronze medal qualified them for the 2004 Olympics.

He was partnered by Shear L'Eau at the European Championships in Punchestown, Ireland, in 2003. They not only helped the British team to retain their title but also finished fourth in the individual standings to press their claims as a likely combination in Athens. A short format was introduced for the 2004 Games, omitting the roads and tracks and steeplechase phases. The likelihood of medals being won and lost on a single show-jumping error became all the greater.

Although Shear L'Eau did an impeccable dressage test to lie 10th after the first discipline (Britain were fractional leaders at that stage), Law believed that there were too many outstanding riders ahead of him to think seriously of an individual medal. It was indicative of the gentleness of the cross-country course that Britain's five riders – the best three to count – all went clear but the team still slipped back to third because of time penalties. Third became fourth when Fox-Pitt's horse, Tamarillo, was withdrawn with a chipped stifle bone.

Law was 11th in the individual rankings and concerned only with improving the team's position. The 12-year-old Shear L'Eau had never produced a clear round in the show-jumping phase of a major competition but ear covers helped to combat his sensitivity to noise. Despite rattling the planks at the final fence, he was able to reserve his best for the biggest stage. Law and Shear L'Eau leapt up to fifth place, one behind Funnell on Primmore's Pride. A team bronze was assured.

By the time the riders came out for the evening jumping, which would sort out the individual medals, judgment had been made in Hoy's favour. Law kept his eye on the prize. "It would have been easy to be distracted by all the confusion and discussion that was going on about Bettina's score," he said later, "but I think that's where age and experience helped me." His place was unaltered after another clear round, but mistakes by Funnell and the American, Kimberley Severson, and an error-strewn round from the leader, Nicolas Touzaint, of France, left him second and satisfied. "The feeling of achievement was incredible," he said. It was all the greater when silver became gold.

Law became only the second Briton to win the individual title and the first since Richard Meade in 1972. Meade applauds his achievement but adds: "I feel very sorry for him in a way because that's not the way you want to win any competition." There was no great spin-off from the success for Law, but a hospital charity benefited to the tune of £760 when a bag of Shear L'Eau's manure was sold on eBay. Law and his fiancée, Trina Lightwood, who had groomed for him since the mid-Nineties, split up at the end of 2005, when Law moved to the United States. He married the Canadian rider, Lesley Grant, in 2007, and the couple run an eventing business in Florida and Virginia.

Aug 19: Yngling class sailing, Shirley Robertson, Sarah Ayton, Sarah Webb

SHIRLEY ROBERTSON was part of the family at the Pink Palace, the British team's rented home from home by the Rushcutters Bay marina in Sydney, and she fancied a less solitary sailing challenge in Athens. The Yngling, adopted as a class for crews of three in 2004, was certainly a challenge, but it represented a leap in the dark for almost everyone. "I had done loads of match racing in keelboats," says Robertson. "So I thought, how hard can it be? I had the gold medal so I was really buoyed by that, but we were really short of money and it was very expensive: it cost 10 times as much as the Europe. I didn't really understand the boat and I couldn't buy knowledge."

In the initial stages of the campaign, Robertson was crewed by Sarah Ayton and Inga Leask. Ayton, though only 20 at the time, had been her training partner in Sydney. Born in Ashford, Middlesex, she began sailing when she was seven and at 10 made her European debut in the Taser class. In 1995, while competing in an event on the south coast, she was taken ill with a potentially fatal strain of meningitis and was in a coma for three days before recovering. Leask, Shetland Islands born and a biology graduate from Southampton, helped Robertson and Ayton to a significant win at the Palma regatta in April 2003 but pulled out ill soon afterwards.

Robertson recalls: "We were at a point, 18 months out from Athens, when we were missing a crew member. Her father had owned the boat, so we were then missing a boat. We had no money and no coach. A garage full of bits and pieces was the sum total of what we had. When I look back on that campaign it's amazing that we managed to turn it round. Winning a gold medal does give you the confidence that you can put a project together, not choke under pressure and make the right decision at the right time.

"The first thing we got was a coach, Ian Walker, who came back from GBR Challenge [the boat which competed in the America's Cup challenger series in 2002]. In essence he chose us. He saw that we had the right ingredients and realised that he could help win us gold. That was a fundamental turning point and then Volvo came in as sponsor. It wasn't easy by any means, but things started to come together and it was a huge relief for me to have another grown-up in the campaign. Ian had great technical knowledge, an incredible work ethic and was very good in a project. You can't have everything and he's very good at prioritising."

Robertson and Walker quickly recruited Sarah Webb, three years older than Ayton (who became known as 'Nipper') but also Ashford-born and similarly affiliated to Queen Mary Sailing Club. Webb was another early starter in the sport and had narrowly missed Olympic selection in the 470 class in 2000. There was now only one missing component. Robertson was determined to have a boat built to their specifications, but the cost, £57,000, was beyond their means so she sold £1,000 shares in 'Blonde Ambition' at a fund-raising evening on the Isle of Wight, where she now lived; 34 Cowes residents bought a stake. "It was lovely," says Robertson. "I felt part of the community and they felt that they were part of what we were doing so it was very special when we won."

Their World Championship results between 2001 and 2004 – 14th, 16th, 7th and 16th – made dismal reading, but they won the test regatta in Athens and qualified for the Games a year in advance. Robertson insisted (and still insists): "We weren't about the World Championships. We were about Athens for two weeks. I never remember thinking we were going to win the gold medal. We just worked really hard every day at becoming faster and smarter, fitter and better at communicating. We talked a lot."

The 'Three Blondes in a Boat' took up residence in Greece two months before the Games began and maintained a consistency of performance which none of their rivals could match. They finished no lower than sixth in the first nine races and, even with an eighth place in race ten they had the luxury of being able to sit out the final day. They celebrated by linking arms and leaping into the Saronic Gulf. Robertson said: "This one is sweeter even than Sydney because there were two other people on the boat with me." She also joked that the day's delay before the medal ceremony would give them "an excuse and time to get their hair done".

Robertson's return to Gatwick was a rather happier affair than it had been eight years earlier:

> They sent a limo to pick up [double gold medallist] Kelly Holmes – we got a helicopter! I hadn't felt at all emotional about it up until then. It was about getting the job done and not letting the girls down and even when we were on the podium I didn't shed a tear, but when we flew over the Downs and I could see the island I burst into tears. I was sitting in the back with a cameraman, whom I knew very well, who was following our journey. And there I was in floods and floods of tears. We were going home to the people who'd really helped us make it happen. It was amazing. We arrived about eight o'clock at night and we got in the only double-decker bus on the island, open top. We did a loop around the town and came along the sea front, all lined with people, and we stopped at my club in Cowes, where we'd had the parting. There were barricades and police. It was really special to share it.

Robertson wanted one more taste of the Olympic experience, but while she was cherishing a chunk of domestic normality, Ayton and Webb were already re-focusing on Beijing and bedding in a new crewmate, Pippa Wilson, a former junior world champion. Robertson gave birth to twins, Killian and Annabel, in July 2006, and was back in a boat 11 weeks later. She maintains that she felt let down more by the British federation, who did not give her sufficient time to re-prove herself (with Annie Nash and Lucy Macgregor), than by her former team-mates. "We were just beginning the journey," she says.

The winning mentality and adaptability have helped Robertson to move seamlessly into the media world, as presenter of CNN's magazine programme, *Mainsail*, and front person for the BBC's sailing coverage.

Aug 20: 1km time trial cycling, Chris Hoy

FOR all his record-breaking successes in Beijing, the race which defined Chris Hoy's career – the one which opened his gold medal account – was the kilometre time trial in Athens four years earlier. Hoy later recalled: "I had never known anything like the pressure I experienced in Athens, but somehow I managed to ride what I consider now to be an almost perfect race: and I did it when it most mattered."

Hoy could easily have missed his date with destiny. A few weeks before setting out for Greece, he was involved in a slow-motion collision with a police van in Manchester. He was winding down from a punishing training session in Athens itself, a week before the start of the Games, when he accelerated in an effort to avoid a bus at a roundabout and skidded on melting tarmac, coming down heavily on his left side. The scars and scabs were still on show when he lined up in the final.

As the favourite and top seed, Hoy was the last to ride. He could only watch as the Australian, Shane Kelly, the German, Stefan Nimke, and France's Arnaud Tournant improved the Olympic record in turn. Tournant's time of 1min 0.0896sec was the first under 61 seconds at sea level. Hoy remained calm, even when the countdown clock was set off prematurely. His split times were all quicker than his rivals, though the advantage with a lap to go was down to 0.07sec. Experiencing lung-bursting pain on a level which he had never known before, Hoy put in a superhuman effort to cross the line in 1min 0.0711sec, 0.185sec faster than Tournant. As he rode round the track in a celebratory daze he could see his mother, sister and, most prominently, his father, madly waving a home-made 'Real McHoy' flag.

David Hoy could have been forgiven for rewinding 20 years, to the time when he commandeered the kitchen of the family home in Edinburgh to upgrade his seven-year-old son's first bike, a £5 purchase from a church jumble sale. Chris was a sport-obsessed child who soon deserted his first love, chess, for more physical pursuits. The story that he was inspired to take up cycling at seven after being captivated by the BMX chase sequence in *E.T.* had the ring of Wikipedia fiction...until Hoy confirmed it was true in his autobiography.

His father, who worked in the building industry, shrugged off budgetary concerns to send Chris and his sister, Carrie, to a mixed-sex independent school, George Watson's, alma mater of Scotland's foremost pair of rugby-playing brothers, Gavin and Scott Hastings.

Chris enjoyed the precision of maths and science and became one of Britain's leading BMX riders within his age group. He was fifth in the Under 12 European Championships in 1987 and also competed in the World Championships in Orlando, Florida, before retiring at the grand old age of 14.

The transition from BMX to track cycling was far from immediate or automatic; mountain biking filled the void in his teens as other sports vied for Hoy's attention. He had been an average footballer and painfully devoted Hearts fan – until they broke his 10-year-old heart by faltering when a league and cup double were within grasp in 1985-86. Hoy was then an erratic rugby fly-half before settling on a sport which resulted in fewer injuries: rowing. It was also his first experience of rigorous training. Hoy represented Scotland as a junior and won a silver medal in the coxless pairs at the British Schools' Championship.

Rowing and mountain biking also became back numbers on the Hoy CV. He later reflected: "I had now 'retired' from five sports, which is not bad for an 18-year-old." Finally, road and track cycling gave him an outlet in which he could shine on a longer-term basis. He was inspired by the deeds of Chris Boardman and, more particularly, Graeme Obree; both broke the world hour record in 1993 and Obree added the world pursuit title. "Obree ticked every box as far as I was concerned," wrote Hoy. "He was the best in the world, he was an original, he was inspirational…and he was from Scotland."

Hoy made his own breakthrough on the track in 1994 when he finished second in the sprint at the British Junior Championships. In the same year he started a degree in physics and maths at St Andrews University; the social life appealed but the course did not and he dropped out at the start of his second year, returning home to work in a bookshop before embarking on a sports science degree at the University of Edinburgh. He won British and Scottish titles in 1995 and, for the first time, glimpsed a trophy-laden future in the sport. Hoy competed at his first World Championships the following year, teaming up with Jason Queally and his close friend and fellow Scot, Craig MacLean, at the newly opened Manchester Velodrome. Their sprint challenge lasted just as long as it took for Queally's foot to slip off the pedal at the start.

A cheque for £10,000, part of the first tranche of payments under Lottery funding, enabled Hoy to cycle full-time when he graduated in 1999. His Olympic ambitions came into sharper focus when he, MacLean and Queally took the silver medal in the team sprint at the

1999 World Championships. Although British cycling was moving forward – Chris Boardman's coach, Peter Keen, had been installed in the newly created post of performance director – the organisation was still far from the well-oiled machine in place for Athens and Beijing. The sprinters, regarded as maverick trouble-makers, had neither a specialist coach nor state-of-the-art carbon fibre bikes as the Sydney Olympics drew closer. In the end, with the appointment of the French-Canadian, Martin "Marv" Barras, they got both.

Queally's thoroughly unexpected victory in the kilometre time trial raised the bar of possibility for the whole British team. Hoy later admitted: "Jason's gold medal winning ride was by far the most significant thing that had happened during my career. It opened my eyes to what might be possible; it brought new horizons into view; and it altered the course that I would take in the years after Sydney." The immediate knock-on effect was a silver medal in the team sprint – the best that Britain could hope to achieve against an outstanding French trio.

They were still on a high when they competed at the World Championships in Manchester the following month. Hoy celebrated his status as an Olympic medallist by having the five rings unskilfully tattooed on his shoulder. The team sprint followed the same script as in Sydney and, though Hoy was not yet dissatisfied with silver, he knew that nothing less than gold would satisfy him in the future. The catalyst for Hoy's emergence as a world-class individual was his decision to start competing in the kilo and the change of emphasis was quickly vindicated when he won a World Cup race in the discipline, riding the bike Queally had used in Sydney (Queally, according to Hoy, believed that it should have been occupying pride of place in a museum, instead). Hoy's time would have been good enough for the bronze medal in the Olympics.

Despite Queally's misgivings about the bike, he was selflessly supportive to Hoy, outlining his training programme in detail and emphasising the importance of rest periods. In time, Hoy evolved his own, more intensive routine and he showed brilliant form in 2002, denying Tournant a fifth successive world title and also winning the team sprint in Copenhagen. Even before that he had become only the fourth rider to record a time below 1min 2sec to win the Commonwealth Games kilo in Manchester.

In 2003, Hoy struggled to cope with the weight of expectation; he failed to defend his world title and third place in the National Championships even threw up the possibility that he might miss selection for Athens. He sought guidance from Shane Sutton, the straight-talking Australian who helped to improve morale after Barras left his post in 2002; he tapped into Boardman's meticulous methodology; a single session with psychiatrist Steve Peters helped him to quarantine negative thoughts and 'keep the chimp in its cage'. Hoy was back on track, actually and metaphorically, when he improved his personal best to win the time trial at the 2004 World Championships in Melbourne.

Hoy did not have long to dwell on his kilo victory in Athens: the team sprint got under way the following day. Despite recording the second fastest ever time, Hoy, Jason Queally (drafted in for a below-par Craig MacLean) and Jamie Staff lost to Germany in the second round. Hoy's downbeat mood after the Games owed more to a post-gold sense of anti-climax and his motivation all but vanished when, in June 2005, cycling's world governing body, the UCI, announced that the kilometre time trial was being omitted from the Olympic programme to accommodate a BMX competition. "Personally, it felt like a kick in the teeth," Hoy admitted.

Perversely, he came out of the shake-up with more rather than fewer events, adding both the individual sprint and keirin to his competitive repertoire. The kilometre time trial was retained in the World Championship schedule. Hoy took so readily to the keirin (a lucrative sport within a sport in Japan) that he won world titles in both 2007 and 2008. On each occasion, he doubled up successfully, winning the time trial in 2007 and the individual sprint in 2008. An attempt to claim Tournant's kilometre world record of 58.875sec, which took Hoy to the extreme altitude of the Bolivian capital, La Paz, ended in narrow failure in 2007, though he did post a world best time over 500m on the same day.

Aug 21: Individual pursuit cycling, Bradley Wiggins

POST-GOLD syndrome is a complaint for which time is the only known cure. Typically, feet begin to touch the ground again after a month. In Bradley Wiggins's case the disorientation was harder to shake off. "My bender after the Olympics lasted a good eight or nine months," he admitted in his autobiography, "and I wasn't quite right for at least a year. I wasn't just drinking for England during this period. I wasn't quite at the races mentally either."

Wiggins's father, Garry, would have approved (and probably wished he had been on his son's bar tab for the duration). Wiggins snr gave his son talent and very little else; he was an Australian cyclist who based himself in London in the mid-Seventies as he chased the franc and the deutschmark in gruelling six-day races on the Continent. He married for the second time in January 1979 and promptly moved to the Belgian city, Ghent, home of one of the best-known six-day events. Bradley Wiggins was born the following year.

In 1982, his father fled again, leaving Bradley to learn later of the drinking, drug-taking (he once smuggled amphetamines in his toddler son's nappy on a flight into Belgium) and violence; even team-mates were not exempt from the occasional left hook. Fourteen years passed before he tried to resume contact with Bradley, who eventually agreed to meet him while on a GB training camp in Australia early in 1999. Garry Wiggins's three children, by three different wives, met for the one and only time.

Finally, in January 2008, Bradley took the call at his home in Eccleston, Lancashire, breaking the news that his father had died after being found, beaten up and unconscious, on the streets of a small town in New South Wales. Dave Brailsford, the Team GB performance director, put a business-class ticket at his disposal, but Wiggins bailed out on the way to the airport and threw himself into manic training for the upcoming World Championships.

Until the age of 12, Wiggins's sporting horizons began and ended with football. A new world opened up for him when his mother, Linda, called him in from a kickabout to watch Chris Boardman's 4,000m pursuit final in Barcelona. Wiggins was entranced and over the next few days he was seduced by the whole Olympic package. "That week or so in front of the TV watching the pictures from Barcelona changed my life," he admitted.

> **'That week or so in front of the TV watching the pictures from Barcelona changed my life'**

Within a few weeks he had joined his first club, in south London, and suffered his first serious spill on a bike – he was knocked unconscious after being hit by a car. A compensation award of £1,700 allowed Wiggins to buy his first racing bike and at 15 he won a British age group title. The following year, competing against the best juniors in the country, Wiggins won three medals, including the gold in the kilometre time trial, and in 1998 he became world junior champion in the individual pursuit. He also competed in the Commonwealth Games as an 18-year-old and qualified for full Lottery funding of £20,000 a year.

Another solid season effectively guaranteed Wiggins's Olympic place and he was part of the pursuit team who broke the British record three times to win the bronze medal. In context, he regarded it as an achievement comparable with his future gold medals at Olympic and World Championship level. Fourth place followed in the madison, the 50km points race which Wiggins contested with Rob Hayles.

Shortly afterwards, Wiggins signed for the short-lived Linda McCartney Pro Cycling team, and his longer-term ambitions to compete in the Tour de France came into sharper focus when he joined Française des Jeux, funded by the French national lottery. By coincidence, one of his team-mates was the Australian, Brad McGee, whose victory over Wiggins in the pursuit final at the Commonwealth Games in 2002 was a critical toughening-up exercise for the Briton. "It hurt badly," he admitted, "and if one single thing drove me on to win the Olympics two years later it was my humiliation at the hands of Brad McGee in Manchester."

Boardman began to play a mentoring role, badgering an initially reluctant Wiggins – "this full-on military approach was like taking a cold shower every morning" – into detailing his objectives, racing and training schedule. In McGee's absence, Wiggins restored his self-belief by winning the pursuit title at the 2003 World Championships in Stuttgart, but he began Olympic year on a downbeat note and only claimed a discretionary place in the individual pursuit when his team-mate, Paul Manning, urged the British selectors to pick Wiggins ahead of him. Wiggins was also starting to doubt the wisdom of his decision to sign for the French team Crédit Agricole the previous winter.

The anxieties were banished as he clicked into gear in the last three months before going out to Athens. The objective in the qualifying round of the individual pursuit was 4min 17sec, but Wiggins went almost two seconds quicker, setting an Olympic record. He was able to preserve a little energy in his next ride and still book his place in the following day's final where, almost inevitably, he would meet McGee. Wiggins's brain was awash with random thoughts as he struggled to sleep that night, but when the race itself began he felt invincible. McGee kept pace with him for the first 2,000 metres, but Wiggins increased his advantage lap on lap to go through the line in 4min 16.304sec.

Despite feeling mentally drained, Wiggins took his place in the British pursuit team who were a distant second to the Australians. He was persuaded against opting out of the madison by his girlfriend,

Cath, whom he married shortly after the Games. The outcome was a third medal, a bronze, in league with Hayles. In the process, Wiggins became the first British Olympian since Mary Rand in 1964 to win three medals at a single Games, and the first British man to achieve the feat since cyclist Benjamin Jones and swimmer Henry Taylor in 1908.

Wiggins tried to fit in cycling commitments around functions and media demands, but it was a losing battle. He described the Tour of Britain as "a gloriously liquid lap of honour". The bike was put away for two months as Wiggins settled into a routine of all-day sessions at his local pub in the Derbyshire village of Chapel-en-le-Frith. "Perhaps, like many cyclists," he theorised, "I am just over the top and have to max out on whatever I am doing." He also had time to indulge his obsessive passions. Wiggins, a devoted Jam and Oasis fan, had already assembled a collection of guitars to go with his boxing memorabilia; now he set his sights on Belgian beers.

He negotiated a 50 per cent pay increase with Crédit Agricole – his annual basic salary went up to £45,000 – but Wiggins found that the gold medal did not bring automatic wealth. Another team, Codifis, more than doubled his money in 2006, when he competed in the Tour de France for the first time. He also earned a reputation as an ever-quotable spokesman for the keep-cycling-clean brigade. Back on the track, Wiggins won gold medals in both the individual and team pursuit at the 2007 World Championships in Palma, Majorca.

Even that achievement paled into insignificance beside Wiggins's astonishing three gold medals in four days at the World Championships in Manchester in March 2008. Again, he did the pursuit double (the team, also featuring Ed Clancy, Manning and Geraint Thomas, broke the world record), and the bonus was victory in the madison with Mark Cavendish.

Aug 21: Finn class sailing, Ben Ainslie

BEN AINSLIE gave way to the lure of the America's Cup in 2000. Shortly before the Sydney Olympics, he met Peter Gilmour, the Australian skipper of the OneWorld challenge. A handshake was followed by the security of a three-year contract; the distant target was to wrest the cup from the defenders, Team New Zealand, in 2003.

Ainslie was caught up in the rich history of the event. He wanted to be part of a team, he wanted to learn about big-boat sailing and, gold medallist or not, he approached the challenge with a wide-eyed humility. That, as he readily acknowledged later, was part of the problem – there was no designated role for him on the boat. Ainslie was little more than a dogsbody, managing the backstays and then scaling the 90ft mast itself to check for the best wind on the course.

A non-compete clause in his contract prevented Ainslie from joining the GBR Challenge as a back-up helmsman – a $1 million dollar 'transfer' fee was laughed off – but he knew that he wanted out. In 2009, he described his few months with OneWorld as "quite possibly the worst experience of my life". His final ordeal was having to explain to the whole team why he was leaving.

Ainslie had already decided that he would bid farewell to the Laser and turn his attention to the "more technically complex and demanding Finn class". A full campaign with OneWorld would have given him little more than a year to prepare for the Athens Games; now he had the luxury of two-and-a-half years to establish himself as king in a new realm. A heavier boat demanded a heavier man at the helm. By the time Ainslie went out to Athens, he had gained almost three stone through weight-training, a carefully controlled diet and protein shakes.

> **'I would hate to be under the microscope like David Beckham. I can still walk down the street unrecognised'**

David "Sid" Howlett, who had coached Iain Percy to the Finn gold medal in 2000, brought his expertise to Ainslie's campaign. His familiarity with the boat – Howlett had competed in the class at the Montreal Games in 1976 – helped Ainslie to make a fast start. He won both the European and World Championships in 2002 and 2003, qualifying for Athens in the process, and completed a hat-trick of world titles with a victory in Rio de Janeiro in February 2004. The only blip was a bout of glandular fever which kept him off the water (and out of the gym) for a total of 10 weeks.

As a result he under-performed at the European Championships and was also beaten by the Pole, Mateusz Kusnierewicz, at the Spa regatta. Kusnierewicz, an A list celebrity at home, was rumoured to be the highest-paid sportsman in Poland. Ben Ainslie made it clear, as he prepared for the regatta to begin in Athens, that he was happy to stay out of the limelight. "I would hate to be under the microscope like David Beckham," he said. "I can still walk down the street unrecognised."

Robert Scheidt remained in the Laser class, but Ainslie knew that he could rely on Guillaume Florent for Gallic bluster…and a protest.

Florent guaranteed that a bad first day for Ainslie – he finished ninth in the opening race – became a whole lot worse. Ainslie and Kusnierewicz, who already had a second place under his belt, both led before the Pole made the decisive manoeuvre. Ainslie was reflecting contentedly on his second place when he discovered that Florent had protested, claiming that Ainslie had crossed in front of him.

Ainslie insisted he had done nothing wrong and he was angered by Florent's failure to indicate at the time that he would protest, thus giving Ainslie the chance to cover himself by doing a penalty turn. The jury sided with Florent, disqualifying Ainslie. He fumed: "If I win the gold I might say nothing and just wander past him. I think I might dangle it in front of his face or something. I was very upset with what he did and the way things turned out but I'm sure his time will come." The fact remained that Ainslie was 20th overall; even he feared that the gold medal was already out of reach.

The press were starved of further Ainslie quotes as he focused obsessively on hauling himself back into contention. Despite the additional worry of a back spasm as he lifted the boat, he was so successful in his mission that two days later, revelling in conditions which were made for aggressive sailing, he had won three races and finished fourth in the other, to take the overall lead. Ainslie continued to dominate the regatta, to the extent that he reflected on the last day's racing as an anti-climax. He needed only to finish within 12 places of Rafael Trujillo in the final race to clinch the gold medal and managed 14th to the Spaniard's 13th. Ainslie was delighted to receive his gold medal from Jacques Rogge, the IOC president, who had himself competed in the Finn class in three Olympic Games.

Ainslie was still keen to challenge himself in fresh arenas; he competed in the highly demanding Sydney to Hobart race in 2005 and the America's Cup became his priority once more when he joined the Team New Zealand challengers as strategist. This time he was determined to see it through, but when London was awarded the 2012 Games any doubts about his participation in Beijing were removed.

Team New Zealand came through the qualifying series to challenge Alinghi for the America's Cup in 2007, but Ainslie was a frustrated spectator as the Swiss syndicate retained the cup. He had moved from his role as strategist on the race boat to helm the B boat, effectively becoming Dean Barker's sparring partner. The campaign ended in July 2007, giving Ainslie a year to prepare for the Beijing Games. He acknowledged the risk, but he had already won the pre-Olympic test regatta in 2006 (his only race that year) and repeated the success in 2007. Team Ainslie was back on course.

Aug 21: Coxless fours, Steve Williams, James Cracknell, Ed Coode, Matthew Pinsent

MATTHEW PINSENT might have been rowing in a pair in Athens; in the end he was part of a four. But he knew, deep down, that his performance would be measured in relation to one person who wasn't even competing. "Whatever I said to people, and the press, in particular," he wrote later, "I knew that it was a public test of me being able to produce the goods without Steve Redgrave being there. The epitaph of my career would have simply read, 'He couldn't win an Olympic Games without Redgrave'."

Pinsent's fourth gold medal, one short of Redgrave's collection, was achieved in the toughest of circumstances and in the closest of finishes. Pinsent, James Cracknell, Ed Coode and Steve Williams did not know, until reassured by the shrieks of delight from the British supporters, that they had beaten the Canadians by eight hundredths of a second. Pinsent likened the feeling to being released from a submarine. Both in the boat and after receiving his gold medal from the BOA chairman, Craig Reedie, he struggled to keep his composure.

Jeff Powell wrote in the *Daily Mail*: "After the agony of 2,000 back-breaking metres came the ecstasy by a matter of inches. Then, as the Union flags went up to hail glory, the emotions overflowed. The oarsman of oak wept uncontrollably, his wife holding him like a giant baby, and those poignant images were beamed around the world." Even chief coach Jürgen Grobler, a man less prone to the trembling lip, was overcome. "This is the most emotional situation I have ever had," he said.

Grobler had taken stock after the Sydney Games and concluded that there would be little point in trying to follow in the footsteps of the Redgrave four. An ideal solution appeared to present itself in the form of a Pinsent-Cracknell pair. Cracknell even anticipated the new combination, which involved his switching from the stroke-side to bow-side of the boat, by brushing his teeth with his left hand.

For two years they were spectacularly successful, even doubling up at the 2001 World Championships in Lucerne to win both the coxless and coxed pairs (with Neil Chugani). The following year was memorable on both the sporting and personal front. In September, they retained their coxless title in Seville, breaking the world record and pocketing a £40,000 bonus from their sponsors, Camelot. The following month, both were married, Pinsent to Greek-Canadian business consultant Demetra "Dee" Koutsoukos and Cracknell to Beverley Turner, a model turned television and radio presenter.

The game plan changed abruptly when Pinsent and Cracknell rowed a ragged race to finish fourth at the 2003 World Championships in Milan; suddenly previous records and titles counted for nothing. A silver medal for a coxless four which included Williams (a reserve in Sydney) persuaded Grobler to change tack, though Redgrave still voiced the opinion that Pinsent and Cracknell should line up together in Athens. In February 2004 it was confirmed that they would join Williams and Josh West in a four. West lasted only two months before being replaced by Alex Partridge who, in common with Williams, was a product of the Bath public school, Monkton Combe, and Oxford Brookes University.

A week later Cracknell had a rib stress fracture diagnosed, Coode taking his place in the crew who won at the World Cup regatta in Poznan, Poland in early May. The intended Olympic four did not race together until the World Cup regatta in Lucerne, less than two months before the start of the Games. They finished third and preparations were thrown into disarray at the start of July when a collapsed lung ended Partridge's hopes of competing in Athens. Coode, the rower dropped to accommodate Tim Foster in the Sydney four, was back on board.

Although they won the Stewards' Challenge Cup at Henley, competing under the Leander club colours, the British four were still on a voyage of discovery when they arrived in Athens. Only some of the questions were

'After the summer we have had, I would be happy to win a one-on-one with Zululand'

answered when they won their heat. Pinsent gave the performance "six or seven out of 10", admitting: "After the summer we have had, I would be happy to win a one-on-one with Zululand." They were far more impressive in their semi-final though, significantly, their time was almost identical to that posted by Canada, the reigning world champions, in the other semi-final.

The difference between the two boats could be measured in fractions throughout an astonishingly tense final. The Canadians were renowned as quick starters, but Pinsent stroked the British crew into a slight lead which they retained at halfway. Canada then eked out a half-second advantage in the third 500 metres, only for the British four to respond. "Crank it," urged Cracknell as they sneaked back in front. The Canadians, too, refused to accept defeat, and all but overhauled the Pinsent crew in the final few strokes.

Pinsent described it later as "by far the hardest Olympic race I had experienced. I had dug deeper into my energy reserves than I ever had before." Cracknell admitted at the time: "There has been a lot of crying and shouting in the last 48 hours. Four years of emotion went into those six minutes." Williams said he had rowed the final stages of the race on pure anger. They had named the boat after Alex Partridge and called it the 'coxless five'. Now Radio 5 Live linked them to Partridge in the London studios. He had been unable even to travel because of his collapsed lung, but his selfless support had been unstinting and inspiring in the build-up to the Games. "I told you, I told you," he shouted.

Partridge was part of the British eight who won the silver medal in Beijing; of the Athens four, only Williams remained in the sport, joining the ranks of double gold medallists in 2008. Coode trained as a solicitor and joined the Cornwall-based family law firm. Both Cracknell and Pinsent kept a comparatively high profile, Cracknell as an adventurer and Pinsent as a versatile sports reporter for the BBC.

Cracknell has rowed the Atlantic and traversed the South Pole with television presenter Ben Fogle. In 2010 he competed in the Marathon des Sables and shortly afterwards he fractured his skull and suffered memory loss after being struck on the back of the head by the wing mirror of a truck while cycling in a trans-American endurance race. On a more sedate level, Cracknell has been a columnist for *The Daily Telegraph* for more than 10 years.

In the immediate aftermath of his fourth gold medal, Pinsent declared that he was 70 per cent certain that he would retire, but added: "I must consider if I can live without rowing, see what else I want to do with my life and decide if I have the mental ability to carry on." He concluded that he did not and, after being knighted in the 2005 New Year's Honours, went in search of new challenges. As presenter of the BBC's *World Olympic Dreams* series, Pinsent has travelled widely in the build-up to the 2012 Games.

Aug 23 and 28: 800m and 1500m, Kelly Holmes

TWO images, 24 hours apart, symbolise the ethereal highs and suicidal lows of the Olympic experience. The first freeze-frames Paula

Radcliffe's despair after pulling out of the marathon in Athens; the second captures Kelly Holmes's pop-eyed expression of pure joy as she crosses the line to win the 800m.

Five days later, Holmes ran a brilliantly controlled race to add the 1500m title and seal the greatest performance by a British athlete at a single Olympics. She dropped to her knees on the track afterwards, more out of disbelief than tiredness. "To get two golds feels like somebody else in my body has done it," she admitted. "It doesn't feel like me." At 34, she was the oldest woman to win an Olympic title at either distance.

For much of her career Holmes had been buffeted by injury. In statistical terms, she was already Britain's finest ever female middle-distance runner, but she needed the imprimatur of a world or Olympic title to prove that she was a competitor as well as a time trialist. The sheer talent had been evident from the moment she finished runner-up in her first cross-country race at the age of 12. Athletics gave Holmes a sense of achievement which she could not find in school work.

Holmes's mother, Pamela, had been only 17 when she became pregnant by her Jamaican boyfriend. The stark choice presented to her was: leave home or have the child adopted. The relationship collapsed before Kelly had celebrated her first birthday and she spent time in a children's home (on one occasion seeing her mother and grandfather appearing on the *Generation Game* on television) before being reunited full time when her mother and stepfather-to-be, Mick Norris, set up home together in Hildenborough, near Tonbridge, in Kent. Kelly faced another period of adjustment when her white step brothers were born.

She was only 13, already tactically aware and sporting a giant Afro hairstyle, when she won the junior 1500m at the English Schools' Championships in Plymouth. Television coverage from the Los Angeles Games the following year, and in particular Seb Coe's 1500m victory, fired her imagination even further. By now, Holmes had already decided that she wanted to be a Physical Training Instructor in the Army when she left school, turning down the offer of an athletics scholarship from the University of Minnesota.

Before that, there were family matters to deal with. She 'met' her father, Derrick, discovering in the process that she had a half sister and half brother. She was so disgusted to find that her mother had begun a new relationship that she dragged the man from his car before punching him in the eye and refused to have anything to do with her mother for almost a year.

Holmes underlined her promise as an athlete when she won the senior 1500m at the English Schools' Championships in 1987, but she turned her back on competitive sport after joining the Army in February 1988. Her specialist 'event' was buffing shoes. She also qualified as a Heavy Goods Vehicle driver and began her training as a PTI at Marchwood, near Southampton. One of the instructors was 400m hurdler Kris Akabusi, who also encouraged Holmes to start training with Southampton Athletics Club. She began competing again in 1989, but Army duties still took precedence, especially after she had taken up her first instructor posting at Imphal Barracks, near York, in 1991.

Two factors combined to convince Holmes she could explore her potential as a middle-distance runner without compromising her Army career. One was the persistence of Wes Duncan, a coach with Middlesex Ladies, who had seen her compete at the Inter-Services Championships. The other was the sight of a distance runner whom she had beaten regularly as a junior, Lisa York, competing at the Barcelona Olympics. In 1992, Holmes ran regularly for Middlesex Ladies and, by now based in Beaconsfield, Buckinghamshire, she set her sights on qualifying for the 1993 World Championships in Stuttgart. This was also the stage in her life when Holmes, irked by speculation about her relationship with fellow athlete Jason Dullforce, vowed to keep her private life private. She wrote in her autobiography: "I realised that people assume what they want without bothering to find out whether or not it's anything close to the truth."

Holmes had beaten her personal best to qualify for Stuttgart and, after swapping guard duty, she was free to line up in her first major championships; despite breaking the English record with a time of 1min 58.64sec, she was eliminated in the semi-finals. Holmes still believed that she could fulfil her athletics ambitions from within the Army and she began working again with her original coach, Dave Arnold. In 1994 she followed a 1500m silver medal at the European Championships in Helsinki with gold at the Commonwealth Games in Victoria, British Columbia.

She deferred a PTI training course so that she could train more effectively for the World Championships in 1995, and went through the early part of the season unbeaten before losing to the Algerian, Hassiba Boulmerka, in the 1500m final in Gothenburg. She then broke the British record in the 800m, running 1min 56.95sec to win the bronze medal, and went even quicker in Monte Carlo a few weeks later.

A placement with the Army Youth Team in north London was another compromise which allowed Holmes to prioritise the Atlanta Games in 1996. Her training was hampered, not for the first or last time, by ovarian cysts. Holmes's mood improved during a training camp in South Africa but, as she confided in the BBC's *Olympic Diaries*, she was short of confidence and self-belief. "I'm feeling very negative and being a moody cow," she admitted. "But nobody knows what I'm going through."

A stress fracture to her left leg put Holmes's participation in doubt, but she ran with the aid of pain-killing injections to finish fourth in the 800m, just a tenth of a second behind bronze medallist Maria Mutola, and last in the 1500m final. She came home on crutches, but was in altogether better spirits when she shattered Zola Budd's British record for the 1500m, which had stood for 12 years, running a time of 3min 58.07sec at the Sheffield Grand Prix meeting in June 1997. Five months earlier Sgt Kelly Holmes (W0804968) had despatched the letter confirming her resignation from the Army before spending three months in South Africa.

Her immediate focus was on the World Championships in Athens. Holmes was the favourite for the 1500m, but she suffered a recurrence of an Achilles tendon injury a fortnight beforehand and pulled up in agony in her heat; a torn Achilles and ruptured calf muscle were diagnosed. The following season was all but a write-off, though Holmes recovered sufficiently to win a silver medal in the 1500m at the Commonwealth Games in Kuala Lumpur. She was also awarded the MBE for services to the Army. In 1999, Holmes's training was so badly restricted by illness and injury – she also fell out with Dave Arnold – that she competed solely in the 800m at the World Championships in Seville, failing even to reach the final.

Arnold was back in favour for Olympic year, when Holmes allowed herself an isolated, drunken lapse to mark her 30th birthday in Potchefstroom. A calf injury refused to clear up and Holmes was forced to rely on the British selectors giving her discretionary places for both the 800m and 1500m in Sydney. Her expectations were minimal, so a bronze medal behind Mutola and Stephanie Graf, of Austria, in the 800m (and her fastest time for five years) constituted a major achievement. An astonished Holmes said afterwards: "You couldn't have written it like this. A bronze is a gold to me." She was still in a bubble of contentment when she finished seventh in the 1500m final.

The all-too-familiar pattern returned to haunt Holmes in 2001 (the loss of her Nike contract was another blow to morale). She was diagnosed with chronic fatigue syndrome at the start of the year and was still short of fitness when she competed in the World Championships in Edmonton; in the circumstances sixth place was an adequate outcome. The season finished on a positive note and though Holmes had to have an ovary removed at the end of the year, after suffering persistent stomach pains, she was back on a high in 2002 when she won the 1500m at the Commonwealth Games in Manchester. Holmes lacked the basic speed to challenge for the 800m title at the European Championships soon afterwards, finishing third.

She landed herself in a quagmire of controversy after telling the BBC's trackside interviewer, Sally Gunnell, that she was pleased to have won the medal "cleanly", a reference which was taken to infer that the winner, Jolanda Ceplak, of Slovenia, was bending the rules. Holmes insisted that she meant nothing of the kind, but her embarrassment was compounded by the fact that her manager, Robert Wagner, also looked after Ceplak. Holmes lost motivation but recaptured her appetite for the sport when she began training with Maria Mutola in Johannesburg at the end of 2002. She was also helped by Mutola's coach, the American, Margo Jennings, convincing her that as a 1500m specialist she was not a true threat to Mutola in the 800m. Holmes stayed at Mutola's nine-bedroom house and was even entrusted with the responsibility of cooking Christmas lunch.

A successful indoor season at the start of 2003 added to Holmes's sense of well-being, only to be stopped in her tracks by a persistent calf injury. The low point came when Holmes was sharing an apartment with Mutola and Jennings in the Pyrenean ski resort of Font Romeu. She wrote in her autobiography, *Black, White and Gold*:

> After one particularly frustrating day, I suddenly felt as if I couldn't cope any longer. I stood in the bathroom of our room in the apartment, locked the door and stared in the mirror, feeling utterly miserable. I was crying uncontrollably but tried to drown out the sound by running the tap into the basin and keeping down the noise of my sobs. There was a pair of nail scissors in a cup on a shelf. To this day, I don't know what made me do this, but I picked them up, opened them and started to cut my left arm with one of the blades. One cut for every day that I had been injured.

The cutting episodes continued until the pain in her calf finally eased under treatment. She was still short of confidence at the World Championships in Paris, but made an eleventh-hour decision to compete in the 800m and showed unexpected energy to finish second behind Mutola. Again the rumour mill stirred into mischievous life. Holmes and Mutola were first accused of running as a team then of being in a relationship. Holmes admitted that her friendship with Mutola was affected but refused to rise to the bait.

Mutola had remained largely injury-free for the bulk of her career, but at the start of Olympic year she injured her hip (ironically after tripping when she tried to get past Holmes in an indoor 1500m in Birmingham). Holmes herself was so used to setbacks that even when fit – as she was in the build-up to Athens – she remained suspicious of her good fortune. She eventually decided to double up, forcing Jennings to make it plain that her primary loyalty was to Mutola in the 800m.

Holmes completed her preparations at the GB team's holding camp in Cyprus. There were still false alarms to confront – she initially interpreted the sharp pain from a millipede bite as a heart attack – and superstitions to accommodate. Holmes was desperate to have her hair re-braided before the start of the Games and a chance meeting on a Cypriot beach with Patricia Akaba, an English holidaymaker who had her own hairdressing business, saved the day.

The schedule required Holmes to run a potential six races in nine days, but she was able to win both her heat and semi-final in the 800m without expending too much energy. She adopted the Alicia Keys song *If I Ain't Got You* – 'everything means nothing if I ain't got you' – as her theme tune for the Games. For Holmes, the you in question was the Olympic gold medal. Knowing that the first person she spoke to after each round would be Sally Gunnell, she asked the athlete-turned-interviewer to come equipped with water and peanuts.

As she whiled away the time before the evening final, Holmes watched a DVD of *Saving Nemo*. Out on the track Jennings said simply, 'Be strong'. Holmes was content to sit near the back of the field as the American, Jearl Miles-Clark, set a fierce pace, and used the accelerating Mutola as her marker to make up the deficit on the second lap. They vied for the lead in the final straight, but Mutola's injury-hit preparations were starting to tell. Holmes kept her form better, just managing to hold off the fast-finishing Moroccan, Hasna Benhassi, and Ceplak. She celebrated wildly before momentary doubt entered her mind. The eyes began popping again when the result was confirmed. Holmes's time, 1min 56.38sec, was her fastest since 1995.

"I was expecting something to go totally wrong, even tonight," she admitted afterwards. "But it didn't. I took the risk of staying back on the first lap so I could use my strength and power at the finish – and it worked." Mutola, who finished fourth, commented cryptically: "She knows my weaknesses." Seb Coe, an appropriate choice to present Holmes with her gold medal, praised her for running the "perfect race".

Less than 24 hours later Holmes was lining up in the 1500m heats, any mental tiredness offset by an aura of calm self-belief. On the rest day before the final she had her hair plaited by the sprinter, Aleen Bailey, who a few hours later helped the Jamaican team to win the 4 x 100m relay. Jennings advised Holmes to hang back in the final and though there were moments when she appeared to have allowed too big a gap to open up she was in such control of the race that she was able to look around her at the start of the final straight before launching her decisive attack.

The economy of her success made it even harder to grasp the magnitude of Holmes's achievement. She became the first British athlete to win two gold medals at a Games since Albert Hill (in the identical events) in 1920. She joined Charlotte Cooper and Ethel Hannam, who won the singles and mixed doubles tennis titles in 1900 and 1912 respectively, as the only British women to win twice at an Olympics. There was no rival for the honour of carrying the British flag at the closing ceremony.

The day after her 1500m victory, Holmes reflected on a low-key wind-down: "I went back to the Games Village hoping to go out for a party, but by the time I got back most of the people were gone. No cabs materialised so I ended up eating my dinner at 4am and sat on the balcony talking to my mum on the phone." Holmes's mother had been prevented from travelling by her fear of flying (and lack of a passport); her father, tracked down to a working men's club near his home in Tunbridge Wells, was keen to deflect some of the credit: "If it wasn't for me," he said, "she wouldn't be here. It's all from me, it's in the genes. Her mother couldn't run."

Newspapers threw some figures in the air and settled on £25 million as Holmes's potential reward. She would not be easily seduced. "I've not made a lot of money from my sport," she said. "You make the money by running, and every year I was injured and not running. It was a struggle, living off my dad [stepfather] and my Army wage. But I never wanted anything but my medals. Whatever comes now will be a bonus."

A crowd estimated at 80,000 turned out to see Holmes's open-topped bus ride through Tonbridge and Hildenborough. She won the BBC Sports Personality of the Year award and wearily turned down Tom Cruise's personal invitation to the British premiere of his film, *Collateral*, after they had both appeared on *Parkinson*. She retired from athletics in 2005, shortly after the announcement was made that London would host the 2012 Games (cue for another eye-popping moment).

As Dame Kelly, she has shed her former reticence and unease in the public eye. Drawing on her Army background, she launched the 'On Camp with Kelly' initiative in 2004, and the Dame Kelly Holmes Legacy Trust was set up in 2008 to 'create life chances for young people'.

Aug 28: 4 x 100m relay, Jason Gardener, Darren Campbell, Marlon Devonish, Mark Lewis-Francis

BRITAIN'S triumph in the 4 x 100m relay in Athens could be written off as an insignificant exercise in papering over the cracks – for the first time in Olympic history the men's athletics team failed to win a single individual medal – but it was an achievement of huge satisfaction for the four sprinters who showed well-drilled (and unusual) togetherness to beat the seemingly unbeatable Americans.

Jason Gardener, Darren Campbell, Marlon Devonish and Mark Lewis-Francis all had something to prove, even if recent Olympic history excused a cynical view of their relay prospects in 2004. The baton never reached Campbell during Britain's heat in Atlanta, where the rested Linford Christie was denied the chance of a final taste of glory. Campbell himself was thwarted when a foursome including Gardener and Devonish were disqualified in their heat in Sydney. Disaster struck once more at the World Championships in Edmonton, Canada the following year, and even when they were masters of the smooth changeover they could be tripped up. Britain won the silver medal behind the United States at the 2003 World Championships, only to be disqualified when Dwain Chambers failed a drugs test.

Man for man, the Americans clearly had the potential to run faster than Britain in Athens. Maurice Greene had won both the individual

100m and the relay in Sydney and fully expected to stage a repeat performance in Athens; Justin Gatlin was the reigning world champion over 100m; Shawn Crawford had already won the 200m; even the lesser-known Coby Miller had run under 10 seconds at the US trials. Gardener was the only one of the Britons to have beaten the 10-second barrier – and that was back in 1999.

The British team could be summed up as two athletes past their best (Campbell and Gardener), one who had never quite broken through in world-class company (Devonish) and an outstanding junior (Lewis-Francis) whose career had regressed. Campbell was 30, Gardener and Devonish both 28 and Lewis-Francis a month short of his 22nd birthday.

Gardener, Bath-raised and educated, struggled to fulfil the promise of his 9.98sec run in Lausanne; his reputation as an individual athlete rested largely on his prowess as a 60m runner indoors. He won the European title four times over the distance and capped that by denying Crawford a widely predicted gold medal at the World Championships in Budapest in March 2004. A hernia operation soon afterwards put Gardener's Olympic preparations behind schedule, but he only just failed to reach the 100m final.

Campbell, from Manchester, announced himself as a sprinter of great potential when he won the sprint double at the European Junior Championships in 1991. Injury hampered his progress and he played in the higher echelons of non-League football for two years before returning to athletics. He won a European title over 100m in 1998 and made an astonishing breakthrough in the 200m in Sydney, clocking 20.13sec in the quarter-final then 20.14sec in the final to finish second to the Greek athlete, Kostas Kenteris.

When Kenteris pulled out of his home Games after missing a drugs test, doubt was inevitably cast over the validity of his previous performances. Campbell's sense of grievance was nothing compared to his anger at remarks from Michael Johnson, the American athlete turned TV pundit. After Campbell had finished last in his 200m semi-final and blamed his poor performance on a hamstring injury, Johnson said on the BBC: "I felt like I'd been taken advantage of, as a viewer and a supporter of Darren. When you tear a hamstring, you're out for six weeks. You can't run."

Campbell, who confronted Johnson in an Athens nightclub and even considered legal action, insisted that he was still suffering from discomfort when he took his place in the relay. Johnson's BBC colleague, Colin Jackson, had also been highly critical of Britain's sprinters, and Campbell said pointedly after the relay final: "After what certain people have said about me I did contemplate going home. I had a meeting with the guys and said if they wanted me to keep going I would. Once they put their faith in me, I had full faith in them."

Devonish's added motivation stemmed from the belief that he should have been competing in the 200m as well as the relay. In 2002, he had clocked a personal best 20.19sec to win the silver medal at the Commonwealth Games in Manchester and was even closer to his home city of Coventry when, the following year, he won the world indoor title over the distance at the National Indoor Arena in Birmingham.

Lewis-Francis's failure to make the 100m final in Athens merely confirmed suspicions that the West Midlander might not, after all, be Christie's automatic successor as a gold-chasing sprinter. If Christie was a late developer, Lewis-Francis resembled a flashy firework which burned out almost as soon as it was lit. He ran 10.10sec for the 100m when 17, 10.12sec just after his 18th birthday to win the world junior title in Santiago, Chile and 9.97sec – the time was ruled out for record purposes by a faulty wind gauge – a year later, in 2001. As a clear indication of his lack of progress, Lewis-Francis's best legal time remains 10.04sec in 2002.

The solidarity in the British squad did not inure them from mishap: they came within inches of disqualification in the semi-final when Lewis-Francis took the baton from Devonish just inside the permitted exchange zone. They were relieved to finish second, half a second behind the American quartet and, despite Gardener's false start in the final, their disciplined exchanges hustled the favourites into error. Crawford's handover to Gatlin was less than perfect; Gatlin, in turn, almost trod on Miller's foot, allowing Devonish to give Lewis-Francis a one-metre advantage over Greene. The American closed with every stride, but Lewis-Francis maintained his form and focus to cross the line in 38.07sec, one hundredth of a second ahead of the Americans. Lewis-Francis, aware almost immediately that he had got the verdict, skipped in delight before being engulfed by his team-mates in a delirious huddle. Campbell insisted afterwards: "The craziest thing is we knew we were going to win it." In an apparent, if clichéd riposte to Michael Johnson, he added: "I just tried to let my feet do the talking."

The main interest centred on Lewis-Francis and the impact that a gold medal would have on his career. In the immediate aftermath of the race, he said: "The adrenaline came from the bottom of my feet to my mouth. I am still tingling all over. A 21-year-old at his first Olympics and going back as a gold medallist. I know now it will come for me. I can look at this medal every day now before training and know nothing is impossible."

Neil Wilson wrote in the *Daily Mail* that Lewis-Francis's "two leaps of delight may have been the launch pad for the second phase of his meteoric rise". Dave Moorcroft, the then chief executive of UK Athletics, predicted confidently: "Mark will be the best in the world one day." Lewis-Francis has done little to endorse Moorcroft's view since. In 2005 he tested positive for cannabis at the European Indoor Championships, only avoiding a lifetime ban from the Olympic Games after UK Athletics ruled that the offence was not performance-enhancing. He missed the Beijing Games through injury instead and seems destined to be remembered as one of great unfulfilled talents of British athletics.

Campbell bowed out of athletics on a controversial note in 2006, a few days after helping the British team to win the 4 x 100m relay at the European Championships in Gothenburg. Campbell boycotted the lap of honour in silent protest at team-mate Dwain Chambers, whose drugs ban had cost him relay medals at the 2002 European Championships and 2003 World Championships. Campbell has become a regular voice on the BBC's 5 Live radio station and also works as a sprint consultant with football and rugby teams. Gardener retired in 2007, shortly after winning the European indoor title over 60m for the fourth time. He coaches and works as a motivational speaker and sports consultant through his company Bullet Management Group.

Devonish has shown Christie-style longevity as an athlete. He improved his personal best for the 100m to 10.06 sec in 2007 and won his fourth World Championship relay medal when the British team finished third in Berlin in 2009. The previous year had brought a sobering reminder that nothing much is guaranteed in sprint relays: the British team were disqualified from their Olympic heat when Devonish's handover to anchor man Craig Pickering took place outside the permitted zone.

2008

THE 'GREAT HAUL OF CHINA'

THE modern Olympics had already celebrated their 100th birthday when British sport – with more than a little help from Lottery funding – finally unlocked the key to consistent success at the Games. The cycling team took another great leap forward when they won seven out of the 10 gold medals contested on the track in Beijing. The 'great haul of China' was conceived with forensic precision in Manchester and brilliantly executed at the Laoshan Velodrome.

Rebecca Romero, as an Olympic sculler turned cyclist, was in a unique position to judge. "Everybody can learn from what we do," she said after winning the individual pursuit. "We have a system that everyone should replicate. I've been involved in two top sports, cycling and rowing, and there is no comparison. We have the best of everything and that's why it works. Cycling gives me the whole package of what I need to win as an athlete.

"British sport should model itself on us. The country is not going to dominate at the London Olympics otherwise."

As Chris Boardman's coach when he won the individual pursuit in Barcelona in 1992, Peter Keen had seen how a spark of inspiration could fizzle out if left untended. There was no system in place and thus no legacy, but Manchester's government-financed National Cycling Centre, which opened in September 1994, at least gave the sport a proper home. The British Cycling Federation remained directionless and disorganised and its wholly owned subsidiary, Manchester Velodrome Ltd, would have gone out of business if the city council had not picked up a £130,000 bill for gas and electricity. The World Championships were held in Manchester in 1996 and Keen was presented with a £2.5 million budget and a blank canvas when he became the first performance director the following year. The chosen focus, on track cycling, had a lot to do with the endemic use of drugs in road racing (exemplified by the Tour de France).

There was a seamless transition when Keen moved to UK Sport in 2004. His successor, Dave Brailsford, was also a former international cyclist; he, too, had a background in sports science. Brailsford worked under Keen and shared his vision, but he also excelled in the area of man management. After Bradley Wiggins's father, Garry, died in suspicious circumstances in 2008, Brailsford offered to pay for a business-class ticket so that Wiggins could fly out to Melbourne for the funeral. The would-be medallists could call on all the advice and assistance available – by 2011 there were 58 staff on the GB team payroll – but ultimately they were the authors of their own programme.

Brailsford struck gold by recruiting Steve Peters, a clinical psychiatrist who worked at Rampton Secure Hospital in Nottinghamshire. On a basic level, Peters became a non-judgmental sounding board for the cyclists. He encouraged sportsmen to think of him as a 'brain mechanic' (they could also book in for a 'mental MOT') and taught them to control primitive emotions (the chimp) and negative thoughts (the gremlin).

The success of Wiggins and Chris Hoy in Athens was a powerful endorsement for the Brailsford regime, overseen by a four-man management committee of Brailsford himself, Peters, Boardman and the assertive Australian, Shane Sutton, who became manager of the track team. The attention to detail was unrelenting; Brailsford banned the C-word – complacency. He even arranged for a hygienist to brief the Beijing-bound cyclists on the best method for washing their hands in China.

Britain's domination in 2008 brought jealousy and insinuation. Paul Hayward wrote in the *Daily Mail*: "Britain's cyclists will have to be willing to explain their success over and over again until the science speaks for itself. Their 'garage' is now approaching Formula One complexity. It is also noticeable to the infrequent visitor that the cyclists and support staff hunt entirely as a pack. They radiate intent."

Aug 10: Individual road race cycling, Nicole Cooke

NICOLE COOKE had enough composure to keep a tight grip on the handlebars as she crossed the line at the end of the most arduous of Olympic road races – she had seen titles conceded by a premature fist pump – but her emotions poured out in an ear-splitting scream of delight which, she later joked, could have been heard in her home village of Wick, in the Vale of Glamorgan. "As I crossed the line I was just so overcome – so happy, so many emotions were coming out," she said. "I made so much noise, but I guess that's the girl that I am."

The riders had expected heat and humidity; instead they were confronted by an unseasonal chill, torrential rain and strong winds for all but the early stages of the 126km race. Runner-up Emma Johansson said afterwards: "At times it felt like I was drowning because there was so much water on the road." Cooke, understandably, put a more positive spin on the conditions: "I'm glad the Chinese authorities laid on some nice Welsh weather for me." She also had good reason to be grateful to her team-mates, Emma Pooley, a surprise silver medallist in the time trial, and Sharon Laws, whose selfless graft allowed Cooke to race defensively before timing to perfection her move through the field.

Ivan Speck wrote in the *Daily Mail*: "Four years ago in Athens, Cooke was part of a five-woman breakaway until she took a bend too wide in the final run to the line and trailed in a disconsolate fifth. The parallels were eerie yesterday as, once more, she bridged a gap to turn a gang of four into a pack of five on the descent from Badaling back to the finish in Juyongguan. This time there was to be no mistake. On team orders, the 25-year-old even risked all as she held back on a dangerous bend 500 metres from the finish and allowed the others to forge clear – to avoid being brought crashing down had one of them fallen."

The impression, to the uninitiated anyway, was that Cooke had run out of steam, but she surged through as the line approached to finish a bike length clear of the Swede, Johansson. Both were given the same time, 3hr 32min 24sec. Earlier in the year, Cooke had been laid low, physically and mentally, by a persistent knee injury. Now she was Britain's first gold medallist at the Beijing Games, the 200th in the modern Olympics and only the second Welsh woman, after swimmer Irene Steer in 1912, to win an Olympic title.

Six weeks later, the conditions were rather better in Varese, Italy, as Cooke became the first woman to win the Olympic and world road race titles in the same year. She reflected beforehand on her achievement in Beijing: "I couldn't be more fulfilled or proud if I was Michael Phelps with his eight gold medals. I won the longest women's event in the whole Olympics against the biggest field in the worst weather in what I would argue is the toughest event. It was an epic race against great competitors and I rode as well as I have ever ridden when

301

the pressure was greatest and the challenge the most testing. I'm a very happy lady."

The first evidence of a prodigious talent – and the dedication to match – could be traced back to a family cycling holiday on the Isle of Wight, when Cooke was only five. She rode tandem with her mother, Denise, and her physics teacher father, Tony, teamed up with her younger brother, Craig. Cooke began competing when she was 11 and soon pronounced that she would become an Olympic champion; she even repeated the prediction on a television programme a year later.

At 16, Cooke became the youngest winner of the British road race title and felt aggrieved to be overlooked – on the grounds of age – for the Sydney Olympics the following year. She was bright enough to get three A grades in her A Levels at Brynteg Comprehensive School (she was a near contemporary of rugby player Gavin Henson) and single-minded enough to choose a professional contract in Italy over a degree course at the university of her choice. She was also fiercely independent – at the Athens Games she preferred a private apartment over accommodation in the Olympic village. Her father generated his own headlines when he was detained on the eve of the road race while trying to paint his daughter's name on a street in Athens.

Cooke, who subsequently won both the Giro d'Italia and the Grand Boucle, the small-scale women's equivalent of the Tour de France, continued to choose the solitary approach over the Team GB environment, opting out of the pre-Beijing training camp in Newport to prepare in the Italian Alps. The Olympics were not an automatic springboard to further successes and in 2009 Cooke's attempts to set up her own professional team floundered for lack of sponsorship. Her reputation as a self-seeking racer was underlined last year when team-mate Lizzie Armitstead accused her of riding only for herself at the World Championships in Copenhagen.

Aug 15: Team sprint cycling, Chris Hoy, Jason Kenny, Jamie Staff

CHRIS HOY summed up the British sprint team's victory in Beijing with the matter-of-fact observation: "It's very rare that all three riders are in the form of their life on the same day, but that's what happened tonight." Even the French, overwhelming favourites on the strength of a hat-trick of world titles, seemed to accept their fate after Jamie Staff, Jason Kenny and Hoy had made history by dipping under 43 seconds in the qualifying round. Hoy equated the achievement to a knockdown in the first round of a boxing match. "The French were on the canvas," he wrote in his autobiography.

If the across-the-board brilliance of the British trio made them an irresistible force – they were only fractionally slower against the United States in the second round and France in the final – the individual game-changer was Jason Kenny, the 20-year-old Boltonian drafted in to replace Ross Edgar after Britain had finished half a second down on the French at the World Championships in Manchester five months earlier.

Kenny, a world and European junior champion in 2006, refused to be overawed by the occasion or by the prospect of teaming up with riders who were 12 and 15 years older than him. He adapted so quickly to the Olympic environment that he recorded the fastest ever second-lap time in Britain's astonishing clocking of 42.950sec. Hoy matched the feat on the final lap of the 750 metre race. Kenny admitted later: "When I saw the time for the first ride on the board I thought I must have read it wrong." The only fleeting concern for Britain was in the final, when the fatigued Hoy threatened to lose touch with Staff and Kenny, conserving just enough energy and momentum to cross the line in 43.128sec.

There was no hiding the delight of British Cycling's performance director, Dave Brailsford. He described the result as "a real kick in the goolies" for the French. Hoy viewed it as both an inspiration and a warning. "I hope everyone will draw strength," he said. "Anything is possible...no one is invincible." Neither Hoy, Staff nor Kenny revealed at the time that two days earlier they had got hopelessly lost on a rest-day outing and spent two-and-a-half anxious hours trudging through downtown Beijing in 100 degree heat.

Paul Hayward, the *Daily Mail* columnist, reflected: "You come all this way and it all boils down to the British beating the French in an event preceded by classic cross-Channel needle. If this dominance is maintained right through next week, there are bound to be mutterings in other camps about other, hidden ingredients. We should face that possibility now. No team has the right to hide behind the conspiracy of silence that has kept dopers and their junkies in business for the last 40 years."

Hoy and Kenny still had individual races in front of them. Staff, the BMX world champion who switched to track cycling in his late twenties, could enjoy all the back-slapping and bonhomie in the Olympic village. Two days after winning the gold medal, he admitted in an interview: "I want to wear it all the time, but you won't believe it, the ribbon is already fraying after one trip out. Made in China. You do want it looking good on your mantelpiece, but for now it gets you anywhere in the world. It gets you free drinks. You want to make the most of the damn thing. Maybe I'll have to see any beer stains as just part of it. I could look into laminating the ribbon."

The lure of London was too strong for Staff to contemplate immediate retirement, but a chronic back injury forced him to give up in the spring of 2010. Three months later he took up a job as manager of the US sprint team.

Aug 16: Individual pursuit cycling, Bradley Wiggins

BRADLEY WIGGINS set the bar high for himself in Beijing, attempting the 'impossible' hat-trick of individual and team pursuit titles and madison. "I was going to have to race seven times at the very limit of endurance in five days," he wrote in his autobiography. Wiggins had managed the feat in the World Championships five months earlier, but there was a critical difference between the schedule in Manchester and Beijing. This time he would not have the luxury of a rest day.

Three weeks earlier, Wiggins had gone from elation to despair in the space of 24 hours at the team's training camp in Newport, Wales. First, he ducked under Chris Boardman's world best for the 4,000m, 4min 11.114sec; the following day he awoke to find that he could not move. A virus was diagnosed and three anxious days elapsed before Wiggins began to recover mobility and strength.

He was restored to full health by the time the British team flew out to Beijing and established his pre-eminence in the individual pursuit with a qualifying time of 4min 15.031sec which beat the Olympic record he had set in Athens and was almost four seconds quicker than the next fastest rider, New Zealand's Hayden Roulston. "I think anyone is beatable," said Roulston afterwards, "but to beat Bradley you have to cut your head off."

'Anyone is beatable, but to beat Bradley you have to cut your head off'

Wiggins followed up with another imperious ride in his heat, beating the Russian, Alexander Serov, and later reflected: "It was completely effortless. I felt I was at about 60 per cent gas and have worked up more of a sweat cleaning my teeth in the morning." Roulston, his head still intact, was Wiggins's token

Rebecca Adlington celebrates as she discovers that she has broken Janet Evans's world record to win the 800m freestyle

Victoria Pendleton flies the flag after winning the sprint final

The delight shows as Iain Percy and (right) Andrew Simpson clinch the Star class gold medal

Tim Brabants roars with joy as he wins the 1,000m kayak singles

A strong finish brings Christine Ohuruogu victory in the 400m

James DeGale scores with a solid punch during his middleweight final against Cuba's Emilio Correa

Jamie Staff, Chris Hoy and Jason Kenny celebrate their team sprint success in the Laoshan Velodrome

Paul Goodison steers his Laser to victory

Bradley Wiggins leads pursuit team-mates Ed Clancy, Paul Manning and Geraint Thomas to victory and a world record

Britain's Yngling trio, (top) Sarah Ayton, (left) Sarah Webb and Pippa Wilson, show gold medal winning teamwork

The British coxless four of (from left) Andy Triggs Hodge, Pete Reed, Steve Williams and Tom James show a mixture of delight and exhaustion

Nicole Cooke beats the opposition and the appalling weather to win the road race

Zac Purchase and Mark Hunter (right) acknowledge the cheers of the British supporters after their win in the lightweight double sculls

A flag-wielding Rebecca Romero celebrates her win in the individual pursuit

opponent in the final. Although the New Zealander led after the first kilometre, Wiggins was in total control of the race and as Roulston weakened he extended his advantage to almost three seconds, winning in 4min 16.977sec. Steven Burke emphasised the depth of talent in the British squad by taking the bronze medal.

Afterwards, Wiggins stressed that he had conserved as much energy as possible. "I had to play it safe, not chase world records," he said. "Three other guys [his team pursuit colleagues] deserved to be in this race. It was the least I could do for them." Asked to sum up the difference between 2004 and 2008, Wiggins said: "In Athens I was a mature rider but an immature bloke. Here I am still a mature rider, but I've grown up as a bloke as well."

Aug 16: Keirin cycling, Chris Hoy

THE odds may have been upset by Britain's team sprint victory, but Chris Hoy proved the following day that favourites could live up to their billing in glorious fashion. The keirin was not so much a race as a three-round procession cum coronation for a sporting giant whose third Olympic gold medal confirmed him as Scotland's most successful Olympian.

The nature of the event, in which riders are paced by a moped-like vehicle known as a derny for all but the last two-and-a-half laps of the 2,000m race, emphasised Hoy's dominance (established by a sequence of 24 successive victories in World Cups and World Championships). On each occasion, the derny accelerated from 30km to 50km an hour before leaving Hoy unchallenged at the front of the field. If there was residual tiredness from the team sprint, he barely showed it. Hoy took almost as much pleasure from the silver medal won by his fellow Scot, Ross Edgar, the rider ousted from the team after their defeat by France at the World Championships.

"It's a day we'll remember for a long time," said Hoy afterwards. "I'm very emotional, but I'm trying to keep a cap on it because I've got another race to go." He added, reflectively: "After the kilo was dropped after Athens there were parts of me thinking that it could be the end of my individual career, but to come back to win a different event altogether is just fantastic." Edgar admitted that the medal was partial compensation for his omission from the team event. "The team sprint was hard to watch," he said, "but the guys put in a phenomenal ride."

The aftermath was much tougher for Hoy than the races themselves. He was confronted by one official whose grasp of English was almost non-existent and a ham-fisted dope tester. "She fumbled and stabbed," Hoy wrote, "as though she'd never conducted the procedure before, and made a right mess of my arm, which was bruised and painful the next morning." Hoy did not return to the Olympic village until midnight and had to get up at 6am to prepare for the qualifying rounds in the individual sprint.

Aug 17: Individual pursuit cycling, Rebecca Romero

REBECCA ROMERO reluctantly accepted that she had run out of events – and sports – when she confirmed her retirement last October, at the age of 31. "Having suffered several setbacks at crucial points," she announced with dull precision, "I believe I'm no longer on a pathway which will see me fulfil my ambition to win a second Olympic gold medal."

Romero's thrilling journey from sculling silver medallist in Athens to cycling gold medallist four years later deserved a less mundane send-off. After her victory in the individual pursuit in Beijing, her coach, Dan Hunt, described her as "the most driven athlete I have met – male or female".

The winding road to success began in a council house in Wallington, Surrey, where Romero and her younger sister, Rachel, soon learned to do without. Their Spanish father and English mother divorced when Rebecca was six, leaving Beverley Romero to bring up her daughters single-handedly. Rebecca showed limited sporting potential before taking up rowing when she was 17. After completing a degree in sports science and English at St Mary's College, Twickenham in 2002, she became a full-time athlete.

Romero was part of the quadruple sculls crew who were left with too much ground to make up by Germany's fast start in the Olympic final in 2004. She said afterwards: "Today we filled up the tank with premium ultra super unleaded petrol and exhausted every drop of that." Satisfaction and disappointment mingled, but the following year brought a measure of revenge with a narrow victory over the Germans at the World Championships in Gifu, Japan.

Word of Romero's growing disillusionment with rowing filtered through to British Cycling and when Hunt phoned her in April 2006 she was instantly receptive to the idea of becoming part of the cycling revolution – even if meant taking a drop in pay. As a rower and Olympic medallist she received £21,000 a year in Lottery funding. In 2008, with a student loan of £8,000 still hanging over her, Romero was making do on £16,000.

She adapted so quickly to pursuit cycling that she won a silver medal at the 2007 World Championships and claimed gold medals in both the individual and team events in Manchester in March 2008. Wendy Houvenaghel, Romero's team-mate, was fractionally quicker in qualifying in Beijing, but Romero retained her form more convincingly to clock 3min 28.321sec in the final, shrieking with delight as she crossed the line to beat Houvenaghel, her flat-mate in the Olympic village, by two seconds. She became the first British woman to win Olympic medals in two sports and admitted: "I would have been absolutely crushed to have won silver again. If I hadn't done it today I don't know where I would be – probably on the floor, dead somewhere." Hunt drove home the point, saying: "Basically, Becks doesn't do silver."

Romero, disappointed that her mother and sister had been unable to afford to travel out to Beijing to watch her, learned just before her race that Britain's quadruple scullers had again finished second. "I was gutted for them because they deserved gold, but it spurred me on," she said, also stressing the structural differences between the two sports. "In cycling it's about taking responsibility for your own performance and having the back-up to do it. I'd never have reached this potential as a rower."

She was deflated by the "ludicrous" decision to drop the individual pursuit from the Olympic programme and even considered taking up canoeing. The inference was clear when Romero was omitted from the team pursuit at last year's World Championships in Apeldoorn, Holland. Victory for Laura Trott, Houvenaghel and Dani King simply vindicated the selection.

Aug 18: Team pursuit cycling, Ed Clancy, Paul Manning, Geraint Thomas, Bradley Wiggins

THE headlines were predictably grabbed by Bradley Wiggins and his ever-growing Olympic medal collection – he matched Steve Redgrave's career total of six when Britain won the team pursuit – but for selfless endeavour there was nothing to match Geraint Thomas's contribution. The Welshman put collective need before personal ambition, turning down the chance to compete in the individual pursuit, and was the energetic strongest link in a scintillating series of rides.

Wiggins, drained physically and emotionally by his exploits in the individual event, admitted as much. He also acknowledged that if Thomas had competed against him the gold medal would have been much less of a formality.

The Beijing quartet proved to be an ideal mixture of experience and youth. Wiggins and 31-year-old Paul Manning, an earth sciences graduate from the University of Birmingham, were both in the team who upgraded their bronze medal in Sydney to silver in Athens. Thomas and Ed Clancy, though only 22 and 23, were already double world champions in the discipline. Thomas, a former junior world champion, had refused to be deflected by a serious training crash in Australia in 2005, when he required blood transfusions after rupturing his spleen, which had to be removed. Yorkshireman Clancy was an unfulfilled talent until being re-programmed by 'brain mechanic' Steve Peters in 2006.

Wiggins was under strict instructions to preserve energy by baling out with 1,000 metres remaining in the qualifying ride (the rules of the event require only three riders to finish). The British team went even quicker later in the day, clocking 3min 55.202sec to beat the world record they had set in Manchester earlier in the year. They found yet another gear the following day, all but catching their opponents in the final, Denmark, to reduce the record to an astonishing 3min 53.314 sec. The euphoria was understandable.

Wiggins: We were perfection. Absolute bloody perfection.

Thomas: We knew it was fast, but 53.3, I can't believe it. It will go down in history.

Manning: It was an incredible feeling to be part of that.

Clancy: There were a few nerves but we knew we were the best team out there.

Wiggins also singled out their Australian coach, Shane Sutton, for praise. "Paul and I were saying on the podium tonight what an eight years it's been. We went nowhere for a few years, just cruising around that four-minute barrier. Then Shane came in and gave us a kick up the arse. Geraint and Ed don't seem to know the meaning of the word fear. They're young kids. They'll go out on the piss tonight and have a good time. They'll lap it up until Christmas. It keeps us relaxed in the team."

The madison, a 50km event in which two-man teams accumulate points in a series of sprints, was a race too far for Wiggins, and a crashing disappointment for sprint specialist Mark Cavendish, who had quit the Tour de France to prepare for the Games; the British pair, winners of the same event at the World Championships earlier in the year, could finish only ninth.

Manning retired after Beijing, taking up a management position with the company which built the velodrome for the London Games and coaching the next generation of pursuiters. Clancy showed his versatility at the 2010 World Championships by winning the omnium, the multi-event discipline which makes its Olympic debut in London (he still confirmed his unwavering commitment to the team pursuit). Wiggins and Thomas are both part of the Team Sky outfit which was launched in 2010 with the initial objective of producing a first British winner of the Tour de France within five years. Wiggins went on record as accepting that he would not be the breakthrough rider, but he exceeded general expectations by finishing fourth overall in 2009.

Aug 19: Individual sprint cycling, Victoria Pendleton

VICTORIA PENDLETON would have happily pinned her gold medal on the chest of team psychiatrist Steve Peters after conquering her insecurities to win the individual sprint in Beijing. She admitted: "I can honestly say that I wouldn't be here if it wasn't for Steve and the work he has done with me."

Four years earlier, Pendleton was consumed with negative thoughts when she competed in Athens. The outcome was a deeply disappointing ninth place in the sprint and sixth in the 500m time trial; she gave serious consideration to retiring. Peters later explained: "Vicky had the skills on the bike, the power and the ability, but what she couldn't do was control the fears and the anxieties, so when she came to competition she massively underperformed. She wanted to disengage, to actually get off the bike."

The sensitivity was part of the Pendleton psyche from an early age and threatened to derail a considerable natural talent. Born in Bedfordshire, she started competing at the age of nine, following initially in the footsteps of her father, Max, a former national grass track champion. After completing her A Levels, Pendleton did a degree in sport and exercise science at Northumbria University in Newcastle and became a full-time cyclist when she graduated in 2002.

Pendleton's fourth place at the 2003 World Championships gave her high hopes of winning a medal in Athens, but she failed to do herself justice. "Not everybody has the perfect mind-set to deal with everything that's thrown at them and I needed a bit of help," she later admitted. "Steve helped me to retrain my brain to think in a different way. It was all about trying to take the self-expectation and pressure away and focusing on doing a job as well as I could."

She also benefited from a weight-training programme designed to add muscle to her slight frame and broke through to win the individual sprint at the 2005 World Championships in Los Angeles. Pendleton was so dominant in 2007 that she carried off world titles for the individual and team sprints, as well as the keirin. She accepted the favourite's tag in Beijing as a compliment rather than an encumbrance, but had to wait until the final day's racing before joining the medal party.

An Olympic record of 10.963sec gave Pendleton the fastest qualifying time and her self-belief remained intact as she won both her semi-final, against Holland's Willy Kanis, and final, against Anna Meares, of Australia, in two of the best-of-three rides. Meares, who had broken her neck in a fall at the start of the year, was happy just to be able to compete. Pendleton said afterwards: "Watching all week on the TV at the athletes' village has been really emotional for me to see people winning medals. I've been so proud. Honestly, I was in tears before the keirin heats even started."

'The fact that the men have seven medals on the track and we only have three stinks to be honest'

Her father admitted: "She was close to being convinced she would get it, but not totally." Pendleton herself said a few weeks later: "I was an emotional wreck beforehand because, while I was happy for everyone else, I was apprehensive about my ride. I worried that I would be the one person who let down the team. So winning was just a relief. And even that felt like a complete anti-climax. It was very surreal on the podium and as soon as I stepped off it was like, what on earth am I going to do now?" She added: "I'm terrible. I beat myself up the whole time because I'm striving for something I'll basically never achieve."

Pendleton's victory gave her the soapbox from which to rail against the Olympic programme, something which *Guardian* cycling correspondent William Fotheringham described as "grotesque in what passes for an age of equality". Pendleton said: "I would have liked to have the opportunity to try to do what Chris has done, because my form is good. Unfortunately, I had only one chance of winning a medal at the Olympics, which is really sad. The fact that the men have seven medals on the track and we only have three stinks to be honest. Something should be done about it, hopefully by 2012. It wouldn't happen in other sports like swimming, would it?"

In the after-glow of her Olympic triumph, Pendleton had plenty of opportunities to indulge her love of glitter and glamour. She modelled for designer Stella McCartney's Adidas show in London Fashion Week and met the Foo Fighters' front man, Dave Grohl, at the GQ Men of the Year awards. She celebrated her 30th birthday, in September 2010, in idiosyncratic fashion, by having 'today is the greatest day I've ever known' – a line from the Smashing Pumpkins' song, *Today* – tattooed on her right arm.

Pendleton's sprinting dominance was only interrupted when, after four straight world titles, she finished third in 2011. The plans for 2012 remained unaltered: a successful defence of her Olympic crown, retirement, then marriage to her Australian sports scientist fiancé, Scott Gardner.

Aug 19: Individual sprint cycling, Chris Hoy

CHRIS HOY felt strong, physically and emotionally, when he arrived in Beijing. He managed a personal best full squat lift of 227.5kg at the team training camp in Wales and dipped under 10 seconds for the 200m for the first time. He was also convinced that the anchored contentment he drew from his relationship with lawyer Sarra Kemp had a beneficial knock-on effect.

The individual sprint unfolded over three days, Hoy making a powerful declaration of intent when he recorded an Olympic record time of 9.815sec to head the qualifiers. He was left to wonder whether, fully rested, he might have been capable of beating Dutchman Theo Bos's world best of 9.772sec. Jason Kenny was second quickest and announced himself as Hoy's heir apparent by coming through four match-racing rounds to confront his fellow Briton in the final. The British coaching team, unable to favour one over the other, left Hoy and Kenny to make their own plans.

Hoy, delighted to beat the formidable Frenchman, Mickael Bourgain, in his semi-final, was the tactical master in the best-of-three gold medal match. He forced Kenny to lead and twice muscled past him off the final bend; the decider was not required. A tearful Hoy celebrated with his girlfriend and parents in the stands. "I can't believe it," he said repeatedly to his father. He became the first British Olympian since freestyle swimmer Henry Taylor in 1908 to win three gold medals at the same Games.

"I would have laughed if you'd told me even two years ago that I'd win three golds here," Hoy admitted. "It's only in the last two or three years that we've had real sprint coaches to guide us and give us the technical know-how. I've always had the power, the speed, but it's about converting that speed, the timing of knowing when to use that speed. In the past, I didn't have a clue what I was doing. I would make mistakes and not learn from them whereas now, if I make a mistake, we look at the video and the coaches say: 'Right, do this, do that.'"

He added: "Jason is going to be the best sprinter in the world in a very short space of time. I just hope I can hang on to him until London. It's got to be a four-year plan. I'll have to take my foot off the gas a little next year and get over what's happened, then really start to build up for London. I just love what I do. I feel very fortunate to have a job that I genuinely get up and look forward to doing."

In theory, Hoy was free, after five days of non-stop endeavour, to enjoy a triple-strength celebration. In practice, he was "absolutely knackered, completely drained, physically and emotionally". He had a sense of what to expect on his return to Britain when his previously under-employed agent began to relay offers and requests which Hoy had previously thought were reserved for real celebrities. Business was completed in Beijing when he carried the British flag at the closing ceremony.

Nothing could quite prepare Hoy for the shock of seeing himself, in enormous poster form, as he drove to an open-topped bus parade in Edinburgh. A crowd estimated at 50,000 turned out to welcome Hoy and the other Scottish medallists. The sense of unreality scarcely let up; first there was a call from publicist Max Clifford. Did he want to make big money or still regard the annual Lottery funding of £25,000 as his main source of income?

Even without Clifford's assistance, Hoy found little difficulty in capitalising on his new-found fame. He became the face which stared across breakfast tables from packets of Kellogg's Bran Flakes. He even had the unnerving experience of Hollywood actor Samuel L. Jackson introducing himself, "a little unnecessarily" Hoy admitted, at the

National Film Awards in London. He estimated that in the course of 84 days he never slept in the same bed for two successive nights.

He saw off some formidable opposition to win the Sports Personality of the Year award and received a knighthood in the New Year's Honours. He was equally delighted to hear that his mother had been made an MBE for services to nursing. Hoy also took the opportunity, while recovering from a crash at a World Cup meeting in Copenhagen early in 2009, to arrange a short trip to Prague, where he became engaged to Sarra Kemp. Hoy donned kilt and sporran for their marriage in Edinburgh in 2010.

Both Hoy and Kenny have struggled to keep pace with the immensely strong Frenchman, Gregory Baugé, over the past few years. Kenny scored a significant win over Hoy in the sprint semi-final at last year's World Championships (the more so because new regulations limit each country to one representative per discipline in the Olympics). Baugé overpowered Kenny to win a third successive world title, only for Kenny to be promoted when Baugé was banned for missing an out-of-competition drugs test.

Aug 11 and 16: 400m and 800m freestyle, Rebecca Adlington

THE shoes and the chocolate were a trivial diversion from the real Rebecca Adlington story: of utter dedication on a shoestring budget and an individual performance to rival almost anything else achieved in Beijing. Janet Evans was poolside to see Adlington break her 800m freestyle world record, which had stood since 1989. "An incredible swim," was the American's hyper-impressed verdict.

Adlington's early motivation, when she began swimming at the Sherwood Colliery club in Mansfield at the age of seven, was to beat her elder sisters, Laura and Chloe. That achieved, her goals became less parochial. She joined Nova Centurion in Nottingham when she was 13 and began working with coach Bill Furniss, a sports science graduate. Adlington narrowly missed the qualification time for the Olympic 800m in 2004, when she won the European junior title, but a bout of glandular fever, followed by post-viral fatigue, effectively denied her the chance of competing in both the 2005 World Championships and the Commonwealth Games the following year.

Finally, all the 5am starts, weekly regime of 65,000 metres (40 miles) in the pool, weight training and aerobics brought their reward.

Adlington's initial focus was purely on the 800m in Beijing, but after winning the 200m, 400m and 800m at Britain's Olympic trials in April 2008 she decided to double up. Adlington's expectations were limited over the shorter distance, in which the Italian, Federica Pellegrini, was favoured to repeat her world record beating success in the European Championships earlier in the year.

Pellegrini set an Olympic record in her heat, but Adlington was only five hundredths of a second behind. Pellegrini's challenge evaporated in the final, leaving Adlington and team-mate Jo Jackson to chase the American, Katie Hoff. Adlington was only fifth after 300 metres and even her father, Steve, watching at home in Mansfield, was losing faith. "She wasn't even in the frame when it came to the last turn," he said later. "We knew she has a very fast finish but we all thought she had left it too late."

Adlington still had half a body length to make up on Hoff in the last 10 metres, but a final lunge enabled her to win in 4min 3.22sec, seven hundredths of a second ahead of Hoffs. Jackson also produced a stirring finish to take the bronze medal. Even afterwards, Adlington needed reassurance that she had touched first. "I saw the race again when the BBC played it back for me and even then I didn't think I'd won. I said, 'I didn't win that', but they showed it under water and my hand just got there." Anita Lonsbrough, the last British woman to win an Olympic gold medal in the pool (in 1960), said: "It has been too long coming."

The tales of sacrifice were put on hold; the press were much more interested in Adlington's shoe collection. A £275 pair of kitten heels by Christian Louboutin were already on order – as reward from her parents for reaching the Games – and the mayor of Mansfield, Tony Eggington, had promised her Jimmy Choos if she won a gold medal. Adlington's mother, Kay, confided to the nation: "When she gets back I want to get her a huge chocolate cake made in the shape of a Christian Louboutin shoe – chocolate's her other great love."

Adlington's parents had lost almost £1,100 in an internet scam after ordering non-existent tickets for the 800m heats and final; they managed to obtain restricted-view replacements from another source and a little media pressure ensured that they did not, after all, have to peer round pillars to watch their daughter. Despite her victory in the 400m, she was gripped by nerves before the longer race, but she posted the quickest heat time and led from the second lap in the final. She was six seconds clear of second-placed Alessia Filippi at the end and her time of 8min 14.10sec was more than two seconds quicker than Evans's record, set when Adlington was six months old. Furniss described her performance as "frighteningly fast" and called it "one of the great all-time swims".

This time the newspaper coverage read like a charity appeal. The *Daily Mail* reported: "She survives on £250 a week, drives to training in a battered Vauxhall Corsa and struggles to pay for goggles…It is only thanks to her parents helping out that the 19-year-old can afford the costs of swimming such as hats, goggles and the £33 costumes which she gets through at the rate of at least one a month. She also receives an annual £1,000 travel and hotel grant from the council in her beloved Mansfield, without which she might not even have found the £300 to make it to the Olympic trials." Adlingon said diffidently: "If Speedo or any brand are interested, I'd love to have a kit deal."

A contract was duly signed with Speedo the following January, but although the financial clouds lifted Adlington did not find it easy to adapt to her new-found celebrity or to regain her competitive edge. Victory in the 800m and second place in the 400m at last year's World Championships hinted at a rediscovery of her 2008 form.

A crowd estimated at 15,000 turned out to mark Adlington's post-Beijing return to Mansfield in a golden Rolls-Royce; the equally golden Jimmy Choos were handed over with a ceremonial flourish. The Yates Wine Lodge was temporarily renamed the Adlington Arms and the pool where she took her first hesitant strokes became the Rebecca Adlington Swimming Centre.

Even in the immediate wake of her double triumph – she was the first British swimmer since Henry Taylor in 1908 to win more than one gold medal at a Games – Adlington insisted that 2012 was her "main target". She stressed the fact that she was "only 19", but there was a straightforward maturity about her comments to the *Mail on Sunday* a few days later:

"There is a tendency for some young people to think that they can get something for nothing these days. But you are never going to achieve anything unless you work hard. If you want your 15 minutes of fame, go on your reality TV show – that's fine. But if you want to achieve something that will last, something fantastic, put the work in. It will pay off. It is so satisfying that I have achieved what I have myself. I haven't had sponsorship deals. I have had to train in a small, 25-metre pool without the best facilities and I haven't had the money behind me. But I got there by working hard."

Aug 16: Coxless fours, Tom James, Steve Williams, Pete Reed, Andy Triggs Hodge

ANDY TRIGGS HODGE and Tom James were both part of the British eight who finished last of the nine participating crews in Athens. It was a powerful incentive to avoid future humiliation. "For four years I thought, I never want that to happen again," reflected Hodge amid the elation of the coxless four's victory in Beijing. "But I knew what went wrong and did something about it."

For two years the solution seemed ready-made and simple. Although there were obvious perils in trying to follow in the giant footsteps of Steve Redgrave and Matthew Pinsent, the ghosts appeared to have been exorcised in a 27-race unbeaten sequence taking in two world titles. Steve Williams, the last link with Pinsent's swansong success in Athens, was joined by Alex Partridge, Hodge and Pete Reed.

Partridge, robbed of his place in the boat in 2004 by a collapsed lung, became the scapegoat when the four's streak ended with an unexpected fourth place at the World Championships in 2007 (his consolation prize was a place in the eight who won a silver medal behind Canada the following year). The critical factor in the crew's return to form was James's promotion in Olympic year, but there were still doubts about the new line-up's ability to cohere successfully in Beijing.

They were short of neither brain nor brawn. James was a Chester-educated engineering graduate, who took a year out from Cambridge to prepare for the 2004 Olympics, only to miss the eight's heat because of illness. The Seattle-born, Cotswolds-raised Reed was a marine engineering officer in the Royal Navy who had been dubbed the 'commander' by Jürgen Grobler, Britain's head coach. "I'm hoping if we win in Beijing, he will promote me to admiral," Reed joked. Hodge had read environmental science at the University of Staffordshire before embarking on a masters degree in water science, policy and management at Oxford. Reed and Hodge were team-mates in Oxford's Boat Race winning crew in 2005 (James was in the opposing boat).

The British quartet beat Italy by a length to win their heat and scored a psychologically important victory over their main rivals, Australia, in the semi-finals. Hodge, the blond-haired self-appointed spokesman for the crew, said before the final: "I have to be this animal.

It is not pure evil, but I want to rip the heart and soul out of everyone around me. It's what works for me, to sit on the start-line and be this person I don't like being. I want to see the other crews cross the line and be wretched, destroyed, because that it is the only way I get what I want. That is how over the top I have to go. It is that summoning of something inside you, letting yourself be overcome with aggression. It is a bloodlust, if you like, and as far as I am concerned this is the last race of my life."

Hodge also offered snap shots of his colleagues (and himself):

Hodge on Reed: "He's a James Bond wannabe. He will be the one showing off his physique.***"***

Hodge on Williams: "The silent assassin, the guy you never see."

Hodge on James: "TJ is the perfectionist, the technician wanting everything to be just right."

Hodge on Hodge: "I'm the one who pisses them off."

The race was anything but comfortable for the Britons. They ate into the fast-starting Australians' lead but were still half a length down with 300 metres to go. Hodge admitted afterwards: "I thought, oh s***, maybe they were saving more in the semi-final than we thought. It was very scary. We always had the confidence that we would move through them but no one gives up on a race." The British crew's vivid acceleration – Williams described the effort as "primaeval" – not only made up the leeway but gave them a 1.28sec advantage over the Australians as they crossed the line in 6min 06.57sec.

A few months later, Reed reflected on the whole experience: "I thought about the Olympics all day and then went to bed and dreamed about it. I thought about winning, losing, race strategy, the opposition, the rigging of the boat, how to eke out small percentages, what kit I was going to wear, the hotel, your girlfriend, whether you want to see your girlfriend. It takes you over, consumes you." Hodge said: "When I got home people were coming up and telling stories of what they were doing when we crossed the line. I've never reached into people's lives like that."

Williams retired as an under-the-radar double gold medallist. James, as he had done after Athens, took time out before returning to the four who won the world title last year in a season of complete dominance. Hodge and Reed settled into a pair who were capable of beating everyone…apart from Hamish Bond and Eric Murray. The New Zealanders completed a hat-trick of world titles at Lake Bled, Slovenia, last year.

Aug 17: Lightweight double sculls, Zac Purchase, Mark Hunter

BRITAIN'S win in the lightweight double sculls in Beijing could have been scripted as a commercial for the new meritocracy: working-class East Ender teams up with public schoolboy to win Olympic title. The differences between Mark Hunter and Zac Purchase went much deeper, but the sporting alchemy (once they had swapped places in the boat) was unmistakeable.

Neither fitted comfortably into the lightweight category – maximum weight 72.5kg (11st 6lb) – first introduced at the 1996 Games in Atlanta. Hunter, seven years older, switched from the heavyweight ranks in 2001. Purchase was a younger convert, making his World Cup debut as a single sculler when still in his teens and winning the world title in 2006 at Dorney Lake, Windsor, the venue for the 2012 Games, in a world best time.

Purchase's route into rowing was traditional – via the on-tap facilities at King's School, Worcester. Hunter, by contrast, had to circumvent the mud and supermarket trolleys to learn to row with the Poplar Blackwall and District club. He completed a six-year apprenticeship as a waterman (passengers) and lighterman (goods) before earning the right to skipper passenger and freight boats on the Thames as a freeman. He was part of a coxless four who made little impression at the Athens Games in 2004.

Hunter and Purchase sculled together for the first time in 2006; they were modestly successful in 2007 and spectacularly so in 2008, when the decision to put Hunter in the stroke seat was fully vindicated – they went through the season unbeaten. Hunter relished the day-to-day training workload, whereas Purchase described himself as "a racer, not a trainer". Hunter learned to accept that results were all that mattered.

They underlined their superiority in Beijing by posting the fastest heat time and had a second and a half in hand on Italy in their semi-final. In the final, Hunter and Purchase made their statement of intent in the second 500 metres. They led by almost two seconds from Greece at halfway and contained the Greeks' committed finish to win in 6min

10.99sec, .73sec ahead. Purchase said afterwards: "The last 10 years came down to six minutes of hell."

Mike Dickson wrote in the *Daily Mail*: "Mark Hunter descended into what he called his 'dark place' yesterday and, once he had finished throwing up through sheer exhaustion, emerged to the ecstasy of winning Olympic gold. Hunter had passed out when he pulled up to the pontoon after winning his longed-for gold and had to be dragged out of the boat by his partner. A few minutes later he was prostrate in the car park, vomiting on to the grass verge, while Purchase, 22, looked like he had done nothing more strenuous than lazily cross the Serpentine." Hunter explained: "I always push myself to the limit and unfortunately that means being sick. When Zac gets to my age then he can start being sick as well."

The partnership was put on hold after Beijing. Hunter took up a short-term coaching position at the University of California. Purchase was given a pair of gold, limited-edition wellington boots by the Hunter Boot company – "because I won a gold medal with Mark Hunter" – and embarked on an extended celebration. He also suffered from post-viral fatigue, but the competitive zest returned when he and Hunter won world titles in both 2010 and 2011.

Aug 17: Finn class sailing, Ben Ainslie

BEN AINSLIE hardly needed the ego massage, but he got one anyway. As Ainslie honed in on a third gold medal, Britain's team manager, Stephen Park, warned the world: "If it comes down to a medal race between Ben and another boat, Ben will kill him. It is not even a discussion worth having. Bet your house on it. Bet your mate's house on it. In fact, bet the nation's house on it. He will just annihilate anybody else that he has got to beat. You just don't want to be in the boat that is going to stand between Ben and a gold medal. He will absolutely drill him."

Ainslie was as good as Park's words. He went into the final race needing only to finish within six places of the American, Zach Railey, but the weather – so calm that the medal race was postponed for a day – finally took a turn for the worse and Ainslie was in his element. He established a lead which he would never relinquish; he described it as "a great race in awesome conditions".

The anxieties of 10 days earlier, when he had been isolated from his team-mates after having mumps diagnosed, were all forgotten. Ainslie's ailment was kept under wraps and he went into the series as the firmest of favourites – he had not been beaten in the class since the Athens Games. The first race, when he slipped from first to 10th as a light wind suddenly changed direction, and a mischievous, threatened protest from Railey on the second day, illustrated the vagaries of regatta sailing.

Four first places and two seconds in the nine races told their own story of consistency and at the end his sense of relief quickly gave way to "profound satisfaction". Ainslie wrote in his autobiography: "There was an outpouring of emotion with the realisation that I'd achieved something that I had been focused on for so long. This was, by far, my most exciting and exhilarating win."

Bronze medallist Guillaume Florent, a regular source of annoyance to Ainslie over the years, paid genuine tribute: "He's like Mike Tyson at his peak," said Florent. "When he has bad days and we have good days it's possible to beat him. When he's sailing at this level it's impossible." The local media were equally impressed, as evidenced by a brief exchange at the press conference after the medal race.

Chinese News Agency: "Are you Superman or from another planet?"
Ainslie: "Thanks for that. As far as I know, I'm human."

The reality was three gold medals, dethroning Rodney Pattisson as Britain's most prolific Olympic sailor. "It is probably 10 times harder to win now, which is where Ben is so amazing," said Pattisson in tribute. "The difference between Ben and I is that I did it all ably assisted by a crewman, but Ben has done it on his own."

There was a full diary of engagements for Ainslie when he returned home. He found Prime Minister Gordon Brown "much warmer in person than he appears on the television". He was "very impressed" by David Cameron, then in opposition, and very unimpressed by a pre-filmed item for the BBC's Sports Personality of the Year award, in which he was asked to don a dinner suit…and fall backwards into a freezing Weymouth Harbour.

Ainslie complained: "The piece which was shown was like an out-take and, frankly, came across as more of a piss-take. I was furious with the BBC and it annoys me that some people show such little respect for sailing. They seem to view it as a joke sport because they don't understand it. It's due to ignorance of the highest level."

The dream was still of an all-British assault on the America's Cup in 2013, but the ambition had to be put on hold once more when Sir

Keith Mills disbanded Team Origin in 2010. At least the decision gave Ainslie the chance to re-focus on 2012. He won the test regatta at Weymouth, only for his 2011 World Championship campaign to finish in anger, controversy and disqualification. Ainslie swam over to the television boat covering the series and jostled both the skipper and cameraman, accusing them of passing too close to his boat, before diving back into the water.

Aug 17: Yngling class sailing, Sarah Ayton, Sarah Webb, Pippa Wilson

SARAH AYTON and Shirley Robertson shared the elation of victory in 2004, but their post-Athens priorities could hardly have been more different. "After Athens I was a 24-year-old who was feeling on the top of the world," Ayton recalls, "and I just wanted to get on and start another campaign. Shirley was at a stage where she wanted to have a family." The complicating factor was Ayton's determination to take charge.

"The biggest thing for me has always been about being the best that I can be at what I do," she says. "I was that at the front of the boat and I needed a new challenge, so for me it was the right thing to go to the back of the Yngling. I'd tried different boats before that, but when you've learned so much about a boat, all the things that people never tell you, you better put that into practice."

As a mother herself, Ayton now acknowledges that she could have taken a more understanding view of Robertson's sabbatical. "As I've matured I've come to realise that in an Olympic campaign there is a window in which you have to have children. Now, looking back on that, I totally respect the position that Shirley was in. Maybe I could have handled things a bit differently."

Sarah Webb remained from the 2004 crew and, after a year-long search, they recruited 20-year-old Pippa Wilson, a former junior world champion who had passed up a psychology degree to sail full time (she also passed the Three Blondes in a Boat test). If Robertson operated a benign dictatorship, Ayton believed in power-sharing. At the start of 2008, Wilson referred to "the total respect I was given the moment I stepped on the boat. We are equals and, as a crew, that's the best position to be in."

Sponsorship from the Swiss bank, Mirabaud, allowed them to sail without distraction and they dominated the class in the build-up to

Beijing, winning back-to-back World Championships – victory in Cascais, Portugal in 2007 clinched their selection for 2008 ahead of Robertson's boat – and the Olympic test event at Qingdao. The medal race in Cascais also proved to be perfect preparation for the finale to the Olympic regatta, in which Ayton, Webb and Wilson trailed the Dutch by a single point. "We'd been in that situation before against Shirley to get the spot for China," Ayton explains, "so we knew what had to be done. We'd trained a lot for that very match-race-style scenario so that we would be able to come out on top." A 24-hour postponement because of still conditions also played into their hands – "it blew 15-20 knots the following day and that's where the Brits excel."

In preparation for their marriage a few weeks later, Ayton and her windsurfer fiancé, Nick Dempsey, who finished fourth in Beijing, had bought wedding bands for each other at the airport, on their way out to China. Webb accepted a marriage proposal from her boyfriend, Adam Gosling, as she was about to climb on to the medal podium; the couple married in February 2009.

Ayton insists that 2004 and 2008 were equally memorable: "I loved every minute of the campaign for Athens and I learned so much from Shirley about how to go about winning a gold medal. Of course, moving to the back of the boat there's just that bit more responsibility. Ultimately you are in charge of where the boat is – you have got the tiller in your hand. I really thrived on that new challenge. Both those medals were special in their different ways. Up to 2004 we were pretty much about boat speed, whereas the focus in 2008 was more about being the best racers that we could be. Also we had the knowledge from 2004 in our favour."

After the Yngling's omission from the programme for 2012, Ayton teamed up with Saskia Clark in a 470 class boat before deciding, in February 2011, that bringing up a small son, Thomas, and supporting Dempsey in his fourth attempt to win an Olympic gold medal, were incompatible with another campaign of her own. She admitted, when we spoke in January, that she was missing the Olympic buzz – "working towards a final goal and knowing what the Games mean" – and does not rule out a return to competitive sailing in the future.

Aug 19: Laser class sailing, Paul Goodison

PAUL GOODISON was introduced to sailing as a four-year-old, but there was little room for other sports in a childhood dominated by football and his devotion to Sheffield United. It was only at the age of 12, when Goodison was confined to the touchline for six months by a cartilage injury, that he allowed himself to be lured to the Ulley club reservoir on a more regular basis.

He was selected for the Royal Yachting Association's youth squad and began to make an impact in the Laser class while completing a maritime studies degree at Southampton Solent University. Ben Ainslie fuelled Goodison's ambition with his silver medal in Atlanta; he also blocked his path to Olympic selection in 2000, though Goodison readily agreed to be Ainslie's training partner for his gold medal winning campaign in Sydney and claimed the Laser berth when Ainslie switched to Finns for Athens.

Fourth place in 2004 left Goodison "utterly demoralised". He admitted: "It was worse as all my team-mates were winning medals and although I was happy for them, it felt so bad that I had missed out. Initially I thought, 'I never want to put myself through that again'. I took about two months off, but the only way to get over it was to prove to myself I could do it and get back in the boat."

Five successive European titles between 2005 and 2009 underlined Goodison's continental dominance – the world title was more elusive – and despite a three-month lay-off after he broke his wrist in a fall from his mountain bike (Goodison is something of an adrenaline sport junkie) he went to Beijing armed with the confidence of victories in both the test events in Qingdao. He made an inconsistent start to the regatta, but reached the medal race in pole position and employed the same containing tactics which had secured the gold for Ainslie in Sydney.

The 'victim' was the Swede, Rasmus Mygren, who needed to win and relegate Goodison to ninth of the 10-boat fleet. Goodison explained afterwards: "I went after him because he was the only one who could beat me to the gold if he won. I feel sorry for him but it is just sport and you have to do what you have to do. I apologised but I think he was a bit stressed and upset. He was screaming at the race officials all through the second half of the race to abandon it when the wind died. If the wind had been a little bit stronger, it would have just been a case of going out and sailing the race and just finishing it off. But with the conditions as they were, you could go from 100 metres behind to 100 metres in front on one puff of wind." Goodison's mother, Cynthia, watched tearfully as he stood on the medal podium; his father, Roy, had been prevented from travelling by a back injury.

A Sheffield brewery, Kelham Island, brought out a beer, Goodison's Gold, in his honour. Eleven days after his win in Beijing, Goodison paraded his gold medal in front of 30,000 fans at Sheffield United's Bramall Lane ground, and was so determined to watch their Championship play-off final against Burnley (they lost 1-0) the following May that he towed his Laser to Wembley before going on to a training camp in Belgium. Goodison's mood was rather brighter when he won the world title in August 2009.

Goodison and his long-time girlfriend, Saskia Clark, who live in Weymouth, the venue for the sailing events in 2012, were able to prepare for the Games secure in the knowledge that their selection was confirmed almost a year in advance; Clark teamed up with Hannah Mills in the 470 class after Sarah Ayton decided to retire in February 2011. Nick Thompson, Goodison's heir apparent as Britain's top Laser sailor, finished second to Goodison's fifth at the 2011 World Championships before agreeing to be his rival's training partner in 2012.

Aug 19: 400m, Christine Ohuruogu

CHRISTINE OHURUOGU was acclaimed by Lord Coe as "the consummate championship runner" after she stormed through from fourth to first in the home straight to win the 400m in Beijing; it was a near carbon copy of her victory in the World Championships a year earlier. Ohuruogu looked a little puzzled when asked to explain her race strategy. "It never goes according to plan so why have one?" she said.

The admission could have been taken as a wider metaphor for someone who seemed to float above day-to-day minutiae, the sort of athlete who *could* have missed three out-of-competition tests through sheer forgetfulness. The *Times* columnist, Simon Barnes, suggested that Ohuruogu's one-year ban was more "a matter of sloppy diary-keeping rather than drug-gobbling wickedness". Fellow athletes, often the fiercest critics of drug offenders, were mostly sympathetic, and a lifetime Olympic ban was lifted on appeal in November 2007.

The significance of that reprieve extended well beyond Beijing. Ohuruogu, one of eight children of Nigerian parents who moved to London in the Seventies, was born and brought up in Newham, within shouting distance of the Olympic Stadium. School came before sport, though Ohuruogu was a junior netball international. She converted to athletics in her late teens and competed at the Athens Games – she reached the semi-finals in the 400m – the year before completing a linguistics degree at University College, London. A relay bronze medal at the 2005 World Championships was followed by a gold medal in the individual event at the Commonwealth Games in 2006.

Five months later her athletics career was in limbo. An appeal to have the suspension lifted early was dismissed in April 2007 and Ohuruogu returned to competitive action only three weeks before the World Championships, rediscovering her race sharpness so quickly that she led Nicola Sanders to a British one-two in Osaka and ran under 50 seconds for the first time. "The race was very close," Ohuruogu said afterwards, "but all the negativity which has been said about me and written about me just spurred me on."

She was largely inured against the fresh round of sniping which accompanied the build-up to the Beijing Games and underlined her medal prospects by running 50.14sec to win her semi-final. The American, Sanya Richards, an absentee in Osaka, was the favourite, and led for most of the race before weakening (she cited a 'hamstring tug' after 320 metres as the culprit) on the run-in. Ohuruogu held her form more convincingly than any of her rivals and crossed the line in 49.62sec, a hundredth of a second slower than she had managed in the World Championships and the slowest winning time in an Olympic final since 1972.

Ohuruogu admitted afterwards: "I was worried because when you go into a final you want to believe you're in your best shape. But I had a headache and it was hot and it was the final and everything was getting to me." Predictably asked whether she felt the medal was tainted, she shot back: "I don't really think about what people think or care. As far as I am concerned, I won a gold medal and that is all that matters."

She sounded the same defiant note when the questioning moved on to 2012. "I'm going to be there whether you like it or not," she said. "When you go to the Olympics you catch the bug. I used to walk to Stratford station every morning on my way to uni and it's 15 minutes from my house. I hope I can treat it as not just a random meet."

Injuries have severely restricted Ohuruogu's racing programme since Beijing. She finished a distant fifth behind winner Richards at the 2009 World Championships and suffered the "gut-wrenching" humiliation of being disqualified for a false start in her heat at last year's championships in Daegu, South Korea.

Aug 21: Star class sailing, Iain Percy, Andrew Simpson

IAIN PERCY'S decision to team up with Andrew Simpson for the Beijing Games made perfect sense – they had been close friends for more than 20 years – but Percy still found it agonisingly tough to break the news to Steve Mitchell, his Star class partner at the Athens Olympics. "Finishing with a woman is easy by comparison," he admitted in an interview in 2009. "I was taking away a man's job, his passion, his dream, all at the same time."

Percy had recruited Mitchell, a former world and European title winner in the Etchells class, after competing alongside him in the Farr 40 World Championships in 2001. The partnership clicked so effectively that they won the Star world title the following year, but sixth place in Athens was well below their expectations. Percy immersed himself in the America's Cup as helmsman on the under-funded Italian boat, +39 Challenge, before re-committing himself to another Olympic campaign. Simpson's skill in the light winds expected to predominate in Beijing was a critical factor in Percy's decision to change crew.

Simpson, the younger by nine months, had first met Percy when they began competing in Optimist dinghies as seven-year-olds. Percy recalled that they were both entered for an Under 15s competition. "Everyone else was behind the bike sheds trying smoking and kissing," he said, "and we were playing with Lego." Simpson, born in Chertsey, Surrey, went to Pangbourne College, in Berkshire, the alma mater of double sailing gold medallist Rodney Pattisson, before, like Percy, reading economics at university. He, too, imagined himself as a City trader (the schoolboy dream of playing football for Tottenham had been reluctantly abandoned a few years earlier).

> '**Everyone else was behind the bike sheds smoking and kissing. We were playing Lego**'

Predictably dubbed 'Bart' when the cartoon series entered the public consciousness in the 1990s, Simpson found himself perennially in the competitive shadow of Percy and Ben Ainslie. "I have sailed hard against Iain and Ben in the past and sadly they had that little bit extra against me," he admitted. "But they are very special." Simpson was good enough in his own right to finish second in the Finn European Championships in 2001, only a year after switching from Lasers, and third at the 2003 World Championships (won by Ainslie). He also gained some reflected glory as training partner for Percy in Sydney and Ainslie in Athens.

He and Percy only began campaigning in 2007 and the promise of third place in that year's World Championships evaporated with a start penalty and disqualification which left them 52nd in the standings in 2008. Their challenge for gold in Beijing was activated by two first place finishes and two seconds between the sixth and ninth races. They still trailed the Swedes, Fredrik Loof and Anders Ekstrom, going into the medal race, but the storm clouds gathering over Fushan Bay filled them with self-belief. Percy said later: "When we got up and saw the wind and the rain, we knew we would win. We are Brits, we live for that stuff. We had to be more concentrated than we've ever been and there was no room for fun. We knew we could do it because we had more talent on board than anyone else."

Fifth place to the Swedes' 10th settled the debate in the Britons' favour and Percy paid emotional tribute to his crewman. "He is a special guy to have given up all his time to help us [Percy and Ainslie]," he said. "Now, to do it here and win gold with your best mate of 25 years means everything. My last medal pales into insignificance against this. We worked so hard. Doing it with the big fella means so much."

Percy found himself paying tribute again (with a joke or two thrown in) as the best man at Simpson's wedding in 2009; Ainslie was chief usher. Back on the water, Percy and Simpson won the World Championships in Rio de Janeiro at the start of 2010. Their pre-selection for London was confirmed in September, but they were forced to pull out of December's World Championships, in Perth, Western Australia, when Percy injured his back.

Aug 22: 1,000m kayak singles canoeing, Tim Brabants

TIM BRABANTS admitted after winning the 1,000m kayak singles canoeing event at the Beijing Games that his other great love, medicine, had been forced to take a back seat for much of the previous 10 years. "It's been a disjointed career," he said. "It's a sacrifice but it's sport and if you are passionate about it, that's what you do."

The passion was ignited at Elmbridge Canoe Club in Surrey when Brabants was 10. He was a tunnel-visioned achiever who put school work and sport before more frivolous activities. By the time he left Salesian School, a Chertsey comprehensive, with three top-grade levels he was already a world junior champion in the 500m kayak pairs. He chose Nottingham University as much for the National Watersports Centre at nearby Holme Pierrepont as for the reputation of the medical faculty.

The juggling act between studies, sport and home life became ever harder to sustain. After winning a singles bronze medal over 1,000m at the Sydney Olympics in 2000 and marrying his South African girlfriend, Michelle, the following year, Brabants set himself the goal of bowing out in Athens – with a gold medal. The promise of a world best time in his heat evaporated in the acute disappointment of fifth place in the final and Brabants knew that something had to give.

"I did think about finishing," he said, "but I felt there was something more to come so I just took a break." Brabants worked for a year in Nottingham then spent an intensive six months in the accident and emergency department of the hospital on the Channel Island of Jersey. Working up to 90 hours a week, he kept fit by following nightshifts with sessions on a rowing machine. Appetite regained, he won the European title four months after returning to the mainland and the gold medal at the World Championships in 2007.

In the 18 months prior to the Beijing Games, Brabants was once more a full-time sportsman, relying on his annual Lottery funding of £24,000. He missed the varied challenge of A&E but reflected: "For now I'm in the privileged position of being able to do two things I love."

Brabants was the quickest paddler in the heats in Beijing and an ultimately comfortable winner in the final, finishing almost a boat length ahead of Norway's Eirik Veraas Larsen. He was asked at what point in the race he felt confident of victory. "I know it's easy to say when you've won," he responded, "but I really did know off that start line. I hit it hard off the start and I knew after those first two strokes that without a doubt I was going to win that race. No one was going to touch me. I felt fantastic."

He dedicated the gold medal to his mother, Liz, who had introduced him to canoeing and watched him compete in Sydney. She died of leukaemia in December 2005. Brabants said: "She supported me all the way and it was a huge regret that she didn't live long enough to see me win the World Championships last year. I went to her grave and left the flowers they gave me for winning. It was a very emotional moment."

The follow-up in Beijing was a creditable bronze medal in the 500m event before Brabants repeated the post-Athens routine, swapping paddle for plaster in another 18-month sabbatical from sport during which he switched on the Christmas lights in Nottingham and, so he claimed, picked up the celebrity invitations which Rebecca Adlington was forced to turn down. He finished second in the 1,000m at the 2010 World Championships, but the prospect of Brabants being unable to defend his Olympic title loomed when he was beaten by fellow Briton Paul Wycherley in a race-off for a place at last year's World Championships.

Aug 23: Middleweight boxing, James DeGale

JAMES DEGALE's father 'watched' his son's Olympic final from the sanctuary of a wardrobe. After all, there was more than parental pride at stake. Leroy DeGale had taken odds of 80-1 before the Olympics began and stood to win £11,000. "I get physically sick watching him," he admitted. "During the finals I was in the wardrobe praying. Each time I heard them shouting I would poke my head out and ask what the score was."

Neither Leroy nor his wife, Diane, would have backed James with any confidence when, in his early teens, he was expelled first from the Barbara Speake stage school in west London and then Whitefield School, Barnet, for disruptive behaviour. His route to self-discipline was through boxing, a sport he had first taken to at the age of 10 before being adopted by Harlesden's thrill-seeking set.

DeGale's progress through the amateur ranks was stealthy. He won ABA middleweight titles in 2005 and 2006 and lost to the eventual silver medallist, Venezuela's Alfonso Blanco, in the 2007 World Championships. DeGale was only regarded as an outside bet for a medal in Beijing, but he guaranteed a bronze at worst by beating Kazakhstani Bakhtiyar Artayev, the welterweight champion from Athens, and made light of a 1-4 record against the Irishman, Darren Sutherland, to reach the final (Sutherland committed suicide in 2009).

The final, in which DeGale was confronted by Cuba's Emilio Correa, was effectively decided by a productive opening round for the Briton. He built a 6-1 lead, helped by a two-point deduction for Correa after he bit DeGale on the chest. The fight then, according to the *Mail on Sunday*'s Rob Draper, descended into "a bar-room brawl which lacked only a honky tonk pianist". The report continued: "The Briton entered the last round with just a two-point advantage, and with the Cuban swinging dangerously. The fight degenerated further, with both boxers falling over each other as they crashed simultaneously to the floor. But each time Correa picked up a point, DeGale equalised with a counter-punch and he would never hold less than a two-point lead, despite Correa's desperation."

DeGale, the 19th and last of Britain's gold medallists in Beijing, countered Correa's biting denial at the press conference by showing the teeth marks. He also felt that he had been fighting to save the job of Britain's head coach, Terry Edwards. Asked after his semi-final whether he would remain amateur if Edwards was replaced, DeGale insisted: "I would not. Terry doesn't get the respect he deserves. He's like a second dad to me."

Edwards was made an MBE in the New Year's Honours…and still sacked. DeGale made some token, principled noises about staying in the amateur ranks…and in December 2008 signed a £1 million plus deal with promoter Frank Warren. He was booed after a laboured points victory in his debut super middleweight fight, suffered a first defeat in the pro ranks against fellow Briton George Groves in May 2011 and claimed the European Super-Middleweight title by beating the Pole, Piotr Wilczewski, in Liverpool last October.

ROLL OF HONOUR 1948-2008

Adlington, Rebecca (b. 1989): 400m and 800m freestyle, 2008

Ainslie, Ben (b. 1977): Laser class sailing, 2000; Finn class sailing, 2004; Finn class sailing, 2008

Allhusen, Derek (1914-2000): Team three-day event, 1968

Attrill, Louis (b. 1975): Eights rowing, 2000

Ayton (- Dempsey), Sarah (b. 1980): Yngling class sailing, 2004; Yngling class sailing, 2008

Barber, Paul (b. 1955): Hockey, 1988

Batchelor, Steve (b. 1961): Hockey, 1988

Bhaura, Kulbir (b. 1955): Hockey, 1988

Boardman, Chris (b. 1968): Individual pursuit cycling, 1992

Bond, David (b. 1922): Swallow class sailing, 1948

Brabants, Tim (b. 1977): 1,000m kayak singles canoeing, 2008

Braithwaite, Bob (b. 1925): Single trap clay pigeon shooting, 1968

Brasher, Chris (1928-2003): 3,000m steeplechase, 1956

Budgett, Richard (b. 1959): Coxed fours, 1984

Burnell, Richard (1917-1995): Double sculls, 1948

Bushnell, Bert (1921-2010): Double sculls, 1948

Bullen (- Holderness-Roddam), Jane (b. 1948): Team three-day event, 1968

Campbell, Darren (b. 1973): 4 x 100m relay, 2004

Christie, Linford (b. 1960): 100m, 1992

Clancy, Ed (b. 1985): Team pursuit cycling, 2008

Clift, Robert (b. 1962): Hockey, 1988

Coe, Sebastian (b. 1956): 1500m, 1980; 1500m, 1984

Coode, Ed (b. 1975): Coxless fours rowing, 2004

Cook (- Carroll), Stephanie (b. 1972), Modern pentathlon, 2000

Cooke, Nicole (b. 1983): Road race cycling, 2008

Cooper, Malcolm (1947-2001): Small-bore rifle three positions, 1984; Small-bore rifle three positions, 1988

Cracknell, James (b. 1972): Coxless fours, 2000; Coxless fours, 2004

Cross, Martin (b. 1957): Coxed fours, 1984

Davies, Chris (b. 1946): Flying Dutchman class sailing, 1972

Davies, Lynn (b. 1942): Long jump, 1964

DeGale, James (b. 1986): Middleweight boxing, 2008

Dennis, Simon (b. 1976): Eights rowing, 2000

Devonish, Marlon (b. 1976): 4 x 100m relay, 2004

Dodds, Richard (b. 1959): Hockey, 1988

Douglas, Rowley (b. 1977): Eights rowing, 2000

Edwards, Jonathan (b. 1966): Triple jump, 2000

Ellison, Adrian (b. 1958): Coxed fours, 1984

Faulds, Richard (b. 1977): Double trap clay pigeon shooting, 2000

Faulkner, David (b. 1963): Hockey, 1988

Finnegan, Chris (1944-2009): Middleweight boxing, 1968

Foster, Tim (b. 1970): Coxless fours, 2000

Fox, Jim (b. 1941): Team modern pentathlon, 1976

Garcia, Russell (b. 1970): Hockey, 1988

Gardener, Jason (b. 1975): 4 x 100m relay, 2004

Goodhew, Duncan (b. 1957): 100m breaststroke, 1980

Goodison, Paul (b. 1977): Laser class sailing, 2008

Gordon-Watson (- Low), Mary (b. 1948): Team three-day event, 1972

Grinham (- Rowley - Roe), Judy (b. 1939): 100m backstroke, 1956

Grimley, Martyn (b. 1963): Hockey, 1988

Grubor, Luka (b. 1973): Eights rowing, 2000

Gunnell (- Bigg), Sally (b. 1966): 400m hurdles, 1992

Harrison, Audley (b. 1971): Super heavyweight boxing, 2000

Hemery, David (b. 1944): 400m hurdles, 1968

Herbert, Garry (b. 1969): Coxed pairs, 1992

Hill, Bertie (1927-2005): Team three-day event, 1956

Hodge, Andy Triggs (b. 1979): Coxless fours, 2008

Holmes, Andy (1959-2010): Coxed fours, 1984; Coxless pairs, 1988

Holmes, Kelly (b. 1970): 800m and 1500m, 2004

Hoy, Chris (b. 1976): 1km time trial cycling, 2004; Individual and team
    sprint cycling, 2008; Keirin cycling, 2008

Hunt-Davis, Ben (b. 1972): Eights rowing, 2000

Hunter, Mark (b. 1978): Lightweight double sculls, 2008

James, Tom (b. 1984): Coxless fours, 2008

Jones, Ben (1932-1990): Team three-day event, 1968

Kenny, Jason (b. 1988): Team sprint cycling, 2008

Kerly, Sean (b. 1960): Hockey, 1988

Kirkwood, Jimmy (b. 1962): Hockey, 1988

Laurie, Ran (1915-1998): Coxless pairs, 1948

Law, Leslie (b. 1965): Individual three-day event, 2004

Leman, Richard (b. 1959): Hockey, 1988

Lewis (- Finan), Denise (b. 1972): Heptathlon, 2000

Lewis-Francis, Mark (b. 1982): 4 x 100m relay, 2004

Lindsay, Andrew (b. 1977): Eights rowing, 2000

Llewellyn, Harry (1911-1999): Team show-jumping, 1952

Lonsbrough (- Porter), Anita (b. 1941): 200m breaststroke, 1960

Manning, Paul (b. 1974): Team pursuit cycling, 2008

Martin, Steve (b. 1959): Hockey, 1988

Matthews, Ken (b. 1934): 20km walk, 1964

Meade, Richard (b. 1938): Team three-day event, 1968; Individual and team three-day event, 1972

MacDonald-Smith, Iain (b. 1945): Flying Dutchman class sailing, 1968

McIntyre, Mike (b. 1956): Star class sailing, 1988

McTaggart, Dick (b. 1935): Lightweight boxing, 1956

Moorhouse, Adrian (b. 1964): 100m breaststroke, 1988

Morris, Stewart (1909-1991): Swallow class sailing, 1948

Nightingale, Danny (b. 1954): Team modern pentathlon, 1976

Ohuruogu, Christine (b. 1984): 400m, 2008

Osborn, John (b. 1945): Tornado class sailing, 1976

Ovett, Steve (b. 1955): 800m, 1980

Packer (- Brightwell), Ann (b. 1942): 800m, 1964

Pappin, Veryan (b. 1958): Hockey, 1988

Parker, Adrian (b. 1951): Team modern pentathlon, 1976

Parker, Bridget (b. 1939): Team three-day event, 1972

Pattisson, Rodney (b. 1943): Flying Dutchman class sailing, 1968; Flying Dutchman class sailing, 1972

Percy, Iain (b. 1976): Finn class sailing, 2000; Star class sailing, 2008

Pendleton, Victoria (b. 1980): Individual sprint cycling, 2008

Peters, Mary (b. 1939): Pentathlon, 1972

Phillips, Mark (b. 1948): Team three-day event, 1972

Pinsent, Matthew (b. 1970): Coxless pairs, 1992; Coxless pairs, 1996; Coxless fours, 2000; Coxless fours, 2004

Potter, Jon (b. 1963): Hockey, 1988

Purchase, Zac (b. 1986): Lightweight double sculls, 2008

Queally, Jason (b. 1970): 1km time trial cycling, 2000

Rand (- Toomey - Reese), Mary (b. 1940): Long jump, 1964

Redgrave, Steve (b. 1962): Coxed fours, 1984; Coxless pairs, 1988; Coxless pairs, 1992, Coxless pairs 1996; Coxless fours, 2000

Reed, Pete (b. 1981): Coxless pairs, 2008

Robertson (- Boag), Shirley (b. 1968): Europe class sailing, 2000; Yngling class sailing, 2004

Romero, Rebecca (b. 1980): Individual pursuit cycling, 2008

Rook, Laurence (1921-1989): Team three-day event, 1956

Sanderson (- White), Tessa (b. 1956): Javelin, 1984

Scarlett, Fred (b. 1975): Eights rowing, 2000

Searle, Greg (b. 1972): Coxed pairs, 1992

Searle, Jonny (b. 1969): Coxed pairs, 1992

Sheen (- Donaldson), Gillian (b. 1928): Foil fencing, 1956

Sherwani, Imran (b. 1962): Hockey, 1988

Simpson, Andrew (b. 1976): Star class sailing, 2008

Spinks, Terry (b. 1938): Flyweight boxing, 1956

Staff, Jamie (b. 1973): Team sprint cycling, 2008

Stewart, Duggie (1913-1991): Team show-jumping, 1952

Taylor, Ian (b. 1954): Hockey, 1988

Thomas, Geraint (b. 1986): Team pursuit cycling, 2008

Thompson, Daley (b. 1958): Decathlon, 1980; Decathlon, 1984

Thompson, Don (1933-2006): 50km walk, 1960

Trapmore, Steve (b. 1975): Eights rowing, 2000

Vaile, Bryn (b. 1956): Star class sailing, 1988

Webb (- Gosling), Sarah (b. 1977): Yngling class sailing, 2004; Yngling
    class sailing, 2008

Weldon, Frank (1913-1993): Team three-day event, 1956

West, Kieran (b. 1977): Eights rowing, 2000

Wells, Allan (b. 1952): 100m, 1980

White, Reg (1935-2010): Tornado class sailing, 1976

White, Wilf (1904-1995): Team show-jumping, 1952

Wiggins, Bradley (b. 1980): Individual pursuit cycling, 2004; Individual
    and team pursuit cycling, 2008

Wilkie, David (b. 1954): 200m breaststroke, 1976

Williams, Steve (b. 1976): Coxless fours rowing, 2004; Coxless fours
    rowing, 2008

Wilson, Jack (1914-1997): Coxless pairs, 1948

Wilson, Pippa (b. 1986): Yngling class sailing, 2008

BIBLIOGRAPHY

A wide selection of national and local newspapers, individually referred to in the book, were consulted in the course of research.

The following books were consulted:

Ainslie, Ben, *Close to the Wind: The Autobiography of Britain's Greatest Olympic Sailor*, Yellow Jersey Press, 2009

Besford, Pat and Long, Tommy, *Wilkie*, Kemps, 1976

Brasher, Chris (edited by), *The Road to Rome*, William Kimber, 1960

Brightwell, Robbie, *Robbie Brightwell and his Golden Girl: The Posh and Becks of Yesteryear*, Kindle Edition, 2011

Bryant, John, *Chris Brasher: The Authorised Biography*, Aurum Press, 2012

Buchanan, Ian, *British Olympians: A Hundred Years of Gold Medallists*, Guinness, 1991

Bullen, Jane, *The Galloping Nurse*, Stanley Paul, 1970

Burnell, Richard, *The Complete Sculler*, Sports Book Publisher, 2000

Butcher, Pat, *The Perfect Distance: Ovett and Coe, The Record-Breaking Rivalry*, Weidenfeld and Nicolson, 2004

Christie, Linford, *To Be Honest With You*, Michael Joseph, 1995

Cleaver, Hylton, *Wilf White and Nizefela: The Story of a Great Show-Jumping Partnership*, Panther, 1957

Cleaver, Hylton, *A History of Rowing*, Herbert Jenkins, 1957

Cross, Martin, *Olympic Obsession: The Inside Story of Britain's Most Successful Sport*, Breedon Books, 2001

Finnegan, Chris, *Finnegan: Self-Portrait of a Fighting Man*, Macdonald and Jane's, 1976

Folley, Malcolm, *Jonathan Edwards: The Authorized Biography of an Olympic Champion*, HarperCollins, 2001

Grinham, Judy, *Water Babe: My Life in Swimming*, Oldbourne, 1960

Gunnell, Sally, *Running Tall*, Bloomsbury, 1995

Hampton, Janie, *The Austerity Olympics: When the Games Came to London in 1948*, Aurum Press, 2008

Harrison, Audley, *Realising the Dream*, Granada, 2001

Hemery, David, *Another Hurdle*, Heinemann, 1976

Holmes, Kelly, *Black, White and Gold*, Virgin Books, 2006

Hoy, Chris, *Chris Hoy: The Autobiography*, HarperSport, 2010

Law, Leslie, *Shear Gold*, Methuen, 2005

Lewis, Denise, *Personal Best*, Random House, 2001

Liggett, Phil, *Fastest Man on Two Wheels: In Pursuit of Chris Boardman*, Boxtree, 1994

Llewellyn, Harry, *Passports to Life*, Hutchinson Stanley Paul, 1980

Llewellyn, Harry, *Foxhunter in Pictures*, Hodder and Stoughton, 1952

Lonkhurst, Bob, *East End Idol: The Amazing Story of Terry Spinks*, BL Associates, 2002

Miller, David, *Sebastian Coe: Born to Run, A Life in Athletics*, Pavilion Books, 1992

Moore, Richard, *Heroes, Villains and Velodromes: Chris Hoy and Britain's Track Cycling Revolution*, HarperSport, 2008

Ovett, Steve, *Ovett: An Autobiography*, Collins Willow, 1984

Peters, Mary, *Mary P: Autobiography*, Stanley Paul, 1974

Phillips, Bob, *The 1948 Olympics: How London Rescued the Games*, Sportsbooks, 2007

Pinsent, Matthew, *A Lifetime In A Race*, Ebury Press, 2005

Rand, Mary, *Mary Mary: Autobiography of an Olympic Champion*, Hodder and Stoughton, 1969

Redgrave, Steve, *Steve Redgrave: A Golden Age*, BBC, 2001

Sanderson, Tessa, *Tessa: My Life in Athletics*, Willow Books, 1986

Sheen, Gillian, *Instructions to Young Fencers*, Brompton Library, 1958

Thompson, Daley, *Daley: The Last Ten Years*, Willow Books, 1986

Wallechinsky, David, *The Complete Book of the Olympics*, Aurum Press, 2000

Wiggins, Bradley, *In Pursuit of Glory*, Orion, 2009

Williams, Peter, *Lynn Davies: Winner Stakes All*, Pelham Books, 1970